FAMILY PSYCHIATRIC NURSING

Christine S. Fawcett, RN, MS, CS

Psychiatric Mental Health Nurse and Consultant
Philadelphia, Pennsylvania

illustrated

 Mosby

St. Louis Baltimore Boston Chicago London Philadelphia Sydney Toronto

Executive Editor: Linda L. Duncan
Developmental Editor: Teri Merchant
Project Manager: Patricia Tannian
Production Editor: Betty Hazelwood
Manufacturing Supervisor: Betty Richmond

Printed in the United States of America

11830 Westline Industrial Drive
St. Louis, Missouri 63146

Library of Congress Cataloging in Publication Data

Fawcett, Christine S.
    Family psychiatric nursing / Christine S. Fawcett.
      p.   cm.
    Includes bibliographical references and index.
    ISBN 0-8016-0159-2
    1. Family—Mental health.   2. Psychiatric nursing.   3. Family
nursing.   I. Title.
    [DNLM: 1. Family. 2. Psychiatric Nursing. WY 160 F278f]
RC455.4.F3F43 1993
610.73'68—dc20
DNLM/DLC
for Library of Congress   92-48204
                                        CIP

93 94 95 96 97 GW/DC 9 8 7 6 5 4 3 2 1

Contributors

Joan K. Austin, DNS, RN, FAAN
Professor, Department of Psychiatric/
Mental Health Nursing, Indiana University
School of Nursing, Indianapolis, Indiana

Ann F. Baker, RN, MS
Staff Nurse/Consultant, Battle Creek
Adventist Hospital, Battle Creek, Michigan

Ann Ottney Cain, RN, PhD, CS, FAAN
Professor, Graduate Program in
Psychiatric Nursing, University of
Maryland at Baltimore,
Baltimore, Maryland

Valerie Telford Cotter, MSN, RNC
Clinical Lecturer, University of
Pennsylvania School of Nursing,
Philadelphia, Pennsylvania

Terri A. Cutillo-Schmitter, RN, MSN, CS
Supervisor, Geriatric-Psychiatry Unit,
Will's Eye Hospital, Philadelphia;
Private Practice,
Lancaster, Pennsylvania

Anne M. Delengowski, RN, MSN
Oncology Clinical Nurse Specialist,
Thomas Jefferson University Hospital,
Philadelphia, Pennsylvania

Jeanne Watson Driscoll, MS, RN, CS
Psychiatric-Mental Health Clinical Nurse
Specialist, Psychotherapy/Consultation/
Education Private Practice,
West Roxbury, Massachusetts

Laila Farhood, RN, MSN, CS
Associate Professor and Chairperson,
Psychiatric-Mental Health Nursing,
American University of Beirut School of
Nursing, Beirut, Lebanon

Joan L. Fopma-Loy, DNS, RN
Associate Professor of Nursing, Indiana
University School of Nursing, Indiana
University East, Richmond, Indiana

Charlotte M. Gilbert, PhD, RN, ARNP
Assistant Professor, University of South
Florida College of Nursing,
Tampa, Florida

Linda Cade Haber, DNS, RN, CS
Clinical Specialist, Veterans Affairs
Medical Center, Marion, Indiana

Patrick E. Kenny, MSN, RN, C, CNA
Education Specialist, The Germantown
Hospital and Medical Center,
Philadelphia, Pennsylvania

Dixie Koldjeski, PhD, RN
President, Health Education Seminars &
Consultation, Inc.; Adjunct Professor, East
Carolina University School of Nursing,
Morehead City, North Carolina

Pamela E. Marcus, MS, RN, CS
Psychotherapist in Private Practice,
Upper Marlboro, Maryland

Donna Martsolf, MN, RN
Doctoral Student, University of Pittsburgh
School of Nursing,
Pittsburgh, Pennsylvania

Deanna Gray Miceli, MSN, RN
Gerontological Nurse Practitioner,
University of Medicine and Dentistry of
New Jersey School of Medicine, Center for
Aging, Stratford, New Jersey

J. Sherry O'Grady-Cocozza, MA, RN, CS
Psychotherapist in Private Practice,
Medford, New Jersey

Barbara Parker, PhD, RN
Associate Professor, University of
Maryland School of Nursing,
Baltimore, Maryland

Margaret M. Pike, RN, MS, EdD
President, Grief, Ltd., Covington, Indiana

Kathryn R. Puskar, DrPH, CS, RN
Director, Graduate Program, Psychiatric
Mental Health Nursing, University of
Pittsburgh School of Nursing,
Pittsburgh, Pennsylvania

Sara Rich Wheeler, RN, MSN
Associate Professor, Lakeview College of
Nursing, Danville, Illinois; Certified Grief
Counselor and Consultant, Grief, Ltd.,
Covington, Indiana

Beatrice Crofts Yorker, JD, RN, MS
Chair, Psychiatric/Mental Health Nursing,
Georgia State University School of
Nursing, Atlanta, Georgia

Foreword

The publication of this book represents another step forward in the gradual development of psychiatric nursing. *Family Psychiatric Nursing* was prepared for psychiatric nurses because it is especially necessary for them to have knowledge of problems of families with whom they work. This work is also addressed to *all* nurses because they also encounter family problems that require informed nursing services. Similarly, this work is helpful for students in nursing education programs because they, too, are preparing themselves for nursing practice, which surely will include problems of families.

Psychiatric nursing is an area of specialization within nursing as a whole. This textbook may be ushering in a trend toward the development of family psychiatric nursing as a subspecialty within psychiatric nursing. This trend would be appropriate and timely. Research is scarce on family problems that come to the attention of nurses in their practice. Few graduate level nursing education programs emphasize family theory and family therapy. This work addresses that gap.

Family Psychiatric Nursing is a natural progression in the development of psychiatric nursing as it is practical in the United States. In this century many changes have been made in this area of nursing care. At the turn of the century, a custodial/companionship mode of practice was most prominent. At mid-century, the relations between nurses and psychiatric patients began to be studied; the aim was to make nursing more therapeutic for patients. In the 1960s, attention shifted toward the community, and psychiatric nurses began to be employed in mental health centers, often as psychotherapists. About the same time, nurses began to prepare themselves for work as group therapists and for providing family therapy.

Families of psychiatric patients have always received the attention of psychiatric nurses. However, the focus of their attention changed over time. At first, in public mental hospitals particularly, families were discouraged, or actually excluded, from visiting a mentally ill family member who was hospitalized. Later, families, and particularly mothers, were in effect blamed for improper nurturing that presumably helped to produce the psychiatric disturbance of their afflicted offspring. At the same time family members were considered an important source of family history information. In the mid-1950s, psychiatric nurses began to explore the possibilities of family therapy. In working with family groups, the problems and systems dynamics of families then entered the purview of psychiatric nursing. The emptying of public mental hospitals, which coincided with the development of psychotropic drugs in the 1960s, led to employment of nurses in a new way. They provided surveillance of psychiatric patients living at home, in foster homes, and in community facilities other than hospitals. In this work, inevitably, with limited time for intensive therapeutic sessions with families, nurses recognized that a broader form of family psychiatric nursing service was needed.

Today families face problems that were seen only infrequently in the 1900s. Three observations about the changing nature of families and the social context in which they live suggest the probability that families having problems will increase. The attention of psychiatric and general nurses to these matters would therefore seem essential, so that the professional services they provide are competent, of the highest quality, and beneficial.

1. Families are the context in which psychiatric problems emerge; of necessity, families must cope. This assumption has validity regardless of whether causation of mental illness is attributed to brain pathology, genetic or biochemical effects, and/or family dysfunction. Furthermore, today, once an individual is diagnosed as having mental illness and treatment is begun, the family retains responsibility. In some instances the "identified patient" regains independence and ability to live apart from the family. In other instances, the family must provide continuing care within the home or take economic and/or supervisory responsibility for such care given in a community facility.

2. In recent decades, the concept of family has been changing radically. Formerly, the two main categories were the *nuclear* and *extended* families. Currently the term has been broadened to include single (male or female) parents; unmarried couples who have children; remarried, divorced individuals who have his, hers, and their children; "domestic companions" who adopt children; gay or lesbian partners who adopt children; foster families; and others. Surrogacy also enters this picture. Two-career families and ethnically mixed marriages are common. Clearly the norms for "family" are undergoing revision.

3. Currently, virtually all societies worldwide are in the midst of tremendous social change. In part, this is the result of a shift from industrialization to a high-technology, information era that is underway. Economic and political factors are also at interplay. In the United States the social transformation has produced great stress, anxiety, and many social problems that affect families. Unemployment, poverty, homelessness, and downward mobility of the middle class are evident. There are population shifts and demographic changes in cities and regional areas because of mobility and immigration. Problems, including crime, arising from the use of drugs and alcohol have become more common. Sexual harassment, spouse abuse, child abuse, and incest are "coming out of the closet." The health care system is in disarray. Many other such problems mirror the major social transformations that are occurring and are having direct and

indirect impact on families and their life-styles. Stress, anxiety, and conflict exist as traditional values are questioned or eroded and new norms are being formulated.

The significance of this textbook is that it provides a theory-based nursing approach to understanding current and emerging problems of families during this period of major and massive social transition. Nurses who have a theoretical grasp of such problems will be well armed to determine constructive nursing services for families with whom they work.

Hildegard E. Peplau, RN, EdD, FAAN
Professor Emerita
Rutgers University

Preface

Mental health nursing has recently focused on the family as the critical component in correcting the problems of the individual. It is now held as truth that much that is right in our lives is the result of the love, support, and guidance of our families and that much that is wrong in our lives results from the problems, shortcomings, and dilemmas faced by our family and family members.

The contemporary health care system has "understood" about the family for years but continues to offer treatment only to individual members. Acceptance of the family form has been and continues to be questioned by the health care system.

It is hoped that the reader of this book will gain a perspective that in working with the individual, there is an equal need to work with the family and that as we work through our issues to deal more openly and effectively with individuals, we must also do the same with family members, families, and family groups.

The purpose of this book is to help nurses and others who care for family members and families to become more aware of special problems, needs, and issues in the life of the present and future family.

The book is organized into three sections. Unit I offers background information in gaining a perspective that will assist the nurse in the organization of thoughts around family principles. Unit II offers definition to the transitional periods that many families frequently maneuver. The chapters of Unit III develop specific areas that cause families and family members unique and possibly severe distress.

The book is intended for students of nursing, as well as practicing clinicians in all areas of nursing. Psychiatric nurses are not the only nurses who see families or who deal with the stresses discussed in this book.

Sincere thanks are offered to each of the contributing authors for their spirits of cooperation and their proficiency in expert practice. Their abilities made this book a reality.

Thanks, too, to the people at Resource Applications and Mosby—in particular, Teri Merchant. The book certainly would not have been completed without her assistance, persistance, and support.

Finally, ongoing thanks need to be expressed to my family and its members. Without them, I would not have been able to complete this task.

Christine S. Fawcett

Contents

Unit I

Theory and Conceptual Framework

Chapter 1

The Contemporary Family

Christine S. Fawcett

The contemporary family is a family unit in transition. What is currently defined as "family" may greatly resemble past family prototypes or bear no apparent resemblance at all. This chapter offers a definition of family, discusses the current model of the concept of family, and discusses various stages of family development.

Family Definition

Every individual holds a belief about what constitutes a family. This belief is shaped by the individual's personal experience with his or her own family and his or her observations of other families, both real and fictional. Examples of well-known and emulated families include the Kennedy family and families from television shows such as "Father Knows Best," "Lassie," "The Simpsons," and "Murphy Brown."

In concept and reality, the term and being "family" has come to resemble the members of a shared household who hold similar values and participate in shared goals. By tradition, this family usually comprises persons bonded by blood relations and by legal actions of marriage and adoption.

WHAT IS A FAMILY IN CONTEMPORARY SOCIETY?

Webster (1986) defines family as a group of individuals living under one roof, a group of persons with common ancestry.

Howard (1978) distinguishes the term with the following: "A family cares for itself. It is a separate entity larger than each of the members. It has feelings — sadness, happiness, peaks and valleys." She further states that the family, not the individual, is the real molecule of society, the key link in the social chain of being.

Carter and McGoldrick (1980) define family as a small social system made up of individuals related to each other by reason of strong reciprocal affections and loyalties, comprising a permanent household that persists over decades and generations, and any subdivision of this kind of social unit that possesses attributes of affection, loyalty, and durability of membership.

Families are each of these things and more. To some, a family may be a group of emotionally involved persons who choose to live in geographic proximity. To others, a family represents relationships of heritage and blood connectedness. To others, a family is a cluster of people to whom something is owed.

Families may consist of those individuals who band together because of shared values, goals, or other motivations. They may be linked together because of marriage or partnerships, blood linkages, or adoption. They may interact together in social roles of husband, wife, mother, father, sister, and brother.

The family may live together in a household and share a common culture. This culture may be unique but will always bear a reflection of society.

Susan and Bill, both in their 30s, live together with their two dogs. They consider themselves a family.

Carol and Fred, newly married, live with two children from Fred's first marriage, three from Carol's two former marriages, and with Carol's elderly Aunt Marie. They call themselves a family.

Neville and James, in their 40s, could not imagine living apart from each other and look forward to discussing the day's events together and sharing their love and support. They call themselves a family.

Families offer a supportive screen between the individual and the rest of the world. How the family defines itself affords those of us who study and work with the family the information on each individual, the family's collective values, the family's defined purpose, and the family's ability to buffer stress and conflict.

Formerly it was easier to define and establish family boundaries. Shared last names, similarities in ages, and having a childbearing focus were all assumptions made to declare what constituted a "family." These assumptions do not hold true in today's world. Persons are deciding to define and select the partners they want to call supportive friends or perhaps family.

Among the shared characteristics that appear in families are the following:

- Blood relationships: parents, children, siblings, cousins
- Marital partnerships
- Feeling love and affection
- Showing caring and compassion
- Feeling sense of belonging and connectedness
- Having history and linkage to posterity
- Practicing rituals to rejoice
- Having a sense of place
- Accepting their membership even with shortcomings
- Honoring their elders
- Having system of earning and spending money
- Having competent manner of parenting or caretaking
- Dividing chores and labor

There are more family characteristics; each family certainly defines itself through the establishment of what is unique to them and in what they pride themselves.

Current Model of Family

With regularity, the family unit has been changing its values and rituals and demanding new roles, outputs, and concerns of its members. With regularity, the family unit has also been upholding its values, rituals, and roles of past breeds. Not surprisingly, in light of this need to change and to remain constant, the family of today is undergoing severe stress.

Changes of gender issues, movement and flexibility of women's and men's roles, sexual mores, and marriage and divorce are key among current discussions of family stress.

Divorce, which was once rare and unorthodox, is not uncommon in families. This dissolution of marriage may offer confusion concerning roles, economics, responsibility, and loyalty.

This stress is responded to with conflict, anxiety, confusion, and the use of stereotyped roles and mores. We are constantly confronted with "role models" from the media, political figures, and others who offer explanations on how to decrease the conflict and pain of this stress. For some, this is further increasing the stressful feelings.

American families have always moved to areas of opportunity. In doing so, they have moved their values, culture, rituals, and role behaviors with them, modifying them as they adapted to the demands of the new situation.

These demands include leaving a family of origin, identifying the company or outside persons as the new extended family, establishing new support systems, isolating from previous supportive networks, fitting in with the new culture or feeling lonely and ostracized from it, and maintaining family values and traditions while dealing with economic constraints.

The family has also been a system embroiled with social change. The move to automation in the 1950s, the social and sexual revolutions of the 1960s, the individual focus of the 1970s, and the value of materialism of the 1980s has impacted greatly upon every family system. Each family has translated these changes into their own way of seeing, understanding, or translating what each of these changes mean and how it impacts on them.

Sandy regarded herself as a "liberated woman" who came into being herself in the early 1970s. She raised three daughters after a divorce and while she was continuing a career in teaching. She became very distressed when one of her daughters eloped. Much conflict and much discussion ensued among the family members concerning the role of women and the value of marriage versus living together.

Barry, age 25, has returned to his parent's home after completing college. He works for a well-established firm in an entry-level accounting position, but "could not consider" living on his own because he could not afford his present car or clothing or have the money to spend on entertainment if he had to pay for housing. Barry's parents looked forward to launching the children and having the house and time to themselves, but are reluctant for him to move out.

In generations past, the family of tradition was seen as one with two different gender parents, children, and a generational connection. Norms for family life were set by how the majority of families were portrayed.

Contemporary families do not necessarily meet a norm by their membership selection. Families may be singly parented, have parents who are of the same sex, or be made of children from more than one or two marriages. Terms such as *blended families, partnerships, co-parenting, nuclear* and *extended families,* and *step-families* are all used to describe the new configurations of this grouping.

Many models of family exist in current culture. Traditional families of two different gender parents were the norm for many years until a variety of family types began to reflect the changes in society. Currently, family types include the following:

- Two adults, female and male with children from the past or present relationship(s)
- Two adults, same gender with children from past or present relationships
- Two opposite gender adults without children
- Two same gender adults without children
- One adult, female or male with children
- Multigenerational — adults, children, grandparents
- Grandparent(s) with grandchildren
- Other blood relatives living together or supporting each other
- Good friends who share same values, beliefs, and support
- Individuals

Children or offspring of the families may be conceived and born into the family, they may be adopted, or they may be children of former marriages or liaisons.

Family Stages

Every family progresses through stages or cycles of life. These stages are predictable, orderly, and normative (Carter & McGoldrick, 1988). Each stage offers challenges and rewards and is marked by particular events, such as change in membership (marriage, birth) or change in activity (retirement).

Carter and McGoldrick (1980), Haley (1973), and Duvall (1977) each developed categories of orderly progression for noting family change.

Duvall's Family Life Cycle considered the traditional two-parent family and gave time frames for gauging development. The stages that she named are the following:

- Marriage of the couple
- Childbearing
- Preschool-age family
- School-age family
- Teenage
- Launching center
- Middle-age parents
- Aging family members

Haley began the incorporation of a multigenerational approach into plans for a strategic family therapy approach. He noted that continual reformation of this tool was necessary to update its usefulness in light of cultural changes. The stages he enumerated are the following:

- Courtship period
- Marriage and its consequences
- Childbirth and dealing with the young
- Middle marriage difficulties
- Weaning parents from children
- Retirement and old age

Carter and McGoldrick (1980) separated family developmental epochs into two categories: normative and paranormative. Those in the first category are the following:

- Marriage
- Birth of child
- Child enters school
- Child enters adolescence
- Birth of grandchild
- Retirement
- Senescence

The paranormative cycle includes the following:

- Miscarriage
- Marital separation and divorce
- Illness, disability, and death
- Relocations of household
- Changes in socioeconomic status
- Extrinsic catastrophe with massive dislocation of the family unit

Membership and activity changes are among the major variables in considering stages framing the contemporary family. Also of prime consideration for health care professionals are illness markers; individual growth and developmental levels, taken together with cultural considerations; ethnic backgrounds; educational abilities; and ability to navigate necessary changes.

Bridges (1980) noted that individuals progress continually through transitions. He defined this process as having three stages: endings, neutral zone, and beginnings.

This transitional progression may also be incorporated into the changes necessary for family growth, movement, and stabilization.

The contemporary family may use the current models of family life cycle to mark their transitions, or other events or aspects may be used. A few families mark their movement through notations of geographic changes, through employment changes, through illness transitions, and through membership modifications. Any or all of these are valuable to this family.

REFERENCES

Berkey, K.M., & Hanson, S.M.H. (1991). *Pocket guide to family assessment and intervention,* St. Louis: Mosby–Year Book.

Bridges, W. (1980). *Transitions: Making sense of life's changes.* Reading, MA: Addison-Wesley.

Carter, E.A., & McGoldrick, M. (Eds.). (1980). *The family life cycle: A framework for family therapy.* New York: Gardner.

Carter, E.A., & McGoldrick, M. (Eds.). (1988). *The family life cycle: A framework for family therapy* (2nd ed.). New York: Gardner.

Duvall, E.M. (1977). *Marriage and family development* (5th ed.). Philadelphia: J.B. Lippincott.

Haley, J. (1973). *Uncommon therapy: The psychiatric techniques of Milton Erickson, M.D.* New York: W.W. Norton.

Harriss, J. (Ed.). (1991). *The family: A social history of the twentieth century.* Oxford: Oxford University Press.

Howard, J. (1978). *Families.* New York: Simon & Schuster.

Johnston, M. (1981). *The health of families in a culture of crisis.* Kansas City, MO: American Nurses Foundation.

Webster's Ninth New Collegiate Dictionary. (1986). Springfield, MA: Merriam-Webster.

Chapter 2

Selected Theories of Families

Christine S. Fawcett

There are many ways to describe a family. This chapter offers selected theories that propose explanation and description of families and discusses the role of the nurse when working with families.

General Systems Theory

Most theories of the family derive their basis from concepts of general systems theory (von Bertalanffy, 1968; Laszlo, 1972). Underlying systems theory is the notion that the whole, the family, is greater than the sum of its parts, the individual members.

System and Subsystem

The family is also composed of individual members, or subsystems, which are parts of the greater system. The nuclear family is made of parents and children. This unit combines with its sibling systems to form the family of origin, which is also a member of a community, and the community is also a member of state, country, and world.

Each member may be considered a subsystem. All of the children may be viewed as the sibling systems. The parents may be seen as a subsystem; and the grandparents collectively and separately are subsystems members. Each of these subsystems is interdependent on one another to form the collective group, family, or system.

Change

Family systems are living and dynamic. Because of this, parts, relationships, and values are ever-changing. Change occurs naturally through the maturation process. It occurs when family members interact with the world and even in relationships between and among family members. Change in one member of the family affects all family members. Change may happen very quickly, as in the unexpected death of a family member, or more slowly, as a child grows to adulthood.

Change is defined as the modification of behavior to each other and to other systems as needs arise or systems demand the adaptation.

Boundary Issues

A family is truly a living system. It continually interacts and exchanges matter, energy, and information with the outside environment (Weinberg, 1975). All families have a degree of permeability: a filtering system protects and allows only selected information, matter, or energy into or out of the family. Examples of the semipermeable membrane are (1) parents screening television and movies for their children to view and (2) adult children keeping traumatic information from their elderly parents because they fear that it would "upset" them too much.

Families also have boundaries or lines of demarcation that aid in identification of individual identity and responsibility and issues that are the domain and responsibility of one part of a system rather than of a suprasystem.

Open Versus Closed

General systems theory judges a system's ability to be in an open or closed state. If a family system is open, it is believed that the exchange of matter, energy, and information is free. During times of severe stress, it is thought that some family systems may move toward being closed. An example of this is the immediate response of a family unit after the death of an important member. Another example is a family whose communication with the outside world is blocked because of political intervention.

Communication

All families interact through communication. Communication serves at least two purposes: it gives information; and it demands a behavioral response (Miller & Winstead-Fry). Verbal exchange is the most commonly used form of communication.

However, all verbal exchanges are accompanied by a nonverbal exchange. Many parents use a glance at their child to attract the child's attention and make a change in the child's behavior.

Role

Each family member plays a role in the family unit. A role may be defined as a part played by a family member. Examples of roles are mother, grandmother, wife, and daughter. Each role has certain socially expected obligations and demands certain behaviors as a result of assuming the role and the responsibility for maintaining it. The role of mother or parent and every other family role has specific obligations set by society and by various family systems.

In addition to the roles of mother, father, and grandparents, siblings play roles because of the order of their birth. Research by Toman (1969) clarified the various demands on first-born and last-born children. Further research has offered more clarity in this area.

Hierarchy and Power

Systems are organized in a particular fashion. Families are arranged so that the generation producing or selecting the offspring is the one that has power to make decisions for the group. In most cases, parents are in positions of authority above children and grandparents are above parents in the same hierarchy.

Power in a family may be connected with the ability to make decisions, the ability to earn and spend money, and the ability to regulate family recreation.

Multigenerational Theory

Bowen (1976) developed an approach to viewing a family that is one of the major theories used in this book. The perspective of this theory is one that views the family as interacting through patterns of emotional interaction. All members of the family use their own intellect to guide their emotions. If all members of the family are able to be themselves, be differentiated, they are able to be individuals, as well as a collective family. In Bowen's words, "They can be separate as well as close."

Bowen (1986) defined the term *emotional* as the force that motivates the family system. The goal of this theory and approach is to help members of families understand intellectually the family emotional system and develop means to reduce fusion or lack of differentiation of self. Eight concepts further describe this emotional system (see box below).

Multigenerational Theory Concepts

Differentiation of self.   The ability of an individual to separate his or her intellectual and emotional functioning.

Triangles.   Three-person emotional system made up of two comfortable persons and a less comfortable outsider. Under stress, the less comfortable outsider becomes less powerful.

Family projection process.   The process in which children learn the family emotional processing system.

Multigenerational transmission process.   The modality for communicating the family emotional and relationship system to each generation.

Sibling position.   Based on the research of Toman (1969), which states that an individual's personality characteristics mesh with the sibling position into which he or she was born and developed.

Emotional cut-off.   Severing the emotional ties with certain members of a family.

Nuclear family emotional system.   Patterns of emotional functioning in a particular family.

Societal regression.   The processes of the family are replicated in society.

Family Adjustment and Adaptation

McCubbin and Thompson (1987) offer another perspective in understanding the family. Their model, T-Double ABCX Model of Family Adjustment and Adaptation, is useful in understanding the family in *crisis* and then in two later phases, *adjustment* and *adaptation.*

Based on Hill's model (1958), ABCX examined the family's response to stress. Each of the letters was a formulation in an equation that configured how well a family was able to cope with stress.

A Stressor
B Resources of family
C Family's perception of event
X Crisis adjustment

McCubbin and Patterson (1981) modified the initial proposal to become the Double ABCX Model with the inclusion of the developmental transitions of each of the individuals in the family.

The T-Double ABCX (1987) offers inclusion of family types and family vulnerability. Family types are defined as including traditional, regenerative, resilient, rhythmic, and balanced. Family vulnerability focuses on the organization and interpersonal condition of the family at the time of the stress.

Role of the Nurse with Families

In many settings, nurses find themselves continuing to focus on individuals. One focus of this book is to assist the nurse to understand the need to focus on the family along with the individual. All of the dynamics covered in this book consider individual family members and their families.

Treatment or interventions with only the individual may certainly assist in the change of the individual; however, some of that change will be limited without the assistance of the family. Treatment or interventions with the family will greatly assist not only the individual, but also the rest of the family members.

REFERENCES

Bell, J.M., Watson, W.L., & Wright, L.M. (1990). *The cutting edge of family nursing.* Calgary, Alberta: Family Nursing Unit Publications.

Berkey, K.M., & Hanson, S.M.H. (1991). *Pocket guide to family assessment and intervention.* St. Louis: Mosby–Year Book.

Bowen, M. (1976). Theory in the practice of psychotherapy. In Guerin, P. (Ed.), *Family therapy.* New York: Gardner Press.

Bowen, M. (1986). *Family therapy in clinical practice.* Northvale, NJ: Jason Aronson.

Carter, E., & McGoldrick, M. (1988). *The changing family life cycle: A framework for family therapists* (2nd ed.). New York: Gardner Press.

Friedman, M. (1992). *Family nursing: Theory and assessment* (3rd ed.). Norwalk, CT: Appleton-Century-Crofts.

Gilliss, C.L., Highley, B.L., Roberts, B.M., & Martinson, I.M. (Eds.). (1989). *Toward a science of family nursing.* Menlo Park, CA: Addison-Wesley.

Hall, J.E., & Weaver, B.R. (Eds.). (1974). *Nursing of families in crisis.* Philadelphia: J.B. Lippincott.

Hill, R. (1958). Social stress on the family. *Social Casework, 39,* 142.

Laszlo, E. (1972). *The systems view of the world.* New York: George Braziller.

Leahey, M., & Wright, L.M. (1987). *Families and psychosocial problems,* Springhouse, PA: Springhouse.

Leavitt, M.B. (1982). *Families at risk.* Boston: Little, Brown.

McCubbin, H.I., & Thompson, A.I. (Eds.). (1987). *Family assessment inventories for research and practice.* Madison, WI: The University of Wisconsin-Madison.

McCubbin, H.I., Wilson, L., & Patterson, J.M. (1981). Family inventory of life events and changes. In H.I. McCubbin & J.M. Patteron (Eds.), *Systematic assessment of family stress, resources, and coping.* St. Paul, MN: Family Social Sciences Department, University of Minnesota.

Miller, S.R., & Winstead-Fry, P. (1982). *Family systems theory in nursing practice.* Reston, VA: Reston Publishing.

Toman, W. (1969). *Family constellation,* New York: Springer.

Toman, W. (1988). *Family therapy and sibling position.* Northvale, NJ: Jason Aronson.

von Bertalanffy, L. (1968). *General systems theory: Foundations, development, applications.* New York: George Braziller.

Weinberg, G.M. (1975). *An introduction to general systems thinking,* New York: John Wiley & Sons.

Wright, L.M., & Leagey, M. (1984). *Nurses and families: A guide to family assessment and intervention.* Philadelphia: F.A. Davis.

Chapter 3

Family Assessment

Terri A. Cutillo-Schmitter

Historically, the primary focus for assessment has been the individual. The client (the symptomatic family member) was seen alone to assess his or her functioning. The individual client was seen as the one in the family who needed to change.

The procedure for obtaining assessment information on admission in many in-patient psychiatric facilities has not significantly changed over the past 20 years. Generally, the psychiatrist performs the psychiatric evaluation of the client while the social worker gathers the social history from family members. The psychiatric nurse involves the client and family in a tour of the unit and in social exchanges as the belongings checklist is completed. Usually the family is then dismissed as the nursing admission assessment is completed. Even if family members are permitted to stay, the questions asked center around the individual client's functioning.

Within this same 20 years, however, a small portion of the admission focus has shifted to assessing family functioning and interaction. Systems theory has contributed to this shift in focus. The concepts of systems theory encompass a family relationship process and a connection between that process and individual functioning (Kerr & Bowen, 1988).

Besides family systems therapists, other medical and psychiatric health practitioners see the relevancy of some of the premises of the systems framework, such as *no individual exists in a vacuum* and *what has an effect on one family member affects all others to a greater or lesser degree.* Many support the belief that illness of one member influences all members to some extent and that supportive interventions and supportive services are important to not only the functioning of the symptomatic one but the functioning of the family as a whole. Flor, Turk, and Rudy (1987) contend that it makes good clinical sense to include the family in the assessment of clients experiencing chronic pain, given the findings that some families suffer considerably from the presence of a chronic pain problem and undergo major changes as a consequence. According to them, chronic pain and chronic illness can have negative impact on the family and reciprocal negative effects on the client. They have studied the uses of family functional assessment instruments, and they assert that more research is needed about how to use such tools in treatment-specific efforts. However, they concluded that such assessments provide practitioners with important additional information from which to evaluate potential family variables that contribute to the problem and hence to better determine whether, when, and to what extent the family should be included in treatment.

Many practitioners think that that which is helpful to the family contributes to increasing the amount of time the client will remain symptom-free. Many also think that to treat a client without sufficient consideration of the family will undermine the treatment. And others see the value of assessing and observing family interactions, especially for the purpose of making decisions about safe placement after discharge. Silliman, Sternburg, and Fretwell (1988) assert that evaluation of family function should be part of the functional assessment of the demented client with disruptive behavior, because not only does dementia place a burden on the caregivers, but a disturbed family creates a stressful environment for the demented client, who in turn responds with disruptive behavior.

Greater numbers of health centers are evolving into family-centered care programs where families are receiving greater roles in the admission, treatment, and discharge processes. Rushton (1990) maintains that as the critical care setting becomes increasingly dominated by technology and as healthcare systems restructure to meet the needs of sicker patients, successful implementation of family-centered care will become crucial.

Also, little by little, greater numbers of mental health centers and psychiatric in-patient departments are valuing the involvement of families in assessment and treatment of individuals. Nurses who have been involved in family model programs can readily cite examples from their practice of positive clinical outcomes when the broader system was assessed at the outset of treatment. Colson, Grame, and Coyne (1990) believe that ample evidence exists from both clinical and research realms demonstrating that family intervention can be crucial for the process and outcome of psychiatric hospital treatment and aftercare. They state that "it profits no one to ignore the powerful mutual interaction of patient and family in the course and outcome of treatment."

Although evidence is growing to support the family systems view that the family contributes to the cause and to the maintenance of the symptom in the individual, few therapists support the goal of systems psychotherapy, which is to effect change in the family relationship system. According to Combrinck-Graham (1990):

> That depression has profound interpersonal effects is not new information. That relational treatment of affective disorders has longer lasting effects and lower relapse rate is also not new information. The possibility that depression can be brought about in interpersonal contexts may be surprising. Nevertheless, researchers examining families in which an adult has a major depression have made intriguing observations about modifying influences of certain kinds of interactions on dysphoria.

In family systems model mental health programs, the purpose of the family assessment process is to engage the family in the healing process and to support the membership in finding its own solutions to the problem. More nurses should promote comprehensive nursing assessments of families to gather important information about family variables that contribute to the problems in individuals. Nurses who purport to treat the client's response to illness will need to evaluate the relationship between the individual's physical and emotional pain response to the family relationships and to the happenings in the systems of which the client is an integral part.

Case Studies that Support the Need for Family Assessment at Admission

The first family case in a systems model in-patient unit involves a 16-year-old girl who was hospitalized after an attempted suicide. A family assessment was conducted while the team that would be involved with the client during her hospitalization observed on a monitor and phoned questions into the therapy room as additional questions were warranted. Caroline's family, which consisted of a younger sister and her parents, had recently moved to another state several hundred miles from their lifetime residence. Her mother was being treated, in a nearby well-known medical center for a blood dyscrasia disease, using a drug known to be highly effective for that disorder. However, the mother was not showing progress as was anticipated by her treating physicians.

The admission assessment revealed that this middle-aged woman was very enmeshed with her own parents and that she and the family had resided in the same town with them since her marriage until the recent move. Caroline and her father were also very close. Intensive family therapy, three times per week, was planned, and the maternal grandparents agreed to be involved in the family therapy as therapy evolved. Positive clinical outcomes occurred for both this young client and her mother within 3 weeks. Caroline's depression abated (without the use of psychopharmacology), and her mother's physical illness began to respond positively to the drug therapy previously initiated. Family assessment at admission permitted the team to plan efficaciously at the outset of treatment.

In contrast, at another 600-bed metropolitan hospital, a 6-year-old boy (Eric) was hospitalized for tactile hallucinations. The family pediatrician had consulted a psychiatrist, who assessed the patient. In the meantime the pediatric clinical nurse specialist (CNS) elicited help from the child and adolescent psychiatric CNS and together they interviewed the child utilizing play. During a brief period the young boy related the following data to the nurses: Eric's young mother's boyfriend had recently left the home. The maternal grandfather was very sick, possibly with terminal cancer. The house was in disrepair, possibly with a leaking roof and bats in the attic that had gotten into the boy's bedroom. The house was infested with bugs, possibly with ants, spiders, and roaches. At home Eric was receiving regular daily doses of medication for "itching." Benadryl was still being administered on the unit. Both CNSs collaborated with the attending and consulting physicians, and the focus of treatment changed because of the additional family data.

The mother was offered supportive counseling, and needed services were arranged for discharge. Also, treatment with Benadryl was discontinued to see if the neurologic symptoms that Eric was experiencing would abate. If relevant family information had been gathered on admission by the pediatric nurse who interviewed the mother about the child's present symptoms or even before admission by the nurse in the physician's office, both time and energy would have been saved, resulting in more cost-effective treatment, possibly with out-patient therapy being sufficient. It should be noted that the treating pediatrician promoted supportive networking with the families she treated in her office whenever she became aware of such a need. Perhaps a more reliable format for gathering relevant family data would have permitted her to treat this overly stressed young woman and her son more effectively at the outset of treatment.

Relevance of Family Assessment for the Psychiatric Nurse

Over the last decade psychiatric nurses have become increasingly observant of client and family transactions during hospital admission and of membership responses during family visits. Some nurses have been documenting and reporting their observations about how different family members elicit different behavior from their client and vise versa. By assessing these exchanges and discussing these in treatment team planning, psychiatric nurses have supplied relevant data that have changed the way the team perceives the problem and plans treatment. This has made a difference in the care that clients receive.

By asking relevant questions of family members, nurses can elicit family information that broadens the team's focus to include the well-being of the entire system. For example, in a collaborative interview held by a psychiatrist and a nurse with a demented client, the client's wife, and their son, the nurse asked the members toward the end of the interview if they had any other concerns for the family. The son immediately focused from his father's disruptive behaviors and onto his concerns about his mother and her heart problems, her insufficient attention to treatment options, and her neglect of his offer to help her. The conflict between the mother and son about family priorities became readily apparent as the client's spouse addressed her son's concerns. Because of the additional information, the focus of the team could be broadened to include the goal for the mother and son dyad to resolve the conflict between them. This endeavor provides a calm to the system and support for memberships affiliations while they attempt to adjust to changing roles brought about by the rapid mental deterioration of the demented family member.

Each family member's perspective of the problem and the family patterns of relating together are valuable clinical data for the nurse, for the treating psychiatrist, and for all members of the team. Nurses can use the data collected from families on admission to successfully plan family experiences that promote a change in the way family members relate to each other. Psychiatric nurses can promote family interventions that influence change in family transactions when they gather family assessment data at admission and when they continue to reassess family involvement as they help clients and families attempt new options as treatment evolves.

For example, focusing on the developmental issues, alone, that contribute to problems in individuals permits the psychiatric nurse to be more sensitive and more competent about selecting topics for teaching and counseling strategies. Nursing interventions should incorporate assisting clients and families with family tasks, as outlined by Duvall (1971), and with the critical emotional issues with which the family struggles in their present life-cycle stage, as presented by Carter and McGoldrick (1980). Life-cycle changes create strains and stress on family members, who must readjust and adapt to the ebb and flow of entrances and exits of family members through such events as births, marriages, leaving home, migrations, and deaths. As life-cycle transitions progress, members to some degree must absorb new attitudes, new roles, and new tasks or shift relationships, give up roles, accept exits, and eventually prepare for death. Besides these stressors, family styles of relating transmitted down the generations provide stressors to family and individuals. See the box on p. 19 to understand the two-directional flow of family stressors.

In the first case history, the nurse could hypothesize that Caroline's mother was never able to separate successfully from her family of origin and that the closeness between Caroline and her father was also interfering in the present with Caroline's differentiating from the nuclear family. In the family with adolescents, increasing flexibility of family boundaries is needed to include the child's independence. Using developmental theory, nurses assessing adolescents like Caroline may want to encourage tasks that would provide the adolescents with opportunities to gain a sense of competence in their own abilities. Nurses also may explore with the adolescents options that would encourage positive peer involvement outside the family. And nurses may want to provide the adolescent time to role play age-appropriate ways for discussing his or her needs and wants with the parents in preparation for family sessions. The nurse also could help teens who have difficulty talking on the unit to share opinions with peers and get feedback from them. Nurses can help teens identify an "I" position and then defend it. In this way the adolescent can begin to differentiate a self in relation to the peer group and in relationship to the family of origin.

In the second case study, major variations existed in the young mother's normal life cycle that stressed the system further, thus reducing her functioning to a degree, necessitating her to reach out to health professionals for help with her symptomatic child. This case emphasizes the importance of a full family assessment and the need for inquiry about upper generations, even when the presenting problem appears somewhere else in the family system. The symptom may function in the service of the family in crisis, as did Eric's tactile hallucinations. Eric's mother needed to deal with her boyfriend's separation, as well as with her father's disability and the possibility of his death at an early age. Dealing with terminal illness is an immensely difficult task for any family to absorb.

The Family Life-Cycle Perspective

This perspective demands a shift from thinking about the individual to thinking about the family as an emotional unit. In thinking about the family as a unit, one views family members in relationship to each other; i.e., the interplay of numerous forces at work over time is assessed and evaluated. It is a different way to think about the human condition. The symptom in the identified person (IP) is seen as a product of the total family problem. The symptom is not just a symptom of what is going on physiologically and internally (psychosocial conflicts), but is related to the emotional events in the larger family unit.

Stressors occur from two directions

Horizontally

Developmentally
Predictable transitions for all families as they move forward through time coping with the natural changes and transitions of the life cycle.

External
Unpredictable events that occur, such as untimely deaths, birth of defective child, war.

Vertically

Patterns of relating and functioning that are transmitted down the generations in a family, primarily through the mechanism of emotional triangling. It includes all the family attitudes, taboos, expectations, labels, and loaded issues with which people grow up.

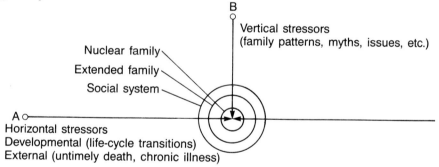

Given enough stress on the horizontal axis, any family will appear extremely dysfunctional, and even a small horizontal stress on a family in which the vertical axis is full of intense stress will create great disruption in the system.

It is important to look at both dimensions when treating an individual or family. i.e., the current life-cycle transitions and their connection to family themes, triangles, and labels coming down in families over historical time.

The central underlying process to be negotiated is the expansion, contraction, and realignment of the relationship system to support the entry, exit, and development of family members in a functional way. Once the key principles of the transition process have been acknowledged, the family can move onto the various shifts involved in entering and proceeding developmentally through the next stage of the family life cycle.

Note. Modified from *The Family Life Cycle: A Framework for Family Therapy* by E.A. Carter and M. McGoldrick, 1980, New York: Gardner.

When assessing a patient in a similar situation, the nurse may help the client to gain accurate information about her family member's illness and prognosis. She may want then to explore issues surrounding the client's concerns for the family. Psychiatric nurses also need to know how to access community services for just such a case. The nurse may want to explore alternatives in living arrangements and to secure help from a social worker and a visiting nurse. He or she may also want to assist similar young clients to gain competence in problem-solving and in finding a wider support network. All of these nursing interventions help calm the system and promote thoughtful considerations of alternative options for handling interpersonal interactions, hence promoting differentiation from one's family of origin while remaining positively attached to the family. In assessing young mothers like Eric's the nurse should further assess her understanding of Eric's developmental needs and then assist his mother in (1) meeting the needs of her offspring and in turn (2) helping him to do for himself age-appropriate tasks. The nurse also should reassess the mother's understanding of administering medications to a young child. Teaching parents how to properly administer medicine to children is another nursing intervention that naturally flows from an admission assessment for such a client.

When nurses assess clients and families developmentally, they can easily refer to developmental theory for guidelines in knowing what kinds of assistance clients adjusting to normal life-cycle changes require. To focus on family life-cycle stages, psychiatric nurses should redesign nursing assessment tools to incorporate the documentation of these normal life-cycle stages and any dislocations, such as divorce, which requires even additional steps for the system to restabilize. Understanding the emotional turmoil experienced at various stages prepares nurses to be sensitive to the client and family who are stuck and who need encouragement to find family resources for healing.

Psychiatric nurses are in a strong position to collect, organize, and integrate family data at admission, because it is usually the nurse who consistently first sees the client and the family at the outset of treatment and during subsequent visits. Actually, psychiatric nurses share a unique responsibility for synthesizing and recording family assessment information and for discussing observed family transactions with the attending psychiatrist to effect relevant planning, pertinent treatment strategies, and positive client outcomes.

Nursing Assessment Tools

Traditional psychiatric initial nursing assessment tools include only biopsychosocial components of the client's functioning. The individual's life-style patterns, allergies, current medications, social involvements, presenting problem, mental status, and past medical, psychiatric, and addictions hospitalizations are the general topics explored.

When a more sophisticated tool is used, it requests information about both individual and family functional status. Recent life changes, life-cycle stage, and current critical life events are explored. Such topics as nightmares, flashback experiences, and traumatic events are investigated to rule out patterns of physical, emotional, and sexual abuse, as well as to assess for episodes of violence in the family. When more sophisticated nursing tools are used, questions that elicit responses about family membership and patterns are asked, such as who lives in the household and who are the significant others; who is antagonistic and who is supportive to the client and family; and who is cut off from the family. Process questions are also asked the client, such as *how does the hospitalization affect you and other members;* and *who in the family does what when you become ill.*

An even more sophisticated tool incorporates asking questions from a group of family members not only about the client's present and past functioning but also about the current family functioning and about their functioning over time. Thus one gains the perspectives of as many family members as possible at admission. When nurses involve family members in the initial assessment interview, a broader view of the problem becomes available from which to consider the available strategies for caregiving.

Sometimes a client will sit silently while another party describes the presenting problem and answers all the nurse's questions. Thus the nurse still receives a narrow perspective of the problem. When the nurse involves everyone who presents at admission in the interview and when he or she even has them answer the same questions, the nurse gains valuable information about everyone's perspective of the problem and about their individual concerns for the family. The nurse also is able to observe the family as they relate together.

When the nurse knows what clients and their families expect and what they want from treatment, the nurse is more apt to plan interventions that will lead to greater compliance. He or she is more apt to know what issues to talk about later with them when the family is involved in telling the nurse their story. The nurse is also in a better position to advocate for families when he or she has heard their concerns directly from them. When nurses gather family assessment data at admission and share it at the initial team planning session, which should occur within the first 24 and 72 hours of admission, treatment is planned more efficaciously.

Following are two simple tools that nurses can redesign and use for family assessment at admission. From both types of assessments discussed in this chapter, hypotheses can be generated about family patterns, family issues, and the life-cycle stages in which the family is struggling. Therefore the nurse who uses one of these methods is more apt to plan strategies that will promote individuation while having members positively involved in the family to-getherness process. When nurses are actively connected with family members at admission, they can be extremely helpful in coaching family members during visiting times to appropriately listen to each other and to meet the needs of self and one another in more thoughtful, calm, and mature ways. Also, nurses can plan more beneficial education and counseling sessions when they know the family knowledge deficits and the family's major concerns and desired changes.

A TOOL ADAPTED FROM JAY HALEY

The first tool presented was adapted from Haley (1976). In his book *Problem-Solving Therapy* he defines four stages for conducting an initial family interview. The process and structure that he offers are pertinent and useful for nurses. The tool gives relevant family information at a glance (Figure 3-1). It

List family members' names and titles: _____   _____
                                        I.P.   Spouse

_____   _____   _____
Children / Sibs   Parents   Parents

_____   _____   _____
Other   Grandparents   Grandparents

Names of members who reside with the I.P. _____

Record each member's perspective of the problem (concerns of the membership):

Record the changes the different members desire to have changed prior to ending treatment:

Record goals for beginning treatment:

_____   _____
    Signatures of family   Signatures of staff

Copyright 1991, Terri Cutillo Schmitter, RN, MSN, C.S.

Figure 3-1   Nursing family assessment tool.

presents easy access to the perspectives of the client and other family members because it summarizes in members' words their current concerns about the family and about the changes they seek through treatment. It also summarizes the goals that the family as a whole are willing to set with the professional nurse on admission.

The first stage of the Haley interview is labeled the *social stage,* in which the family is greeted and made comfortable by the interviewer. This is an important part of the interview and involves *joining* with the family, which is critical to treatment and which will be discussed later in the chapter.

The second stage is called the *problem stage,* in which the inquiry is about the presenting problem. In this stage I merely suggest that the nurse ask two questions and have each family member answer: "What are the problems that bring you here today?" and "What are your concerns for your family?" The nurse is also instructed to politely tell the family that it is extremely beneficial to have the family members take turns in giving information one at a time, without interrupting the one telling his or her story.

The third stage is labeled the *interaction stage,* in which the family members are asked to talk to each other. I have purposefully chosen, however, not to use the third stage of the Haley interview, which I omitted from the format (structure) of the nursing interview. I believe that it has relevance only when one is more fully trained and qualified for or is being supervised to provide family therapy. Family enactments can cause the intensity in the family relationship process to erupt in the room. Skilled as well as unskilled therapists find it hard to effectively manage the emotional reactivity of the family without assistance.

The fourth stage is the *goal-setting stage,* in which the family is asked to specify just what changes the family wishes to occur before ending treatment. This part of the interview sets up a partnership with the family from which to begin working. After the family give their answers, the nurse should summarize with them beginning goals from which to begin care.

These goals must incorporate the family focus but should also include the nurse focus so the goals reflect that which the treatment center realistically can offer the family. The interview is then ended by explaining to the family what will happen next. In an in-patient unit it might be a tour of the unit or it might be distributing cards with names and phone numbers of the care providers. And if the family is to return for treatment, an appointment is also given by the nurse.

I have used this process for providing brief family assessments with staff nurses to engage the family at admission to more effectively involve them in the treatment phase. The format comprises one page, so it is easy to record and to access. At a glance, other nurses and care providers can digest the family's multiperspectives and their reasons for being in treatment. They can easily grasp what the family hopes to change or have changed through treatment. Focusing on this kind of data allows the nurse to know more about the issues that he or she should initially explore with the client and family. And as the nurse continues to gently confront wider issues, he or she can continue to plan nursing strategies and family experiences that will more likely help the family resolve the problem that initially brought them into treatment.

To use this first tool, however, several family members who are directly involved in the client's life must be present at admission for the interview. When the client presents for treatment alone, another appointment may be arranged for a family interview during the initial 72 hours of admission. Or if this is not possible, another format such as the genogram can be used to elicit applicable family data.

Results for nurses who have used the tool. Nurses who have used the tool adapted from the Haley interview consider the experiences useful and helpful to their practice. According to several of them, the experience with the family enabled them to know the family better and to have the family relate to them on a more therapeutic level. The admission interview seemed to have encouraged nurses to seek family out in helpful ways. For example, in a busy adolescent program where 18 to 26 teens were hospitalized at any given time, the nurses who were involved in the family assessments became more involved with families in a variety of ways throughout the adolescents' stay. They initially formulated the mutual goals with the parents, which established a way for working together on the unit in the future as treatment evolved. Hence when families visited, the nurses were prepared to get involved and they took advantage of opportunities to coach parents and children to interact more effectively together, instead of just making social exchanges with families or ignoring them as in the past.

These nurses also spent more time on the phone with family members, not as in the past merely to listen to parents lament about their child's behavior but instead to assist the parent with decisions about a relevant consequence for their teen's behavior. The nurses also began to phone parents at home more readily when parental feedback was warranted by events happening on the unit. Hence the nurses helped parents develop skill in providing positive feedback to their child when the teen's behavior was more age appropriate.

Nurses who worked with adults in another psychiatric setting with initial family assessments also reported better success in engaging clients and their spouses in relevant problem-solving during family visits to the units on which they were employed. All of these nurses commented that they more easily engaged families in setting pertinent family goals for passes outside the hospital. And they reported that these families also gave more useful data upon return from pass than that which nurses had received before performing the initial family admission interviews.

THE GENOGRAM AS A NURSING ASSESSMENT TOOL

Using a genogram at admission is another format for obtaining useful family data and for recording large amounts of data in a concise manner. A genogram is a format for drawing a visual map of the family that lists data about significant members of a three- or four-generation family, such as names, birth and death dates, education, occupation, marriages, migrations, divorces, remarriages, medical, social, and psychiatric illness, and cutoffs (Figure 3-2). Genograms display family information graphically in a way that readily provides a gestalt of complex family patterns and a rich source of hypotheses about how a clinical

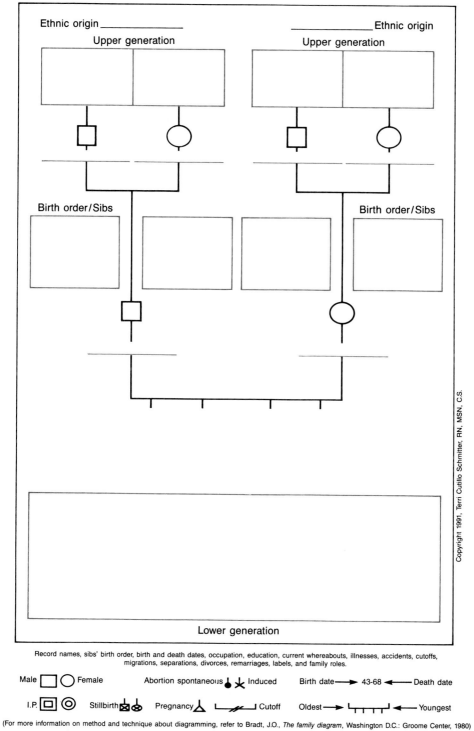

Figure 3-2 Genogram.

problem may be connected to the family context and the evolution of both problem and context over time (McGoldrick & Gerson, 1985).

Performing a genogram on each admission would provide nurses with a systematic way for learning and recording important family information in a compact format for easy reference. For most nursing staff in a busy center, it is almost impossible to review a chart on all new clients before providing care to them on any given day. It is, however, most important for nurses to know about the new client so that they can be sensitive to the client situation. A genogram (a family map) records important summary information succinctly so that it can be gleaned quickly and efficiently by any nurse or care provider who needs to have pertinent information in a short time.

Relevancy for using a genogram. Rogers and Cohn (1988) found that genograms captured more family information than physicians' routine family histories and that the ability of a genogram to detect psychosocial problems in family members was superior to that of routine histories. In addition, they found that genograms will lead to increased physician exploration of family issues. It is my experience that the additional family information enriches the psychiatric team's perspective of the presenting problem and how to begin helping families resolve pertinent family issues.

I have also found that the additional family data often change the attitude and the behaviors of the staff. This became apparent to me while I was involved in the treatment of a sexual abuse perpetrator. It was difficult for the nurses and other clinicians to provide care to this male client who was admitted to our busy adult in-patient center after an attempted suicide after disclosure of his crimes. Most staff avoided him unless he requested something from them. A genogram format was used to collect and to record additional current and past family data. The family map afforded easy access to much of the family history in which extreme abuse was documented. This additional data sensitized the staff, who were then more able to be empathetic of this traumatized individual. Even though staff still had distinct distaste for the client's behavior, they spent more time with him, attempting to engage him in conversations and in groups. They were also able to appreciate the need for family work and to cooperate in such a way that the family sessions could occur on the locked unit.

An admission nursing assessment using the genogram format can be used by the nurse to gather necessary client and family information. It can serve as the nurse's part of the comprehensive team assessment. It can be gathered from whomever presents at admission even if the client presents alone or when information must be taken from a family member because the client is unwilling or unable as a result of his mental state to give applicable admission data.

A genogram on each client chart would serve as an excellent tool for updating information and for correcting information as the nurse continues to obtain additional family data. It would also provide all team members with a rich data base about the family and client. Such relevant information contributes to the formulation of realistic team treatment goals and interventions. It offers all team members a way to keep track of the family membership, nodal family events, and client and various members' roles in their present family and families of origin. The genogram also presents family labels and family patterns that have significance in the ongoing care of the client. In their book *Genograms in Family Assessment,* McGoldrick and Gerson (1985) offer invaluable assistance in the types of questions to ask and in the hypotheses one can make while assessing and treating individuals and families using a genogram format. A genogram format permits the nurse to draw conclusions about the family and client function over time, about emerging family patterns, and about such unresolved issues as issues of loss.

Genogram information can also be gathered throughout the client's stay and recorded in such a way that it can be copied and given back to the client as a historical keepsake that can then be used and shared by family over time. (Currently the geriatric unit where I am employed is using a family map and a life review format for gathering family information. The information is then copied for the client record, and the original is sent home with the family. The format for life review work was also loaned to a University instructor for use by junior nursing students with residents in a long-term care facility.)

Herth (1989) found the genogram to be useful as both an assessment tool and an appropriate intervention strategy in certain specific situations. She believes that genograms can provide a comprehensive, holistic picture of elderly clients and their environment. In addition to collecting family data, when Herth engaged the elder in the participation of the diagraming process, she was able to assess the elder's functioning in sensoriperception, memory function, functional communication, fine motor skills, and behavioral domains. The genogram offers nurses many choices in application so as to gather pertinent assessment data for a variety of client populations.

A suggested procedure for the genogram nursing assessment interview. Just as with the first tool, in the beginning of the interview it is important to hold a brief social stage, making introductions and determining the best way to join with the members. It helps to explain to the family the purpose of using a genogram, such as to gain a visual map of the family. Also, somewhere in the interview, families should be warned before the nurse probes into difficult areas that questions may be difficult and that the family may choose not to explore any area that it does not wish to discuss.

After the preliminaries, the nurse begins the second stage of the interview by recording the members present and listing on the genogram diagram the names of the people who reside with the identified client (see box, p. 28). The genogram format for the nursing assessment includes additional data the nurse should gather about the individual to meet standards.

Because the family is eager to tell their story, the interviewer begins by asking about the problem that brought the client and family to the center. It is important to start with the family focus, concentrating on the present problem as the family see it. It helps to include questions about what has been tried and what has failed and to gradually build up to exploring similar problems in the client's and family's past. This should be done only as the family is comfortable and wishes to share the larger context of the problem. In other words, the process of gathering family data to capture relevant historical information

---

Nursing Assessment: Genogram Format

I   Facilitate social stage and introductions

II   List members present for interview (member who initiated treatment)
     List members of identified person's (IP's) household
     Explore history of presenting problem (reason for the family coming for treatment)

III Explore history of IP's hospitalizations/treatments: medical; psychiatric; addictions
     Explore IP's current medical problems: acute and chronic; how currently managed;
     current medications; allergies

IV   Explore other family history (begin with nuclear family)
     Ask about who else in the family is symptomatic; past similar problems/symptoms
         of other members
     Explore recent life events: family transitions and situational stressors/changes
     Explore marital couple and functioning of spouses over the years
     Explore roles and labels; close affiliations and cutoffs in the family over time
     Explore serious illnesses, problems in nuclear family and extended membership
         (serious illness—medical, psychiatric; chronic pain syndrome, addictions to
         prescribed medications, drugs, alcohol; violence and abuse)

V   Ask about current concerns for IP; for other members; for family in general
     Ask about the changes that the family desire to see before ending treatment
     Formulate mutual goals

VI   Perform client mental status and physical assessment
     List family strengths and liabilities
     Record impressions and nursing diagnoses
     Record recommendations for nursing interventions and strategies

---

should extend from exploring the current household and members closest to the client to the wider extended family and the broader social systems, such as close friends, school, job, and community associations. It is extremely important for the nurse to constantly refocus on the present when the client or family see no point in exploring extended relatives and past events.

Once the family tell their story, and especially if they present the problem as a "client problem," it helps if the nurse directs the next set of questions about the client. Exploring such topics as the IP's current and past medical conditions, allergies, current medications, and management of acute and chronic conditions, as well as history of past psychiatric or addictions treatment, helps reassure the family that the nurse's focus is similar to the family focus. This completes the third part of the interview, and the nurse next begins to focus on collecting more data about family during the fourth stage. The nurse should initially investigate and use the diagram to record nonthreatening information about other family members. Exploring birth dates, birth orders, education, occupation, and health status should occur before delving into more difficult data, such as the causes and circumstances of family members' deaths; serious

***Questions When Using a Genogram History: At Admission; Within 72 Hours
of Admission; or Over Time for Life Review Work***

When, from where, and why did the family migrate to this country

What have you heard about or experienced as life in the old country
What are the whereabouts of extended family members
What have you heard about your grandparents, great uncles, aunts, and cousins
What have you heard about grandparents', aunts', and uncles' reasons for leaving home

Discuss mother's family and then father's family

Birth order of mother (father) and siblings
Education, occupational history, geographic locations over time, health history
Birth and death dates; from what did each die or how did each die
What do you know/remember about your mother's (father's) family and specifically
  about mother (father)
What do you remember most about mother (father)
What was mother (father) like
What traits of theirs do you own
What traits have you passed on to your children; others
Share an event between you and your mother (father)
To which parent did you feel closer; share reason
Was there any distance/conflict between you and one parent (ask reason)

What do you remember about your parents as a couple

How did they meet; what attracted them to each other
How long were they married; what did they like to share
Explore issues in the marriage: separations, divorce, other marriages (if any)
How did they relate to each other (how do they relate now)
What kinds of things do/did they share together

Who in the family was named after another member/significant person

Who inside and outside the family has been important to your family/to you
Who were your favorite aunt/uncle/cousin/sister/brother
Has anyone else ever lived with your family (where are they now; what happened to
  them)
What is the birth order of your siblings

How did family members react to a specific family member's birth

How did family members react to a specific family member's *leaving home/marriage*
How did family members react to a specific family member's *death*

Are any family members especially close

Who helps whom out when help is needed
In whom do family members confide

Do any family members not speak to each other

(or who have ever had a period of not speaking to each other; issues of conflict)
Explore problem(s): how have relationships been influenced by the issue/problem

Continued.

Questions When Using a Genogram History: At Admission; Within 72 Hours of Admission; or Over Time for Life Review Work — cont'd

What does the future hold for the family

What will happen in the family if the problem continues; if it goes away

What has been your family's experience with professionals or agencies

Discuss early childhood memories

What are your most vivid childhood memories
What are your earliest recollections as a child
What is the first song that you recollect hearing
What is your earliest recollection of being sick; did parents/sibs treat you differently
Inquire about family play; chores; trauma; relationship with each sibling

Discuss teenage and young adult years

Ask about adventuresome moments and about activities shared with peers, sibs, cousins, others; first sexual experience
How did they declare independence/first leave home

Discuss your courtship and marriage(s)

Ask about what each was doing when they met
What attracted you to your spouse and your spouse to you
Explore where each was born; education; work history
Ask if either had any physical, emotional; social symptoms prior to their meeting; during courtship; early marriage, etc.
How/where/when did you and your spouse(s) meet
What else was happening in the family when you were contemplating marriage
Explore the length(s) of courtship/marriage
Ask about the wedding; who came; who didn't and the reason; who was not invited/reason
What kinds of things did you enjoy doing as a young couple together
Explore earlier marriages/divorces and issues of conflict
Where are ex-spouse(s) and children by that marriage now and current relationship
Inquire about any moves and issues involved; either couple returning to school; change in occupations
Who lived with the couple over time
All couples have some disagreements; what did you and spouse disagree about
What sorts of conflict and problems have you had (currently have)
Explore the birth order of the spouse and relevant family members; issues and patterns

Discuss child(ren) conceived inside or outside of the couples' marriage(s)

How did you/your spouse/family members react to your pregnancies/birth(s) of your child(ren)
Was anyone in the family sick during any pregnancy; early months of any birth
How do/did you get along with each of your children
Who is/was closest to whom

Questions When Using a Genogram History: At Admission; Within 72 Hours of Admission; or Over Time for Life Review Work — cont'd

What kinds of things did you and spouse enjoy doing with your children growing up
What were the most pleasurable ages/stages of development
Did any of your children have problems as young children/teenagers/young adults
Are any of your children having any difficulty now
Does anyone in the family not speak to another member
Have any recent job changes, unemployment, or other work changes occurred
Which child(ren) have gotten married/separated/divorced
Which child(ren) have children; how many; how old; any in college, service, careers
Do any problems exist between any of the children/grandchildren
Do any of your family members frequently take prescribed medications
Do any of your children/grandchildren have problems with drugs/alcohol
Has anyone in the family been ill, moved away, had an accident, died, been arrested

What do you think the future holds for your family/for particular members

Explore the present and provide a personal evaluation

Describe your present life-style and daily activities: nutrition; sleep and rest patterns; smoking habits; alcohol consumption; usage of prescribed medications, as well as street drugs
What are your present living conditions; with whom do you live
If given a choice, is this where you would like to live
How is your present health; are you as active as you would like to be; are you as active as most people your age
Does your church affiliation play an important part in your life/any other affiliations
Are any situations in your neighborhood/community affecting you emotionally

What things are going on in your life right now that are worthwhile to you

Who are the important people in your life
What are your greatest pleasures; accomplishments

What things are making it hard for you right now

Persistent thoughts, feelings, fears, regrets

If you could repeat any part of your life, what would you like to change

Note. Modified from *Family Evaluation: An Approach Based on Bowen Theory* by M.E. Kerr and M. Bowen, 1988, New York: W.W. Norton; and from *Genograms in Family Assessment* by M. McGoldrick and R. Gerson, 1985, New York: W.W. Norton.

emotional and social diseases in the family; and issues behind cutoffs and other family conflict.

Generally, the nurse will want to explore the nuclear family first and then explore the upper and lower generations in the direction that seems appropriate to the family focus, until three or four generations are captured to some degree. The exploration of extended family data should not continue past ½ hour unless it is beneficial to the client and family. Further exploration can continue in follow-up sessions. Before ending the genogram interview, I believe it is valuable to explore the concerns of the people in the room and to request information from them about the changes that they desire to see before ending treatment. During this fifth stage the nurse should then solidify with the family a goal for beginning treatment. To end the interview she should give the family information about what to expect about their involvement in the client's treatment and with the nursing staff and other team members. The sixth stage begins after the family is comfortably situated. The client's mental status and physical assessment should be completed; impressions and nursing diagnoses formulated; and recommendations for treatment recorded (see box, pp. 29-31).

A Case Study From a Genogram Admission Assessment

To elaborate on the data recorded on the IP's genogram (Figure 3-3), the interpretations will follow the categories outlined by McGoldrick and Gerson (1985).

CATEGORY 1: FAMILY STRUCTURE

The 88-year-old client lives with her 49-year-old adopted son. He is her only child. He moved into the client's home 1 day after his father's death 9 years ago. His wife and he had been having marital problems at the time, and they have remained separated but not divorced since then. Also residing with the client and her son is a male boarder, who also had marital difficulty when he was given refuge by the family. According to the client, the boarder has overstayed his visit by 9 months. The daughter-in-law, who was never accepted by the client, lives in a home previously owned by the client and her husband and given to the son and his family when the couple moved to a new home shortly before the death of the husband. It is unclear if both of the son's children live in the home, but at least one of them resides there with her own child(ren). More complete data about the lower generations and their functioning still need to be collected. What is interesting to note is that in the upper generation the client's father was unable to convince his wife to come to America for 6 years after he migrated here. One suspects she had difficulty leaving her parents. The same family configuration exists in the present, with the son living with the client and conflicted about remaining in the home.

The living arrangements alone give clues to possibilities for strains, rigid triangles, cross-generational boundaries, alliances, and loyalty conflicts. The client's son presents with some depression, as well as somatic complaints. And

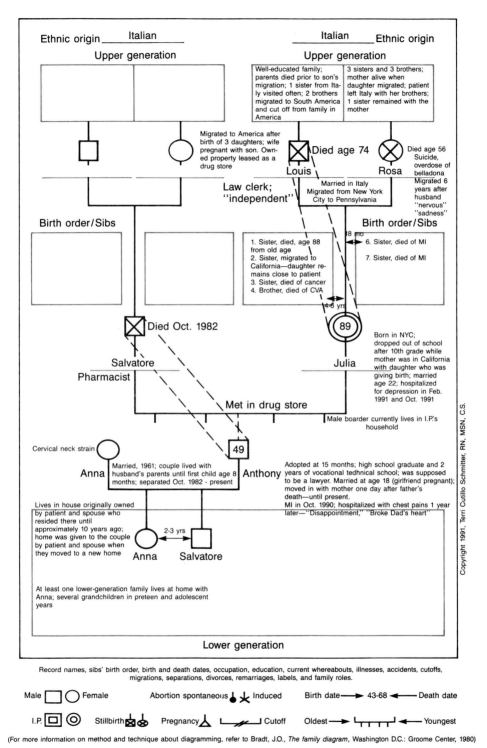

Ethnic origin _____Italian_____   _____Italian_____ Ethnic origin

Upper generation

Well-educated family; parents died prior to son's migration; 1 sister from Italy visited often; 2 brothers migrated to South America and cut off from family in America

3 sisters and 3 brothers; mother alive when daughter migrated; patient left Italy with her brothers; 1 sister remained with the mother

Migrated to America after birth of 3 daughters; wife pregnant with son. Owned property leased as a drug store

Died age 74

Louis

Law clerk; "independent"

Married in Italy Migrated from New York City to Pennsylvania

Rosa

Died age 56 Suicide, overdose of belladona Migrated 6 years after husband "nervous" "sadness"

Birth order/Sibs   **Birth order/Sibs**

1. Sister, died, age 88 from old age
2. Sister, migrated to California—daughter remains close to patient
3. Sister, died of cancer
4. Brother, died of CVA

18 mo → 6. Sister, died of MI

7. Sister, died of MI

4-6 yrs

Died Oct. 1982   89

Salvatore
Pharmacist   Julia

Born in NYC; dropped out of school after 10th grade while mother was in California with daughter who was giving birth; married age 22; hospitalized for depression in Feb. 1991 and Oct. 1991

Met in drug store

Male boarder currently lives in I.P.'s household

Cervical neck strain

Anna   49   Anthony

Married, 1961; couple lived with husband's parents until first child age 8 months; separated Oct. 1982 - present

Adopted at 15 months; high school graduate and 2 years of vocational technical school; was supposed to be a lawyer. Married at age 18 (girlfriend pregnant); moved in with mother one day after father's death—until present.
MI in Oct. 1990; hospitalized with chest pains 1 year later—"Disappointment," "Broke Dad's heart"

Lives in house originally owned by patient and spouse who resided there until approximately 10 years ago; home was given to the couple by patient and spouse when they moved to a new home

2-3 yrs

Anna   Salvatore

At least one lower-generation family lives at home with Anna; several grandchildren in preteen and adolescent years

Lower generation

Copyright 1991, Terri Cutillo Schmitter, RN, MSN, C.S.

Record names, sibs' birth order, birth and death dates, occupation, education, current whereabouts, illnesses, accidents, cutoffs, migrations, separations, divorces, remarriages, labels, and family roles.

Male ☐ ○ Female   Abortion spontaneous ● ✕ Induced   Birth date ──→ 43-68 ◄── Death date

I.P. ☐ ◎   Stillbirth ⊠ ⊗   Pregnancy △ └─✕─┘ Cutoff   Oldest ──→ └┬┬┬┘ ◄── Youngest

(For more information on method and technique about diagramming, refer to Bradt, J.O., *The family diagram*, Washington D.C.: Groome Center, 1980)

Figure 3-3   Recording information on genogram.

according to the information collected, as an only child he was under much pressure to excel and to become the lawyer that the maternal grandfather had wanted to become. Of course the son may have been in conflict with following his own father into pharmacy school. It is interesting to note that the client's son named his son after his adopted father. And one wonders if this son is expected to become a pharmacist by the father and some other profession by the mother or if the son feels compelled to remain loyal to his father by not achieving a profession at all, but obtaining vocational schooling instead.

CATEGORY 2: LIFE-CYCLE FIT

The family over time has consistently had difficulty declaring independence and leaving home. The maternal grandmother remained home in Italy with three daughters and finally left when her three brothers joined her husband in America, while another sister stayed behind with the mother. The client's second eldest sib left home and settled in California, across the continent from Pennsylvania. The patient herself declared pseudoindependence by dropping out of school while her mother was far away helping the second eldest with a new birth. Now the client's son is looking after his mother while at least one of his own married children is at home with his wife. The family over time continues to find difficulty adapting to the separateness of the young adults. The current psychologic deterioration of the client no doubt has heightened the family stress, reactivating generational interconnectedness (1) at least of an emotional nature, given the somatic complaints of the client's son; (2) possibly of a financial nature, since adult children remain at home; and (3) possibly at a functional level.

CATEGORY 3: PATTERN REPETITION ACROSS GENERATIONS

Still to be assessed is repetitive patterns of suicide. Questions about how the maternal grandmother died, as well as sibs in her generation, should be asked. For example, the client declined to discuss the death of her second sib, leaving the possibility of other suicides. No information about the husband's family is available to date. The intense enmeshment and role confusion makes one question the possibility of incest in the family. The functional states of members need further assessment. What is known is that the client and her mother are labeled as fragile and anxious individuals and that both spouses were well-educated and most likely assumed overresponsible and dominant positions in the marital and parental subsystems. Perhaps the client's grandmother was afraid to travel to America with her family. The client states she was too scared to fly there to visit.

CATEGORY 4: LIFE EVENTS AND FAMILY FUNCTIONING

Dates are missing, and so it is hard to try to track events with changes in family members' functioning. In question is how many years there were between the deaths of the client's mother and grandmother. And was there an anniversary reaction to the maternal grandmother's death when the client's mother committed suicide? In the present, the son had a heart attack in October, 8 years after his father's October death; the client is psychotically depressed in October, 1 year later (and 2 weeks afterwards, on exactly the same date as last year, the son will be readmitted to the hospital with similar symptoms as last year). Intense emotion surrounds the client's spouse's death. In the interview the client accuses the son of breaking his father's heart and causing his death. She herself desired to keep the suicide of her mother a secret, and only with her son's support could she disclose the information, a clue (1) that she still feels guilt and remorse about her mother's death and (2) that she has not sufficiently grieved the loss.

CATEGORY 5: RELATIONAL PATTERNS AND TRIANGLES

Several cut-offs exist in the maternal family of origin, and no information about significant others emerged about the client's spouse's family from questions asked (that part of the diagram was left uncompleted because of lack of time and the fatigue of the patient). Parent-child relationships are fused, and rigid cross-generational triangles appear over time. The maternal grandmother was enmeshed with her daughter who did not move away with her young husband. The client and her father were tightly joined, and the father permitted the daughter to disobey his wife and leave school. The client has permitted the son to remain at home, even though she was physically fit and financially independent at the time of her husband's death and able to afford any kind of assistance needed for homemaking. This permits the son to focus on the failing health of his mother in order to not deal with the marital issues — the wife can blame the client for keeping her husband away, while the client complains about the daughter-in-law not being good enough for her son, and the son can remain irresponsible to his family. At least one child remains home (with children of her own) with the daughter-in-law, and one of these children (4 weeks after the client's hospital admission) has threatened to not see the grandmother because "Grandmom always puts me down." Triangles and conflicts abound in this enmeshed family that require further exploration and family therapy interventions to encourage detriangling of family members.

According to Bowen, each family member, in order to differentiate, needs access to all other members without the interference of a too closely joined relationship that interferes with a person-to-person relationship with both members of the dyad. Outside influences in the family should be explored also, and experiences for the client with roommates and the other residents should be encouraged by the nurses to loosen rigid boundaries that exclude family members from relying on others outside the family for the attainment of some self-needs.

CATEGORY 6: FAMILY BALANCE AND IMBALANCE

The sibling relationships of marital couples in the family should be explored to analyze the complementary fit. One can hypothesize about other patterns of balance and functioning levels of spouses and offsprings. The patient's son is currently unemployed and living off of stock investments. However, it was implied that the son's wife is employed and therefore may be overfunctioning in efforts to maintain financial assistance to her own children and the entire household. Over the generations in this Italian family, under-responsible members seem to marry spouses who are overfunctioners. Roles also may be in conflict in both households as to who is the parental head, with adults vying for the role of caretaker. In this family in the upper generations, differences in class and background may be an issue, since the patient refers to a difference in class values between her father's family at least and the daughter-in-law's family. These values and their impact on current issues in the family also should be explored in family therapy. The nurses can use the data to open discussion about values-clarification in one-to-ones and in group work with the client.

Considerations for Selecting a Family Assessment Format

The format chosen for the admission assessment will depend largely on the following:

- Type of population and ages
- Family model with which one feels most comfortable
- Philosophy of program at nurses' workplace
- Admission procedure for completing comprehensive team assessment process

For example, if other disciplines are already involved in completing a genogram or recording similar information and no other discipline meets all together with the family to elicit the pertinent data stressed in the first tool, that first tool might be more applicable. It is valuable to elicit from all members in the presence of the family membership what each wants from therapy. In this way the nurse and other care providers (1) will be less apt to collude with the client or other family members and (2) will know up front what the family expectations are so that they can plan relevant treatment goals and interventions.

A family diagram is extremely valuable to construct when the client presents alone in treatment. The use of a genogram can give nurses valuable clinical data without probing, and they are free to ask the types of questions that are most suitable to the client's condition for whatever purpose and time frame they have. Both tools offer a way of gathering pertinent data, which should eliminate wasted effort and time trying to establish goals for treatment that do not include the client's responses to the relationship system or what the family and client want from treatment. Both formats have a legitimate place in nursing.

IMPORTANT PROCESS VARIABLES

The process by which one conducts a family interview is even more important than the format chosen to gather the data. Psychiatric nurses have a good foundation in interviewing skills from which to initiate wider uses in their practice. The following guidelines offer the process steps or the "how to" for conducting initial and ongoing family interviews. The way one uses self to make connections with other people and to affirm others is an art that takes time to develop. But important components for working effectively with distressed individuals are worth consideration.

First, staff nurses, like all other clinicians working with families, should be cognizant that they can easily be pulled into the emotional reactivity of the family. According to Kerr and Bowen (1988):

> At the outset, in subtle and in not so subtle ways, a family automatically attempts to incorporate a therapist into its problems and in addition to wanting to influence the thinking of a therapist . . . and to have him as an ally . . . an anxious family may also try to get a therapist to take the problems off its shoulders by pressuring him to provide "answers."

It is extremely important to attempt at all times to be as neutral, as objective, and as distant to the family's emotional process as is possible. However, while remaining somewhat separate from the emotional reactivity of the family, the nurse must not appear detached, cold, noncaring, and too professional to them either. This is a tricky balance to achieve, but one that the nurse must believe is necessary if he or she is to work effectively with families.

During interviews, when nurses recognize that they have stopped asking questions and are instead doing a lot of talking, that is a cue to them that they have been "hooked" by the family and therefore their cue to refocus back to the family and the interviewing questions. It is important to ask questions and not to give answers for the family; in that way the nurse gets to know the family better and the family gets to know itself.

The process of interviewing families is enhanced when one understands to some extent the roles one plays in one's own family. When one realizes usual patterns of behavior in one's own family, one will have a better chance of remaining neutral at least to some degree in one's work with families. Performing family of origin work in one's own family can be valuable in remaining calm and outside the triangling process of the family in treatment.

Second, maintaining the self-esteem of each member is also critical during the admission interview. It is most significant to achieve if one wants to have each member sufficiently engaged in the admission process and willing to return to participate in treatment. Each family has a member who is primarily responsible for keeping the family in treatment. Each member is important to the health and healing of all others. All members deserve to be understood and accepted by the nurse, no matter how they present themselves. Nurses should make this first experience a comfortable one for all the family members.

When providing the first interview, the nurse should not share his or her opinions or interpretations about whatever information is being shared by a family member. Nurses cannot impose values—values that do not matter to the family, that they do not understand, and that they do not care to own. Nurses must remain nonjudgmental and tolerant of unpleasant material and the strong feelings shared by the membership in the room to be effective interviewers. Normalizing emotion-laden issues, refraining from putting blame on any member, and treating each person with respect should occur as each family member tells his or her version of the family story.

Third, nurses providing family interviews should learn how to *join* with families at the outset of treatment. *Joining* involves helping to make each member feel important to the healing process. Minuchin and Fishman (1981) define *joining* as the umbrella under which all therapeutic transactions occur. They state that joining is more an attitude than a technique and that it is letting the family know that the therapist understands them and is working with and for them. They believe that joining is the glue that holds the therapeutic system together.

For example, it is important that the tone of the nurse reflect the mood of the family. If the mood appears sad, the nurse will want to be quiet, somber, and slow-paced as he or she conducts the interview. For some people, the approach should be very formal, whereas for others a casual attitude might be more effective. Reading the family and recognizing cultural influences help set the family at ease at a time when it is usually very hard for them.

Finding opportunities to connect with each member should occur during the social stage of the interview. Involving oneself in play with young children is one useful way to join with some parents. Listening to members discuss a basketball game and sharing in their interest are ways of joining other individuals. Joining should be a consideration in all transactions with patients, but it is extremely critical at admission, since admission is the time when most family members decide whether to remain involved in treatment.

Fourth, the nurse should also be able to give the family a sense of hope that they can find solutions to the problems and to the emotional pain that they share with the nurse. A healing relationship solicits the client's internal and external resources and empowers the client by bringing hope, confidence, and trust (Benner, 1984). The nurse will want to end the interview with an upbeat note, providing the family with new options for relating and possibly closing off old ones.

When a chaotic family presents, it is often hard not to absorb their frustration and sense of helplessness and then transfer it back to the family. Sometimes it may be necessary for the nurse to remove himself or herself from the room before ending the session, to take a break from the emotional stimuli of the family. This opportunity allows the nurse to reflect alone on a hopeful frame for ending the session. Or at that point he or she may want to discuss the case with a colleague to obtain another perspective of how to reframe the problem to help the family deal with other possibilities for change. Actually, at any time during a session when the nurse feels emotional or hooked by the family, he or she may ask to be excused from the interview. This strategy allows the interviewer the opportunity to reflect on a focus away from the stimuli in the room in order to return and to maintain leadership during the remainder of the session or to decide on a frame for ending the session.

Fifth, every individual struggles to maintain autonomy while attempting to remain a part of the family. Minuchin (1974) writes that "in all cultures, the family imprints its membership with self-hood." He states that "human experience of identity has two elements: a sense of belonging and a sense of being separate." He further asserts that "the laboratory in which these ingredients are mixed and dispensed is the family, the matrix of identity." When nurses attempt to understand this ultimate struggle, they can use the assessment data to design strategies that consider both the autonomy of the individual members and the need for them to belong to their family. The hospital or health center can become a learning laboratory where nurses are the teachers and where families are helped to experience themselves in new ways.

Finally, *caring* is most likely the critical element that enables a practitioner to become expert in the art of helping individuals to heal themselves. The individual and family want help with the pain and the stress that they are experiencing, and nurses want to help them change the situation that is maintaining their discomfort. Caring clinicians operate from a committed, involved stance that does not take over and smother. According to Benner and Wruble (1989), caring sets up the condition of trust where help can be given and help can be received. These nurse theorists describe the *caring phenomenon,* which illustrates for nurses the kind of caring that must happen if one is to significantly impact the healing process of individuals. In attempting to understand and to utilize his or her conceptualization, I put caring on a continuum, with ceasing to care at the extreme left and overinvolvement in another's personhood at the extreme right end. In the middle is the ability to remain autonomous but yet to be in a position of belonging to the membership of the group. From that position one respects the autonomy of each member and permits differences to exist. Caring individuals do not seek to dominate or to control, but neither do they cease to set priorities and become apathetic. In maintaining a middle position, the nurse working with patients would neither advise the family about what they ought to do nor disengage from the family discomfort. Rather, the nurse would attempt to understand the family and promote their creativity to find a solution to the problem—a solution that makes sense to them and is workable for them (Table 3-1).

Using the caring continuum for visualizing where the person seeking help is located is somewhat helpful when assessing and planning for an individual's needs. For example, some individuals whom nurses will treat will have lost their ability to care and will be located at the extreme left end. To them, nothing will seem to matter more or less than anything else. When assessing this, nurses will know that these are individuals who need nourishment and nurturing from the nurse and especially from their family to engage again in life. Another family member located at the right end will be controlling and dominate others, obstructing family members' sense of separateness. These individuals will require the nurse's patience and assistance in helping them to learn to feel powerful without taking over and dictating to others. This individual will need firm kindness and may even require a strong ultimatum from the family if he or she does not wish to change behaviors that obstruct others in the family.

Assessing where clients are located on the caring continuum can provide the nurse with increased options for planning experiences for the individual, as well as for the family. A significant role that a nurse performs is that of a family coach. In one context the nurse may need to do for a client, whereas in another context he or she will coach the person to do for self to complete a task

Table 3-1   The Caring Continuum

The person comprises three components:
1. Embodied intelligence (mind and body; reflective and reflexive), which allows persons to live in the world and understand it in relationship to themselves.
2. Background, which is composed of cultural, family, and school influences that provide the content of what is understood.
3. Concern, which is the way one is involved in one's own world in which people, events, and things matter. It describes a phenomenologic relationship in which the world is apprehended directly in terms of its meaning to self. Concern is the reason people act. It is necessary for life.

Caring ties the three components together. It is an enabling condition of connection and concern. It enables a person to discern problems, recognize possible solutions, and to implement those solutions.

0	o	0
Detached	Engaged	Over-engaged
Disconnected	Connected	Overly-connected
Loss of a sense of belonging	Autonomy and sense of belonging intact	Dominant/dependent
		Oppressive
		"Leaps in" and takes over the other
All things appear equal, nothing stands out as relatively more or less important or inviting—nothing really matters.	From a place of care, the person can neither claim complete autonomy nor be the absolute source of all meaning	From this place of "controlled caring" the person dictates what matters in order to create a safe place and exercise freedom to stop caring when the person is being threatened
There is no direction for choosing one over another.	Sets up possibilities for helping patients to recover caring, to appropriate meaning or reestablish connection	
The person needs rest and respite, as well as reintegration of concern and involvement	Knows what to offer without overextending or assuming more responsibility for the stiuation than necessary	
	Acknowledges pain & discomfort—offers what one can even though not enough.	
Patients who have perceived being cared for by nurses who seemed detached describe feeling dehumanized, devalued, angry, and fearful	Patients feel supported, comforted, tuned-into, and attended-to; e.g., patients are able to grieve a loss and maintain hope	Patients describe feeling smothered, powerless, controlled

Note. Modified from *Primacy of Caring: Stress and Coping in Health and Illness* by P. Benner and J. Wrubel, 1989, Menlo Park, Calif: Addison-Wesley.

unassisted. Or the nurse may in one case coach a family member to provide assistance to another member, whereas in a similar situation coach someone to stand aside and let the family member struggle to complete an assignment alone.

In summary, psychiatric nurses who encounter families and who wish to help them, will need to *follow* in order to lead, to *accommodate,* and to *submit,* as well as to *support, direct,* and *suggest* as Minuchin and Fishman (1981) assert. Caring nurses will tread graciously and respectfully as they enter the system of families experiencing pain and turmoil. Staff nurses can provide opportunities for families to heal themselves. The first opportunity presents at admission.

Teaching Family Assessment Skills

Psychiatric clinical nurse specialists who have received education and experience in family systems theory and techniques are in a good position to collaborate with psychiatric nurses to design nursing assessment tools and to train registered nurses to perform initial family assessments at admission. Carter (1988) describes a process for teaching child and family assessment skills to medical students doing brief out-patient clinical experiences. Carter believes that his method is consistent with Bandura's social learning theory and that it is strong because it does the following:

- Allows for guided practice with corrective feedback
- Allows students to learn vicariously by the modeling of supervisors
- Breaks the interviewing process into component parts that can be separately learned and then combined
- Allows the student to develop an increased sense of self-efficacy, which may be critical to future performance

Recommended in Table 3-2 is a similar teaching method. This method is used for teaching psychiatric registered nurses practicing in adolescent and adult hospital settings to perform family assessments and to carry out effective transactions with families.

Initially the nurse elicits interest and motivation to learn family systems theory by collecting family data from families on the unit and discusses this in treatment team meetings and nursing rounds. Simultaneously in-services are held on systems theory and application and consultation completed with at least one psychiatrist. Some nurses remain closed off to systems thinking until it is validated by at least one respected attending psychiatrist or unless family therapy has been used as an effective modality for treating individuals on the units.

Staff nurse involvement is encouraged when treatment moments with families occur on the unit. This leads to (1) beneficial discussion about observed patterns of behavior of family members and (2) exploration of reasons for the approaches taken with the family and of strategies and techniques that can be employed in various situations.

Table 3-2   Teaching Family Assessment Skills Outline

Stage 1	Clinical nurse specialist (CNS) collaborates with staff psychiatrist Conducts family assessments Discusses family perspective in team Conducts family theory inservices
Stage 2	CNS elicits interested registered nurses Provides handouts/reading assignments Makes arrangements for supervision Provides training seminars Joins family and staff transactions
Stage 3	CNS supervises and model interviews Provides before and after feedback RN arranges the environment and session
Stage 4	CNS consults and affirms RN conducts sessions alone CNS supervises discussion at team meeting RN discusses in nursing rounds

Stage two begins when interested staff are scheduled for meetings to establish effective ways for setting up training. At this time handouts are given to begin reading for future discussion: Chapter 1 of *Problem-Solving Therapy* by Haley (1985) and Chapter 21 of *Family Therapy in Clinical Practice* by Bowen (1978). They are encouraged to read *Uncommon Therapy: The Psychiatric Techniques of Milton H. Erickson, M.D.* by Haley (1986). Logistics for receiving experiences and supervision in admission assessments are developed according to unit policies. Head nurses were contacted to arrange changes in staff scheduling and to decide on blocks of time for training sessions.

The third stage involves training seminars approximately 2 hours long for 6 to 8 weeks in which readings, other handouts, and the actual assessment sessions are reviewed and discussed. Simultaneously, family assessment sessions with before and after feedback sessions are employed, which are at first observational for the nurse. Once nurses gain competence in their process skills and in using the format of the tool, they begin to conduct the session with supervision.

Before conducting sessions, presession meetings take place to plan the level of participation of the facilitators and to discuss how to set up the interviewing room and how to conduct the session. It is important at that time to remind nurses that one purpose of the interview is to gather information about content and the other is to gather information about the family process. On occasion, when I encouraged involvement without preinstructions, a staff nurse sympathetically moved to calm an upset family member, therefore ruining an opportunity to observe the family's automatic responses to the individual. Establishing parameters for staff participation during the actual session is necessary before the session gets underway.

The postinterview meeting is extremely important for discussing such issues as staff joining and rationale for the ways the CNS or the RN handled family transactions. Critiquing the session also permits discussion of other ways that things can be handled for future work with different families. And yet another important purpose is to discuss the assessment data to design some strategies for continued work with the family and with the individual client.

The fourth and final stage of training begins when the RN conducts the family admission interview alone as part of the initial assessment process for his or her primary clients. Nurses are expected to discuss the family view, their perception of the problem, relevant family issues, and what they think might work for the family at the initial treatment planning session. In this way, nurses' assessment data are consolidated into the team's treatment plan. Nurses are free to consult with the CNS at any time, and they are expected to discuss their primary clients in nursing rounds periodically for peer review. This permits ongoing supervision and affirmation for staff nurses who are assessing and working more intensely with families.

Nursing's Future Work with Families

Family assessments lay a firm foundation from which to plan relevant nursing and psychiatric team interventions that lead to positive client outcomes. Therefore it behooves nurses to decide on a format for collecting relevant family data. Knowing the client and his or her relationships better will provide the nurse with a wider perspective from which to plan interventions that have a greater chance of success, since they will be more on target with client and family needs and expectations. When nurses use current theory and past experiences and strive to care, they will enhance client caretaking by including the client and family in problem-solving and caregiving efforts. Family care and interventions promote growth, health, and healing in individuals. Nurses who get involved with families will make a difference in the outcome of treatment for psychiatric clients.

REFERENCES

Benner, P. (1984). *From novice to expert: Excellence and power in clinical nursing practice.* Menlo Park, Calif: Addison-Wesley.

Benner, P., & Wrubel, J. (1989). *Primacy of caring: Stress and coping in health and illness.* Menlo Park, Calif: Addison-Wesley.

Bowen, M. (1978). *Family therapy in clinical practice.* New York: Jason Aronson.

Carter, E.A., & McGoldrick, M. (1980). *The family life cycle: A framework for family therapy.* New York: Gardner.

Carter, I. (1988). Teaching child and family assessment skills to medical students during brief outpatient clinic experience. *Canadian Journal of Psychiatry, 33,* 546-549.

Colson, D.B., Grame, C., & Coyne, L. (1990). Scales for assessing family intervention during psychiatric hospitalization. *Bulletin of the Menniger Clinic, 54*(3), 368-383.

Combrinck-Graham, L. (1990). Developments in family systems theory and research, *Journal of the American Academy of Child and Adolescent Psychiatry, 29*(4), 501-512.

Duvalle, E.M. (1977). *Marriage and family development.* Philadelphia: J.B. Lippincott.

Flor, H., Turk, D.C., & Rudy, T.E. (1987). Pain and families. II. Assessments and treatment. *Pain, 30,* 29-45.

Haley, J. (1976). *Problem-solving therapy: New strategies for effective family therapy* (2nd ed.). Philadelphia: Harper & Row.

Haley, J. (1986). *Uncommon therapy: The psychiatric techniques of Milton H. Erickson, M.D.* New York: W.W. Norton.

Herth, K.A. (1989). The root of it all: Genograms as a nursing assessment tool. *Journal of Gerontological Nursing, 15*(12), 32-37.

Kerr, M.E., & Bowen, M. (1988). *Family evaluation: An approach based on Bowen theory.* New York: W.W. Norton.

McGoldrick, M., & Gerson, R. (1985). *Genograms in family assessment.* New York: W.W. Norton.

Minuchin, S. (1974). *Families and family therapy.* Cambridge, Mass: Harvard University Press.

Minuchin, S., & Fishman, H.C. (1981). *Family therapy techniques.* Cambridge, Mass: Harvard University Press.

Rogers, J., & Cohn, P. (1988). The genogram's contribution to family-centered care. *New Jersey Medicine,* April, *85*(4), 300-306.

Rushton, C.H. (1990). Strategies for family-centered care in the critical care setting. *Pediatric Nursing, 16*(2), 195-199.

Silliman, R.A., Sternburg, J., & Fretwell, M.D. (1988). Disruptive behavior in demented patients living within disturbed families. *Journal of the American Geriatrics Society, 36*(7), 617-618.

Chapter 4

Family Mental Health

Dixie Koldjeski

Family mental health has long been a concern of mental health nursing. However, like other mental health disciplines, the specialty has focused for the most part on families who have system dysfunctions or a member who has an identified psychiatric problem. Significant contributions have been made by nurses to such families and their members by providing special kinds of therapeutics. The specialty, however, can make an equally significant contribution in family mental health by providing prevention counseling to mentally healthy functioning families to help them stay healthy.

Attention should be given to helping healthy families stay healthy. This focus is part of a general movement toward preventive health programs and activities. Many people agree that they must be responsible for their physical health by engaging in nutritional, exercise, and daily living patterns that enhance health and reduce stress. At the same time, education and activities that help people maintain and enhance the mental health of healthy functioning families have received less attention.

The strengthening of families is a favorite theme when national health policies are discussed. Until now, however, the debate has focused on such problem areas as lack of child day-care facilities and the need for flexibility in parental work schedules to cover a variety of family needs. A global view is needed of family health: one that encompasses the aspects just mentioned but also goes far beyond to provide assistance to families in monitoring and maintaining both physical and mental health, establishing health-promoting relationships, and providing education that identifies patterns of living that characterize healthy family living and member development.

Family system functioning and the mental health of family members are interrelated and influence one another. This interrelationship exists because families are small interacting social systems and as such create intensive learning environments for members. In this context, health education that includes both mental and physical health aspects assists families to understand and maintain optimal personal and systemic health status. This focus on health promotion and primary prevention is at the core of all programs designed to prevent the health troubles of individuals and families from developing into clinical problems.

Mental health promotion programs and prevention activities focus on concepts that often are abstract and therefore are more difficult to grasp than indicators of physical health, such as blood pressure and other measurable vital signs data. Families need assistance in understanding what healthy family functioning means and how it interrelates to personal, interactional, and familial relationships. They need assistance in making connections between family functioning and member health, growth, and actualization. Prevention counseling is one approach by which this can be achieved.

An important aspect of prevention counseling is the need to redefine mental health as an integral part of health. This redefinition should use language and images that do not evoke stereotypes traditionally associated with mental illness and insanity. Mental health services have long been provided in systems that make them appear separate and unrelated to physical health. Further, mental and emotional illness is often equated in usage with the term *mental health.* In the 1960s move to establish community mental health centers as part of a new approach in mental health, Grinker (1966) noted that the term *mental health* had a sweet sound and had come to replace the feared term *mental illness.* A decade later, Cowen (1977) noted that diffuseness and abstractness continued to define mental health. And more than a decade still later, what mental health means for both individuals and families remains vague and open to different definitions.

Psychiatric mental health nursing, rooted in the discipline of nursing, is in a unique position to provide leadership for development of theory and therapeutics from a primary prevention perspective. These advancements guide and inform nursing actions in family mental health. Using both a prevention and holistic perspective, as well as knowledge and experience from its own and other disciplines, mental health nursing can make a significant contribution in this area by providing approaches that are effective and visionary.

In this chapter, selected models of healthy family functioning provide useful knowledge and direction about prevention counseling in family mental health nursing. Characteristics of healthy family functioning from several perspectives show many indicators of such functioning. Perspectives and issues, as background, offer a rationale for this focus in nursing. And last, some general guidelines for use of a prevention counseling program with healthy functioning families are noted.

Mental Health Perspectives

In the field of mental health, different perspectives have guided the development of services by which to address the emotional and mental needs of individuals and families. One perspective has guided the development of direct services to be provided by professionals to families and people who have recognized emotional and psychiatric disorders. Another has focused on the development of indirect services by professionals to other professionals in case or program consultation. Mental health education may also be provided to people in key social roles who in turn provide services to interested persons in such areas as parenting, coping, and disciplinary practices.

Two types of theoretic perspectives have been identified by Jones and Diamond (1982): a family theory perspective developed primarily by the social sciences; and a family therapy perspective developed by clinicians in various family and mental health disciplines. Both perspectives have advanced knowledge and therapeutics about family health and family functioning.

From a public health perspective by levels of prevention, activities in mental health have been mostly secondary and tertiary in nature. Targets have been individuals, families, groups, or populations known to be *at risk* for some disorder, behavioral pattern, or condition or where clinical problems already exist. Knowledge about health problems that have a significant mental health component has been used successfully in such programs. Phenylketonuria (PKU), a genetic disorder that if left untreated causes mental retardation, has been virtually eliminated by routine testing of the urine of newborns for an excess of the offending chemical and by instituting early treatment.

A primary prevention nursing perspective for family mental health is advanced here. It is based on the premise that the specialty has both a disciplinary perspective and the clinical flexibility to draw together the accumulation of nursing and related knowledge and therapeutics from other disciplines and synthesize these into novel formulations. These reformulations may then be used to provide prevention counseling to healthy functioning families. Such counseling addresses specifically the mental health aspects of general health but does not ignore other aspects. For example, the character-istics of strong families and the normal processes of healthy family functioning are known. Such knowledge can be used to help families as systems maintain their strengths and improve intrafamilial relationships, both of which influence in subtle and explicit ways the mental and physical health of family members.

A primary prevention perspective that focuses on healthy family functioning departs from the specialty's traditional approach of focusing on the phenomena of family dysfunctions, the psychiatric illnesses of member(s), and related problems. However, these perspectives represent two vital dimensions of psychiatric and mental health nursing, albeit the traditional approach is the more used model for knowledge application and reimbursement for services.

A basic goal of a primary prevention perspective in family mental health is to assist healthy functioning families to maintain and enhance the health of both the family system and family members. It embodies the notion that families usually need assistance in evaluating and learning new competencies for maintaining and/or augmenting family health — both physical and mental — as new situations arise that must be handled. It also assumes that healthy functioning families have strengths and the desire to help their members develop into productive, coping, and reasonably satisfied members of society. Overall, the focus is on helping such families recognize and alter variations in family systematics and dynamics to reduce the possibility of warping in intrafamilial relationships and patterns of living. Another area of concern is the need to strengthen the self-concept of individual members, lessen the intensity of problems of daily living, and enhance member growth, development, and actualization.

Need for an Emphasis on Family Mental Health

Revolutionary changes have occurred over the past 4 decades in family structures, functions, values, and beliefs. Significant areas of family living have experienced rapid changes in long-established practices and beliefs. They include but are not limited to such areas as two working parents, modes of sexual expression, parenting beliefs and practices, coping under novel situations without tradition or elders to offer advice, and an increased responsibility for family and personal health. The adequacy of education for children is a great worry for many parents, and many feel helpless to alter existing situations. And drugs and crime in schools and the streets create perilous environments that force many children to learn a preponderance of survival coping skills, although these skills may not be appropriate for other environments in which jobs are performed and careers established.

Scanzoni (1987), a family theorist and practitioner, noted a need for a paradigm change in conceptualizations of family functioning. This change would move from a traditional focus on nuclear family units, roles, structures, career transitions, interconnections between child/adult relationships, and family development to a more contemporary focus on marriage and family relationships, alternative relationships, close relationship situations, sexuality as a fundamental indicator of a unique relationship, and the value of permanence in family relationships.

Such a shift would reflect the pace and substance of rapid social change on families as society's most basic and enduring structure. Families need help in understanding and coping with the consequences of such shifts in society. Coping in a world that has altered so drastically in such a short time leaves parents with gaps in knowledge and experience by which they can guide themselves and their children to cope with today's daily risks and tomorrow's uncertainties. Education and counseling that interrelate family functioning and the mental and physical health of members are two such areas. Families can learn to evaluate old coping approaches and try out new ones for handling both the aggravations and crises of daily family living as these evolve around both old and new situations. They can be taught to recognize and use health-promoting behaviors and to recognize the role of family strengths in healthy family functioning. Suggestions can also be provided to assist families to take active roles in the development and actualization of family members.

Vaugh, Huntington, Samuels, Bilmes, and Shapiro (1975) emphasized that the nature of primary prevention programs in mental health was quite different from that of programs that focused on treatments at various stages of mental conditions and illnesses. The message then, which has even greater relevance now, was that prevention in mental health must focus on mental health—mentally healthy people, mentally healthy families, and mentally healthy environments. In this conceptualization, no designated patients, no designated problematic families, and no stigmatic labels of mental or emotional illness are associated with participation in counseling programs. Primary prevention counseling can serve as one connector between family systematics and member dynamics and the mental and physical health of family members.

Concepts and Meanings

Mental health prevention counseling requires a new conceptual paradigm and a new health perspective. Mental health for families and members cannot be assayed through the lens of personal and familial pathologies. Old concepts must be given new meanings and new relationships given a different focus.

Preventions in mental health are *primary* in nature; that is, they are nursing actions designed specifically to strengthen and enhance the general well-being, growth, and performance of *healthy functioning family systems and members.* Such actions are offered or provided before the development of ostensible mental or emotional problems and illness and, in a sense, provide some immunity against their development.

Primary prevention actions include but are not limited to consideration of the patterns of interrelationships that the family characteristically uses in coping, communication, and affective responses. For family members, such actions encompass the psychologic, physical, and behavioral dimensions of personal development and actualization of self. Actions also include preparing for the assumption of adulthood responsibilities and experiencing satisfaction and joy in relationships with others. The realization that the necessary activities of life and living, such as education and work, can have positive and health-promoting aspects for one's self and for significant others is an important part of such growth.

Those who design activities to promote and strengthen family and member mental health assume that family systems and members have repeated experiences over time. In this context, system and individual dynamics undergo a process of blending, melding, interacting, and fusing of experiences in complex ways as the system becomes a crucible for human growth, development, and actualization.

Promotions for mental health are *general* actions that may be taken to inform and educate the general public about mental health in general and certain kinds of mental illness in particular. Mental health promotions are not targeted to specific families or individuals. Rather, they provide general information and education about mental health and mental illness. They foster awareness, influence attitudes, and identify alternatives so that people can make informed choices. Through such choices, people can decide whether and how to change their behavior in ways that would achieve an optimal level of physical and mental health, as well as improve their social and physical environments. This focus follows from a general concept of health promotion and clinical applications (Taylor, Denham, & Ureda, 1982).

Mental health promotions also provide to the general public education and information about the prevalence and scope of mental illness in the population. Some promotions include simple checklists of signs and symptoms designed to help people recognize a possible relationship between what they are experiencing and a mental health problem. Minimizing the stigma associated with mental and emotional illness and early seeking of professional treatment have long been important messages in mental health promotion efforts.

It should be noted that in the nursing literature over the past 2 years, the concept of health promotion has been given an emphasis that is similar to what is defined here as primary preventions. However, these new interpretations may become a standard for the discipline, so they are noted here. Parse (1990, 1991) defined prevention as actions that thwart disease processes and impede the progress of pathophysiologic disorders. She states that health promotion comes from a different perspective and refers to one's personal integration with one's world. In this view, health promotion refers to actions taken to enhance the quality of flow of life in the human-environment process. It leads to changes in patterns of living and enhances the quality of life; it is much more than controlling disease. M. C. Smith (1990) considers health promotion to be a unique nursing focus. It is more than and different from disease prevention and encompasses the whole client: person, family, and community. She identifies an intensive interhuman process as the vehicle for health promotion rather than health teaching and providing health information.

Prevention counseling in mental health nursing is a specialized nursing process by which preventions having an emphasis on mental health are provided to clients from a holistic nursing perspective. It addresses the phenomenon that mental health nursing is uniquely prepared to address potential health problems that may arise from interactions of person/family health environment.

Prevention counseling is provided *before* the occurrence of mental health problems. Behaviors, repetitive responses, conditions, or interactions have not become patterned to the extent that they create emotional and mental stress and perhaps some discomfort and lessen the likelihood of optimal functioning for family systems and their members.

Prevention counseling encourages the development of effective coping responses and self-actualization of members. Because of the participation of members, it promotes a sense of family identity and unity and contributes to the overall strengths of family systems. Such counseling serves as a catalyst by providing feedback on system functioning, member actions, perceptions, and visions of the future. Family involvement in self-evaluation and self-instituted changes is encouraged. Prevention counseling provides opportunities for the mental health nurse (1) to activate and participate in family systematics in ways that promote system heterostasis (that is, balances in functioning around many dimensions of family functioning) and (2) to show how functioning balances relate to member growth.

Secondary preventions are actions designed to prevent the development of particular behaviors or frank disorders in individuals, families, groups, or populations *at risk* for such development.

Secondary prevention activities are an integral part of the range of mental health services provided today in comprehensive mental health centers. Such activities are distinguished by their relatively narrow focus and targeted on known populations with known risks.

Healthy family functioning is a holistic indicator of family systems in which environments have been established in which the needs of members and the needs of the system have achieved heterostasis along the major dimensions of family living in ways that foster member growth.

Healthy family functioning is characterized by affectional bonds being expressed both verbally and behaviorally and where caring attitudes are valued. Members have the freedom to develop a separate identity and selfhood. Family structure is clear, yet flexible enough for harmonious interactions to occur in the general patterns of family life and living. Basic family processes, such as coping and communication, are effective and open to examination and change. The family as an entity has interchanges with other environments and takes from and contributes to these because they are important contexts in which aspects of family and member growth takes place. In such families, there is respect for members and their views. Self-actualization for all members, irrespective of age and stage, is valued and supported. Overall, healthy functioning families indicate happiness and enjoyment among family members and with life in general.

$$\bullet \quad \bullet \quad \bullet$$

A conceptual note: the concepts of healthy family functioning, strong families, functional families, and adaptive families are used interchangably throughout the chapter. All refer to family mental health and mental wellness.

Issues Related to Prevention in Mental Health

Issues about the use of primary preventions in mental health must be revisited from time to time. Since the turn of the century, services have focused on the needs of the emotionally and mentally ill because of their seriousness and scope. A broader service goal has evolved over the past decade to include populations known to be at risk for some particular disease or condition. But the idea of providing primary prevention services to families and individuals continues to raise issues. Five recurring issues in relation to prevention counseling with healthy functioning families are identified.

ETHICS

The first issue focuses on the ethics of providing primary prevention counseling in mental health—in this instance, to healthy functioning families. In the first decade of the community mental health movement, such activities were discounted on the grounds of an inadequate knowledge and research base; therefore there was a real possibility that problems could be created where none existed. These concerns of the past have been overtaken by the development of a vast knowledge base about healthy functioning families: how they can be identified and how they can be assisted to stay healthy. Further, where family strengthening programs have been provided, no evidence has been found that shows problems have been created for participants. Rather, families have striven toward better functioning and, in this process, have had both the knowledge and option of withdrawing from activities that might be perceived or experienced as threatening their integrity.

The ethics of making available mental health prevention counseling that focuses on healthy family functioning can be rephrased today: is it ethical *not* to offer families counseling assistance where knowledge is available? A further question is whether unusual issues and requirements are being raised to justify *not* offering prevention counseling to families because this offers few opportunities for reimbursement from health insurance payers. The combination of informed consent, an available broad knowledge and research foundation on which to base such counseling, and the needs of healthy functioning families in a rapidly changing society make a compelling rationale for offering mental health prevention counseling.

DEFINITIONS

A second issue of prevention counseling for healthy functioning families is that of definitions. What characterizes a healthy functioning family? The question is difficult to answer as is a similar question about the mental health of individuals. For more than 40 years, different definitions have been proposed. A recurring problem is that such definitions are derived from particular theories of family functioning and individual mental health arising from psychiatric illness perspectives; thus consensus is difficult.

Today, however, a substantial body of knowledge is available about healthy family functioning that is quite different from knowledge developed from perspectives and theories of individual emotional and mental illness that focused on dysfunctions. Strong and healthy functioning families are no longer defined as those with an absence of dysfunctions and diseases; rather, they are defined as unique and dynamic learning environments that have structure, dynamics, roles, and functions of their own. The issue of definition today can be answered by different perspectives that provide new insights and open up new possibilities for both prevention and therapeutic actions.

LIMITED RESOURCES

A third issue concerns the use of limited resources in the field of mental health. In question is why limited resources should be used to help healthy families stay healthy when so many different and serious needs exist for treatment services. The answer to this is that resource allocation policies for mental health services should be based on the public health principle that prevention services are the long-term approach to reduction of treatment services.

The legislation that established community mental health centers mandated that a core of services be provided, two of which are consultation and education. These have long been considered prevention services, although in practice their use has often focused on case consultation and other secondary prevention activities. Funds allocated for these purposes over the years have been small, but the provision of such services has become an integral part of mental health service systems. Prevention counseling to both families and individuals is an extension of this public health principle.

PROFESSIONAL PERSPECTIVES

The issue of perspectives as held and used by mental health professionals and their influence on mental health services and education continues to be recognized. A dominant perspective is the "medical model" of mental illness. The strength of this prevailing view creates barriers to the establishment of mental health perspectives that conceptualize such through an entirely different set of lenses.

The fuzziness of meaning about mental health carries over to the services provided by professionals. Cowen (1977) noted that mental health clinicians have for so long and so singularly espoused therapeutic-restorative services that it is difficult for them to distinguish other kinds of therapeutics.

Porter-O'Grady (1985) pointed out that nursing has developed a highly refined internal vision of a world that focuses on illness-generating living, unhealthy business and social practices, destructive life-styles, and a number of excesses that contribute to illness and disease. He believes that a new orientation for nursing must shift emphasis from illness and illness-based health services to health and health-based ones. The hospital-medical-healthcare complex supplies powerful reinforcement for the illness vision, as do third-party reimbursement policies. Meleis (1990) noted that although health is central to nursing, it is not recognized as such by the public and other disciplines. But one may also ask to what extent nursing actually uses the wellness aspect of health to orient its education, policies, practices, and world-view. And Phillips (1990) noted that to move toward a holistic perspective of health, there must be a move away from disease perspectives tied to specific sciences.

A clear concept of family mental health embodies a mental health nursing perspective that has a clear concept of mental wellness. In reference to families, mental wellness is equated with healthy functioning families. Promotions and preventions are the therapeutics that address mental wellness.

The issue of prevention counseling with healthy functioning families must be answered in contexts unlike those when the same issue was raised years ago. Knowledge has taken a quantum leap in most areas of mental health. Failure to move forward on the use of such knowledge and to encourage innovations in applications chills and blocks the emergence of new approaches to family mental health.

MEASUREMENT

The last issue is that of measurement. In clinical assessments or clinical evaluations, baseline data typically are obtained from subjects before initiation of actions or interventions designed to have some kind of outcome. These data are then used to make comparisons during the actions or interventions and after they are completed. Traditionally, methodology focuses on determining whether significant differences occurred as a consequence of whatever actions were taken.

The before/after data in prevention counseling have a different set of expectations and hence need a different kind of interpretation. The goal of prevention counseling is to *maintain or enhance* healthy family functioning over time around an established baseline. Theoretically, it would not be expected that before and after data would show significant differences; rather, such data would be expected to form a mosaic around the baseline aspects of healthy family functioning that were selected to guide the counseling process. This conceptual assumption is consistent with research that has found that no single aspect of family functioning makes families different.

An unexpected consequence of prevention counseling is an observation that ostensible deviations exist from the anticipated response pattern on some aspect of family functioning being considered. If such observations are made, appropriate statistical tests can be made to determine whether such differences are significant. The point to be made, however, is that in prevention counseling, there is no intent to try to effect changes of such magnitude in family functioning that standard statistical tests would deem them to be significant. Rather, the intent is to maintain or enhance the strengths families already have.

Models of Healthy Functioning Families

Several models of healthy family functioning can provide theory and applications for family mental health. They have been developed by both clinicians and academicians.

OTTO'S FAMILY STRENGTH MODEL

In 1963 Otto, a humanistically oriented psychologist, began development of a model of healthy family functioning because he saw a need for "healthy" or "normal" families to strengthen family life and family systems. His indicators of healthy family functioning covered the physical, emotional, and spiritual needs of the family and its members; communication; personal and social support; self-development; role flexibility; and a concern for family unity, loyalty, and cooperation.

From research, Otto (1962, 1963, 1964, 1971, 1972, 1975, 1976) identified 12 strengths (see box, p. 55). In family strengthening programs, the model provided direction and focus for working with families in areas of family functioning that could be enhanced. Baseline data on the just-noted strengths can be collected by arranging them in a Likert-scale format. Families may respond as a whole by having members arrive at a consensus as to the degree they may be present and as individual members. Such data provide information about the totality of strengths the family has as a whole; they also provide information about the extent that members think their families have such strengths. This information is useful in prevention counseling because it shows areas in which strengthening may be needed.

Otto's Indicators of Healthy Family Functioning

1. Provision of spiritual, emotional, and physical needs of members
2. Sensitivity to needs of individual members
3. Effective communication
4. Provision of support, encouragement, and security
5. Initiation of growth-promoting experiences
6. Initiation and maintenance of family, community, and governmental relationships
7. Growth for adults through the experiences of children
8. Flexibility of family roles
9. Mutual respect and individuality for members
10. Growth through crisis experiences
11. Development of family unity, loyalty, and cooperation
12. Acceptance of help by family members when appropriate

STINNET'S FAMILY STRENGTH MODEL

For more than 2 decades, Stinnet and his colleagues (Rowe et al., 1985; Stinnet, 1985; Stinnet, Chesser, & DeFrain, 1979; Stinnet, Chesser, DeFrain, & Knaub, 1980; Stinnet, DeFrain, King, Knaub, & Rowe, 1981; Stinnet, DeFrain, Lindgren, Van Zandt, & Williams, 1982; Stinnet, Knorr, DeFrain, & Rowe, 1981; Stinnet, Lynn, Kimmons, Fuenning, & DeFrain, 1984; Stinnet & Sauer, 1977; Williams, Lindgren, Rowe, Van Zandt, & Stinnet, 1985) have explored the roots of family strengths in more than 3000 families around the world. This research group searched for the *qualities* that make strong families, irrespective of family structure. In general, strong families have troubles like other kinds of families, but they handle these more effectively by maintaining a sense of "we-ness," by members pulling together, and by using effective problem-solving approaches (McCubbin & Patterson, 1981).

Stinnet and DeFrain (1985) identified from the vast body of research that the team had generated six universal *qualities* that characterize strong families (see box, p. 56).

When this model is used to guide clinical programs to strengthen families, before-and-after assessment of prevention counseling can be obtained by using the instrument developed by the research group. It consists of the six strengths in a Likert-scale format and asks families to rate themselves. The strengths are oriented toward families as interacting systems. Interpretation is straightforward: the higher the overall score on strengths, the greater the strengths of the family. While this tool provides a form of global measurement of family functioning, it has a convenient clinical use: that of serving as a selection indicator for strong families for involvement in prevention counseling. This research group has been responsive to requests for information.

Stinnet and DeFrain's Universal Qualities of Strong Families

1. **Commitment**   Family members are dedicated to promoting each other's welfare and happiness, and unity is valued.
2. **Appreciation**   Family members express appreciation on the actions and achievements of others.
3. **Communication**   Family members have good communication skills and spend a lot of time talking to one another.
4. **Time**   Family members spend time—quality time—in large quantities with one another.
5. **Spiritual wellness** Family members have a strong sense of a greater good or power in life, and that belief gives them strength and purpose.
6. **Coping abilities**   Family members are able to view stress and crises as opportunities to grow.

MCMASTER MODEL OF FAMILY FUNCTIONING

The McMaster Model of Family Functioning has a long history of development and evolved from a combination of theory and clinical research (Epstein, Baldwin, & Bishop, 1983; Epstein, Bishop, & Baldwin, 1982; Epstein, Bishop, & Levin, 1978; Westley & Epstein, 1969). Six dimensions of healthy family and member functioning have been identified:

1. Problem-solving competence
2. Communication exchange and clarity
3. Established patterns of roles
4. Affective responses over a broad range of stimuli
5. Affective involvement in activities and achievements of other family members
6. Behavioral control

The sixth dimension refers to the ways in which families maintain standards of conduct for members. A seventh dimension, general family functioning, is available for use in assessment and serves as a holistic indicator of whole family functioning.

A family assessment device (FAD) has been developed for both clinical and research use. The device obtains dimensional measurements on each family member, as well as on holistic functioning of the family as a unit. It can be easily administered to families and individual members before and after clinical actions to determine change. The researchers provide instructions for scoring the FAD and have computer services available for this purpose. This research group has been responsive to written and telephoned requests and questions.

CIRCUMPLEX MODEL OF FAMILY FUNCTIONING

The Circumplex Model of Family Functioning has been under development for several years (Anderson, 1986; Olson, 1986; Olson, Portner, & Bell, 1982;

Olson, Russell, & Sprenkle, 1983; Olson, Sprenkle, & Russell, 1979; Sprenkle & Olson, 1978). More than 300 research projects were conducted or are under way testing the model or determining some aspect of instrumentation developed for measuring the various dimensions of family functioning.

A distinctive feature of the model is that it postulates curvilinear relationships rather than linear ones within family systems; that is, family relationships are considered to develop and be maintained by bending, revolving, turning, and curving around a few established dimensions rather than to develop in increments through a series of steps or phases as on a continuum.

Two primary dimensions of family functioning are adaptability (the ability of families to change their structure) and cohesion (emotional involvement). Families may vary from very high to very low on these. Because of the cirvilinear nature of relationships, the model generates a total of 16 family types of functioning, which are grouped in three categories: *balanced, midrange,* and *extreme.* Communication serves as a facilitating dimension and is considered the essential dynamic by which families and members shift on the dimensions of adaptability and cohesion.

The model has been subjected to an unusual amount of scholarly criticism and dialogue. One issue is whether the curvilinear model actually "fits" the processes of family functioning; this is still an open question. Another is whether the large number of family types can be readily used in clinical applications because they require a precise set of discriminations that would be difficult to obtain in clinical assessments and processes. As a result of such dialogue, instruments designed to measure the family dimensions have undergone a number of revisions. However, the basic assumptions and theory have not substantially changed.

Instrumentation exists for measuring the dimensions of family functioning. The most recent revision can be obtained from the research group. A number of other instruments are available for use in clinical assessments, such as family strengths and quality of life. Information about scoring and interpretation of data is made available when instruments are secured. This research group is responsive to written and telephoned questions and requests.

BEAVERS SYSTEMS MODEL

The Beavers Systems Model evolved out of both clinical and research data. Its application to normal functioning families was tested in the 6-year Timberlawn Study of Healthy Families. The results were published by Lewis, Beavers, Gossett, and Phillips (1976) and in later reports by Beavers (1982) and members of the team (Beavers, Hampson, & Hulgus, 1985; Beavers & Voeller, 1983). An excellent comparison of this model with the Circumplex Model was conducted by Lee (1988).

The Beavers Systems Model emphasizes normal rather than pathologic family functioning. Normality is judged by growth, adaptation, and change over time. Normal health is equated with optimal health and placed on a continuum of competence rather than "normality." The model assumes that healthy and unhealthy family functioning is a matter of degree rather than differences in kind. Further, it assumes that the degree of normality can be specified, measured, and assigned a place on the competency continuum. The model's structure generates more unhealthy family types than healthy ones.

Two major dimensions of family functioning are competence and family style. Five degrees of competence are possible on the competency continuum; the endpoints are *severely disturbed* and *optimally healthy*. Three types of family styles cross section the competency continuum, two of which are extreme and connote severely disturbed families. A mixed style is associated with competent families. Adequate and optimally competent families with mixed life-styles fall into the healthy range.

Characteristics of optimally competent families were identified by a number of indicators. They seek and find intimacy, hold respect for the viewpoints of others, and hold respect for individual choices and perceptions. They have excellent group problem-solving and negotiation abilities, with conflicts quickly resolved. Individuation is encouraged and permitted within established boundaries. Hierarchial structures are well defined, and there is flexibility in handling daily living and family member relationships.

Optimal functioning families (healthy) had a variety of interrelationships and no particular way of doing things. In these families there were expectations for caring, a respect for one's own views and those of others, and exploration of numerous options for handling life experiences. Numerous interconnections were found that reached outside families to other environments. Stable and caring parental relationships were characterized by considerable role definition and accurate appraisals of family competency. Personal autonomy of members was valued. Openness of expression of affect reflecting warmth, affection, and caring was evident, and family interactions had a high degree of spontaneity. Of considerable import was the finding that no single thing seem to make the difference between optimally adequate families and adequate ones.

In adequately competent families, effective functioning was more akin to less-effective functioning families than to optimally functioning ones. Of import was the finding that children in these families were just as competent as those in optimally functioning families. This finding suggests that family members have an independent capacity to grow and actualize in family systems having a variety of structures and dynamics. It also suggests that some aspects of family functioning may have more impact on member growth and actualization than others.

An assessment tool was developed for measuring family functioning based on the structure and assumptions of the model. A major drawback to its use is that both observers and raters are needed to make clinical judgments from actual observations or from videotapes. Whether the measurement format can be modified to involve families and members in the clinical assessment remains to be seen.

OTHER PERSPECTIVES AND RESEARCH

Healthy family functioning has been approached from a number of other perspectives in both theory and research. Pless and Satterwhite (1973) identified healthy family functioning as measures that influence the health of family members. Deykin (1972) associated healthy family functioning with the indicators of decision-making, emotional gratification, perceptions of crises, perceptions of community, responses to crises, and responses to community. Hume, O'Conner, and Lowery (1977) found healthy family functioning and member experiences affected by environmental surroundings and settings, degree of involvement in environments, the extent to which satisfaction was achieved in interrelationships, and achievement of goals. They found that a focus solely on family systems was inadequate to understand and assist individual members in their growth and health. Weakland (1977) examined family somatics, which he considered a neglected area of family functioning.

Reiss (1980) found healthy functioning families were open and growing systems that used innovative responses to change things and to handle daily situations. They had clear power structures, encouraged individual member uniqueness, had reality confrontations, freely expressed warmth and optimism, and showed awareness of the behavior of others.

Hansen (1981) lived with three "normal" families to observe members in daily functioning in their natural contexts. Differences in interactional problems were usually small but repetitive and pervaded other parts of living. Selected characteristics of functional (normal) families showed a smooth and relaxed rhythm of living; marital relationships had a lower priority than parental and parent/child ones. Outside sources were used to help resolve problems. There was an overall pattern for addressing family problems, as well as a high level of spontaneity and agreement between marital and parental relationships.

From a slightly different perspective, Anderson (1973) related family growth to the essential competencies of coping, satisfying family interactions, and actualizing dormant potentials of family members. Barnhill (1979) analyzed a number of theories on family functioning and found several dimensions involved in promoting a "family health cycle." They are as follows:

1. Individualization for family members
2. Emotional closeness that allows for individual identity expression and development
3. Flexibility in responses to change and living
4. Stability and security in family interactions and relationships
5. Clear communications
6. Clear role boundaries
7. Clear generational boundaries for relationships

Walsh (1982) compiled a number of normal family perspectives and processes, which has helped to shift an emphasis from abnormal to normal family functioning. She noted that past emphases on defining "normality" as the absence of disease caused a skewed notion of normality, because normality and health are often confounded and myths about the normal family abound. From a systems perspective, normal family processes have been identified as transactions and include integration, maintenance, and growth of the family unit in both individual and social systems.

More recently, healthy functioning families having different structures from two-parent families have been examined. Hanson (1986) recently examined characteristics of healthy single-parent families and found them to be similar to healthy two-parent families. Patterns of functioning in families of remarried and first-married couples were examined by Peek, Bell, Waldren, and Sorrell (1988). They found that different family structures had similar patterns of functioning on the dimensions of cohesion, adaptability, expressiveness, flexibility and openness, interaction skills, problem-solving, organization, and control of family functioning. And from a slightly different perspective, Walker, McLaughlin, and Greene (1988) compared family functioning in families having healthy and unhealthy adolescents. Cohesion and adaptability were different in healthy adolescent families.

In summary, several models based on research related to healthy functioning families have been developed from a number of perspectives. Although shifts in paradigms have occurred over the past 25 years, they will continue to focus on a better understanding of normal or healthy functioning families.

Conceptualizations of Family Mental Health

MENTAL HEALTH NURSING PERSPECTIVE

Vital interrelationships exist between family mental health and the mental health of family members. Family mental health may be characterized by healthy family functioning. Family health and individual member health fuse to form holistic family mental health: one is not possible without the other.

Assumptions. The following assumptions focus and guide the conceptualization for family mental health and healthy family functioning:

1. Family systems as open systems operate on the principles of general systems theory; however, the unique aspects of family systems may alter to some extent in both subtle and explicit ways their applicability to various subsystems, particularly the personal systems of members.
2. Family systems are primary social systems in which members across the life span must be nurtured, socialized, humanized, and provided support to reach adulthood.
3. Families have an organizational structure of roles, authority, and functions, which develop into patterns by which to handle daily living situations and growth of members.
4. Change in any part of a family system resonates throughout the entire system; it may be experienced in different ways and with different intensities by members and by the system as a whole.
5. Healthy family functioning is more than the absence of dysfunctional patterns of functioning; it has a structure and dynamic of its own that is different in kind, direction, and aim.
6. Family system functioning shapes and alters the sociobehavioral, psycho-

logic, and physiologic dimensions of member health; at the same time, member health shapes and alters family systems.

7. Therapeutic actions and interventions that derive from a perspective and synthesis of nursing and related science knowledge about family functioning have different emphases, relationships, and outcomes from those that are primarily medically, socially, and behaviorally oriented.

PERSPECTIVE ON FAMILY MENTAL HEALTH

Moos and Moos (1976) and Moos (1976, 1979, 1984) have identified three common dimensions of family environments that have behavioral consequences for members: (1) the relationship dimension; (2) the personal growth dimension; and (3) the system maintenance dimension. These dimensions interrelate and may be translated more specifically into indicators. This orientation has served as part of the general organizing framework for the conceptualization of family health with a mental health nursing perspective.

Interrelationships in family systems are unique in many ways because as they develop and evolve, they serve as intense and intimate learning environments. In these environments, members acquire values, beliefs, and patterned behaviors. They learn health-protecting behaviors, develop and use ever-expanding coping dialogues, acquire communication styles and patterns, and undergo both overt and subtle changes in growth that foster the emergence of an adult selfhood.

In families, a certain amount of tension exists to stimulate and motivate growth and exploration of new approaches to life and living. Contemporary families, irrespective of structure, generate such tension in the normal course of events of daily living in their assumption of family responsibilities. This tension gives a touch of sharpness to novelty and challenge. It helps families to adapt to rapid and evolutionary changes in values and beliefs, as well as structure and function.

Family systems are also unique in that they experience considerable differences in kind and degree of interrelationships. All families have *variations* in their multidimensional patterns of interaction. Through prevention counseling, such variations can be identified, altered, and singled out for consideration of change. Potential problematic variations and patterns in such normal family processes as communication and coping can be examined. A need exists for members to develop selfhood with support and tact. Parenting practices, relating to persons of the same and opposite sex, and the development of social, interpersonal, and personal competencies needed for successful adulthood are part of the complex tasks families face and can correct with guidance.

Families are unique in other ways. They tend to have members at different ages, stages, and places in their life trajectories. Hence, members have a variety of ever-changing needs that must be met and wishes that should be considered. Irrespective of age and stage, all members need nurturance to some extent and continued support to develop independence and selfhood. Each of these differences sets the stage for normal stresses and strains to arise in family systems.

Healthy functioning families, like other kinds of families, have varied and competing claims and goals made by members. In these small dynamic social systems, the tensions and strains of daily living amplify and resonate easily throughout the system of interrelationships. Small variations in attitudes, values, and behaviors can have surprisingly large consequences for family members and for the system. Strong families have the strengths and resources to handle such variations. If such variations become repetitive to the point that a level of chronic aggravation is generated, points of contention can often be alleviated through skilled counseling.

Families have special responsibilities for member growth and development if potentials are to be actualized (Bruhn, Cordova, Williams, & Fuentes, 1977). The mental health of members may be considered along three dimensions: psychologic, sociobehavioral, and physiologic. The *psychologic dimension* is concerned primarily with development of self-esteem, independence, and selfhood. In this process, learning, empathy, motivation, locus of control, and development of a world view are important personal dynamics. The *sociobehavioral dimension* is concerned with learning and using coping dialogues appropriately, communication, roles, relationship establishment and maintenance, problem-solving, handling authority, development of core values, and development of cohesion and actions that support family health and welfare. The *physiologic dimension* is concerned with managing stress, assuming responsibility for personal health-promoting behaviors and life-styles, monitoring general health indicators, and recognizing that an emergence of somatic behaviors may be an indicator of stress and dissatisfaction that are coming from other dimensions of personal health and from the family system functioning as an entity.

At a systems level, families must learn how to cope competently in a variety of routine situations and stresses encountered in daily living. A family systemic is learning that healthy family functioning involves a delicate balancing act along many dimensions (i.e., a heterostasis) in ways that members have both stability and instability in a mix that propels both system and members to new growth and in new directions. Families must develop and use social and organizational competencies to interconnect themselves to other systems in communities that address general and special interests of the family.

Conversely, family members must develop competencies in personal and social relationship formation and maintenance, both of which are essential for growth at timely phases of development (Johnson, 1991). Competency-building has long been identified as a pervasive prevention strategy for promoting positive mental health for individuals (Bloom, 1979; Gladwin, 1967). Adler (1982) found the same thing applied to families. Their interactional abilities are a key to development of interpersonal competence of members and are related to positive mental health for both families and members.

From a mental health nursing perspective, family mental health includes but goes beyond general health concerns arising from a systems perspective. The mental health nursing perspective includes the nursing perspective, its caring ethic, and special qualities of nurse/client relationships. These guide the nurse to focus on interrelationships related to family systematics and member dynamics. This focus is implemented through use of special nursing knowledge and theory and a perspective screen that is sensitized to nuances and actions in interpretations of such data.

M. J. Smith (1990) called attention to some of the implications of use of "clinical" as a description of nursing activities. She thinks it has come to mean nursing activities in hospital settings. The mental health nursing perspective recognizes that this association of clinical with settings could be a constraint. Instead, it emphasizes health—in all its aspects—and focuses on the person/environment/health process and related nursing practice and is based on patterns of functioning evolving from this process.

Prevention counseling, as a mental health nursing process, is a unique health-promoting and growth-actualization process. Its knowledge bases may be generated by many disciplines and synthesized into particular nursing formulations about health/wellness phenomena that nursing is uniquely prepared to address as its domain of practice.

More specifically, mental health nursing uses the holistic perspective of nursing and special ways of being, relating, and acting with families. This basic paradigm guides the organization of nursing phenomena and leads to a consideration of the multidimensional aspects of health in both family functioning and member health.

The psychiatric mental health nurse comes to mental health nursing with the unique perspective of nursing and basic and specialized systems of knowledge about health and mental health in family systems. Therapeutic use of self is central to therapeutic strategies. A psychiatric mental health nursing perspective is different from that of other disciplines in this field. This view can now be supported in a more substantive way. Graves and Corcoran (1989) found that the structure of nursing knowledge is substantively different and uses different problem-solving and knowledge-structuring principles from other disciplines.

MENTAL HEALTH NURSING PERSPECTIVE: A FAMILY STRENGTHENING MODEL

Koldjeski (1984) is one of the few nurses in the specialty who has focused on the theory and research of healthy functioning families from a mental health nursing perspective. From this early work, she went on to develop a Family Strengthening Model that was used to develop a prevention counseling project. Consistent with the general conceptualization of family mental health, she synthesized from research a number of characteristics of healthy functioning families (see box, p. 64).

From nursing, a holistic perspective of health orients a focus on both physical and mental health. Nursing roles and relationships are considered unique when compared with those of other health professionals. The core notion that behavior is a person/environment/health-interaction process provides direction for counseling activities. Phenomena so generated are those that nursing is

---

Koldjeski's Characteristics of Healthy Functioning Families

1. Encouraging intimate, loving, and supportive experiences among members without loss of personal identity and sense of self.
2. Establishing a climate in which the unique aspects of members and their views are respected without undue punishment or negative valuation.
3. Having open and varied interrelationships in which social and personal competencies can be learned and experienced as rewarding.
4. Promoting and experiencing cohesion as a family and member.
5. Having a set of cultural and spiritual values, beliefs, and expectations that are understood by members.
6. Participating in a wide range of social and cultural activities so as to develop problem-solving and social competencies.
7. Helping members to see beyond the present and encouraging the development of aspirations and goals that are future-oriented.
8. Maintaining social, kin, and community networks and linkages for support, learning, and enjoyment.
9. Having a general structure of roles and relationships that is open enough to readily support changes.
10. Having a pattern of organization for handling daily living that is open to change and unexpected happenings.
11. Ensuring that expectations and responsibilities related to authority are known to all members.

---

uniquely prepared to address in its focus on promotion of health and prevention of potential health problems.

Interconnections between whole family functioning and individual family member health and nursing process are conceptualized as coming together in a fusion process. That is, they blend together and unite such that the original things continue to exist but become transformed into different things by the energy immanent in the things themselves. In family systems, the result of such fusion provides energy and motivation to fuel total family functioning.

While keeping in mind the characteristic interrelationships of healthy family functioning, researchers selected certain indicators to signify the characteristics to facilitate their use in counseling activities. Indicators selected for this purpose are the following:

1. Family strengths (Otto, 1964, 1972; Stinnet, 1985)
2. Family interrelationships, interactions, and communications patterns (the Beavers Systems Model, 1976, 1977, 1981, 1983; Barnhill, 1979.)
3. Family coping patterns (Circumplex Model, 1978, 1979, 1986)
4. Family health beliefs and health practices (Breslow & Somers, 1977; Hopkins, 1959; Peachey, 1963; Pender, 1987, 1990)

For member mental health, indicators were consolidated into three interrelating dimensions for parsimony in usage: (1) the *psychologic dimension* expressed the empathic tendencies, locus of control, and self-esteem; (2) the *sociobehavioral dimension* expressed through coping, communication, role, and general holistic life adaptation for individual members; and (3) the *physiologic dimension* expressed through the indicators of stress management, health beliefs and values, health practices, and patterns of illness.

Using the general conceptualization of family mental health and the more specific indicators of family and member health in their physical and mental aspects, guidelines for the development of a prevention counseling program with a bias toward the mental health component of health were developed. A comprehensive assessment tool is needed and may be augmented by special assessments for articulation dimensions of family functioning. Both whole family functioning and individual member health data are considered essential in understanding variations in family systems and dynamics over the course of a program in prevention counseling.

FAMILY FUNCTIONING: CONTROL-CONGRUENCE MODEL

A second example of synthesis of knowledge from nursing and other sciences that has resulted in a reformulated model of family functioning is the control-congruence (CC) model. The model was developed at Wayne State University to formulate a mental health nursing approach for working with families who have physical, emotional, interpersonal, social, and environmental problems (Friedman, 1989a, 1989b). A study of this reformulated model suggests that its assumptions, propositions, concepts, structure, and overall goal are appropriate for use with healthy functioning families. Further, it has flexibility in the emphases that can be selected to guide particular nursing interventions and actions.

The model was developed by synthesizing selected aspects of nursing theory from Rogers (1980), Newman (1979, 1983), and Parse (1988, 1987). Family theory developed in a number of disciplines was also used to formulate a unique perception of relationships between theory and nursing process (Constantine, 1986; Haley, 1976; Kantor & Lehr, 1975; Minuchin, 1974).

Systemic organization, control, and congruence are the major dimensions of family functioning. Through use of the nursing process, the goal is to strengthen behaviors relative to personal, interpersonal, and family levels of functioning. The CC model addresses all system levels of family functioning, although the author states the ultimate aim is to reduce anxiety at the individual level. However, interventions may be targeted at any one of the subsystems because of their interdependence within the larger family system.

Family processes are conceptualized as regulating earthly conditions, or accessing conditions of time, space, energy, and matter to achieve control and congruence for each individual within the system. Control is achieved by new knowledge and stability that allow the development and transmission of stable patterns over generations and growth periods. Congruence for family members focuses on emotional bonding based on interactional patterns, values, and their meanings. These are acquired through new knowledge, inquiry, and realizations.

Four major processes operate as dynamisms within family systems to interconnect space, time, energy, and matter for purposes of stabilizing growth, affect, and meanings about togetherness, system change, system maintenance, and individuation. The resulting relationships are expressed in interaction patterns that result in congruence and control and regulate the collective behavior of the family system.

An assessment guide based on the conceptual model is available. In addition, a second guide is available that gives steps involved in providing nursing therapeutics.

FAMILY FUNCTIONING MODEL: USING ROGERS' THEORY

Operating from an assumption that a discipline needs to develop and use its own knowledge base in clinical practice and research, Whall (1986) and her colleagues made a significant contribution in this idea. They showed how derivations, reformulations, and applications to family therapy and theory can be made. These formulations do not specifically address nursing activities for healthy family functioning; however, the root theories are general ones and should apply. One example of theory clarification using a well-known nursing theory is described.

Using Rogers' theory of unitary man (1970, 1980, 1983a, 1983b), Johnston (1986) focused on applications of family interventions. The theory assumes unity between individual, family, and other kinds of systems, so data are intended to apply to all. Families are conceptualized as irreducible energy fields and have discernible and observable patterns of functioning. These patterns cannot be identified from knowledge of individual members. Families have the capacity to participate knowingly in changes in family and environmental fields. Such participation can be directed toward family-selected goals. This approach means that actions or interventions focus on the family as a whole rather than on individual members.

Johnston reframed and clarified the basic assumptions and principles in Rogers' theory to make them more explicit to family systems as the unit of care for nursing. They are (1) the family system is a unified whole and cannot be understood by a summation of various parts; (2) family and environmental fields are in continuous mutual interaction; (3) life processes are nonlinear, nonrepeating rhythmicities; (4) patterns identify the family field; and (5) the family system has a coherence — a whole — that is more than and different from the sum of each member's contributions to family functioning.

These assumptions and principles guide nursing assessment as to what are relevant phenomena and how they are to be clustered and interpreted by use of the special meanings inherent in the original theory. Johnston noted that in Rogers' theory, there is a striving always for synthesis rather than analysis. This means that assessment focuses on energy fields, such as family and environment in mutual simultaneous interaction, patterns, and four-dimensionality. Interventions may focus on redesigning patterns, valuing diversity and change, exploring life-style variations aimed toward conflict resolution, and participating in change processes. Johnston suggested questions by which interventions could be evaluated, such as whether new patterns assist the family in making decisions better than old ones and whether the extent of family participation has changed.

Fitzpatrick, Whall, Johnston, and Floyd (1982) took several nursing models/theories and developed psychiatric mental health applications to show how to apply general nursing formulations to specialty areas of clinical nursing. These efforts should be recognized for their importance. They serve as exemplars for using the unique theory base of nursing to guide and inform the clinical nursing practice.

Nurses are becoming more knowledgeable about using nursing theory/ models to reframe formulations that have direct relevance to family functioning. Further, different theories are being used for different aspects of clinical practice. For example, Quayhagen and Roth (1989) used nursing conceptual models to develop a tool for assessment of mature families. Heinrich (1987) reported on a clinical nursing education experience in which students focus on the psychosocial aspects of family health in healthy functioning families through participant/observer experiences. And Killeen (1990) reported on a project in which mental health promotion was taught to children in Head Start Centers.

In summary, three kinds of models of family functioning based on nursing theory or reformulated from both nursing and theory from other disciplines have been identified for use with a focus on healthy functioning families. The nursing models use knowledge from the sciences in somewhat different ways. They are examples of how mental health nursing can use theory and research to emphasize the general nursing perspective and a special emphasis on mental health.

Guidelines for Prevention Counseling

Five program guidelines found useful in planning and providing prevention counseling services are (1) the need to demystify meanings about mental health; (2) the need to integrate physical and mental aspects of health as a concept of overall health; (3) the need to establish the focus of the program; (4) the need for participation to be freely available to families and their members with opportunities to withdraw from activities if they wish; and (5) the need to maintain strict privacy about the content and dynamics of the counseling sessions themselves.

DEMYSTIFYING MEANINGS OF MENTAL HEALTH

Mental health has long been an umbrella concept under which many meanings find cover and where mental health is often presented as a synonym for mental illness. Scholarly and professional definitions held by mental health clinicians and the meanings of mental health held by the public are often different. Many definitions of mental health can arouse old concerns and stereotypes about mental illness.

Once families have indicated their interest in participating in prevention counseling, one of the first things that must be addressed is demystifying the process by recasting mental health as a dimension of general health. This recasting must avoid the language of mental illness and provide new ways of thinking and talking about mental health. So much of the language of mental health used by mental health professionals conveys illness, so the use of health-oriented language in relation to mental health is an area that needs careful monitoring.

This recasting process can be approached by suggesting that family members not label one another as "sick" when relationships are tension-laden and uncomfortable. The use of such labeling can be a barrier and shows a lack of other ways of naming behavior and/or a reluctance to cope with it. It can also be used as a reason to refer problematic situations to professionals. Recasting also must link family functioning behaviors with indicators of strong or healthy families. Specific behaviors can be identified and discussed in terms of their healthy aspects to help families make connections between mentally healthy functioning and the behaviors to which it relates.

INTEGRATING MENTAL AND PHYSICAL HEALTH

Mental and physical health continue to be viewed as separate aspects of general health. A focus on family functioning is an ideal way to help members interconnect events that happen in family systems and their own health concerns, problems, and feelings. Members usually have no difficulty in coming up with examples that illustrate such connections.

This linking of seemingly disparate aspects of family functioning and personal health concerns and behaviors of family members lays down a rationale for having members examine their health patterns and health-promoting behaviors. In this context, a focus on socioemotional and psychologic aspects of behavior of members is not as threatening as when it seems to be a dominant concern. Finally, a view that families have responsibilities for the health of their systems and their members and that the mental health aspect is not so mysterious that it must be left to mental health professionals can strengthen the role in family maintenance.

ESTABLISHING PROGRAM FOCUS

There is a need early in prevention counseling to establish the focus of the program, and this must be reaffirmed as necessary during sessions. This enlists family participation and minimizes any fears that the program is some kind of therapy in disguise.

Specific objectives can be developed as families provide feedback during counseling sessions and the mental health nurse has an opportunity to observe and experience the interactional system that the family uses in daily living. To accomodate the family input, the framework must have some structure but be open enough that changes can be readily made.

Some examples of establishing a program focus on healthy family functioning counseling and a discussion of a bias toward the mental health aspect in prevention counseling follow.

Helping families recognize strengths. Healthy functioning families should be helped to identify and recognize the things they do that make their family systems positive learning environments for members and for the system as a whole. Prevention counseling can then focus on strengthening or broadening these. In counseling sessions, activities associated with this focus may cover (1) teasing out from experiences characteristic patterns of family functioning, (2) obtaining family views and perceptions about the effectiveness of use of such patterns in general and special situations, and (3) determining gaps in knowledge about what happens when there is discomfort about the way in which families handle certain situations.

Strategies used in prevention counseling should be framed as prevention activities that address health. These activities involve all family members and need openness about shifts in actions that might influence family system functioning and member behavior. This common base of knowledge must be established so that family participation can proceed.

An important part of the role of the mental health nurse is to help family members make connections between *recurring* experiences that may be causing tension and frustration because they are incompletely handled. Residual emotions attached to such experiences must be connected to the experiences themselves. Once this is done, the meanings various members have attached to the experiences can be explored and different approaches for coping considered.

Strategies found useful for helping families recognize their strengths are clarification of communications, examination of relationships, consideration of member views, and giving value to concerns and hassles members find irksome. Another strategy is to demonstrate how situations can be redefined so that social, situational, and environmental factors can be seen to play a part and give a different contextual meaning to events and experiences.

Families may be asked to construct a *family strength ladder,* on which they rank their strengths and potentials. An approach can be used to have family members state private wishes. This often produces information of hidden longings and yearnings for personal actualization that have never been revealed or expressed before and perhaps have never reached a point of awareness until a special opportunity is provided. Cognitive restructuring is also a process that can be used to recast experiences to incorporate new information and interconnect them so that new meanings, insights, and perspectives evolve. Throughout, health and mental health education are used because they are powerful strategies in prevention counseling.

Identifying patterns of family functioning. A focus on examination of patterns of family functioning as they are expressed in interactions, interrelationships, and normal family processes can provide crucial data. This area of knowledge is intimately related to family system maintenance and development of member growth and actualization. Of equal importance are the processes that maintain and enhance family cohesion and family identity.

Programs may include a number of different activities. One is to obtain descriptions of an experience in which families have participated and have each member describe her or his personal feelings and feelings being part of a family.

This approach can involve experiences in which family members were proud of themselves and their family and others in which positive feelings were not as pronounced. Discussion can then identify what the differences between the two are and explore factors that may have contributed to different outcomes. Members can describe approaches they have used or seen others use to handle disagreements and provide information on how effective those approaches were. These types of discussion open opportunities for exploring alternative and perhaps more positive approaches for handling both agreements and disagreements.

For family member growth, development, and health, families may be asked to identify instances of expressions of caring for others. They can provide information on how members help each other in developing self-esteem, identity, autonomy, and locus of control. The multiple dimensions of health and mental health of members must be interconnected to family functioning, a major role for the mental health nurse, because families usually have neither the perspective nor knowledge to make such linkages in ways that minimize distortions.

One strategy useful in prevention counseling is the use of a *family experience calendar*. Members can be asked to identify the kinds of experiences they have had in the recent week or month to get a sense of the scope, diversity, and kinds of experiences engaged in. This is important because it is known that there is a relationship to member and family coping between diverse and adequate number of social and interpersonal experiences and the development of personal and social competencies. The family experience calendar also helps families to remember both pleasurable and unpleasurable experiences because the latter tend to stand out in memory and be cited as examples for handling subsequent behavior. The intent is to not let unpleasant experiences become the prevailing memory and be used as a model for future handling of situations. Exploration of factors that make such experiences have different perceptions, and outcomes often provide clues to coping and changes that may be useful.

Other strategies include "feuding, fussing, and fighting" actions that help members identify experiences that have been tension- or anger-producing. Around these experiences, residual feelings may continue to persist because of incomplete resolution. Role playing and role restructuring can be used to examine ongoing familial interactions and to explore what new interactions around the same situations could be tried. A variety of strategies involving interactional analysis can be used to good advantage when examining family interactions and interrelationships.

Recognizing family structure, roles, and organization. A focus on family structure, roles, and organization is another important area in prevention counseling. It should be remembered that clear concepts about family system structure, roles, and organization usually are not in the knowledge banks of family members and the members may not even understand what is meant by these aspects of family functioning. Yet these concepts are most important to an understanding about the ways in which families function. One role of the nurse early in counseling is to help provide meanings to these concepts and give examples that connect these to empirical examples. Once this is done, members usually have no difficulty in relating various kinds of knowledge and experiences relating to these aspects of the family system. Overall, the nurse must assist families to organize knowledge systems in ways that make sense to families and their members, to identify gaps in knowledge, and to avoid overemphasis on any one aspect.

Of import in such exploration is the interweaving of basic family processes, such as communication, interaction, interrelationships with social and community networks, and values and belief systems. All of these must be linked in a meaningful way to the supports and strengths available in families for supporting the personal development of members. The perceptions of family members about who is "boss," the role of parents, and the role of different family members must be made known — information that may elicit considerable surprise. Family potential and strengths can be used to assist members to learn additional social and personal competencies as maturation occurs. Personal interests and career goals are also opportunities that should be brought out into the open and discussed.

Strategies useful for highlighting such activities are family mapping, role mapping, sociogramming, and genogramming. Sculpting, an approach that allows feelings to be expressed in actions without verbalizations, is useful when members are asked to act out what their perceptions of family interrelationships are in the family system. Repeopling, that is, the placement of different members in different family roles for examination of the experience, is another approach to open up communication and provide new insights for participants. Anticipatory guidance and values clarification are other strategies useful in prevention counseling.

Handling daily living relationships. A focus on handling daily living relationships gets to the heart of family functioning, because it is these interactions that profoundly affect family systems and members. They represent the reality of daily living. Daily hassles and unanticipated events and experiences are part of the pattern of enjoyment and satisfaction that members experience. Daily living intimately involves roles and divisions of labor in family systems that are necessary for the system to survive and maintain a hospitable environment for satisfaction and growth of members.

System dynamics — that is, relationships, interrelationships and interactions, and member actions — involve coping and handling both satisfying and frustrating experiences. Recurring experiences that are energy-demanding but not terribly innovative and exciting must be dealt with. In family systems, members must learn to express concern for others and experience closeness among members. Emotional involvement fosters the development of competencies that set the stage for positive adult intimate experiences. And, in family environments, the toleration of failures without undue negative valuation establishes a base for risk-taking as adults.

An integral part of family organization concerns the inculcation of values and belief systems about important aspects of life and living. One such system relates to health and mental health and the health practices that the family uses to promote and maintain health. Breslow and Somers (1977), in a classic article, have outlined a lifetime plan for health monitoring to increase longevity and prevent illness.

The role of the mental health nurse is key to the success of prevention counseling. Obviously, a focus on the interactions in family systems will arouse concern, anxiety, guilt, and anger among members, and placing blame should be expected. Skillful counseling assists members to recognize the healthiness of such emotion, to accept it in a nonjudgmental way, and to accept a view that such emotions are "normal." Once the emotional aspects are dealt with, a more objective look at interactions can get under way.

Activities in this area also include identification of characteristic patterns of how crisis situations are handled. Consideration should be given to the effectiveness of such approaches, as well as to the family's plan for health promotion and maintenance. Very often, in the context of such discussions, difficulties not heretofore mentioned are identified and can be given special consideration.

Strategies useful for this aspect of counseling are coping pattern identification, problem-solving approaches, and exploration of the family/environment "fit" to determine whether the family recognizes contributions to member growth from sources and resources outside the family milieu. Last but not least, families need to recognize that a variety of emotions will bubble up at unexpected times and about unexpected things. Such bubbling-up is to be expected and accepted as routine and handled without undue valuation.

Interrelating family and community systems. A focus on interconnections between family, community, and social systems provides important information. Such networks of interrelationships mutually support, replenish, and provide novel experiences for one another. These interconnections link the health of families and communities.

Activities useful in addressing this area are those that sensitize families to the notion that communities are more than geographic locales — they have a life of their own. Linkages to the mental aspects of health of communities and the health and mental health of family systems can be identified. The community as an invaluable resource for the family can be highlighted, and the contributions that families make to community activities and health should be cited.

Strategies useful for this aspect of counseling are to have families define their community with the purpose of determining how constrained or specialized their view may be. Gaps in use of community resources can be identified. Families usually find the idea of their community having mental health aspects quite novel. The mental health nurse can help to structure knowledge in this area to broaden and strengthen the linkages between families and their communities.

PARTICIPATING BY INFORMED CONSENT

Informed consent is of course needed for families and their members to participate in prevention counseling. This consent should be based on discussions about the nature of prevention counseling and what it involves. It includes an understanding that families may withdraw from sessions whenever they wish with no questions asked and without any consequences of this action on subsequent health care that may be needed in any system of services.

MAINTAINING PRIVACY

Families need to arrive at an agreement about the availability of information from counseling sessions. If such sessions are conducted under the sponsorship of already established mental health or community health services, families may balk at participation because they do not want their records intermingled with those of families and clients with a variety of health problems, especially mental health ones. If sessions are provided by entrepreneurs or educational services, arrangements about privacy can usually be established to family satisfaction, because no institutional rules govern the retention and dissemination of client information. In these settings, legal advice on what kinds of records are required by law is recommended.

• • •

A conceptual approach and rationale for prevention counseling with healthy functioning families is one approach for providing prevention counseling activities. Models of healthy functioning families from the social and behavioral sciences and selected research show both knowledge and experience bases for this focus. Three models for guiding nursing activities of a prevention nature with an emphasis on mental health show the diversity by which available bodies of knowledge can be synthesized and reformulated. Guidelines for programs in prevention counseling with healthy functioning families include demystifying mental health; identifying patterns of family functioning; recognizing family structure, roles, and organization; handling daily living experiences; interrelating family and community systems; participating under informed consent; and maintaining privacy of data generated.

Program development includes activities designed to address the areas in which prevention is to be provided, seeking family participation, and developing or identifying strategies that encourage participation and change. Of import is the need to minimize language and communication that evokes negative stereotypes associated with mental illness. Much care should be exercised to ensure that prevention counseling does not cause families to become labeled as having "mental health problems."

A prevention counseling approach from a mental health nursing perspective is different in both degree and kind from counseling provided by other mental health disciplines. Like family therapy, prevention counseling uses an array of generic strategies, but the special qualities and characteristics that such counseling derives from nursing are what make a difference. Mental health promotion and primary prevention in mental health will become increasingly important as the decade advances because treatment approaches can never handle problems after they have developed—the hope for the future is to prevent problems to the extent that knowledge and experiences permit.

REFERENCES

Adler, P.T. (1982). An analysis of the concept of competence in individuals and social systems. *Community Mental Health Journal, 13,* 24-25.

Anderson, D.A. (1973). The family growth group: Guidelines for an emerging means of strengthening families. *Family Coordinator, 23,* 7-13.

Anderson, S.A. (1986). Cohesion, adaptability and communication: A test of an Olson Circumplex Model Hypothesis. *Family Relations, 35,* 289-293.

Barnhill, L.R. (1979). Healthy family systems. *Family Coordinator, 28,* 94-100.

Beavers, W.R. (1982). Healthy, midrange and severely dysfunctional families. In F. Walsh (Ed.), *Normal family processes.* New York: Guilford.

Beavers, W.R., Hampson, R.B., & Hulgus, Y.F. (1985). Commentary: The Beavers Systems approach to family assessment. *Family Process, 24,* 398-405.

Beavers, W.R., & Voeller, M.N. (1983). Family models: Comparing and contrasting the Olson Circumplex Model with the Beavers Systems Model. *Family Process, 22,* 85-98.

Bloom, B.L. (1979). Prevention of mental disorder: Recent advances in theory and practice. *Community Mental Health Journal, 15,* 179-191.

Breslow, L., & Somers, A.R. (1977). The lifetime health monitoring program. *New England Journal of Medicine, 296,* 601-608.

Bruhn, J.B., Cordova, F.D., Williams, J.A., & Fuentes, R.G. (1977). The wellness process. *Journal of Community Health, 2,* 209-221.

Constantine, L.L. (1986). *Family paradigms: The practice of theory in family therapy.* New York: Guilford.

Cowen, E.L. (1977). Baby steps toward primary prevention. *American Journal of Community Psychology, 5,* 1-22.

Deykin, E. (1972). Life functioning in families of delinquent boys: An assessment model. *Social Science Review, 46,* 90-102.

Epstein, N.B., Baldwin, L.M., & Bishop, D.S. (1983). The McMaster family assessment device. *Journal of Marriage and Family Therapy, 9,* 171-180.

Epstein, N.B., Bishop, D.S., & Baldwin, L.M. (1982). The McMaster model of family functioning: A view of the normal family. In F. Walsh (Ed.), *Normal family processes.* New York: Guilford.

Epstein, N.B., Bishop, D.S., & Levin, S. (1978). The McMaster model of family functioning. *Journal of Marriage and Family Counseling, 4,* 19-31.

Fitzpatrick, J., Whall, A., Johnston, R., & Floyd, J. (1982). *Nursing models and their psychiatric mental health applications.* Bowie, MD: Robert J. Brady.

Friedman, M.L. (1989a). Closing the gap between grand theory and mental health practice with families. Part I: The framework of systemic organization for nursing of families and family members. *Archives of Psychiatric Nursing, 3,* 10-19.

Friedman, M.L. (1989b). Closing the gap between grand theory and mental health practice with families. Part II: The Control-Congruence Model of mental health nursing in families. *Archives of Psychiatric Nursing, 3,* 20-28.

Gladwin, T. (1967). Social competence and clinical practice. *Psychiatry, 30,* 30-43.

Graves, J.R., & Corcoran, S. (1989). The study of nursing informatics. *Image, 21,* 227-231.

Grinker, R. (1966). Forward. In D. Offer & M. Sabshin (Eds.), *Normality,* New York: Basic Books.

Haley, J. (1976). Problem-solving therapy. San Francisco: Jossey-Bass.

Hansen, C. (1981). Living-in with normal families. *Family Process, 20,* 53-75.

Hanson, S.M.H. (1986). Healthy single-parent families. *Family Relations, 35,* 125-132.

Heinrich, K.T. (1987). Refocused family study program sharpens students' assessment skills. *Nursing and Health Care, 8,* 175-178.

Hopkins, P. (1959). Health and happiness and the family. *British Journal of Clinical Practice, 13,* 311-313.

Hume, N., O'Conner, W.A., & Lowery, C.R. (1977). Family adjustment and the psychosocial ecosystem. *Psychiatric Annals, 7,* 32-49.

Johnson, T.P. (1991). Mental health, social relations and social selection: A longitudinal analysis. *Journal of Health and Social Behavior, 12*(4), 408-423.

Johnston, R.L. (1986). Approaching family intervention through Rogers' conceptual model. In A.L. Whall (Ed.), *Family therapy theory for nursing.* Norwalk, CT: Appleton-Century-Crofts.

Jones, S.L., & Diamond, M. (1982). Family theory and family therapy models: Comparative review with implication for nursing practice. *Journal of Psychiatric Nursing and Mental Health Services, 20,* 12-19.

Kantor, D., & Lehr, W. (1975). *Inside the family.* San Francisco: Jossey-Bass.

Killeen, M.R. (1990). Using Head Start Centers for teaching mental health promotion. *Child & Adolescent Psychiatric and Mental Health Nursing, 3*(3), 79-84.

Koldjeski, D. (1984). *Community mental health nursing: New directions in theory and practice.* New York: John Wiley & Sons.

Lee, C. (1988). Theories of adaptability: Toward a synthesis of Olson's Circumplex and the Beavers Systems Models. *Family Process, 27,* 73-85.

Lewis, J.M., Beavers, W.R., Gossett, J.T., & Phillips, V.A. (1976). *No single thread: Psychological health in family systems.* New York: Brunner/Mazel.

McCubbin, M.H.L., & Patterson, J.M. (1981). Broadening the scope of family strengths: An emphasis in family coping and social support. In N. Stinnet, J. DeFrain, K. King, P. Knaub, & G. Rowe (Eds.), *Family strengths 3: Roots of well-being.* Lincoln, NE: University of Nebraska Press.

Meleis, A.I. (1990). Being and becoming healthy: The core of nursing knowledge. *Nursing Science Quarterly, 3*(3), 107-114.

Minuchin, S. (1974). *Families and family therapy.* Cambridge, MA: Harvard University Press.

Moos, R.H. (1976). Evaluating and changing community settings. *American Journal of Community Psychology, 4,* 313-326.

Moos, R.H. (1979). Evaluating family and work settings. In P. Ahmed & G. Cohelo (Eds.), *New directions in health.* New York: Plenum Press.

Moos, R.H. (1984). Context and coping: Toward a unifying conceptual framework. *American Journal of Community Psychology, 12,* 5-25.

Moos, R.H., & Moos, B. (1976). A typology of family social environments. *Family Process, 15,* 357-371.

Newman, M.A. (1979). *Theory development in nursing.* Philadelphia: F.A. Davis.

Newman, M.A. (1983). Newman's health theory. In I.W. Clements & F.B. Roberts (Eds.), *Family health: A theoretical approach to nursing care.* New York: John Wiley & Sons.

Olson, D.H. (1986). Circumplex Model VII: Validation studies and FACES II. *Family Process, 25,* 337-351.

Olson, D.H., Portner, J., & Bell, R. (1982). Family adaptability and cohesion evaluation scales. In D.H. Olson, H.L. McCubbin, H. Barnes, A. Larsen, M. Muxen, & M. Wilson (Eds.), *Family Inventories.* St. Paul, MN: Minnesota Press.

Olson, D.H., Russell, C.S., & Sprenkle, D.H. (1983). Circumplex model of marital and family systems VI: Theoretical update. *Family Process, 22,* 69-83.

Olson, D.H., Sprenkle, D.H., & Russell, C.S. (1979). Circumplex model of marital and family systems: Cohesion and adaptability dimensions, family types and clinical applications. *Family Process, 18,* 3-15.

Otto, H.A. (1962). The personal and family resource development programs: A preliminary report. *International Journal of Social Psychiatry, 8,* 185-195.

Otto, H.A. (1963). Criteria for assessing family strengths. *Family Process, 3,* 329-332.

Otto, H.A. (1964). The personal and family strengths research projects: Implications for the therapist. *Mental Hygiene, 48,* 439-450.

Otto, H.A. (1971). *The family cluster: A multibase alternative.* Los Angeles, CA: Holistic Press.

Otto, H.A. (1972). *The utilization of family strengths in marriage and family counseling.* Los Angeles, CA: Holistic Press.

Otto, H.A. (1975). The human potential movement: An overview. *Journal of Creative Behavior,* 258-265.

Otto, H.A. (1976). *Marriage and family enrichment: New perspectives and programs.* Nashville, TN: Abingdon Press.

Parse, R.R. (1987). *Nursing science: Major paradigms, theories & critiques.* Philadelphia: W.B. Saunders.

Parse, R.R. (1988). *Man-living-health theory of health.* Paper presented at College of Nursing, Wayne State University, Detroit, MI.

Parse, R.R. (1990). Promotion and prevention: Two distinct cosmologies. *Nursing Science Quarterly, 3*(3), 101.

Parse, R.R. (1991). Mysteries of health and healing. *Nursing Science Quarterly, 4*(3), 93.

Peachey, R. (1963). Family patterns of illness. *General Practitioner, 27,* 82-89.

Peek, C.W., Bell, N.J., Waldren, T., & Sorrell, G.T. (1988). Patterns of functioning in families of remarried and first-married couples. *Journal of Marriage and the Family, 50,* 699-708.

Pender, N.J. (1987). *Health promotion and nursing practice* (2nd ed.). Norwalk, CT: Appleton-Century-Crofts.

Pender, N.J. (1990). Expressing health through life-style patterns. *Nursing Science Quarterly, 3*(3), 115-122.

Phillips, J.R. (1990). The different views of health. *Nursing Science Quarterly, 3*(3), 103-104.

Pless, I.B., & Satterwhite, B. (1973). A measure of family functioning and its application. *Social Science and Medicine, 7,* 613-621.

Porter-O'Grady, T. (1985). Health versus illness: Nurses can chart the course for the future. *Nursing and Health Care, 6,* 319-321.

Quayhagen, M.P., & Roth, P.A. (1989). From models to measures in assessment of mature families. *Journal of Professional Nursing, 5,* 319-321.

Reiss, D. (1980). Pathway to assessing the family: Some choice points and a sample route. In C.F. Hofling & J. Lewis (Eds.), *The family: Evaluation and treatment.* New York: Brunner/Mazel.

Rogers, M.E. (1970). *An introduction to the theoretical basis of nursing.* Philadelphia: F.A. Davis.

Rogers, M.E. (1980). Nursing: A science of unitary man. In J.P. Riehl & C. Roy (Eds.), *Conceptual models for nursing practice* (2nd ed.). New York: Appleton-Century-Crofts.

Rogers, M.E. (1983a). Analysis and application of Rogers' theory of nursing. In I.W. Clements & F.B. Roberts (Eds.), *Family health: A theoretical approach.* New York: John Wiley & Sons.

Rogers, M.E. (1983b). A science of unitary beings: A paradigm for nursing. In I.W. Clements & F.B. Roberts (Eds.), *Family health: A theoretical approach.* New York: John Wiley & Sons.

Rowe, G., Lindgren, H., Van Zandt, S., Williams, R., DeFrain, J., & Stinnet, N. (1985). *Family Strengths 5.* Newton, MA: Educational Development Center.

Scanzoni, J. (1987). Families in the 1980s: Time to refocus our thinking. *Journal of Family Issues, 4,* 394-421.

Smith, M.C. (1990). Nursing's unique focus on health promotion. *Nursing Science Quarterly, 3*(3), 105-106.

Smith, M.J. (1990). Clinical: The meaning of the term. *Nursing Science Quarterly, 3*(3), 102.

Sprenkle, D., & Olson, D.H. (1978). Circumplex Model of marital and family systems IV: Empirical study of clinical and nonclinical couples. *Journal of Marriage and Family Counseling, 4,* 59-74.

Stinnet, N. (1985). Research on strong families. In G.A. Rekers (Ed.), *National leadership forum on strong families.* Ventura, CA: Regal Books.

Stinnet, N., Chesser, B., & DeFrain, J. (Eds.). (1979). *Building family strengths 1: Blueprints for action.* Lincoln, NE: University of Nebraska Press.

Stinnet, N., Chesser, B., & DeFrain, J., & Knaub, P. (Eds.). (1980). *Family strengths: Positive models of family life.* Lincoln, NE: University of Nebraska Press.

Stinnet, N., & DeFrain, J. (1985). *Secrets of strong families.* Boston, MA: Little, Brown.

Stinnet, N., DeFrain, J., King, K., Knaub, P., & Rowe, G. (Eds.). (1981). *Family strengths 3: Roots of well-being.* Lincoln, NE: University of Nebraska Press.

Stinnet, N., DeFrain, J., Lindgren, N., Van Zandt, S., & Williams, R. (Eds.). (1982). *Family strengths 4: Roots of well-being.* Lincoln, NE: University of Nebraska Press.

Stinnet, N., Knorr, B., DeFrain, J., & Rowe, G. (1981). How strong families cope with crises. *Family Perspectives, 15,* 159-166.

Stinnet, N., Lynn, D., Kimmons, L., Fuenning, S., & DeFrain, J. (1984). Family strengths and personal wellness. *Wellness Perspectives, 1,* 25-31.

Stinnet, N., & Sauer, K. (1977). Relationship patterns among strong families. *Family Perspectives, 11,* 3-11.

Taylor, R.B., Denham, J.W., & Ureda, J.R. (1982). Health promotion: A perspective. In R.B. Taylor (Ed.), *Health promotions: Principles and clinical applications.* Norwalk, CT: Appleton-Century-Crofts.

Vaugh, W.T., Huntington, D.S., Samuels, T.E., Bilmes, M., & Shapiro, M.I. (1975). Family mental health maintenance: A new approach to prevention. *Hospital and Community Psychiatry, 26,* 503-508.

Walker, L.S., McLaughlin, F.J., & Greene, J.W. (1988). Functional illness and family functioning: A comparison of healthy and somaticizing adolescents. *Family Process, 27,* 317-332.

Walsh, F. (1982). *Normal family processes.* New York: The Guilford Press.

Weakland, J.H. (1977). Family somatics: A neglected edge. *Family Process, 16,* 263-272.

Westley, W.A., & Epstein, N.B. (1969). *The silent majority.* San Francisco, CA: Jossey-Bass.

Whall, A.L. (1986). *Family therapy theory for nursing.* Norwalk, CT: Appleton-Century-Crofts.

Williams, R., Lindgren, H., Rowe, G., Van Zandt, S., & Stinnet, N. (Eds.). (1985). *Family strengths 6.* Lincoln, NE: Department of Human Development and the Family, University of Nebraska.

Chapter 5

Family Law

Beatrice Crofts Yorker

As society becomes increasingly complex, so do the laws governing most intricacies of our professional and personal lives. Healthcare providers must be grounded in a number of evolving legal principles to maintain current practice. The growing area of family law includes statutes, judicial decisions, and legal doctrines that directly influence psychiatric nursing care. Nurses who work with families and the systems that impact families will encounter a variety of circumstances requiring a basic understanding of legal guidelines and precedent. This chapter provides an overview of the major areas that are subsumed under the general heading of *family law*. Implications for psychiatric nursing practice are woven into each topic, and finally, the role of the psychiatric nurse as a legal advocate for the family is covered.

The Role of the State in Regulating Family Matters

HISTORICAL PERSPECTIVE

The traditional common law, derived from English origins, viewed a man as the sole person capable of having legally recognized rights. Wives and children were considered his "property." They had very few rights independent of the adult male figures in the family. Until the twentieth century the laws regarding family life were relatively noninterventionist. What few restrictions did exist were based on biblical sanctions (e.g., adultery) and social taboos (e.g., incest).

The concept of "federalism" is central to understanding the development of family law in this country. According to the founding fathers, states were allowed to regulate most matters of day-to-day life. However, if the state promulgated laws that violated the Constitution or the Bill of Rights, the federal courts could intervene and strike down laws deemed unconstitutional.

Throughout the late 1800s and 1900s, laws that had protectionist and regulatory effects on the family were enacted by the states. Although these laws symbolized the state's recognition of public welfare interests, many of these laws were paternalistic and based on notions of antiquated morality. Because of the federal court system, laws such as those prohibiting interracial marriage

(*Loving v. Virginia*, 1967) and marriage of prisoners (*Salisbury v. List*, 1980) have been declared an infringement of constitutionally protected liberty interests.

When federal courts scrutinize state laws governing family life, the liberty interests of the individual within the family must be weighed against the interests of the state. As Justice Powell explained (*Zablocki v. Redhail*, 1978 at 396):

> The State, representing the collective expression of moral aspirations, has an undeniable interest in ensuring that its rules of domestic relations reflect the widely held values of its people. . . . State regulation has included bans on incest, bigamy, and homosexuality, as well as various preconditions to marriage, such as blood tests.

As state governments enacted laws in the interests of public health and welfare, Constitutional challenges arose whenever an individual or a class of individuals perceived an infringement on their exercise of liberty. A series of Supreme Court decisions on such issues brought about the evolution of the "right to privacy" as we understand it today. Although the United States Constitution does not specifically enumerate privacy as a protected right, the court amalgamated several provisions from the Constitution and the Bill of Rights into what they called *penumbras* (umbrellas) of enumerated rights that implied the fundamental right to privacy.

SEXUAL PRIVACY

The advent of medical technology in the area of reproductive health made laws that regulated contraception and sex education less necessary to meet the state's objective of protecting public health and welfare. The landmark case of *Griswold v. Connecticut* (1965) established the doctrine of sexual privacy. This case was brought by a married couple and their physician, challenging the Connecticut law that prohibited contraceptive use, prescription, or counseling.

The Federal Court of Appeals upheld the state law; however, the Supreme Court overturned this decision. Justice Douglas provided an excellent description of the process the court used to establish the right to sexual privacy (*Griswold v. Connecticut*, 1965 at 484):

> Various guarantees create zones of privacy. The right of association contained in the penumbra of the First Amendment is one, as we have seen. The Third Amendment in its prohibition against the quartering of soldiers "in any house" in time of peace without the consent of the owner is another facet of that privacy. The Fourth Amendment explicitly affirms the "right of the people to be secure in their persons, houses, papers, and effects, against unreasonable searches and seizures." The Fifth Amendment in its Self-Incrimination Clause enables the citizen to create a zone of privacy which government may not force him to surrender to his detriment. The Ninth Amendment provides: "The enumeration in the Constitution, of certain rights, shall not be construed to deny or disparage others retained by the people."

This case symbolized a breakthrough in the tension between human rights versus state regulation. The political atmosphere in the United States was ripe for challenging state regulation of private sexual behavior and morality. On the heels of this decision came many others, expanding the *Griswold* right of a married couple to engage in consensual sexual acts in the privacy of their bedroom to unmarried persons (*Eisenstadt v. Baird,* 1972), and minors (*Carey v. Population Services International,* 1977), based on the Equal Protection Clause.

By the 1970s state laws prohibiting abortion were coming under attack using the sexual and reproductive privacy arguments put forth in the *Griswold* line of cases. *Roe v. Wade* (1973) and its companion *Doe v. Bolton* (1973) were the watershed cases overturning Texas and Georgia laws that made it a crime to procure or attempt an abortion unless it was medically justified to save the life of the mother. The Supreme Court identified the state's purposes for antiabortion laws, and these were addressed in turn. The Court said the first rationale, that of discouraging illicit sexual activity, was based on Victorian social concern and the statute was "overbroad" in its attempt to meet that objective. Second, the state's interest in regulating a risky medical procedure was due for a reevaluation. The Court reasoned what was once a procedure associated with high mortality could be performed quite safely with current medical practices. The state did, however, retain an interest in regulating the relative medical safety of abortions. Finally, the Court examined the competing interest in prenatal life (*Roe v. Wade,* 1973).

The well-known trimester breakdown illustrated the Court's analysis of the maternal, fetal, and state interests and rights. During the first trimester, a fetus is not viable; therefore the fetal right is minimal when balanced against the mother's right to determine her reproductive status. The second trimester poses potential health risk to the mother, so some state regulation is permitted. During the third trimester, the viability of the fetus makes abortion entirely subject to regulation of the state. The status of women's right to make a choice regarding an abortion has been reviewed regularly by the Supreme Court.

Although the recent *Webster v. Reproductive Health Services* (1989) decision did not directly overturn *Roe v. Wade* (1973), it severely curtailed the interpretation of the constitutional right to privacy, including a woman's freedom to make decisions about abortion. The Court upheld Missouri's restrictive statutes disallowing use of public funds for nontherapeutic abortion services and placing a burden on practitioners to determine fetal viability after 20 weeks of gestation. The abortion issue continues to polarize many political and legislative agendas.

Another case that helped shape the area of constitutionally protected sexual privacy was decided in 1986. *Bowers v. Hardwick* (1986) involved a challenge to the Georgia anti-sodomy statute, which reads in part (Ga. Code Ann. 16-6-2 [1984]):

(a) A person commits the offense of sodomy when he performs or submits to any sexual act involving the sex organs of the one person and the mouth or anus of another. . . (b) A person convicted by the offense of sodomy shall be punished by imprisonment for not less than 1 nor more than 20 years. . .

This case involved Mr. Hardwick, a male homosexual who was charged with violating the statute by committing sodomy with another male in the bedroom of Hardwick's home. A married couple joined Hardwick in a federal suit alleging the unconstitutionality of the statute in so far as it "chilled and deterred" them from engaging in such sexual activity in the privacy of their home. The Federal District Court held, however, the married couple had no standing to join the law suit because they were not directly injured by the law.

Hardwick won an appeal in the Court of Appeals for the Eleventh Circuit. The State of Georgia appealed to the Supreme Court, and this decision was ultimately reversed in favor of upholding the state law against sodomy. Justice White wrote the majority opinion, and he summarized the constitutional issue as follows (*Bowers v. Hardwick,* 1986 at 190):

> The issue presented is whether the Federal Constitution confers a fundamental right upon homosexuals to engage in sodomy and hence invalidates the laws of the many States that still make such conduct illegal and have done so for a very long time.

This decision came as a surprise to many, particularly in light of a preceding Georgia case in which the Supreme Court protected a person's right to read illegal obscene material in the privacy of his or her own home (*Stanley v. Georgia,* 1969). The majority justified the discrepancy in these two decisions by distinguishing *Stanley* as a right protected by the First Amendment Freedom of Speech Clause, and *Bowers v. Hardwick* as a "right to sexual privacy" issue.

FAMILY PRIVACY

Although sexual privacy is an area of law that is frequently tested through the legislature and the court system, other issues related to the self-determination of a family have been legally scrutinized. The civil rights movement of the 1960s brought to a halt many governmental attempts at legislating morality and values. Knowledge about culture and religious diversity broadened public awareness of what could be tolerated within a range of socially acceptable behaviors and beliefs.

A 1974 case involving nontraditional life-style typifies many legal controversies of this period. On the North Shore of Long Island, the Village of Belle Terre has a land use ordinance restricting inhabitants of single-unit dwellings to "families," defined as "one or more persons related by blood, adoption, or marriage, living and cooking together as a single housekeeping unit, exclusive of household servants" (*Village of Belle Terre v. Boraas,* 1974 at 2).

Six unrelated male and female students from the State University of Stony Brook rented a house in the Village. The students challenged the ordinance that excluded them for the following reasons (at 2):

> "It bars people who are uncongenial to the present residents; that the ordinance expresses the social preferences of the residents for groups that will be congenial to them; that *social homogeneity is not a legitimate interest of government* [emphasis added]; that the restriction of those whom the neighbors do not like trenches on the newcomers' rights of privacy; that it is of no rightful concern to villagers whether the residents are married or unmarried; that the ordinance is antithetical to the Nation's experience, ideology and self-perception as an open, egalitarian, and integrated society.

On appeal, the Supreme Court held the ordinance constitutional because it did not discriminate against unmarried individuals per se, and no "fundamental" right was at stake. Also, the Court found the state had a legitimate interest in controlling additional parking, noise, and visitors that would naturally occur if the ordinance were exceeded. Justice Douglas supported the government interest as he wrote in the majority opinion (*Village of Belle Terre v. Boraas,* 1974 at 9):

> The police power is not confined to elimination of filth, stench, and unhealthy places. It is ample to lay out zones where family values, youth values, and the blessings of quiet seclusion, and clean air make the area a sanctuary for people.

In contrast to this decision, the following two cases illustrate how the Supreme Court uses a "strict scrutiny" test to evaluate a statute if a fundamental constitutional right is threatened. Governmental regulations that infringe on the rights of families in the area of First Amendment religious freedom invoke strict scrutiny by the courts.

In 1922 the United States enacted laws to require school attendance of all children between the ages of 8 and 16 years. The Compulsory Education Act specifically mandated "public school" attendance. Several private educational institutions, including the Society of Sisters and the Hill Military Academy, protested the Act because it denied the family's right to choose an educational environment for their child (*Pierce v. Society of Sisters of the Holy Names of Jesus and Mary,* 1925).

The Supreme Court agreed with the private educators and stated (*Pierce v. Society of Sisters* at 534 and 535):

> We think it entirely plain that the Act of 1922 unreasonably interferes with the liberty of parents and guardians to direct the upbringing and education of children under their control. As often heretofore pointed out, rights guaranteed by the Constitution may not be abridged by legislation which has no reasonable relation to some purpose within the competency of the state. . . . The child is not the mere creature of the state; those who nurture him and direct his destiny have the right, coupled with the high duty, to recognize and prepare him for additional obligations.

The Court further equated education to a property interest protected by the Due Process Clause of the Fourteenth Amendment.

In the case of *Wisconsin v. Yoder* (1972), a compulsory school attendance law was found invalid when weighed against the fundamental right of religious freedom. The Wisconsin law required all children to attend school until the age of 16 years. Several members of the Conservative Amish Mennonite Church were fined $5 each for violating the statute. People of the Amish religion found formal education beyond the eighth grade a threat to the Amish way of life. Many experts testified to the fact that not only did compulsory education interfere with the apprentice system used by the Amish to educate 14- and 15-year-old children, but the continued exposure to peer pressure and structured academics past the age of 14 years positively threatened continuation of the entire Amish way of life.

The Supreme Court balanced the State's interests against the Free Exercise Clause of the First Amendment. The interests of the State include a *parens patriae* power to act on behalf of a child with absent or incompetent parents. An example of permissible exercise of the *parens patriae* power involves the right to intervene when a child's parents deny lifesaving medical treatment on religious grounds.

Justice Douglas, however, pointed out in his dissenting opinion that the wishes of the children were entirely disregarded by the Court (*Wisconsin v. Yoder,* 1972 at 245):

> It is the future of the student, not the future of the parents, that is imperiled by today's decision. If a parent keeps his child out of school beyond the grade school, then the child will be forever barred from entry into the new and amazing world of diversity that we have today. The child may decide that that is the preferred course, or he may rebel. It is the student's judgment, not his parents', that is essential if we are to give full meaning to what we have said about the Bill of Rights and of the right of students to be masters of their own destiny.

Many states now have laws allowing an exception to compulsory school attendance if parents can demonstrate that in-home instruction is equivalent to that provided in a public school (Waddlington, Whitebread, & Davis, 1983).

Psychiatric nurses should be aware of the complexities involved in constitutional law, particularly as it relates to advocacy for the family unit, for children, or for the power of the state to intervene in so-called "zones of privacy." It is comforting to know that the courts use psychologic research and theory as a basis for difficult decisions. In *Yoder* for example, Kohlberg and Piaget were cited.

The Marital Relationship and Some Alternatives

THE MARRIAGE CONTRACT

Few rights are as basic to the concept of liberty as the right to marry. Yet society has for centuries regulated certain dimensions of this right. The government has an interest in promoting healthy sexual activity and procreation. Because marriage is the legalization of these activities, the state may use marriage as an opportunity to ensure public health and welfare in appropriate ways.

Examples of regulatory activities required by the government before legalizing a marriage contract include the following:

- Blood tests to determine absence of certain sexually transmitted diseases
- Determination of age and, if a minor, requirement of parental consent
- Determination of no prior currently legal marriages of either party
- Determination of no outstanding child support obligations

The Uniform Marriage and Divorce Act (UMDA) and the majority of states require a 3-day waiting period between the application and issue of a marriage license.

Some of the antiquated restrictions on marriage have not passed constitutional muster in the twentieth century. Examples of these include antimiscegenation statutes (laws prohibiting interracial marriage) (*Loving v. Virginia,* 1967) and regulations that disallow marriage if there are outstanding child support payments (*Zablocki v. Redhail,* 1978), although laws remain in most states prohibiting mentally disabled persons from marrying (Areen, 1985).

Psychiatric nurses and other family counselors should be aware that two states have laws requiring premarital counseling in certain situations (e.g., one party younger than 19 years or previously divorced) (Utah Code Ann., 1953, 30-1-30 to 39). These laws were enacted in California and Utah in an attempt to reduce the divorce rate of teen marriages. Perhaps other states will follow, and nurses in community mental health centers may find themselves providing the required premarital counseling.

Incest is a widely recognized legal restriction on marriage. The origins of this restriction are based in cultural taboo and on health and welfare interests of the state. A typical statute prohibiting consanguinity criminalizes marriage between the following degrees of relationship: parent, grandparent, sibling, child, grandchild, aunt, uncle, nephew, or niece; the status of whether cousins are permitted to marry varies from state to state.

Polygamy is another legislated prohibition, even though those practicing it have argued a fundamental First Amendment right to exercise of religious preference. The judicial rationale for the continuation of antipolygamy laws is summarized by the Supreme Court in a case that denied a Mormon the right to practice bigamy (*Reynolds v. United States,* 1878) (at 165):

> We think it may safely be said there never has been a time in any State of the Union when polygamy has not been an offence [sic] against society, cognizable by the civil courts and punishable with more or less severity. In the face of all this evidence, it is impossible to believe that the constitutional guarantee of religious freedom was intended to prohibit legislation in respect to this most important feature of social life. Marriage, while from its very nature a sacred obligation, is nevertheless, in most civilized nations, a civil contract, and usually regulated by law. Upon it society may be said to be built, and out of its fruits spring social relations and social obligations and duties, with which government is necessarily required to deal.

Another regulatory exercise of the state that has been supported by the courts involves premarital blood tests for venereal disease. A new issue has rekindled the balance of privacy interests and the fundamental right to marry versus the public health and welfare interest of the state. The technology to test for human immunodeficiency virus (HIV) is now widely available. AIDS is considered a sexually transmitted disease. Although logic supports a mandatory HIV test before marriage, the civil rights and privacy considerations have prevailed over this logic, and no states have successfully legislated such testing.

Several considerations come into play in the area of AIDS testing. First, the purpose behind syphilis and gonorrhea testing before marriage is more rehabilitative than preventive. AIDS cannot be cured at this point. Certainly, knowledge of HIV-positive status might encourage safe sex, and it might prevent maternal transmission of HIV-positive status to children of the marriage, but the state cannot deny the right to marry based on HIV-positive status. The usefulness of this information is still debatable as treatments and medications that can positively influence the progression of HIV are becoming available.

The government not only restricts marriage, it also recognizes it as a legally binding contractual relationship, fraught with benefits and burdens. Most states, for example, have enacted laws that recognize common law marriage. The requirements typically involve (1) at least one of the parties having reason to believe no prior legally binding marriage exists, (2) the couple agreeing to be married, and (3) the couple living together for a specified period of time (e.g., 7 years). Several societal interests are preserved by recognizing common law marriages: (1) it is financially preferable to have a spouse (rather than the state) be legally responsible for support of a family; (2) children are protected from illegitimacy; and (3) a cultural preference remains for supporting the nuclear family as the primary social unit.

In spite of the legal and social preference for marriage, the divorce rate has reached unprecedented proportions. As a result of the current high divorce rate, some couples enter into marriage with an antenuptial agreement regarding the potential outcome of divorce.

The notorious *DeLorean* case provides an example of the legal status of antenuptial agreements (*DeLorean v. DeLorean,* 1986). The DeLoreans married in 1978 under an antenuptial agreement that provided for separate property acquisition by each of the spouses. Under most state laws, property acquired during the marriage is considered communal and is divided equitably. Mrs. DeLorean protested that the agreement should not be enforced because she had less financial sophistication than her husband and he did not inform her fully of his financial status before the agreement.

In general, public policy supports the use of antenuptial agreements. However, three conditions can invalidate an antenuptial agreement. First, fraud or duress must be used to coerce one party into the agreement. Mrs. DeLorean had the opportunity to consult with an attorney before signing the agreement so the court said the first condition was not met. Second, if the agreement is "unconscionable," it can be invalidated. The mere fact that the DeLoreans' antenuptial agreement was not equitable did not make it unconscionable. Third, a full disclosure of the wealth of the enforcing party must occur. Although Mr. DeLorean did not fully disclose his wealth to his bride-to-be, Mrs. DeLorean was 23 years old, had been married before, and had some knowledge of finances from her modeling career. The court also applied the California law (where the marriage took place), which was not as strict regarding degree of financial disclosure. The court upheld the agreement (*DeLorean v. DeLorean,* 1986).

NONTRADITIONAL COUPLES

The women's movement has had a profound impact on traditional views of marriage. The availability of contraceptive technology has diminished the necessity for legal sanctions before sexual activity. The sexual "revolution" of the 1960s and 1970s greatly reduced the stigma associated with cohabitation without a marriage contract.

The classic case of *Marvin v. Marvin* (1976), known for coining the term *palimony,* involved the property rights of a party in a cohabitation relationship. The plaintiff in this case claimed that she and the defendant entered into an agreement to live together and to combine their efforts and earnings. She agreed to "give up her lucrative career as an entertainer" and to be a full time "companion, homemaker, housekeeper, and cook" in exchange for the defendant's agreement to "provide for all of plaintiff's financial support and needs for the rest of her life." The couple lived together for several years; then the defendant asked the plaintiff to leave. After a little over a year of support payments, the defendant stopped all financial support. Neither party claimed a common law marriage existed. In response to the plaintiff's lawsuit, the defendant said he had no financial obligation to provide continued financial support to his ex-lover. He relied on the general rule that contracts based on "immoral" activities are unenforceable.

The court did not see it his way. Justice Tobriner wrote (*Marvin v. Marvin*, 1976 at 669):

> Although the past decisions hover over the issue in the somewhat wispy form of the figures of a Chagall painting, we can abstract from those decisions a clear and simple rule. The fact that a man and woman live together without marriage, and engage in a sexual relationship, does not in itself invalidate agreements between them relating to their earnings, property, or expenses.

The case illustrates the broadening view of contract law applied to interpersonal familial relationships. Another area of legal challenge involves the rights and obligations of same-sex couples who live together. The case of *Jones v. Hallahan* (1973) typifies the judicial interpretation of the status of same-sex couples. Two women attempted to obtain a marriage license in the state of Kentucky. The Circuit Court denied the issue of a license, and the women brought a suit alleging violations of their basic constitutional rights to marry, to associate, and to the free exercise of religion.

The court used the Webster's New International Dictionary definition of marriage. Based on (1) the definition of joining male and female sexes in order to have a marriage and (2) prior case law that denied legitimacy of same-sex marriages, the Kentucky Court denied the women a right to marry.

There are still no states with laws permitting same-sex marriages (Areen, 1985). The *Bowers v. Hardwick* case just discussed gives family counselors an idea of the Supreme Court's standing on the issues of homosexual rights. Some homosexual couples have gained legal financial rights (e.g., to inherit) through adoption (*Baker v. Nelson*, 1971). Many homosexual couples are creating a durable power of attorney with their partner for the purpose of retaining their decision-making rights over those of blood relatives in the event of terminal illness.

Termination of Marriage

DIVORCE

It is easy to blame modern no-fault divorce laws for the demise of the traditional nuclear family. Several factors must be considered, however, in the evolution toward a no-fault system of divorce. Technology, the Industrial Revolution, and the advent of labor-saving devices have all allowed people the freedom to end marital unhappiness. Individuals have become far less dependent on a nuclear family for survival than in agrarian or even early industrial times. As day-to-day survival becomes easier, the ability to meet needs in the upper range of Maslow's (1970) hierarchy increases. Self-esteem, love and belonging, and self-actualization have moved into the realm of possibilities for ordinary husbands and wives.

It has not only been a growing discontent with marriage that caused a reform in the divorce laws; the civil rights movement has also shown women they could take action to free themselves and their children from oppressive or abusive domestic situations. It was therefore public demand, rather than legislative invention, that simplified the process of divorce.

The traditional grounds for divorce required a showing by the requesting party that he or she was indeed the "innocent injured spouse" (*Benscoter v. Benscoter*, 1963). States generally recognized the following statutory grounds for divorce:

- Adultery
- Cruelty
- Desertion
- Conviction of a felony

A spouse who did not want a divorce had several defenses available. Condonation was a particularly harsh defense if the wife complained of cruelty as a basis for a divorce action. A defense of "condonation" could be used if the complaining spouse tolerated the behavior described as cruelty. Because women were often in a financially dependent position, an abusive husband could get a judge to dismiss the petition for a divorce based on the assumption that the wife must have "condoned" the abuse, or she would not have continued to live in the marital home.

Collusion became increasingly common when laws permitted divorces only on fault-based grounds. A couple who mutually desired an end to the marriage would agree that one spouse would feign adultery or cruelty to meet the statutory requirements for a divorce decree. This was not a particularly fair solution because the result forced one party into a position of alleged misconduct. This often had an adverse effect on property distribution and custody determinations.

CUSTODY

Custody determinations are frequently encountered in the practice of child psychiatric nursing. Not only can nurse practitioners be involved in making custody decisions, but nurses very frequently intervene to minimize the emotional sequelae faced by families as they sort out arrangements for children after divorce.

Before the nineteenth century, common law routinely gave the father custody in divorce situations. This was based on the "property" classification of children. Automatic paternal custody gave way to the "tender years" presumption as the human potential movement provided awareness that children had unique needs and were more than mere property. Without evidence to the contrary, the mother was deemed the proper person to have custody when dealing with children of tender years. The tender years presumption has encountered challenges by fathers claiming it violates their Equal Protection and Due Process rights under the Fourteenth Amendment (*Ex Parte Devine,* 1981).

Increasing concern with child welfare has moved judges, legislators, and attorneys alike toward using the "best interests of the child" as the standard in determining custody arrangements (Goldstein, Freud, Solnit, & Goldstein, 1986). This standard may require a *guardian ad litem* be appointed to represent the child's interests. Some courts have considered the preference of the child among the factors weighed (*Goldstein v. Goldstein,* 1978). Child advocates should allow this only if the child can do so without emotional trauma. It is a tremendous burden on young children if they believe their preference may deny one of their parents custody.

Unfortunately for family counselors who "take on the role of the evaluator, the choices are usually very limited. The issue is often not what is in the child's best interests, but what choice will be least detrimental to the child" (Weiner, Simons, & Cavanaugh, 1985). Psychiatric nurses should be aware of the adversarial nature of the divorce process and the subsequent psychosocial effects on all family members.

Mediation is becoming a viable adjunct to the legal dissolution of marriage. Rather than the typical adversarial process of divorce, mediation offers an alternative approach involving an impartial mental health professional and an impartial attorney, who can facilitate the couple's ability to compromise and cooperate with one another. According to the American Association for Mediated Divorce (AAMD), mediation of custody arrangements involves a three-part process (1) delineating a philosophy of coparenting, (2) maximizing each parent's caretaking responsibilities, and (3) stipulating financial support arrangements. Divorce is viewed not as an end to the family life cycle, but rather as a crisis phase as the marriage ends (Ruman & Lamm, 1983). Psychiatric nurses can be a valuable asset in a mediation team.

Joint custody as a legal option has been very useful in decreasing the adversarial nature of marital dissolution and in eroding the "tender years presumption" that favors maternal custody (Freed & Walker, 1988). Nurses should be aware of longitudinal studies conducted on the psychologic adjustment of children in the years after divorce. Wallerstein and Kelly's (1980) significant research showed that continued parental contact and reduced anger and conflict were the two major factors that minimized trauma and aided psychologic recovery in children of divorce.

The Uniform Child Custody Jurisdiction Act (UCCJA) was enacted to discourage noncustodial parents from kidnapping their children and removing them to another state. All the states have adopted this act, and this means states will recognize custody decrees of another state.

HOMICIDE

In rare circumstances of domestic violence, a wife may end the marriage by killing her husband. A recent development in criminal law occurred when courts permitted psychologic evidence of the "battered wife syndrome" as a defense to murder charges. Courts are recognizing research and expert testimony regarding the cycle of violence and battering that often culminates in the wife's realization that she will either kill or be killed. If children are in jeopardy, women may be further motivated to take this course of action even though the consequences could be life imprisonment. In the case of *State v. Kelly* (1984), the State Supreme Court reversed a conviction of manslaughter because the trial court should have given scientific credibility to expert testimony regarding the battered wife syndrome.

Children and the Law

CHILD ABUSE

All healthcare providers are required to report child abuse. Psychiatric nurses are frequently exposed to matters that might cause them to suspect that either physical, emotional, or sexual abuse is occurring in a family. The mere suspicion of abuse is enough to trigger the force of these laws. Health professionals are sometimes reluctant to report without hard "evidence" of child abuse. The laws are designed to encourage rather than deter child protection, so some type of immunity from suit is usually granted to the reporting professional if the allegations are made in good faith, even if there are no conclusive findings of abuse.

Nurses should report abuse to the appropriate protective services for the state or county of residence. An investigation follows. A child is physically removed from the home only in cases of life-threatening or imminent abuse. Ideally, protective intervention involves monitoring and support of the parents. The role of the state is summarized in the following quote from a judge (*In re: J.S.R.*, 1977 at 863):

> The right of a natural parent to raise one's child is a fundamental and essential one which is constitutionally protected. However, it is not an absolute one. The state has both the right and the duty to protect minor children through judicial determinations of their best interest. To this end, the state has a substantial range of authority to protect the welfare of a child, and the state's legitimate interest in the child's welfare may be implemented by separating the child from the parent.

Research in bonding and attachment has demonstrated to the legal system that the trauma of separation is so profound, removal must be reserved for the most harmful and endangering conditions. Many states are engaged in legislative reform encouraging the speedy termination of parental rights in extreme cases. This should minimize the length of time children spend in foster care. This is required if the parents are deemed temporarily unfit. However, the children are unavailable for adoption because of the typically lengthy period involved in terminating parental rights. Psychiatric nurses are often advocates for children who are victims of an inadequate system of placements.

RIGHTS AND PROTECTION OF MINORS

The courts must balance the rights of parents, the rights and best interests of minors, and the interests of the state in any issue involving a conflict between parent and child. The landmark case of *Parham v. J.R.* (1979) provides a cogent analysis of this balancing process by the Supreme Court. This case involved a class action suit filed by minors committed to the state mental hospital. Georgia law permitted J.R.'s mother to sign a consent to voluntary hospitalization. The Georgia law placed an affirmative duty on each hospital administrator to release only a child "who has recovered from his mental illness or who has sufficiently improved that the superintendent determines that hospitalization of the patient is no longer desirable" (Ga. Code 88-503.2, 1975).

The plaintiff in this suit claimed that the ability of parents to commit minors to state hospitals and the lack of policies for timely review of the need for hospitalization violated their rights under the Due Process Clause of the Fourteenth Amendment. The Court reviewed all of the evidence and determined that the state law did not violate the rights of minors. In their discussion, however, the Court discouraged abuse of the state system by turning out children who were difficult to handle or place (*Parham v. J.R.*, 1979).

Psychiatric nurses must be knowledgeable of due process requirements for any kind of institutional commitment. The issue requires heightened advocacy when minors are involved. "Ultimately nurses can be a powerful influence with their 24-hour access to the child. This information should facilitate the postadmission reevaluation of the child's status and need for continued commitment" (Siantz, 1988).

Reproductive Issues

Reproduction is a core element of family life. It is also subject to some regulation by the state, although the right to reproduce is considered a fundamental component of ordered liberty. Modern reproductive technology is moving into areas of potential conflict so rapidly that the laws cannot keep abreast of all facets requiring regulation.

ARTIFICIAL INSEMINATION

The use of anonymous sperm donor banks by married couple consumers is well regulated and complies with public policy. Some recent applications of insemination technology include use by single women, lesbian couples, and consensual, rather than sperm bank, arrangements.

A California case illustrates the problems that can arise when private arrangements are made. A lesbian couple was introduced to a willing adult male who agreed to donate sperm so that one of the women could conceive a child. The donor continued a friendly interest in the pregnancy and expressed a desire to form a trust fund for the child. The women listed the father's name on the birth certificate, but their agreement was for the two women to be legal guardians of the child.

Once the child reached the age of 1 year, the father petitioned to have paternity rights, but the trial court awarded the mother sole custody. On appeal, the Court rejected the women's argument that family autonomy should exclude a sperm donor from parental rights and held that the father "was not excluded as a member of [the child's] family, either by anonymity, by agreement, or by the parties' conduct" (*Jhordan C. v. Mary K.* 1986 at 395).

SURROGATE MOTHERHOOD

The highly publicized case of Baby M. brought the issues of surrogate motherhood under extensive legal and ethical scrutiny. In that case, a surrogate mother became so distraught after the birth of Baby M. that she refused to give the baby to the adoptive couple even though the sperm had been provided by the husband of the couple and she had signed a contract agreeing to give up all her parental rights in exchange for payment of $10,000. The trial court said the contract fell within the law and awarded custody to the married couple.

The State Supreme Court ultimately declared the state law that had permitted contracts of this type was void and against public policy. Although the Court sympathized with the heartache of infertile couples, they concluded a law that permitted surrogacy contracts was unethical, illegal, and exploitive of women. "The problem involves how to enjoy the benefits of technology—especially for infertile couples—while minimizing the risk of abuse" (*In re: Baby M.,* 1988 at 1264). The judge then awarded parental rights to the two biologic parents, but awarded custody of the child to the married couple based on the "best interests of the child" standard. The surrogate mother was granted visitation rights in a manner similar to that of other separated parents.

Psychiatric Nursing Practice

Nurses who work with families must be aware of the state laws governing their practice. The Nurse Practice Act (NPA) should be examined for language authorizing expanded roles in nursing. Judicial interpretation of NPAs is sparse. What little case law does exist has been generally supportive of nurses who engage in advanced clinical practice. The case of *Sermchief v. Gonzales* (1983) involved a suit against two nurse practitioners by physicians who claimed the nurses' independent practice, which included physical assessment and diagnostic and prescriptive activities under protocols, violated the state NPA and the Medical Practice Act.

The Missouri Supreme Court was deluged by letters and briefs of community support for the advanced practice of the nurses. The Court also recognized evidence regarding education and training beyond the baccalaureate level enabling nurses to function independently. The Court held that the nurses' practice fell within the legislative intent of the Nurse Practice Act (Yorker, 1989):

The *Sermchief* case should provide encouragement for . . . nurses since it illustrates what power we can have in the courts by defining our practice with educational requirements and advanced skills.

Statutes regarding privileged communication and confidentiality are critical to psychiatric nursing practice with families. All clients and patients have a right to privacy. Conditions that require breach of the confidential relationship include knowledge of the patient's danger to self or others, physical or sexual abuse of children, and patient authorization of release of records (e.g., in litigation).

The *Tarasoff* decision expanded a mental health practitioner's duty to protect the patient to identifiable third parties. The decision requires that treating professionals warn potential victims of the homicidal intentions of their clients (*Tarasoff v. Regents of the University of California,* 1976).

In conclusion, nurses who see themselves as advocates should become involved with the legal process in the following ways:

1. Legislative empowerment: Nurses are learning to be politically active in reforming laws so that mental health is promoted.
2. Participation in judicial proceedings: Nurses who care for families may have a variety of opportunities to testify as experts, as witnesses to the facts, and as treating professionals in cases involving family issues.
3. Research in public policy: Nurses should initiate and collaborate in research that examines the effect of public policy on psychologic well-being.

Psychiatric nursing theory and research can make a difference. Courts and legislators pay close attention to current scientific advances in mental health. It is imperative that nurses include legal advocacy as part of their practice.

REFERENCES

Areen, J. (1985). *Cases and materials on family law.* Mineola, NY: The Foundation Press.
Baker v. Nelson, 291 Minn. 310, 191 N.W. 2d. 185 (1971).
Benscoter v. Benscoter, 200 Pa. Super. 251, 188 A. 2d. 859 (1963).
Bowers v. Hardwick, 478 U.S. 186, 106 S.Ct. 2841, 92 L.Ed. 2d. 140 (1986).
Carey v. Population Services International, 431 U.S. 678, 97 S.Ct. 2010, 52 L.Ed. 2d. 675 (1977).
DeLorean v. DeLorean, 211 N.J. Super. 432, 511 A. 2d. 1257 (1986).
Ex Parte Devine, 398 So. 2d. 686 (Ala., 1981).
Freed, D., & Walker, T. (1988). Family law in the fifty states: An overview. *Family Law Quarterly, 21*(4), 417-571.
Ga. Code Ann. 16-6-2 (1984).
Goldstein, J., Freud, A., Solnit, A., & Goldstein, S. (1986). *In the best interests of the child.* New York: The Free Press.
Goldstein v. Goldstein, 115 R.I. 152, 341 A. 2d. 51 (R.I., 1978).
Griswold v. Connecticut, 381 U.S. 479, 85 S.Ct. 1678, 14 L.Ed. 2d. 510 (1965).
In re: Baby M., 109 N.J. 396, 537 A. 2d. 1227 (1988).
In re: J.S.R., 374 A. 2d. 860, (D.C. App. 1977).
Jhordan C. v. Mary K., 179 Cal. App. 3d. 386, 224 Cal. Rptr. 530 (1986).
Jones v. Hallahan, 501 S.W. 2d. 588, (Ky. Ct. App. 1973).
Loving v. Virginia, 398 U.S. 1, 87 S.Ct. 1817, 18 L.Ed. 2d. 1010 (1967).
Marvin v. Marvin, 18 Cal. 3d. 660, 134 Cal. Rptr. 815, 557 P. 2d. 106 (1976).

Maslow, A. (1970). *Motivation and personality* (2nd ed.). New York: Harper & Row.

Parham v. J.R., 442 U.S. 584, 99 S.Ct. 2403, 61 L.Ed. 2d. 101 (1979).

Pierce v. Society of Sisters of the Holy Names of Jesus and Mary, 268 U.S. 510, 45 S.Ct. 571, 69 L.Ed. 1070 (1925).

Reynolds v. United States, 98 U.S. 145, 25 L.Ed. 244 (1878).

Roe v. Wade, 410 U.S. 113, 93 S.Ct. 705, 35 L.Ed. 2d. 147 (1973).

Ruman, M., & Lamm, M. (1983). Divorce mediation: A team approach to marital dissolution. *Trial, 19*(3), 86.

Salisbury v. List, 501 F. Supp. 105 (U.S. Dist. Ct., Nev. 1980).

Sermchief v. Gonzales, 660 S.W. 2d. 683 (Mo. 1983).

Siantz, M. (1988). Children's rights and parental rights. *Journal of Child and Adolescent Psychiatric Mental Health Nursing, 1*(1), 14-17.

Stanley v. Georgia, 394 U.S. 557 89 S.Ct. 1243, 22 L.Ed. 2d. 542 (1969).

State v. Kelly, 97 N.J. 178, 478 A.2d. 364 (1984).

Tarasoff v. Regents of the University of California, 551 P.2d. 334 (1976).

Utah Code Ann. 30-1-30 to 39. (1953).

Village of Belle Terre v. Boraas, 416 U.S. 1, 94 S.Ct. 1536, 39 L.Ed. 2d. 797 (1974).

Waddlington, W., Whitebread, C., & Davis, S. (1983). *Cases and materials on children in the legal system.* Mineola, NY: The Foundation Press.

Wallerstein, J., & Kelly, J. (1980). *Surviving the breakup: How parents and children cope with divorce.* New York: Basic Books.

Webster v. Reproductive Health Services, 492 U.S. 490, 109 S.Ct. 3040, 106 L.Ed. 2d. 410 (1989).

Weiner, B., Simons, V., & Cavanaugh, J. (1985). The child custody dispute. In D. Schetky & E. Benedek (Eds.), *Emerging issues in child psychiatry and the law.* New York: Brunner/Mazel.

Wisconsin v. Yoder, 406 U.S. 205, 92 S.Ct. 1526, 32 L.Ed. 2d. 15 (1972).

Yorker, B. (1989). Scope of practice. *AAOHN Journal, 37*(2), 80-81.

Zablocki v. Redhail, 434 U.S. 374, 98 S.Ct. 673, 54 L.Ed. 2d. 618 (1978).

Unit II

Family Transitions

Chapter 6

The Transition to Parenthood

Jeanne Watson Driscoll

Transition to parenthood: What is it? What does it involve? Is it a one-time event or a continual process? How do people know when they have become parents? When people are asked to describe what being a parent is, they find it difficult to provide a simple description. In fact, the question generally opens the door to a lengthy discussion of feelings, events, memories, beginnings, endings, responsibilities, legacies, generational rituals, and, at times, confusion. Parenthood has been described and defined as a transition, a rite of passage, a situational stressor, or a developmental crisis. (Parenthood marks the change in standing of men and women who give birth or bring forth offspring, thus becoming responsible for a child or children.) Parenthood is, regardless of definition, an irreversible process that changes one's life in all domains: physical, psychologic, and spiritual. It is a process that for many never feels completed or achieved "par excellence." It is, however, an experience that brings with it unexpected growth and development.

Purpose/Model

The purpose of this chapter is to describe the beginning transition to parenthood. Bridges (1980), in his book *Transitions: Making Sense of Life's Changes,* defines transition times as key times in the natural process of self-renewal. His book is based on a theory of personal development that views transition as the natural process of disorientation and reorientation that marks the turning points of the path of growth. He describes three phases of the transition process: the ending of a former stage; then a period when one feels a sense of lostness and emptiness; and finally, beginning anew.

Endings, according to Bridges, are handled by each individual on the basis of his or her experience. He found that four experiential concepts tend to occur during the process of endings: disengagement, disidentification, disenchantment, and disorientation. Often the process of change begins with disengagement. If this change process is clarified, channeled, and supported by the individual and his or her significant others, the change can lead to growth, development, and a sense of renewal.

When people experience disidentification, they tend to break away from old connections. They may experience feelings as "not really sure of who I am anymore." Then they may become disenchanted. This has been called a kind of *limbo experience* — a person floats between the old and the new. The person begins to discover that his or her own world, the way he or she formerly defined it, is no longer real. This recurrent experience occurs in the lifetime of the individual who has the courage and trust to believe it in the first place. To change, one must realize the inner realities, the intrapsychic part of the personal reality, are changing. Disorientation occurs when people recognize that they have been lost and confused and do not know what they are feeling. It is a period of existential crisis; it is not a psychologically comfortable time. It can be a meaningful experience, but does awaken old fears and fantasies of death and abandonment. Individuals may describe feeling confused and empty; things that were familiar may have an unreal quality about them; things that used to be important no longer are. Disorientation affects our sense of space and time; it is, however, a phase that must be lived through, for it is after the endings are experienced that one begins to make way for the new beginning.

It is important to be aware of the fact that the completed state of parenthood is rarely achieved. This is because being a parent involves continuous transitions. Each new phase of development in the child's life will require that parents process through their own transitional experience. Parents have remarked, "I was just getting to the baby stage, and then she began to crawl and became a toddler; then as I was getting the hang of that, she became a preschooler." It is important for the nurse to appreciate these processes and remember that for each "turning point," unique experiences and processes will require an individualized care plan for each member of the family system, as well as family. Being a parent is a dynamic process that has many hellos and goodbyes that require information, validation, and support.

Pregnancy: the Beginning, or Is It the Ending?

Too often the birth of the baby is viewed as the beginning of parenthood; however, for the woman, becoming a parent begins on a physiologic level. The transition to parenthood begins with an ending — the missed menstrual period. The woman may have planned the pregnancy for years, she may be pregnant as an outcome of reproductive technology, or, for some, the pregnancy is a complete surprise — "I can't believe this happened." Immediately she begins to experience a myriad of emotions, even before she is positive that she really is pregnant. For many women, this ending is kept as a special secret, one which she does not share for a while. She will at some point seek support and validation from family and peers. In fact, it may be the nurse who is the first person who is invited into her transitional process.

Before the validation of the pregnancy, the woman may already be experiencing those feelings of detachment, disorganization, disenchantment, and disengagement, as described by Bridges. She needs tremendous support to begin the process of change. Once the pregnancy is validated, she will decide to invite her partner, family, and close friends into her process, but it will be done at her own rate or pace. The disclosure of the pregnancy depends on her prior pregnancy history and how she handled other critical experiences in her life. In the current technologic society of reproductive health care, this woman may be afraid to become attached to this pregnancy until the amniocentesis results have been reported and she knows that her baby is healthy. Each woman takes into the pregnancy her experiences and her development; therefore pregnancy is a unique psychologic, physical, and spiritual experience no matter what her parity. One cannot develop a standard that will fit the universe of pregnant women because of the nature of the human species.

The nurse should conduct a thorough nursing assessment with this pregnant person (Flagler & Nicoll, 1990). It is so important for the nurse to keep the assessment process free of evaluation, critique, and judgment. Neither the woman's feelings about this pregnancy experience nor her feelings about the transition will be known unless she tells you. Nurses need to be aware of their own subjective biases and projections because these will affect how and what the woman discloses. One woman shared that when she told a nurse she was pregnant, the nurse's response was "you must be so excited." What the woman actually felt was terrified, but she was then afraid to share that because she felt that the nurse "would think something was wrong with me that I was not excited."

The transition to parenthood that occurs during the pregnancy contains other key elements. They are discussed and organized into trimester sections.

FIRST TRIMESTER: "Is this really happening?"

The first trimester of pregnancy is when the tangible process of becoming a parent begins. Often one may hear a woman say, "I knew that I was pregnant the next day. I felt different. I did the home pregnancy test and just stared at it. I mean this is what we wanted — had been working to get — and now the test said I was pregnant, and I was terrified; is this what I really wanted?" The theme of ambivalence is prevalent during this trimester, no matter what the circumstances of the pregnancy.

Physiologically, the early pregnancy may not be at all what the woman expected as an exciting experience, but rather as a time when she feels sick and tired: "If I am pregnant, I should be happy. Why do I feel like all I do is throw up and be sick; this is not very much fun." These words may be part of the process of disorientation or disenchantment. In her fantasies of pregnancy, the woman may not have allowed the physiologic aspects to enter the picture; she just thought of how nice it would be to have a baby in her uterus. She is disenchanted: "Is this it?" She begins to daydream, becomes more cognizant of the pregnant women in the store or at the restaurant, finds herself crying easily, and feels irritated, scared, nervous, and lonely. Feelings of ambivalence, concern, and fear, as well as joy and anticipation, should be validated and encouraged. It may be useful for the nurse to encourage the woman to keep a journal of her own passage on this journey of pregnancy and future parenthood and to help her discuss what this pregnancy means to her and her partner. It is important that she feel that she can share any thoughts with the nurse, even those thoughts and feelings that she may feel are bizarre. She needs to feel accepted in her phase of disenchantment. Anticipatory guidance regarding the changes that are occurring in her body physiologically and psychologically should be presented in one-to-one teaching, as well as written materials. The nurse will begin to help this woman pull together her support systems and play an active role in this network.

The nurse should continue to assess and provide anticipatory guidance regarding the "normal" experiences in the first trimester. It is important that the nurse use "permission giving" statements to facilitate the dialogue, as well as promote the therapeutic relationship. For example, "women have shared with me that they often feel disillusioned or disenchanted with the first trimester of pregnancy; they feel that they are supposed to be excited, yet they really just feel sick. Has that happened to you?" The woman does not feel that she must respond with happy, glowing statements; she will hear that this nurse may be able to hear the "not so nice" feelings and that it may "be okay." These interactions are very important for the development of the relationship. It is also important to the woman's self-esteem and self-acceptance that she has a safe place to disclose her feelings and concerns.

What about her partner? How are things going for them? It may help to include both members of the couple during the discussion and anticipatory guidance sessions (Jordan, 1990). Often during those sessions, clarification of misinformation occurs and the couple can reality check. There are many myths and old wives' tales that they will be subjected to by "helpful" family and friends. The supportive role of the nurse cannot be stressed enough. As the woman goes through the processes of disengagement, disorientation, disidentification, and disenchantment, she will need validation, mutuality, and connection.

SECOND TRIMESTER: "It feels funny, a baby inside!"

As she enters this trimester, the woman may have an appointment for an amniocentesis or may be waiting for the results; she may have decided not to have an amniocentesis, or it may not have been recommended that she have one, based on her unique history and age. The woman will be either really starting to get involved with this pregnancy or still carrying around her secret until the test results are back. If she has a history of loss, she is dealing with those issues. The woman may be feeling physiologically better while she begins to experience additional body changes. She may find that her moods are more balanced, that she is not as emotionally labile, but her waistbands do not button anymore and she looks a bit "rounder." This is a critical time to assess her feelings about body image and self-concept as an evolving pregnant woman. A sense of anxiety is pervasive throughout pregnancy; the level of anxiety should be continuously assessed and strategies developed to cope with the different stresses. It is imperative that neither she nor her feelings be invalidated. If she shares with the nurse that she is feeling anxious, the nurse should encourage her to share more about what she means by this, how it feels for her, and what helps her cope. Too often she will be told that "anxiety is normal; it's your hormones; just relax." This statement cuts her off and may lead to an internalized sense of shame and self-doubt. The woman eventually internalizes her fears and concerns and begins to believe that she is the only person who feels this way, so something must be wrong with her. This can cause her to feel that she may be "crazy" and is not coping well: "Everyone else I talk to that is pregnant tells me that they don't feel like I do—is there something wrong with me?" If her level of anxiety is interfering with her activities of daily living, she needs to be evaluated by a psychiatric care provider (Curry, 1990; Lederman, 1990). Her feelings and concerns should be taken seriously; this is the key nursing concept of care.

Kumar and Robson (1984) found in their retrospective study of postpartum women that 10% of the postpartum population were diagnosed with postpartum depression. These women described being clinically depressed during pregnancy but were undiagnosed and untreated. The sad part of these results is that it is during the pregnancy experience that women encounter healthcare providers more frequently than during any other healthcare-based experience.

Occasionally a woman will share with the nurse that she feels sad; that she is not sure this is such a "wonderful experience" (Flagler & Nicoll, 1990). She may be in that phase of transition called *disenchantment.* It is okay to feel feelings; it is even better to have a safe, nonjudgmental place to share these feelings of confusion, uncertainty, fear, and disengagement. She is beginning to mourn the loss of who she was. She is trying to find her new evolving self in this experience (Flagler & Nicoll, 1990). She may be more introspective; her dreams may be vibrant, scary, and clearly remembered. She is having survival fears for both herself and her child. She is beginning the work of preparing for the new beginning—birth.

The woman is changing physiologically, psychologically, and spiritually. She may begin to experience the baby's movements in her uterus; the pregnancy is "really real." It is important to assess her feelings about the baby in her uterus: Is she beginning to make an attachment? Is she denying the pregnancy? Does she feel that she has been taken over by "this thing inside of me?" It is normal to feel a bit anxious about the baby in the uterus—she is beginning to realize that the baby is separate from her although very much attached to her.

Some women take charge of their anxieties at this time at a very cognitive level. They ask for bibliographies and begin to purchase or borrow books and videos. Other women allow the process to happen and do not want to know too much. One nurse hid all her obstetric and pediatric textbooks because she did not want to increase her already high anxiety level by putting more "potential" scenarios in her head. The woman may give all her trust to the healthcare providers and feel that if there was anything that she should know, they would tell her. This is a somewhat learned-helplessness model, but she may not feel that she has anything to worry about: "I am young, and I take good care of myself. Pregnancy is healthy, and I shouldn't have to be all crazy while I am pregnant." Denial can be a healthy defense, as well as a maladaptive coping style; this is where the nurse should continually assess the denial level of the woman.

For some men, it is in the second trimester that they really believe the pregnancy. They may feel their baby move or may accompany their partner during ultrasound and see the baby moving inside her. Now they may begin to discuss, if asked, their dreams and concerns: "Will I be a good father? Will my partner survive this process? What will happen to our relationship after this baby is born? What about our finances? Will the baby be a girl? A boy? Healthy?" The partner/father needs to be helped to share his concerns because he may feel that it is more important to pay attention to the mother—he doesn't want to scare her with his worries, but where does he go? Who is there to listen to him? The nurse's role continues to be one of support and anticipatory education. The range of normal emotional concerns should be shared and physical norms discussed. The partner needs to hear that his concerns are normal and that the nurse is there for him too if he has any questions—that he can call the nurse.

Childbirth classes will appeal to the cognitive and psychomotor skills in that the couple will be provided with information about the physiology of labor and delivery and they will learn breathing and massage techniques that are useful during labor. This experience reflects the philosophy of empowerment through knowledge.

THIRD TRIMESTER: "Will I be pregnant forever?"

The woman really feels pregnant now. The baby makes his or her presence known through the uterine wall. The baby will wake, move, and roll when he or she wants to. The pregnant woman begins to realize, again, that she has no control of this little baby; the baby has a mind of his or her own! Many performance anxieties may begin to surface: "Will I be a good laboring woman? Will my partner be there? Will the baby be all right? Will I live through the experience?"

If the woman goes into premature labor at this time, the normal situation of pregnancy will change because the pregnancy now becomes high risk. The mother may be hospitalized for premature labor, gestational diabetes, pregnancy-induced hypertension, or some other problem. The attention will be focused on maintaining the pregnancy as long as possible for higher probability of survival of the child. The pregnancy now becomes physiologically and psychologically high risk and may potentially alter the parental role development, making nursing assessment critical.

It is important to have the woman and her partner talk about their fantasies about the birth. This will give the provider a sense of what to expect if the reality birth is really very different from the fantasy birth. Many women begin to feel uncomfortable with their changing body size and body boundaries. They verbalize anxiety and fear that something will happen; their dreams may contain fears regarding the death of the baby and/or herself or of being trapped and unable to escape. The woman is reading and taking classes, but assumes that only she is anxious; "everyone else in class looks so calm." She is concerned about work—leaving it and going back to it. It is difficult for her to really focus on the after-birth phase because her survival needs are paramount: "If I make it through the birth, I will figure out how to live with the baby." Now she is going to the healthcare provider's office every 2 weeks to every week; she is anxious that her water will break in the store or at the office; she is afraid that her partner will not be around so she gets him a beeper for 24-hour availability. The nurse should encourage the woman to share her concerns and worries because the woman may feel that she is just "being silly" and may feel as though no other person is worried about any of the things that she is. It does help to have worries validated and supported. Again, if the anxiety/concern level is far above what the nurse believes to be acceptable, he or she may need to refer the woman for additional support and help.

LABOR AND DELIVERY: "There is no turning back"

Labor and delivery mark another dramatic turning point. From the first twinge of a contraction or the rupture of membranes, there is no turning back. Often, in the hospital the woman may hear from one of the staff, "So today you are going to have a baby!" She has been waiting for this day for 9 months, give or take a few weeks. Now she wonders if there is a way to skip this part or if she can go back home: "I am not sure I am ready for this experience; I didn't finish my classes; I didn't read enough books. I don't think this is such a good idea — it is too scary!"

Labor may be "long; day moves into night;" it appears as if the world is on hold except for the fact that the woman has seen two different teams of providers on each shift. "I feel so alone. My husband was so tired. I didn't think I was ever going to deliver this baby." This is a very disorienting experience. If her labor is augmented with Pitocin or if she needs epidural anesthesia, the woman may feel disenchanted: "I took the classes so I could have a vaginal delivery without medication — what did I do wrong?" Labor is a time of feeling confused, relieved, terrified, and yet thrilled. Some women describe labor as feeling "out of touch with reality: "I would just lie there waiting for the next contraction — it was scary." Others feel that it is the most intense, in-tune, physical, psychologic, and spiritual experience: "I never felt so powerful and in control in my life; I really enjoyed pushing her out — it felt great." It is the critical time before "life resumes an intelligible pattern and direction;" it is the time that proceeds "beginning anew" (Bridges, 1980).

This "turning point" experience of labor and delivery can and often does effect the "beginning anew" phase of the transition process to parenthood. The impact of the healthcare provider on the perceived birth experience for this woman and her partner is critical. The woman and her partner need to feel supported, loved, and cared for. Women have described feeling abandoned, ignored, looked and talked over: "They would always look at the monitor; no one looked at me." One woman shared, "The nurse pushed my face away from the monitor; she told me to let her watch the machines. I thought I was going to cry; I felt like a child." The nurse's intent may have been one of reassurance and support, but it was perceived by the woman as threatening. The laboring woman's perceptive reality is intense; she needs to feel the emotional strength and connection from the nurse, again reflecting the concept of care.

One phase in labor is called *transition*. This is when the woman's uterus is completing the dilation process, and it is almost time to push. It is a phase when the contractions are hard, strong, and "unbelievable." This transition phase is similar to the transitions we have been discussing so far. The woman becomes disenchanted with this whole process: "I can't do this anymore; I feel like I am going to die." She becomes disengaged from those around her: "Don't touch me; leave me alone." At times she is disoriented: "What time is it? When do I finish this?" The nurse plays a vital role during this transition by keeping the woman reality based and focused on the work at hand, as well as by constantly supporting and enhancing the woman's self-esteem: "You are doing beautifully; keep up the good work. That's it—a little longer." When the baby is born, it is imperative that as soon as possible, the mother hold, validate, and identify her child. This will allow her to begin to move into the next transitional experience, postpartum.

POSTPARTUM: "Now we have to learn to live with this baby!"

The immediate focus of this transition is often centered on the infant and his or her physical needs. New parents feel compelled to learn "infant care-taking skills," especially in today's healthcare system of shortened length of hospital stay. They are aware that they must leave the hospital within 24 hours and tend to put their own emotional issues on the back burner so they can begin to feel comfortable with the cognitive/psychomotor aspects of infant care. Unfortunately, too many healthcare providers are also focused on these issues with the exclusion of the physical and emotional care of the woman. It is important to remember that the physical and psychologic needs of the mother are not gone, only suppressed for a time. She will place the baby's needs before her own and needs to be protected from that quick response. She needs to be nurtured and cared for during this immediate phase. Her physiologic needs will require the frequent assessment of the nurse. The nurse should focus on the mother's care so that the mother can then care for her child.

If the woman has had a caesarean birth, she has experienced major surgery, which involves pain management that may get in the way of her learning curve for infant care. She begins the process of transition to the role of mother in a very different space and time from her roommate who had a vaginal birth. Intense feelings flood the affect of these women. The transition process begins again, and yet she has not even finished the other one, the physiologic transitions.

What happens psychologically? The mother perhaps begins this transition disenchanted: "I couldn't do it without medications. I really wanted a boy, and I have a girl—is it bad to feel sad? I didn't even want to see my baby after the surgery—I just wanted to sleep. I didn't bond at birth!" She needs to be provided with a safe place to mourn her dreams and fantasies. She needs to verbalize her feelings about her performance expectations, as well as her performance expectations of her partner and the healthcare team. She may say, "Thank God, this is over, I am alive, and the baby is alive. I am going to sleep— I am so tired; it has been such a long 9 months." The woman needs to be encouraged to do the work of integrating the labor and delivery experience into her self system. She needs to share her feelings of personal success, feelings of incompetence, and feelings of inadequacy: "I thought that I would not act like a screaming banshee, but I did; I am so embarrassed."

Rubin (1985) describes that becoming a mother means taking on a new identity and mourning the previous identity. This sounds very similar to the period of "lostness and emptiness" as described by Bridges in response to life's turning points. So it seems, "here we go again." Learning to live with a new baby, whether it is a biologic child or an adopted child, presents major turning points in growth.

A new transition is being welcomed, but was the first one completed? In reality, multiple transitions are going on simultaneously, which is why this is such a critical time for intervention, support, and guidance from the professional healthcare provider, the nurse.

Each member of the family experiences losses. These losses may be real or perceived, but they do occur and should be validated and the grief process should be facilitated. There are issues related to loss of self, role, social status, economic status, and relationships (Driscoll & Sozanski, 1990; Grace, 1978; Peretz, 1970; Rubin, 1985). The resolution of these losses is critical for the development and attainment of parental roles. The nurse, as he or she supports the transition of the couple as the couple grows from two members to a family of three, must encourage the verbalization of the feelings and emotions so that he or she can validate, clarify, and promote the grief process.

Many women experience a period of emotional lability in the first week after the birth. They feel happy, sad, scared, confused, competent, incompetent, ambivalent, irritated, angry, or rageful. They feel out of control: "I looked at the baby and started to cry. Why was I crying—I was happy." Another woman shared, "I would look at my husband with hate; his life had not changed—he could go to work. What did I do now—change diapers and breastfeed?" The emotional aspects of this time are frightening for the new parents. This experience has been called *postpartum blues.* It is a time of great biochemical changes, the time when the body equilibrates to a prepregnant state. The hormones surge and drop, the neurotransmitters are altered, and the emotions are surfacing rapidly.

The key to the care of women during this transition is support, honest reassurance, and physical care. The woman needs to have someone take care of her, but she does not know how to ask. She is so used to being the one who takes care of others and questions whether she deserves help. The nurse should help set up the support networks available to her when she is home with her new baby.

The woman is feeling disengaged from her friends and family: "Everyone else's life returns to normal; my life is completely topsy turvy." She feels disidentified, she does not feel that her old friends without children have any idea how she is feeling, and she perceives that they have pulled away support because they never call or drop over. She is disenchanted: "Is this all it is—change diapers, nurse, burp, wash?" Finally, she is disoriented; being a mother doesn't fit: "What is a mother? What should I feel? I don't feel much except tired, anxious, scared, and, at the same time, relieved."

Healthcare providers should provide additional support for this woman, especially in the current health delivery system that mandates short hospital stays and does not readily reimburse for home services for the purpose of support and mental health. What can the nurse do to promote healthy transition and resolution of losses?

Recommendations for Nurses

The time of early transition to parenthood is an excellent time for preventive mental health. The woman will be in contact with nurses in various disciplines: pediatric nurses, obstetric nurses, mental health nurses, family health nurses, as well as nurses who may be neighbors. Ongoing nursing assessment is critical with each contact. How is the woman doing? How are the members of the family adjusting? Open-ended questions should be asked so that the person can describe his or her own reality. The environment of trust is critical because nurses are asking women and their families to share with them feelings, emotions, and concerns that may not be supported in their network. Permission-giving statements are helpful in facilitating discussion. Using the opening statement, "In my clinical practice women and men have shared with me that the first few weeks at home with a baby are overwhelming, and sometimes they wonder if this was such a smart idea. Have you ever had any of those feelings?"

Postpartum psychiatric disorders may be identified via this warm, open assessment process. If the woman is continuing to experience labile moods, anxiety, and sleep disorders and to verbalize feelings of inadequacy, incompetence, or fears regarding the baby's health and safety after about 21 days, the nurse must refer the woman for evaluation by knowledgeable mental health professionals. These professionals must be sensitive to the potential psychiatric disorders that may occur after the birth of the baby, so the responsibility of the nurse may be to ascertain who these professionals are before he or she offers a referral. (Refer to box below.)

Postpartum psychiatric disorders have an excellent recovery rate if they are diagnosed early and if up-to-date interventions and management strategies are used (Fernandez, 1992).

The transition to parenthood is a prime preventive mental health time, and the nurse plays a critical role in the identification and referral if necessary. Most parents want to do the best job that they can in their new role. Often they will tell the nurse that they are going to do things differently from their parents. They want to change the history of parenting that has been passed down

---

Depression After Delivery — National

Depression After Delivery — National was founded in 1985 by Nancy Berchtold in response to the lack of support available after she experienced a postpartum psychosis and depression. Currently there are at least 70 self-help support groups established in the United States as part of the *Depression After Delivery Network.* There are telephone contact people (women and men) available nationally who may be able to refer nurses to the caring mental health professionals in their area.

Depression After Delivery — National
P.O. Box 1282
Morrisville, PA 19067
1(800)944-4PPD

through generations. It comes as a complete surprise when they hear their parent's voices come out of their mouths! Humor is critical as a strategy in coping with the transition to parenthood.

Many couples may be afraid to disclose "not-so-nice" feelings because they fear that they will be criticized and judged by their thoughts and feelings. Why is it so hard to talk about how one feels? There is a pervasive, subjective belief that the women should be happy because she had a baby. Society does not want to hear the emotions that must be shared to make a successful transition. Is this because the feelings and thoughts deviate from "happy and together?"

The period after the baby is born is called the *postpartum* period. If one uses the medical model, this period lasts about 6 weeks, the amount of time it takes for the uterus to return to its prepregnant state. It takes, however, at least 12 months to make the transition to parenthood, to feel the identity of mother or father.

A 66-year-old mother shared with me that being a parent does not end when the children become adults either. She describes that her continued concern and worry about her children is with her all of the time (her youngest is 30, and her oldest is 44).

The first year after the birth of the first child is filled with many transitional experiences. It is the continuation of the process of transition. It is an experience that is lived individually and collectively for the new family. Each family member has unique needs, feelings, and concerns; who gets the attention usually becomes a very important issue. It is a time when periods of disorientation and disenchantment occur. The woman, whether she is staying home for 6 weeks before returning to work or transitioning to the role of stay-at-home mother, will have periods of joy and sorrow—she will need to disengage from old relationships or acknowledge that the relationships will change and she will make new acquaintances. She wants to talk with women who are "living through this," and to feel validated in her emotions. A need exists for postpartum, new mother, and new father support groups to facilitate the communication necessary to inspire change.

•   •   •

Once the baby is born, does life begin anew? In practice, this really ends the pregnancy and the couple begins a new transitional process, so it continues—with each beginning there is an ending. It is the process of dealing with the transitions, making the emotional adjustments to the transitions, valuing the time, and providing the space for the changes to be embraced, cherished, and learned from. Nursing can provide the safety and the support for this critical transition and plays a priority role in the process.

REFERENCES

Berchtold, N., & Burrough, M. (1990). Reaching out: Depression After Delivery Support Group Network. In NAACOG's *Clinical Issues in Perinatal and Women's Health Nursing, 1*(3), 385-394.

Bridges, W. (1980). *Transitions: Making sense of life's changes.* Reading, MA: Addison-Wesley.

Brown, W.A. (1979). *Psychological care during pregnancy and the postpartum period.* New York: Raven.

Cohen, R.L. (1988). Psychiatric consultation in childbirth settings. New York: Plenum.

Colman, A., & Colman, L. (1977). Pregnancy: The psychological experience. New York: Bantam.

Curry, M.A. (1983). Variables related to adaptation to motherhood in "normal" primiparous women. *Journal of Obstetrical and Gynecological Nursing 12*:(2):115-121.

Curry, M.A. (1987). Maternal behavior of hospitalized pregnant women. *Journal of Psychosomatic Obstetrics and Gynecology, 7,* 165-182.

Curry, M.A. (1990). Stress, social support, and self-esteem during pregnancy. In *NAACOG's Clinical Issues in Perinatal and Women's Health Nursing, 1*(3), 303-310.

Dix, C. (1985). *The new mother syndrome: Coping with postpartum stress and depression.* New York: Doubleday.

Driscoll, J.W. (1990). Maternal parenthood and the grief process. *Journal of Perinatal and Neonatal Nursing, 4,* 1-10.

Driscoll, J.W., & Sozanski, G.K. (1990). Care of the pregnant woman with pre-existing mental illness. In NAACOG's *Clinical Issues in Perinatal and Women's Health Nursing, 1*(3), 186-193.

Fernandez, R.J. (1992). Recent clinical management experience. In J.A. Hamilton and P.N. Harberger (Eds.), *Postpartum psychiatric illness: A picture puzzle.* Philadelphia: University of Pennsylvania Press.

Flagler, S., & Nicoll, L. (1990). A framework for the psychological aspects of pregnancy. In NAACOG's *Clinical Issues in Perinatal and Women's Health Nursing, 1*(3), 267-278.

Grace, J.T. (1978). Good Grief: Coming to terms with the childbearing experience. *Journal of Obstetrical, Neonatal and Gynecological Nursing, 1,* 18-21.

Hans, A. (1986). Postpartum assessment: The psychological component. *Journal of Obstetric, Gynecologic and Neonatal Nursing, 15,* 40-51.

Harding, J.J. (1989). Postpartum psychiatric disorders: A review. *Comprehensive Psychiatry, 30,* 109-112.

Herz, E.K. (1992). Prediction, recognition and prevention. In J.A. Hamilton and P.N. Harberger (Eds.), *Postpartum psychiatric illness: A picture puzzle.* Philadelphia: University of Pennsylvania Press.

Jordan, P.I. (1990). First-time expectant fatherhood: Nursing care consideration. In *NAACOG's Clinical Issues in Perinatal and Women's Health Nursing, 1*(3), 311-316.

Kumar, R., & Robson, K.M. (1984). A prospective study of emotional disorders in childbearing women. *British Journal of Psychiatry, 144,* 35-47.

Lederman, R.P. (1990). Anxiety and stress in pregnancy: Significance and nursing assessment. In *NAACOG's Clinical Issues in Perinatal and Women's Health Nursing, 1*(3), 279-288.

McBride, A.B. (1973). *The Growth and Development of Mothers.* New York: Harper & Row.

Mercer, R.T. (1986). *First-time motherhood: Experiences from teens to forties.* New York: Springer.

Peretz, D. (1970). Development, object relationships and loss. In B. Schoenberg, A.C. Carr, D. Peretz, and A.H. Kutscher (Eds.). *Loss and grief: Psychological management in medical practice.* New York: Columbia University Press.

Rising, S.S. (1974). The fourth stage of labor: Family integration. *American Journal of Nursing, 74,* 873.

Rubin, R. (1985). *Maternal identity and the maternal experience.* New York: Springer.

Schlossberg, N.K. (1984). *Counseling adults in transition.* New York: Springer.

Schoenberg, B., Carr, A.C., Peretz, D., & Katscher, A.H. (Eds.) (1970) *Loss and grief: Psychological management in medical practice.* New York: Columbia University Press.

Chapter 7

Families in Divorce Transition

Linda Cade Haber

Divorce statistics suggest that divorce is a widespread phenomenon. The annual rate of divorce in 1991 was 4.6 divorces per 1000 population (National Center for Health Statistics, 1991). In the United States, currently 26.7% of white women have been divorced, and projections are that about 54% of first marriages for women aged 25 to 29 will ultimately end in divorce (Norton & Moorman, 1987). Martin and Bumpass (1989) predict an even higher rate when they maintain that two thirds of all first marriages are likely to end in separation or divorce. Norton and Glick (1986) estimate that 40% of American children born in the 1980s will eventually live in a one-parent home because of divorce.

As divorce has increased, so has empiric and theoretic work on the subject. In this discussion of divorce as a family transition, research is reviewed and guidelines for nursing prevention/intervention are presented. The focus is on the consequences, not the causes, of divorce.

The Family as a System

To examine divorce as a family transition, it is necessary to view the family as a system. In the general systems theory framework, a family can be seen as a system of interdependent parts forming a whole (Wilson & Kneisl, 1988). A change in any part of the system affects all other parts.

Every system strives to maintain a dynamic equilibrium, or balance, among the various forces that operate within it and on it. Equilibrium, called *homeostasis,* is achieved when a balance exists between that which is valued and to be conserved and the changes that disrupt the system (Wilson & Kneisl, 1988). These changes can originate from within the family or from the external environment. One property of a system is the extent to which it is open or closed. Openness requires that a system be flexible in adapting to changes demanded by the environment. Families whose systems are more closed tend to exclude or distort information to maintain a balance.

Family systems have boundaries as well. Boundaries are limits that define who participates in the system and the subsystems. Boundaries exist between individuals, between subsystems, and between the family system and the environment. Boundaries may be clearly defined and open to change, poorly defined resulting in confusion and chaos, or so rigid that little input can permeate the system (Johnson, 1986).

Structure refers to the organization of the family. The type of family and the value system of the family dictate roles, communication patterns, and power distribution. Family systems theory has identified a strong parental subsystem and clear, flexible boundaries as essential factors for healthy family functioning (Durst, Wedemeyer, & Zurcher, 1985).

When the family is conceptualized as a system containing subsystems, one can see the rippling effects of divorce (Leahey, 1984). Divorce affects roles, communication, and authority within the family. Changes in the marital system affect the ability of the parents to maintain a strong leadership team. In turn, the parent-child subsystem is realigned. These changes make it necessary for the family system to find new ways to meet the needs of its members. In this chapter the focus is on changes in family relationships that occur during the divorce transition.

Theoretic Models for Families of Divorce

Theoretic models that guided early investigations of divorce and that continue to be influential are those based on individual development, such as psychoanalytic theory (Wallerstein & Kelly, 1980), attachment (Bowlby, 1969), and responses to grief (Crosby, Lybarger, & Mason, 1987). Nevertheless, family models have recently become more significant.

Theoretic work on families in divorce can be viewed as extensions of work on family crisis and family stress. Holmes and Rahe's (1967) pioneering work on life-change events identified divorce as a major stressor requiring more adaptation to change than any other single event except for the death of a spouse. Their work has influenced research on divorce, especially the studies related to health. Bloom, Asher, and White (1978) reviewed reports of research on the relationship between divorce and emotional/mental disorders, suicide, homocide, accidents, and illness. Smith, Mercy, and Conn's (1988) study supports the view that the divorced continue to be at higher risk for suicide. Dawson (1991) found that children from disrupted marriages have increased risk of accidents, injuries, and poisonings requiring medical attention. The most recent trend in research on divorce and health is to examine changes in immunologic functioning of persons who are in the divorce transition (Kiecolt-Glaser et al., 1987).

Another approach to theoretic work on family crisis and stress is Hill's (1958) ABCX model. As illustrated in Figure 7-1, the Double ABCX model (McCubbin & Patterson, 1983a) expanded Hill's framework. The stressor (a, here the marital separation) influences crisis adjustment (x) indirectly through existing resources (b) and perception of the event (c). In the McCubbin model, the family's accumulation of life events and added stressors over time (Aa) influences family adaptation both directly and indirectly through adaptive

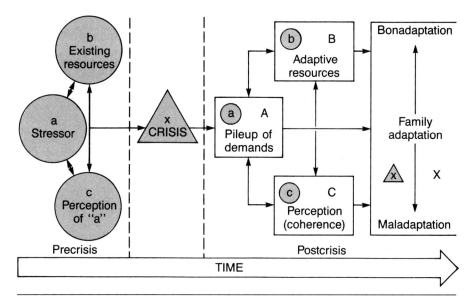

Figure 7-1   Double ABCX Model. (*Note.* Modified from Family Adaptation to
Crisis [pp. 26-47] by H. McCubbin and J. Patterson. In H. McCubbin,
A. Cauble, and J. Patterson [Eds.], 1983a, *Family Stress, Coping, and
Social Support,* Springfield, IL: Charles C. Thomas.)

resources *(Bb)* and perception *(Cc).* As the diagram illustrates, time is an
important variable in the model.

Theories that use the work of Hill and McCubbin to explain the divorce
transition include models of stages of family adjustment (Ahrons, 1980), the
divorce transition model (Buehler, Hogan, Robinson, & Levy, 1985/1986;
Buehler, personal communication, April, 1989), and the theory proposed by
Peterson, Leigh, and Day (1984).* Stages of family adjustment to divorce are
considered further in the section on relationships between former spouses.

In the divorce transition model (Buehler et al., 1985/1986), divorce-related
stressors, such as economic, housing, parent-child, legal, and former spouse
stressors, are the major independent constructs *(Aa).* Other independent
variables are resources (*B* and *Bb*), perceptions of the divorce (*C* and *Cc*), the
couple's divorce history, and background factors. Well-being *(Xx),* the
dependent construct in the model, is a multidimensional construct that includes

---

* Controversy exists about what constitutes family research. Thompson and Walker (1982)
maintain that for a study to be dyadic (or family) research, it must have an assessment of individual
characteristics of both partners (or all family members) or an assessment of the properties of a
relationship. One or more members can provide this information. White and Mika (1983) claim that
failure to incorporate work on divorce into family stress and coping has led to focus on individual
adjustment. Nevertheless, even in research on the Double ABCX Model (McCubbin & Patterson,
1983a,b), the dependent construct is often individual well-being.

family members' self-esteem, parenting satisfaction, economic well-being, and indices of social competence in children. In later work, Buehler presents a model of interactions among parent's well-being, parent-child relationship, former spouse relationship, and child's well-being. Each of these constructs is proposed to be influenced by the other factors.

Using the framework of McCubbin and Patterson (1983a,b), Peterson et al. (1984) emphasize the individual family member's definition of the situation. The principal stressor in this model is the degree of disengagement from family roles by a spouse/parent. The amount of disengagement is proposed to influence the severity of the crisis definition for children, which, in turn, affects the level of the child's social competence. Partner disengagement is believed to also affect the custodial parent's ability to parent. Other elements of the model include such resources as outside support, personal capacities of custodial parents, and regenerative capacities within the parent-child relationship.

Rodgers (1987) has extended the development of theory on postmarital family organization by incorporating elements of developmental theory, social network theory, and family problem-solving theory into stress and crisis theory (McCubbin & Patterson, 1983a,b).

Although the underlying premise of theoretic models is that divorce is a family crisis, most of the relationships statements and empiric tests of the models concentrate on subsystems of the family instead of the family as a whole. Accordingly, the subsystems are examined separately before discussion of dynamics of the family as a whole is undertaken.

Relationships Between Former Spouses

Marital relationships are complex. Marriages differ along such dimensions as level of conflict, intimacy, and satisfaction. It is difficult, however, to predict which couples will divorce on the basis of marital traits. Marital complaints of spouses who later divorced include lack of affection, conflict over gender roles, communication problems, infidelity, alcohol abuse, and physical abuse (Bloom, Niles, & Thatcher, 1985; Kitson & Langlie, 1984; Kitson & Sussman, 1982).*

When one or more spouses perceive that their needs are not being met within the marriage, the process of emotional divorce begins. Cox (1981) describes emotional divorce as involving (p. 462)

. . . a subtle withdrawal of one partner from the other, erecting barriers that slowly shield each from hurt by the other, gradually shifting concern from "us" to "me," meeting more and more psychological needs outside of the marriage and, finally, the erosion of the couple's sexual life together.

Although the actual events vary, one common feature is that each partner

---

* The percentage of female subjects that cited physical abuse as a cause of divorce ranges from 9.9% (Thurnber, Fenn, Melichar, Chiriboga, 1983) to 21% (Cleek & Pearson, 1985). Emotional abuse was cited by 55.5% of females and 24.7% of males (Cleek & Pearson, 1985). One third of Davis and Aron's (1988) subjects cited husband's physical, verbal, or emotional abuse as a cause of divorce.

begins to concentrate on his or her partner's shortcomings and failures rather than on his or her strengths.

The process of how partners move through the stages of divorce is described by Ahrons (1980; 1983) and Ahrons and Rodgers (1987). The first two phases occur before marital separation. In the first phase, *individual cognition,* most spouses initially deny the effects of marital distress on family members. Eventually, conflict escalates and the spouses may begin to blame each other. After one of the spouses (or sometimes both) has identified the source of stress as the marital relationship itself, they seek a solution. Partners may begin the process of emotional divorce early or only after other coping behaviors have failed. The duration of this transition (which may last several years) depends on the coping behaviors employed and other factors related to the family's vulnerability to stress. The next stage, *family metacognition,* occurs when the family system begins to change in recognition of the marital problems. Because of the persistent emotional bonds between spouses, the spouses' feelings are highly ambivalent in this stage.

During the rest of the divorce transition, the focus turns to adjusting to changes in relationships. The third stage, *separation,* occurs when one spouse moves out of the family home. Spouses may separate and reconcile briefly, especially if they have ambivalence about divorce or guilt about their children's distress. In the fourth stage, *family reorganization,* the major stressors are defining the coparenting relationship and deciding child custody issues. Spouses must separate their spousal roles from their parental roles and terminate the former relationship while redefining the latter. The final phase, *family redefinition,* depends on the couple's ability to maintain a child-centered relationship.

Adaptation to divorce entails a grieving response for some people. Crosby et al. (1987) propose that persons who have experienced divorce will display a sequence of feelings, cognitions, and behaviors that progress through the stages of grief. Because of the losses involved, mourning and expressions of grief are generally present. The capacity to consciously tolerate painful emotions involved in divorce is essential for optimal recovery (Count & Sacks, 1985).

In both theoretic models and research reports, time is an important variable. Findings about the influence of time on adjustment to divorce have been contradictory. Some studies of adjustment indicate that symptoms diminish over time (Bloom, Hodges, Kern, & McFaddin, 1985; Hanson & Spanier, 1983; Wertlieb, Budman, Demby, & Randall, 1984). In contrast, other researchers found that time since separation is not related to adjustment (Tschann, Johnston, & Wallerstein, 1989) or to attachment (Brown & Reimer, 1984).

In studying the relationship between time and adjustment to marital separation, Melichar and Chiriboga (1988) did not find a linear relationship. Women for whom the most time had elapsed from separation to interview reported the fewest negative emotions, whereas the group intermediate on time reported the most negative emotions. Women who passed through the period from separation to divorce more quickly seemed more debilitated at the time of interview than women who had more time to adjust.

Marital partners rarely move through the emotional divorce at the same pace and rarely exhibit the same degree of adjustment. Wallerstein and Blakeslee (1989) found that in two thirds of the former couples, one person was much happier than the other a decade after the divorce. Factors that help explain individual differences include attachment, gender, and status of initiator. These factors also interact with each other to influence adjustment.

According to Power (1987), evidence of attachment includes refusal to consider or plan for a pending divorce, attempts to delay the divorce through property and child custody battles, frequent preoccupation with the past, seeking unnecessary interactions with the absent partner, and reluctance to engage in activities that mark the transition to single status. Prolonged feelings of attachment have been found in a substantial percentage of divorces (Berman, 1985; Brown, Felton, Whiteman, & Manela, 1980; Kitson, 1982). For example, Wallerstein and Blakeslee (1989) found that one half of the women and one third of the men were still intensely angry at their former spouse 10 years after the divorce.

Although researchers use various measures of attachment and adjustment, high levels of attachment are consistently related to lower levels of adjustment. Preoccupation with ex-spouse is associated with more distress (Berman, 1988b) and lower well-being (Masheter, 1991). Tschann, Johnston, and Wallerstein (1989) found that both men and women with better divorce adjustment were less attached to their former spouses, either positively or negatively. Berman's (1988a) findings support the view that positive attachment for the former marital partner is a salient part of the divorce and that this attachment may exacerbate subjective distress. In Brown and Remier's (1984) study, subjects who were highly attached to their ex-spouse and who perceived less control over reconciling were moderately depressed.

Although Ferreiro, Warren, and Konanc (1986) maintain that a spouse with a high level of attachment may initiate a divorce because of such behavior as alcoholism, abuse, or infidelity, the initiator is likely to have less attachment to the spouse than the noninitiator (Berman, 1985; Brown & Reimer, 1984; Kitson, 1982).

Researchers find that women are more likely to favor divorce and men are more likely to want reconciliation (Bloom & Hodges, 1981; Bloom & Kindle, 1985; Rands, 1988; Reissman & Gerstel, 1985). In Wallerstein and Blakeslee's (1989) study, 65% of the women and 35% of the men actively sought to end the marriage despite opposition from their spouse. Initiator status is positively related to well-being (Rands, 1988) and acceptance of divorce for men (Thompson & Spanier, 1983) and negatively related to level of distress (Count & Sacks, 1985; Crosby et al., 1987; Wallerstein & Blakeslee, 1989), especially at the time of separation (Pettit & Bloom, 1984).

In addition to feelings of attachment within the marital relationship, parents are connected to each other through their children. Whereas childless couples may be able to resolve their feelings about the divorce and terminate contact with their former spouses, parents must maintain contact with each other. Parents need to resolve feelings about the marital relationship at the same time that they are developing a method of coparenting after divorce. Broom (1981) suggests reasons why cooperative parenting may be difficult. The family positions of parent and spouse are deeply enmeshed in one another. Each adult in a family is both a spouse and a parent; that is, one person occupies two roles. This connection causes difficulty when a person seeks to detach from the spouse role while maintaining the parent role. If separating parents are to become cooperative parents, they will need to resolve their marital discord to develop and maintain a sense of trust and understanding.

According to Broom (1981), a considerable proportion of divorcing couples could develop a cooperative coparenting relationship given understanding and support. In empiric investigation, however, Furstenberg and Nord (1985) found that most parents reported that they rarely discuss matters concerning the child with the outside parent and that the outside parent had little or no influence in the decision-making process. Similarly, only about 21% of Ahrons and Wallisch's (1987) respondents and 25% of Wylder's (1982) subjects reported frequent discussions about school or medical problems, finances, the children's accomplishments, and major decisions in the children's lives. In Maccoby, Depner, and Mnookin's (1990) study, the coparenting pattern for families where the mother was the custodial parent was described as cooperative by 24% of the sample, conflicted by 36%, disengaged by 29%, and mixed by 11%.

Former spouses reported a high level of dissatisfaction and conflict in their relationships (Bloom & Hodges, 1981; Bloom & Kindle, 1985; Goldsmith, 1980; Hetherington, 1989, 1991; Wallerstein & Kelly, 1980; Wylder, 1982). According to Ahrons and Wallisch (1987), at least one half of their sample described their interactions with spouse as negative and their feelings toward spouse as hostile. Basic differences of opinion about childrearing were reported by 62% of the women and 53% of the men. Kressel, Jaffe, Tuchman, Watson, and Deutsch (1980) predicted that about 10% of divorcing couples begin a lifetime of conflict with their ex-spouses.

Parents who cannot reach agreements about child support, visitation, and custody may seek resolution through the legal system. Although a detailed treatment of custody decisions is beyond the scope of this chapter, several points are made here:

- Custody is never really settled because, theoretically, either spouse can return to court at any time to seek change.
- Support is growing for the child's right to independent counsel in legal disputes that involve custody (Solnit, 1983).
- The benefits of joint versus sole custody are controversial.

For an early review of joint custody, see Clingenpeel and Repucci (1982). According to Ahrons and Wallisch (1987), little empiric evidence exists on the long-range effects of joint custody and the abilities of divorced parents to handle shared childrearing.

The current adversary process of divorce can delay and intensify the resolution of losses (Schwartzberg, 1981) and has a negative impact on the psychologic adjustment of children (Saayman & Saayman, 1988/1989). Gardner

(1986) maintains that protracted litigation can produce psychopathology in children and adults. Because of the detrimental effects of prolonged litigation, clinicians have recommended divorce mediation as a means of settling disputes.

In summary, relationship factors such as attachment and initiator status affect individual adjustment to divorce. Individuals who show less distress at divorce are likely to be less attached to their spouse and to have initiated the divorce. Persons who make a good adjustment to divorce are those who are able to resolve their feelings of loss. The relationship between spouses after divorce is quite complex. The level of conflict between former spouses greatly influences their ability to coparent effectively.

Parent-Child Relationships

In addition to the marital subsystem, another important subsystem of the family is the parent-child relationship. Children's reactions contribute to the context within which parent-child relationships change during the divorce transition.

CHILDREN'S REACTIONS DURING THE DIVORCE TRANSITION

During the predivorce phase of marital conflict, children worry about physical violence between parents, friends witnessing the conflict, what the future will bring, and financial hardship (Adams, 1982). According to Wallerstein and Blakeslee (1989), more than half of the children in their study witnessed physical violence between their parents.

In addition to developmental delays (Hetherington et al., 1989), investigators have described a wide variety of adjustment problems in children and adolescents from divorced families. Specific reactions include difficulties in school (James & Wilson, 1984; Kinard & Reinherz, 1984; McLoughlin & Whitfield, 1984; Westman, 1983); anxiety and depression (Cooney, Smyer, Hagestad, & Klock, 1986; Hillard, 1984; Mitchell, 1983); withdrawal and dependency (Kinard & Reinherz, 1984); hostility (Hetherington, 1989; James & Wilson, 1984; Kinard & Reinherz, 1984); delinquency (Adams, 1982; Kalter, Riemer, Brickman, & Chen, 1985); sexual intercourse in adolescents (Flewelling & Bauman, 1990; Wallerstein & Corbin, 1989); substance use (Flewelling & Bauman, 1990; Needle, Su, & Doherty, 1990); and concern about future relationships (Chess, Thomas, Korn, Mittelham, & Cohen, 1983; Hillard, 1984; Mitchell, 1983; Wallerstein & Blakeslee, 1989; Wallerstein & Corbin, 1989). This concern about future relationships is supported by Glenn and Kramer's (1987) finding that adults (especially white females) who grow up in separated and divorced families are more likely to divorce than those who grow up in intact families.

There is great diversity in children's response to divorce (Hetherington et al., 1989). In a review of the literature about the impact of divorce on children, Demo and Acock (1988) maintain that divorce does not have uniform consequences for children. It may well be that divorce is merely a marker event and does not, in itself, cause harm to children. Factors that appear to mediate a child's adjustment after divorce include age, gender, and predivorce adjustment (Long & Forehand, 1987). Although older children and adolescents experience pain and anger as their younger siblings do during the interval immediately after divorce, they are less likely to blame themselves for the divorce and are better able to resolve loyalty conflicts, to cope with stressors such as economic change, and to use individuals who are not kin as support systems (Hetherington et al., 1989). In reviews of research, Zaslow (1988; 1989) concluded that gender differences in children's response to divorce depend on the type of family in which the children live after divorce. Boys respond more negatively than girls if they live with a custodial mother who has not remarried. Girls, however, do not adjust as well as boys to father custody or to living with a stepfather.

Researchers have postulated that a major factor that determines the consequences for children is the level of parental conflict, which does not necessarily decrease after divorce. but may in fact remain constant or even increase (Ahrons, 1981; Hetherington et al., 1989; Webster-Stratton, 1989).* Other factors believed to affect children's adjustment to divorce include the psychologic well-being of the parent (Wallerstein & Blakeslee, 1989) and the child's relationships with both parents. Kalter, Kloner, Schreier, and Okla (1989) found that the best predictors of girls' adjustment after divorce are mothers' self-esteem and level of emotional problems, whereas the best predictors of boys' adjustment are mothers' social adaptation and negative changes in mothers' lives.

CHANGES IN PARENT-CHILD RELATIONSHIPS

The parent-child relationship is important to children's well-being in all families. Researchers suggest that the negative effects of divorce can be greatly mitigated if the child maintains positive relations with both parents (Hetherington, 1989; Wallerstein & Blakeslee, 1989) or the custodial parent (Solnit, 1983).

Parent-child relationships change during the divorce transition as parents are often caught in their own turmoil and have less energy to invest in parenting. A decreased ability to perform nurturing and disciplining functions has been found, especially in the initial period after separation (Abelsohn, 1983; Bloom, Hodges, & Caldwell, 1982; Hetherington, 1991; Kalter, 1990; Mitchell, 1983;

---

* The proposition that parental conflict is a mediating variable that influences children's adjustment to divorce is supported by the following findings: (1) the level of parental conflict was positively associated with children's problems during the divorce transition (Kurdek, 1981; Saayman & Saayman, 1988/1989; Shaw & Emery, 1987; Stolberg, Camplair, Currier, & Wells, 1987; Warren et al., 1987; Woody, Colley, Schlegelmilch, Maginn, & Balsanek, 1984); (2) Adjustment problems were related to parental conflict but not to separation or divorce (Chess, Thomas, Korn, Mittelman, & Cohen, 1983; (3) children from intact families with high levels of marital conflict are as likely to have problems as those from divorced homes (Cherlin & Furstenberg, 1989; Hess & Camara, 1979; Kurdek & Sinclair, 1986; Schwartzberg, 1981); and (4) ongoing high levels of conflict, whether in intact or separated/divorced homes, were related to negative self-concept (Bishop & Ingersoll, 1989). A contrasting view is expressed by Kalter, Kloner, Scheier, and Okla (1989), who found that the level of interparental hostility was not related to any of the child adjustment measures.

Wallerstein & Blakeslee, 1989). A trend toward a coercive, reciprocal cycle of negative parent-child interaction often occurs in the first year after divorce (Hetherington, 1989; Hetherington et al., 1989; Patterson, 1982). Children and adolescents are more likely to act out (Ambert, 1984; Hodges, Tierney, & Buchsbaum, 1984) and to exhibit deviant and noncompliant behavior (Webster-Stratton, 1989), and parents are less likely to set effective limits on children's aggression (Amato, 1987; Crossman & Adams, 1980; Fischer & Cardea, 1982; Webster-Stratton, 1989).

Parallel changes occur in the affection/satisfaction dimension of parent-child relationships. According to Hetherington et al. (1989), as many as one third of older children and adolescents become disengaged from their families. Children from divorced families evaluate both their mothers and fathers significantly less favorably than those from intact families (Parish & Dostal, 1980).

For adolescents, the transition to divorce threatens the previous stability of their external world, as well as their fundamental beliefs about who their parents are (Abelsohn, 1983). Children may respond with anger to revelations about a parent's behavior, such as infidelity. Children often observe considerable changes in their parents' life-style. Adolescents and their divorced parent(s) are often confronting similar issues, such as dating, dealing with one's own sexuality, and learning to be independent (Peck & Manocherian, 1988). When the adolescent's opposite-sex parent dates, it may create feelings of curiosity and excitement; when the same-sex parent dates, it may encourage (through identification and modeling) the acting out of the adolescent's own sexual impulses (Kalter, 1990). Adolescent girls may respond negatively when they observe their mother behaving in what to them is age-inappropriate behavior. For example, girls may perceive their mother as competing with them for male attention by flirting and by wearing clothing suitable for teenagers.

Although some children and adolescents reported a deterioration in their relationships with parents, others acknowledged positive feelings about their parents, for example, satisfaction with relationship with custodial mother (Hetherington, 1989); closeness, trust, and open communication with the parent (Wallerstein, 1984); and gratitude for the support and security that their custodial parents provided (McLoughlin & Whitfield, 1984). A similar situation existed for parents' perception of parent-child relationships after separation/divorce. Whereas some adults listed parent-child relationships as stressors, many reported that parent-child relationships improved (Buehler & Langenbrunner, 1987; Fischer & Cardea, 1982).

Much of the research on parent-child relationships just cited examined the child's relationship with the custodial parent. Statistics indicate that 80% to 90% of children of divorce live with their mother (Cherlin & Furstenberg, 1989; Norton & Glick, 1986). Because the noncustodial parent is likely to be the father, research both about father-child relationships and about visitation must be considered.

Relationship with father. Marital conflict seems to have paradoxical effects on father-child relationships. Although conflict during marriage may lead to unusually close relationships between fathers and children in an attempt to minimize marital interaction (Wallerstein & Kelly, 1980), a typical pattern is for fathers to become more involved in work and other activities outside the home. After divorce, however, some fathers develop a closer relationship with their children than they had when married. As Rowling (1983) and Wallerstein and Blakeslee (1989) note, little similarity is apparent between the father-child relationship before divorce and the visiting relationship.

Regardless of contact, the noncustodial father remains a significant presence in his children's lives (Wallerstein, 1984; Wallerstein & Blakeslee, 1989). To contribute to the child's healthy adjustment to divorce, however, the father must maintain regular contact with his child (Abelsohn, 1983; Ahrons & Rodgers, 1987; James & Wilson, 1984; Kurdek, 1981; Schwartzberg, 1981).

During the divorce transition, children display concern about their relationships with their fathers. Common themes include fear of loss (Adams, 1982); feelings of rejection (McLoughlin & Whitfield, 1984; Mitchell, 1983; Wallerstein & Blakeslee, 1989); longing for and caring about the noncustodial parent (Bonkowski, Boomhower, & Bequette, 1985); desire for more contact (Kurdek & Sinclair, 1986); and an intense desire to make contact with the absent father (Wallerstein, 1984; Wallerstein & Blakeslee, 1989).

Children's feelings of attachment toward the noncustodial parent are likely to be mixed with other emotions. Some children are aware of their negative feelings toward their father and react with anger, especially if they blame him for the divorce. Children of divorce reported low attachment to noncustodial parents (White, Brinkerhoff, & Booth, 1985); rated their fathers negatively (Parish & Dostal, 1980); reported deterioration in their relationships with their father (Cooney et al., 1986); and reported less support from noncustodial fathers (Amato, 1987). According to custodial mothers, 22% of the children objected to visits with their father (Fischer & Cardea, 1982).

Visitation. Children's concern about loss of contact with the absent parent and their feelings of rejection are consistent with the data on visitation. In a national probability sample, Furstenberg, Nord, Peterson, and Zill (1983) reported that frequent contact with outside parent (an average of at least 1 day per week) occurred in only 17% of the disrupted families. (The frequency of once-a-week contact in this study is equal to the typical court-ordered visitation schedule of every other weekend.)

The proportion of children with no contact with their absent parent in the past year is particularly disturbing. Children in this category comprise 18% of Seltzer's (1991) sample; 23% of Seltzer, Schaeffer, and Charng's (1989) sample; 31% of Kurdek and Sinclair's (1986) sample; 51.8% of Furstenberg's et al. (1983) sample; and 60% of McLoughlin and Whitfield's (1984) subjects. The likelihood of having no contact with absent parent increases with time since separation/divorce (Furstenberg et al., 1983; James & Wilson, 1984; Seltzer, 1991). Ambert (1984) found that 50% of the fathers of children in the lower socioeconomic status had completely disappeared at 5 years after separation.

Besides time since separation, other factors that predict frequency of visitation include father's level of education (Seltzer et al., 1989); provision of child support (Furstenberg et al., 1983; Seltzer, 1991); father's sense of competency as a father; the ease with which father can see his children (Tepp, 1983); and the absence of intense animosity between parents (James & Wilson, 1984; Wallerstein & Kelly, 1980). Some noncustodial fathers with high levels of attachment to their children may find intermittent parenting painful and withdraw from their children (Hetherington et al., 1989). In clinical samples, fathers reported that they decreased visitation to avoid their own feelings of sadness about the loss of their children (Jacobs, 1983; 1984).

Most fathers perceived an increased number of problems and decreased satisfaction with parent-child relationships after divorce (Bloom & Hodges, 1981; Buehler & Langenbrunner, 1987). Hess and Camara (1979) maintain that the duration of visits may be more important than frequency in fostering positive relationships between children and noncustodial parents. As Buehler et al. (1985/1986) note, the visitation format may not contribute to the repair of strained relationships. Noncustodial fathers often report that they view visitation as artificial and prefer a deeper relationship with their children.

In addition to characteristics of the father and of the environment that predict visitation, children themselves may influence the frequency of contact with their outside parent. For example, children's pleasure in the visit may reinforce father's continuing contact (Wallerstein & Kelly, 1980); older children who are more independent may seek to spend additional time with their father (Seltzer, 1991); adolescents may prefer to participate in other activities; and children may decide on their own to discontinue visits for a variety of reasons (McLoughlin & Whitfield, 1984).

Nevertheless, Hess and Camara (1979) assert that relationships between noncustodial fathers and their children can be maintained even with variation in such matters as distance, opportunity to visit, and the level of tension between the divorced parents. Of course, maintaining or improving these relationships requires effort from both parent and child, and in some cases, counseling may be helpful.

Sibling Relationships

As family size contracts with divorce and one or both parents become less available to the children, sibling relationships become more important, for better or for worse (Eno, 1985). The changes associated with the divorce transition may bring siblings closer, may increase conflict among them, or may lead to siblings isolating themselves from each other (MacKinnon, 1988/1989; Nichols, 1986). If siblings support each other, the sibling bond may be strengthened. Although it is possible that increased closeness of siblings after divorce may be unhealthy, Hetherington (1988) characterizes less than 10% of her subjects as having an intense, enmeshed, and symbiotic relationship with a sibling. In most families, siblings who turn to each other for solace and support benefit from these contacts. MacKinnon found that in comparison with siblings from married families, siblings in divorced families engaged in more caretaking behavior, such as directing, teaching, and helping.

In other cases, sibling relationships become more negative during the divorce transition. MacKinnon (1988/1989) found that sibling interactions in divorced families were both more negative and less positive than in married families. Similarly, Hetherington et al. (1989) maintain that siblings in mother's custody (both single-parent and remarried families) appear to have troubled relationships, especially if one of the siblings is a boy; Wallerstein and Kelly (1980) report that many children do not consider their siblings to be helpful in dealing with divorce; and Amato (1987) found that adolescents in one-parent families report more conflict with siblings than those in intact families.

Developmental stage influences response to divorce and may contribute to conflict between siblings. Preschoolers usually react to divorce with regressive behavior, whereas adolescents spend more time away from home. Resentments may occur as the older child observes the younger one gaining extra maternal attention and the younger child sees that the older one has gained more freedom. In single-parent families, older children may take on more responsibility for taking care of younger siblings (Hetherington et al., 1989). As Wallerstein and Kelly (1980) note, reactions to older siblings who assume parental responsibilities are mixed. The younger child may respond by objecting to the older siblings's increased authority or by appreciating the care he or she receives.

Shifting family loyalties that occur with divorce, such as parent-child alliances, also affect sibling relationships (Eno, 1985; Nichols, 1986). A strong parent-child coalition may interfere with the developing competence of the excluded child and harm the functioning of the sibling subsystem (Eno, 1985). If each parent has a child as an ally, conflict between the siblings may even mirror the marital conflict. Also, siblings may compete for attention from the noncustodial parent. Of course, this situation is exacerbated if the outside parent favors one child over the others.

Although it may be instructive to examine family subsystems, a complete treatment of effects of divorce must also examine dynamics of the family as a whole.

Triangles

The family systems concept of triangle is helpful in describing complex family dynamics. According to Bowen (1985), a triangle is a predictable emotional process that takes place in any significant relationship when there is difficulty in the relationship. For purposes here, the three corners of a triangle consist of mother, father, and child. When there are marital difficulties, one or both spouses may turn to the child to meet emotional needs. According to Abelsohn (1983), during the divorce transition, it is common for preexisting, dysfunctional, cross-generational coalitions to be accentuated or for new ones to emerge. For example, adolescents may become more enmeshed with the custodial parent and be unable to separate from that parent.

Another dysfunctional pattern involves role reversal, wherein the child feels responsible for taking care of the parent emotionally. Many children feel worry and concern for their parents, often the single mother (Cooney et al., 1986;

McLoughlin & Whitfield, 1984; Mitchell, 1983). Adolescents may become a source of strength and support for their parents (Abelsohn, 1983; Kalter, Pickar, & Lesowitz, 1984). Wallerstein and Blakeslee (1989) maintain that the child's role may become one of warding off the parent's serious depression. The term *overburdened child* was used to describe children in such a role. Single parents may elevate an older child to the level of confidant (Hetherington et al., 1989; Stolberg & Walsh, 1988). According to Schwartzberg (1981), the need of the custodial parent (usually the mother) to have a confidant leads to blurring of generational boundaries, greater difficulty with discipline, and often heightened anxiety and guilt over reawakened oedipal conflicts, especially in boys.

The marital separation often brings implicit or even explicit demands for allegiance from one or both parents. Buehler and Trotter (1988), Patten-Seward (1984), and Westman (1983) note the tendency for children of divorce to become the ally of one parent. Conflicting pressures for loyalty intensify stress for the child (Cooney et al., 1986; Fry & Addington, 1985; Hetherington et al., 1989; Hillard, 1984). Loyalty conflicts are especially stressful when one parent tries to undermine the child's relationships with the other parent. This phenomenon is illustrated by Berman (1983), Buehler and Trotter (1988), and Gardner (1986). These researchers describe parents (often the custodial mother) who handle their anger at their ex-spouse indirectly through the children by enlisting the child as an ally, by encouraging the child to spy on the other parent, and by denigrating the other parent in front of the children. In an empiric investigation, Buehler and Trotter (1988) found that nonresidential parents' (but not custodial parents') report of such behaviors was related to children's withdrawal, aggression, dependency, anxiety, and depression. Similarly, Tshcann, Johnston, Kline, and Wallerstein (1989) report that children whose fathers involve them in conflicts or use them for emotional support display more behavior problems than other children.

The child is an active agent in the triangle. Children may perpetuate or maintain dysfunctional patterns by perceiving one parent as right and the other wrong (Blotcky, Grace, & Looney, 1984); by instigating conflict between the parents (Adams, 1982; Westman, 1983); by trying to reunite the parents; or by distracting their parent from grieving for the loss of the marriage (Fulmer, 1983).

Although the more common triangle during the divorce transition involves forming an alliance with the child, the mother may instead view the child as an enemy (Chethik, Dolin, Davies, Lohr, & Darrow, 1987; Derdyn, 1983; Hodges, 1986). Frequently the custodial parent and the child partially recreate the former spousal relationship. Clinical problems arise when a child becomes the target of the parent's anger at being abandoned by the other parent. Many of these children openly recognize that they have taken the absent parent's place in the conflict (Derdyn, 1983). Chethik et al. discuss two mechanisms that could be operating in these situations. The child could take on negative characteristics of the absent parent as a defense against painful emotions, such as sadness, helplessness, abandonment, and loss of self-esteem. Alternatively, the parent's distorted perception of the child's behavior could serve the parent's need to reestablish previous marital balances or to reactivate early childhood conflicts.

In summary, even though there is wide variation in how family members react to divorce, divorce has the potential to greatly alter family relationships. Roles, alliances, boundaries, communication patterns, and lines of authority are changed. The consensus is that while divorce obviously alters the marital relationship, significant changes occur in parent-child relationships as well. How well the new family unit, labeled a *binuclear family,* can continue to meet the needs of its members seems to depend on the parents' ability to cooperate and the children's maintaining positive relationships with both parents.

Social Support

In addition to being an independent area of research, social support forms an integral component of models of family stress (Ahrons & Rodgers, 1987; Buehler et al., 1985/1986). Lines of inquiry about social support and social networks of families in the divorce transition include the following:

- Differences in the networks of married and single persons (Gerstel, Riessman, & Rosenfield, 1985)
- Changes in network membership after divorce (Ambert, 1988; Gerstel, 1987; 1988; Leslie & Grady, 1985; Rands, 1988; Tolsdorf, 1981)
- Sources of support
- Interference versus support from network members

Gerstel et al. (1985) found that separated/divorced people are less likely than the married to have a confidant, a homogeneous network, or a network composed of a high proportion of kin. Adults in the divorce transition are more likely to feel lonely and to have smaller and more burdensome networks.

Gerstel (1987), Leslie and Grady (1985), Rands (1988), and Tolsdorf (1981) studied changes in network membership. Gerstel and Tolsdorf both found that as network members take sides with one spouse, the structure of the social network changes from one large network into two relatively unconnected subsystems. Each spouse is connected to his or her own subsystem of the network and removed from the former partner's subsystem. Many divorced persons lose friends who feel loyal to the ex-spouse. In Leslie and Grady's longitudinal study, mothers seem to homogenize their networks in the direction of increased density and family membership at 1 year after divorce. In contrast, Rands found that the postseparation network becomes less kin-centered, less heterosexual, and less couple-oriented.

Not surprisingly, Rands (1988) reports that it is unlikely that relations with one's former in-laws will be maintained. Only about 11% of Spanier and Thompson's (1984) sample identified a former in-law as one of the three people to whom they felt closest. Ambert (1988) found that relationships with former in-laws were likely to be either negative (11.6%) or nonexistent (63%) after divorce. Both spouses reported a good relationship with each other's parents in only 11% of the cases. The person most likely to have a positive relationship with former in-laws is the custodial mother who remarried.

A variety of sources of social support have been reported. Mothers report seeking help from social agencies and therapists (Henderson & Argyle, 1985; Storm, Sheehan, & Sprenkle, 1983). Attorneys (Felner, Primavera, Farber, & Bishop, 1982) and grandparent couples (Matthews & Sprey, 1984) report that they provide support to divorced mothers. Although both divorced men and women rely on kin, men are more likely to rely on them in the early stages of divorce, whereas women are more likely to maintain these ties over time (Gerstel, 1988). Women and children report seeking help from family and friends (Henderson & Argyle, 1985; McLoughlin & Whitfield, 1984; Mitchell, 1983; Storm et al., 1983).

Help from relatives may or may not be forthcoming, however. According to Wallerstein and Blakeslee (1989), less than 10% of the children reported that any adult had offered support as the divorce unfolded. Berman (1988a) found that only one third of his subjects viewed their parents as supportive although 63% of them had contact with their parents more than once a week. In contrast, a vast majority (90% of the women and 86% of the men) of Spanier and Thompson's (1984) subjects reported receiving moral support from at least one parent. Help in the form of services was received by 45% of the women and 35% of the men; financial assistance was provided to 51% of the women and 22% of the men. Men and women who had children were more likely than the childless to receive services from their parents. According to Kitson, Moir, and Mason (1982), families are more likely to provide help to separated or divorced persons if family members approve of the decision to divorce and if the separated/divorced individuals have experienced other life events in addition to the divorce.

Milardo (1987) reminds us that it is unreasonable to assume that once a network of intimates is identified, we can judge this network to be supportive. Network members may contribute both hinderance and sabotage in addition to support (Spanier & Thompson, 1984; Tolsdorf, 1981). Milardo maintains that kin are more likely than friends to be critical. Kin more frequently provide a greater degree of both interference and support than friends, and the effects of this interference may outweigh or at least undermine any positive consequences of support. Hetherington (1989) found that divorced women who reside with their parents often report conflictual or ambivalent relationships with them. Sources of conflict include the divorced mother's social life, loss of independence, shared control over the children, and disagreement about disciplining the children.

In summary, theoretic models identified social support as an important resource that may mediate the effects of divorce on family members. More empiric testing is needed to examine under what circumstances social network members enhance or hinder the family's adjustment to the divorce transition.

Guidelines for Treatment

Because of the stress accompanying the changes that occur in the divorce transition, professional help may be indicated. General guidelines for clinicians and families are offered, followed by recommendations for specific interventions directed at individuals or relationships.

To maintain maximal effectiveness when working with divorcing families, the nurse should be aware of his or her own biases and of the potential for triangulation. Countertransference issues that might arise include excessive sympathy for clients, shared perception of the former spouse as the person to blame, and intolerance for client's anger at his or her former spouse. Within therapeutic systems, one spouse may try to obtain the therapist's approval of his or her own position. With an understanding of typical reactions to divorce, as well as an awareness of his or her own responses, the clinician is better able to be objective with families in the divorce transition (Rice, 1989).

Assessment of the stage of divorce is a crucial first step in helping the clinician distinguish between temporary regression and developmental interference (Ferreiro et al., 1986; Musty, 1983; Wylder, 1982). Clients' needs vary according to the stage of the divorce process. Although more distress may be experienced in the separation phase (White & Mika, 1983), children may benefit from treatment for divorce-related issues as long as 4 years after the divorce has occurred (Kalter et al., 1984; Pedro-Carroll, Cowen, Hightower, & Guare, 1986; Stolberg & Walsh, 1988).

To promote optimal adjustment, clinicians can make the following recommendations to parents. Parents should give adequate and clear information about the divorce to the children, inform school officials about the divorce (Funk, 1983; Hodges, 1986), keep the children in the same school if possible (Hodges, 1986), and encourage usual involvement with peers (Stolberg & Walsh, 1988). Hetherington et al. (1989) maintain that day-care centers and schools that provide warm, structured, and predictable environments can offer much-needed stability to children experiencing changes in the family environment.

Persons are vulnerable to disturbances in health during periods of transition and change (Musty, 1983). Therefore clinicians should help families establish good health habits, such as nutritionally balanced meals, predictable and consistent bedtimes, regular eating schedules, and regular physical exercise (Guidubaldi, Cleminshaw, & Perry, 1985; Sprenkle, 1989).

Interventions in the divorce transition might be centered on children, parents, or relationships. Although the choice of intervention depends on the nature of the presenting problem, some goals for therapy are consistent across levels of treatment. All family members need to accept the permanence of divorce, to resolve their feelings of loss, and to adapt to the changed circumstances of living. Both children and parents should be encouraged to use the support systems already available and to identify additional persons that could serve as resources (Sprenkle, 1989). Many adults and children in the divorce transition will benefit from interventions designed to improve their skills in anger control, communication, conflict management, and relaxation.

The formats for accomplishing these goals are quite varied. In addition to individual and family therapy, groups can be helpful. Group experience may generate support and acceptance (Salts, 1989; Sprenkle, 1989; Young, 1989).

Short-term psychoeducational groups have been designed for children (Kalter et al., 1984; Pedro-Carroll et al., 1986; Young, 1989) and for parents (Buehler & Trotter, 1988; Stolberg & Garrison, 1985).

CHILDREN

Many children react to the divorce with intense emotions. In addition to resolving their feelings of grief, children must cope with ongoing parental disharmony, adapt to repetitive separations from a visiting parent or cope with loss of contact with the noncustodial parent, and resolve conflicts that arise over their parents' new partner (Kalter et al., 1984).

Clinicians should be aware of the tendency of children of divorce to see themselves as victims. Children believe that they have no control over this major event in their lives (Nichols, 1989; Wallerstein & Blakeslee, 1989). The challenge for therapists and parents is to reduce feelings of powerlessness in children by pointing out the things over which the child does maintain control (Young, 1989).

Because children frequently deny painful emotions associated with divorce, group programs can be helpful in reducing resistance by providing opportunities for displacement. A variety of activities have been used to facilitate discussion and working through of feelings. These include viewing stimulus films (Young, 1989), role-playing courtroom situations in which custody is decided (Kalter et al., 1984), and writing letters about their feelings about the divorce (Bonkowski, Bequette, & Boomhower, 1984).

Sibling subsystem intervention. The nurse therapist can intervene in the sibling relationship directly by seeing the siblings together without their parents present. Assessment should explore dimensions of the relationship, such as conflict, play, and mutual support, and their perception of the way their parents are involved in that relationship (Eno, 1985). The goal of sessions with siblings is to strengthen and support the subsystem to help it function more effectively and thus provide coping and developmental assistance for the children (Nichols, 1986).

ADJUSTMENT OF PARENTS

Adjustment to divorce can be problematic for many people. It is not uncommon for persons in the divorce transition to seek psychologic counseling. In a longitudinal study, Menaghan and Lieberman (1986) found that the newly divorced were significantly more depressed than they had been when married. Similarly, Doherty, Su, and Needle (1989) report that psychologic well-being of women in their sample declined from before to after separation. In Bloom, Hodges's et al. (1985) study, subjects identified specific problem areas, including feelings of loneliness, guilt and self-blame, incompetence, financial stress, psychologic problems, sexual dissatisfaction, legal problems, securing employment for women, homemaking difficulties, problems with health, and work-related difficulties. Substance abuse also increased from before to after separation (Doherty, Su, & Needle, 1989).

The primary goals for treatment of individuals are to help them attain emotional acceptance of divorce and to restructure their life-style (Power, 1987). Individuals must retrieve the hopes, dreams, plans, and expectations that they invested in their spouse and in their marriage (Carter & McGoldrick, 1988) and establish a new sense of identity (Wallerstein & Blakeslee, 1989). Each spouse needs to examine his or her own role in the marital problems (Brown, 1988). Reducing both positive and negative attachment to the ex-spouse is central to adjustment after divorce (Tschann, Johnston, & Wallerstein, 1989). The extent of attachment to former spouse should be assessed, and clients can be informed that their feelings of attachment are a normal part of the divorce process. Ferreiro et al. (1986) recommend that clients construct a balance sheet of gains and losses. Clients should identify which aspects of the losses are distressing to them, that is, loss of role as a married person, loss of contact with a loved one, and loss of the family home. Individuals should permit themselves to grieve over the losses that divorce entails (Count & Sacks, 1985; Fulmer, 1983; Musty, 1983).

According to Tschann, Johnston, and Wallerstein (1989), conflict with the former spouse during the separation period increases negative attachment to the former spouse and thus interferes with positive adjustment after divorce. The level of hostility toward the spouse should be assessed. Divorce is a crisis in which many people feel that their rage at their ex-spouse is justified. According to Wallerstein and Blakeslee (1989), it is a rage that feels good. Clients may need confrontation about the negative impact of severe expression of rage at the ex-spouse (Derdyn, 1983; Woody, Colley, Schlegelmilch, Maginn, & Balsanek, 1984). Vogelsang (1982) encourages clients to make a list of grievances, rank them in order of importance, and decide which ones they are ready to discard.

Clients often express their grievances through blaming their spouses for all that is happening and considering themselves as helpless victims (Vogelsang, 1982). The therapist must not reinforce a "helpless victim" position (Sprenkle, 1989). It is crucial that the clinician help the divorcing person gain a sense of power and control over his or her own destiny (Granvold, 1989; Sprenkle, 1989).

PARENT-CHILD RELATIONSHIPS

The clinician can assess the parent-child relationship by asking how and what the children were told about the divorce. Children should be told (1) the reasons for the divorce, with each parent accepting some responsibility for the dissolution (Ferreiro et al., 1986); (2) that the children did not cause the divorce; and (3) that both parents remain available to them. Parents can be informed of children's typical reactions to divorce and should be encouraged to permit their children to express their feelings about the divorce. Because of the likelihood of children testing limits and of custodial parents' diminished capacity to respond effectively, the divorced mother may feel overwhelmed by parenting. The first priority is to help the custodial mother to be competent on her own at handling the children's day-to-day needs and assisting in their normal developmental tasks (Brown, 1988). A central dilemma for the single mother is how to enlist the help of others without permitting them to take over for her. In addition to formal therapy, parent education courses may be beneficial.

Relationship with noncustodial parent. The goal of visitation is to maintain the child's contact with the noncustodial parent in order to reduce the sense of loss and facilitate the developmental task of identification for children (Funk, 1983). If the child is not having contact with the noncustodial parent, the clinician should determine the reasons for this decision. In general, visitation with the noncustodial parent is recommended unless the parent suffers severe psychopathology or there is a history of family violence (Broom, 1981; Ferreiro et al., 1986; Hodges, 1986). Because many spouses describe their former partner as emotionally disturbed (Jacobs, 1983), the clinician should interview the noncustodial parent and seek more objective sources of information, such as previous counselors (Lowery, 1989). If the noncustodial parent chooses not to maintain contact with his or her child, the child should be helped to understand that the problem is the responsibility of the absent parent and is not caused by any defect in the child (Gardner, 1977).

Fathers who participate in family therapy may have special needs. Many fathers leave the marriage with little knowledge of their children (Friedman, 1982). According to Hodges (1986), divorced fathers may have difficulty tolerating the ebb and flow of attachment in children. These parents could benefit from learning that it is normal for children to have more intense and less intense affectional ties over time. Clinicians can help fathers (1) to develop basic communication skills, such as awareness and disclosure of their own feelings, (2) to understand children's developmental needs, and (3) to tolerate children's expressions of anger about the divorce (Jacobs, 1983; Schwebel, Moreland, Steinkohl, Lentz, & Stewart, 1982). Fathers should understand that their continuing role with their children includes caretaking, providing guidance, and setting moral and behavioral standards for their children.

Guidelines for the structure of visitation can be discussed. Age differences among siblings lead to difficulty in choosing a common activity (Wallerstein & Kelly, 1980). The noncustodial parent and children may need help in working out a set of realistic expectations for their contacts with each other. The visiting parent should avoid the role of entertainer or "Santa" to the children. Visits should include routine experiences of daily living, such as homework and helping with chores, for example, fixing toys, preparing meals, and doing yard work (Kalter, 1990; Nichols, 1986). Overnight and weekend visits give the child an opportunity to become a more natural part of the father's life. Because parting can be distressing, fathers and children need to establish rituals for saying good-bye until their next contact.

RELATIONSHIPS BETWEEN FORMER SPOUSES

According to family systems theory, a strong parental subsystem and clear and flexible boundaries are essential for healthy family functioning (Durst et al., 1985). When the target of intervention is the relationship between former spouses, an initial goal is to help the members of the divorcing family see themselves as a continuing family system (Ahrons, 1983; Ahrons & Rodgers,

1987; Broom, 1981). The shared perception is necessary for development of a cooperative parenting relationship.

Although Broom (1981) maintains that many former spouses can develop cooperative parenting arrangements, clinicians should be aware that not all ex-spouses are capable of or desire to coparent (Moreland, Schwebel, Fine, & Vess, 1982). According to Maccoby, Depner, and Mnookin (1990), parental conflict persists well after the divorce for a significant proportion of families. To cooperate after divorce, both parents should have a strong commitment to their children's welfare, place a high value on the opportunity to perform the parenting role, view their ex-spouse as a competent parent, and separate perceptions of the parental and former spousal role performance (Ahrons, 1983; Broom, 1981; Durst et al., 1985; Wylder, 1982). In addition, the couple should have attained a high degree of resolution of interspousal conflict. Persons who are not yet ready to cooperate with their former spouses may need individual or group therapy to resolve their feelings about their former spouse.

Divorce counseling or divorce mediation may be helpful for divorced persons who want to improve their coparenting relationships. The teaching of conflict resolution skills may occur in conjoint treatment (Schwebel et al., 1982) or in a group format wherein couples who are able to coparent cooperatively can serve as role models (Ahrons, 1980).

TRIANGLES

The therapist should intervene directly in those situations where the parents have created a triangle by involving the children in their conflict. Parents need to learn how to keep the children out of interparental conflict (Webster-Stratton, 1989). Establishing rapport with the parent(s) who comes for treatment (usually only the mother) is necessary before the parent will be receptive to feedback about family dynamics. The feedback may be presented in an educational manner as the clinician helps the parent(s) understand that using the child as an ally, confidante, or spy interferes with the child's development by causing loyalty conflicts and blurring generational boundaries.

The clinician should indicate that although it is natural for the parent to be angry with his or her former spouse, children rarely share the same negative view of the other parent (Broom, 1981). The mother may have difficulty separating her feelings from her child's feelings (Kalter, 1990). In an example from the author's clinical practice, when the father arrived 15 minutes late to pick up his son for visitation, the mother became enraged and would not permit the child to leave. The boy himself was unconcerned about his father's tardiness, but he became upset when his angry mother cancelled the visit. The mother later acknowledged that her response was related to her own feelings of abandonment and rejection when her father did not visit as scheduled when she was a child. With therapy, some mothers become able to encourage and support visitation.

To decrease the likelihood of involving children in their conflict, parents should be advised to avoid communicating through their children. Otherwise, children are exposed to expressions of anger if they deliver unwelcome news and to other powerful emotions if they are asked to transmit emotionally charged messages (Broom, 1981).

Clinicians should recommend to parents that they refrain from denigrating their former spouse in front of the children because it can damage the child's sense of security and self-esteem (Derdeyn, 1983; Kalter, 1990). For parents who denigrate their former spouses, the clinician should ask them to consider the child's experience as he or she listens to the parent's comments. It may be useful to gently confront the parent by saying, "You believe these things to be true about your former spouse. Do you think it helps the child to hear you say them?" Another intervention is suggested by Sprenkle (1989), who notes that with highly inflammatory clients, he has occasionally used a paradoxical approach, such as asking the client, "If you wanted to be harmful to your children, how specifically would you do it?"

In summary, the therapist can help parents to alter specific behavior patterns that have detrimental outcomes for themselves and their children. While facilitating change in dysfunctional triangles is challenging, there is potential to significantly improve the adjustment of parents and children.

•   •   •

As divorce has become prevalent, families in the divorce transition are seeking professional help. Psychiatric nurses can promote successful adjustments to the changes that divorce entails. The review of research on how individuals, subsystems, and families change in response to divorce provides information about the effects of divorce. Although more research is needed to describe specifically the processes by which family relationships change, some generalizations can be made. Change in the family system affects many of its characteristics, such as the members' ability to carry out their roles, the boundaries between subsystems, and avenues of communication. Factors that contribute to successful coping and adaptation are the parents' ability to maintain positive relationships with their children and to cooperate with each other after divorce.

Clinicians can use a variety of methods to facilitate the achievement of divorce-related tasks. Regardless of method, the goals of clinical treatment are to help family members resolve their internal conflicts created by the divorce and to promote effective functioning in the parent-child and former spouse relationships. To be effective in promoting family change, the nurse must gain the trust of the family members and attend to each one's distress. With a thorough assessment of the unique meaning that individuals attach to their experience, the nurse can plan more specific interventions.

REFERENCES

Abelsohn, D. (1983). Dealing with the abdication dynamic in the post divorce family: Context for adolescent crisis. *Family Process, 22*(3), 359-383.

Adams, G. F. (1982). The effects of divorce on adolescents. *The High School Journal, 65,* 205-211.

Ahrons, C. R. (1980). Divorce: A crisis of family transition and change. *Family Relations, 29*(4), 533-540.

Ahrons, C. (1981). The continuing coparental relationships between divorced spouses. *American Journal of Orthopsychiatry, 51,* 415-428.

Ahrons, C. (1983). Divorce: Before, during, and after. In H. McCubbin & C. Figley (Eds.), *Stress and the family, Vol. 1: Coping with normative transitions* (pp. 102-115). New York: Brunner/Mazel.

Ahrons, C., & Rodgers, R. (1987). *Divorced families: A multidisciplinary view.* New York: W. W. Norton.

Ahrons, C., & Wallisch, L. (1987). The relationship between former spouses. In D. Perlman & S. Duck (Eds.), *Intimate relationships: Development, dynamics, and deterioration* (pp. 269-296). Beverly Hills: Sage.

Ajzen, I., & Fishbein, M. (1977). Attitude-behavior relations: A theoretical analysis and review of empirical research. *Psychological Bulletin, 84*(5), 888-918.

Amato, P. R. (1987). Family processes in one-parent, stepparent, and intact families: The child's point of view. *Journal of Marriage and the Family, 49,* 327-337.

Ambert, A. (1984). Longitudinal changes in children's behavior toward custodial parents. *Journal of Marriage and the Family, 46,* 463-467.

Ambert, A. (1988). Relationships with former in-laws after divorce. *Journal of Marriage and the Family, 50,* 679-686.

Bar-Tal, D. (1978). Attributional analysis of achievement-related behavior. *Review of Educational Research, 48,* 259-271.

Berman, M. (1983). Children as pawns. *Family Advocate, 6*(2), 22-26.

Berman, W. H. (1985). Continued attachment after legal divorce. *Journal of Family Issues, 6*(3), 375-392.

Berman, W. (1988a). The relationship of ex-spouse attachment to adjustment following divorce. *Journal of Family Psychology, 1*(3), 312-328.

Berman, W. (1988b). The role of attachment in the post-divorce experience. *Journal of Personality and Social Psychology, 54*(3), 496-503.

Bishop, S., & Ingersoll, G. (1989). Effects of marital conflict and family structure on the self-concepts of pre- and early adolescents. *Journal of Youth and Adolescence, 18*(1), 25-38.

Bloom, B., Asher, S., & White, S. (1978). Marital disruption as a stressor: A review and analysis. *Psychological Bulletin, 85*(4), 867-894.

Bloom, B., & Hodges, W. (1981). The predicament of the newly separated. *Community Mental Health Journal, 17*(4), 277-293.

Bloom, B., Hodges, W., & Caldwell, R. (1982). A preventive program for the newly separated: Initial evaluation. *American Journal of Community Psychology, 10,* 251-264.

Bloom, B., Hodges, W., Kern, M., & McFaddin, S. (1985). A preventive intervention program for the newly separated: Final evaluations. *American Journal of Orthopsychiatry, 55*(1), 9-26.

Bloom, B., & Kindle, K. (1985). Demographic factors in the continuing relationship between former spouses. *Family Relations, 34*(3), 375-381.

Bloom, B. L., Niles, R. L., & Thatcher, A. M. (1985). Sources of marital dissatisfaction among newly separated persons. *Journal of Family Issues, 6*(3), 359-373.

Blotcky, M. J., Grace, K. D., & Looney, J. G. (1984). Treatment of adolescents in family therapy after divorce. *Journal of the American Academy of Child Psychiatry, 23*(2), 222-225.

Bonkowski, S., Bequette, S., & Boomhower, S. (1984). A group design to help children adjust to divorce. *Social Casework, 65*(3), 131-137.

Bonkowski, S., Boomhower, S., & Bequette, S. (1985). What you don't know can hurt you: Unexpressed fears and feelings of children from divorcing families. *Journal of Divorce, 9*(1), 33-45.

Bowen, M. (1985). *Family therapy in clinical practice.* New York: Jason Aronson.

Bowlby, J. (1969). *Attachment and loss: Attachment, Vol 1.* New York: Basic Books.

Broom, D. B. (1981). No longer spouses, still parents: Toward cooperative parenting after separation. *Australian Journal of Sex, Marriage, and Family, 2*(4), 181-191.

Brown, F. (1988). The postdivorce family. In B. Carter & M. McGoldrick (Eds.), *The changing family life cycle: A framework for family therapy* (pp. 371-398). New York: Gardner Press.

Brown, P., Felton, B., Whiteman, V., & Manela, R. (1980). Attachment and loss following marital separation. *Journal of Divorce, 3,* 303-317.

Brown, S., & Reimer, D. (1984). Assessing attachment following divorce: Development and psychometric evaluation of the Divorce Reaction Inventory. *Journal of Counseling Psychology, 31*(4), 520-531.

Buehler, C. A., Hogan, M. J., Robinson, B. E., & Levy, R. J. (1985/1986). The parental divorce transition: Divorce-related stressors and well-being. *Journal of Divorce, 9*(2), 61-80.

Buehler, C., & Langenbrunner, M. (1987). Divorce-related stressors: Occurrence, disruptiveness, and area of life change. *Journal of Divorce, 11,* 25-49.

Buehler, C., & Trotter, B. (Nov, 1988). The former spouse relationship and children's well-being post-separation: Theory and programmed intervention. Paper presented at the annual meeting of the National Council on Family Relations, Philadelphia.

Carter, B., & McGoldrick, M. (1988). Overview: The changing family life cycle. In B. Carter & M. McGoldrick (Eds.), *The changing family life cycle: A framework for family therapy* (pp. 3-28). New York: Gardner Press.

Cherlin, A., & Furstenberg, F. (March 19, 1989). Divorce doesn't always hurt the kids. *The Washington Post,* p. C3.

Chess, S., Thomas, A., Korn, S., Mittelman, M., & Cohen, J. (1983). Early parental attitudes, divorce and separation, and young adult outcome: Findings of a longitudinal study. *Journal of the American Academy of Child Psychiatry, 22*(1), 47-51.

Chethik, M., Dolin, N., Davies, D., Lohr, R., & Darrow, D. (1987). Children and divorce: The "negative" identification. *Journal of Divorce, 10*(1/2), 121-138.

Cleek, M., & Pearson, T. (1985). Perceived causes of divorce: An analysis of interrelationships. *Journal of Marriage and the Family, 47,* 179-191.

Clingenpeel, W., & Repucci, N. (1982). Joint custody after divorce: Major issues and goals for research. *Psychological Bulletin, 91,* 102-127.

Coleman, M., & Ganong, L. (1990). Remarriage and stepfamily research in the 1980s: Increased interest in an old family form. *Journal of Marriage and the Family, 52,* 925-940.

Cooney, T., Smyer, M., Hagestad, G., & Klock, R. (1986). Parental divorce in young adulthood: Some preliminary findings. *American Journal of Orthopsychiatry, 56*(3), 470-477.

Count, R., & Sacks, A. (1985). The need for crisis intervention during marital separation. *Social Work, 30*(2), 146-150.

Cox, F. (1981). *Human intimacy: Marriage, the family and its meaning* (2nd ed.). St. Paul: West.

Crosby, J., Lybarger, S., & Mason, R. (1987). The grief resolution process in divorce: Phase II. *Journal of Divorce, 10*(1/2), 17-40.

Crossman, S., & Adams, G. (1980). Divorce, single parenting, and child development. *Journal of Psychology, 106,* 205-217.

Davis, B., & Aron, A. (1988). Perceived causes of divorce and postdivorce adjustment among recently divorced midlife women. *Journal of Divorce, 12*(1), 41-55.

Dawson, D. (1991). Family structure and children's health and well-being: Data from the 1988 National Health Interview Survey on Child Health. *Journal of Marriage and the Family, 53,* 573-584.

Demo, D., & Acock, A. (1988). The impact of divorce on children. *Journal of Marriage and the Family, 50,* 619-648.

Derdyn, A. (1983). The family in divorce: Issues of parental anger. *Journal of the American Academy of Child Psychiatry, 22*(4), 385-391.

Doherty, W., Su, S., & Needle, R. (1989). Marital disruption and psychological well-being: A panel study. *Journal of Family Issues, 10*(1), 72-85.

Durst, P. L., Wedemeyer, N. V., & Zurcher, L. A. (1985). Parenting partnerships after divorce: Implications for practice. *Social Work, 30*(5), 423-428.

Eno, M. (1985). Sibling relationships in families of divorce. *Journal of Psychotherapy and the Family, 1*(2), 139-156.

Ferreiro, B. W., Warren, N. J., & Konanc, J. T. (1986). ADAP: A divorce assessment proposal. *Family Relations, 35,* 439-449.

Felner, R., Primavera, J., Farber, S., & Bishop, T. (1982). Attorneys as caregivers during divorce. *American Journal of Orthopsychiatry, 52*(2), 323-336.

Fine, M. A., Moreland, J. R., & Schwebel, A. I. (1983). Long-term effects of divorce on parent-child relationships. *Developmental Psychology, 19*(5), 703-713.

Fischer, J., & Cardea, J. (1982). Mother-child relationships of mothers living apart from their children. *Alternative Lifestyles, 5*(1), 42-53.

Flewelling, R., & Bauman, K. (1990). Family structure as a predictor of initial substance abuse and sexual intercourse in early adolescence. *Journal of Marriage and the Family, 52,* 171-181.

Friedman, H. (1982). The challenge of divorce to adequate fathering: The peripheral father in marriage and divorce. *Psychiatric Clinics of North America, 5*(3), 565-580.

Fry, P. S., & Addington, J. (1985). Perceptions of parent and child adjustments in divorced families. *Clinical Psychology Review, 5*(2), 141-158.

Fulmer, R. H. (1983). A structural approach to unresolved mourning in single-parent family systems. *Journal of Marital and Family Therapy, 9*(3), 259-269.

Funk, J. B. (1983). Special problems in divorce management. *Developmental and Behavioral Pediatrics, 4*(2), 108-112.

Furstenberg, F., & Nord, C. (1985). Parenting apart: Patterns of childrearing after marital disruption. *Journal of Marriage and the Family, 47*(4), 893-904.

Furstenberg, F. F., Nord, C. W., Peterson, J. L., & Zill, N. (1983). The life course of children of divorce: Marital disruption and parental contact. *American Sociological Review, 48,* 656-668.

Ganong, L., & Coleman, M. (1984). The effects of remarriage on children: A review of empirical literature. *Family Relations, 33,* 389-406.

Gardner, R. (1977). *The parents' book about divorce.* New York: Doubleday.

Gardner, R. (1986). *Child custody litigation: A guide for parents and mental health professionals.* Cresskill, NJ: Creative Therapeutics.

Gerstel, N. (1988). Divorce and kin ties: The importance of gender. *Journal of Marriage and the Family, 50,* 209-219.

Gerstel, N. (1987). Divorce and stigma. *Social Problems, 34*(2), 172-186.

Gerstel, N., Riessman, C., & Rosenfield, S. (1985). Explaining the symptomatology of separated and divorced men and women: The role of material conditions and social networks. *Social Forces, 64*(1), 84-101.

Glenn, N., & Kramer, K. (1987). The marriages and divorces of the children of divorce. *Journal of Marriage and the Family, 49,* 811-825.

Goldsmith, J. (1980). Relationships between former spouses: Descriptive findings. *Journal of Divorce, 4,* 1-20.

Granvold, D. (1989). Postdivorce treatment. In M. Textor (Ed.), *The divorce and divorce therapy handbook* (pp. 197-223). Northvale, NJ: Jason Aronson.

Guidubaldi, J., Cleminshaw, H., & Perry, J. (1985). The relationship of parental divorce to health status of parents and children. *Special Services in the Schools, 1*(1), 73-87.

Hanson, S., & Spanier, G. (1983). Family development and adjustment to marital separation. *Sociology and Social Research, 68*(1), 18-40.

Henderson, M., & Argyle, M. (1985). Source and nature of social support given to women at divorce/separation. *British Journal of Social Work, 15,* 57-65.

Hess, R. D., & Camara, K. A. (1979). Post-divorce family relationships as mediating factors in the consequences of divorce for children. *Journal of Social Issues, 35*(4), 79-96.

Hetherington, E. (1988). Parents, children, and siblings 6 years after divorce. In R. Hinde & J. Stevenson-Hinde (Eds.), *Relationships within families.* Cambridge: Cambridge University Press.

Hetherington, E. (1989). Coping with family transitions: Winners, losers, and survivors. *Child Development, 60,* 1-16.

Hetherington, E. (1991). The role of individual differences and family relationships in children's coping with divorce and remarriage. In P. Cowan & E. Hetherington (Eds.), *Family transitions.* Hillsdale, NJ: Lawrence Erlbaum.

Hetherington, E., Stanley-Hagan, S. & Anderson, E. (1989). Marital transitions: A child's perspective. *American Psychologist, 44,* 303-312.

Hill, R. (1958). Social stresses on the family. *Social Casework, 39,* 139-150.

Hillard, J. R. (1984). Reactions of college students to parental divorce. *Psychiatric Annals, 14*(9), 663-670.

Hodges, W. (1986). *Interventions for children of divorce: Custody, access, and psychotherapy.* New York: John Wiley & Sons.

Hodges, W., Tierney, C., & Bushsham, H. (1984). The cumulative effect of stress on preschool children of divorced and intact families. *Journal of Marriage and the Family, 46,* 611-617.

Holmes, T., & Rahe, R. (1967). The Social Readjustment Rating Scale. *Journal of Psychosomatic Research, 11,* 213-218.

Huntley, D., Phelps, R., & Rehm, L. (1987). Depression in children from single-parent families. *Journal of Divorce, 10*(1/2), 153-167.

Isaacs, M., Leon, G., & Donohue, A. (1987). Who are the "normal" children of divorce? On the need to specify population. *Journal of Divorce, 10*(1/2), 107-119.

Jacobs, J. (1983). Treatment of divorcing fathers: Social and psychotherapeutic considerations. *American Journal of Psychiatry, 140*(10), 1294-1299.

Jacobs, J. (1984). The effect of divorce on fathers. *International Journal of Family Therapy, 6*(3), 177-191.

James, A., & Wilson, K. (1984). The trouble with access: A study of divorcing families. *British Journal of Social Work, 14,* 487-506.

Johnson, B. (1986). *Psychiatric-mental health nursing: Adaptation and growth.* Philadelphia: J. B. Lippincott.

Journal of Divorce. (1985) *8*(3), Spring/Summer.

Kalter, N. (1990). *Growing up with divorce: Helping your child avoid immediate and later emotional problems.* New York: The Free Press.

Kalter, N., Kloner, A., Schreier, S., & Okla, N. (1989). Predictors of children's postdivorce adjustment. *American Journal of Orthopsychiatry, 59*(4), 605-618.

Kalter, N., Pickar, J., & Lesowitz, M. (1984). School-based developmental facilitation groups for children of divorce: A preventative intervention. *American Journal of Orthopsychiatry, 54*(4), 613-623.

Kalter, N., Riemer, B., Brickman, A., & Chen, J. (1985). Implications of parental divorce for female development. *Journal of the American Academy of Child Psychiatry, 24,* 538-544.

Kiecolt-Glaser, J., Fisher, L., Ogrocki, P., Stout, J., Speicher, C., & Glaser, R. (1987). Marital quality, marital disruption, and immune function. *Psychosomatic Medicine, 49*(1), 13-34.

Kinard, E., & Reinherz, H. (1984). Marital disruption: Effects on behavioral and emotional functioning in children. *Journal of Family Issues, 5*(1), 90-115.

Kitson, G. (1982). Attachment to the spouse in divorce: A scale and its application. *Journal of Marriage and the Family, 44,* 379-393.

Kitson, G. K., & Langlie, J. K. (1984). Couples who file for divorce but change their minds. *American Journal of Orthopsychiatry, 54*(3), 469-489.

Kitson, G., Moir, R., & Mason, P. (1982). Family social support in crisis: The special case of divorce. *American Journal of Orthopsychiatry, 52*(1), 161-165.

Kitson, G., & Sussman, M. (1982). Marital complaints, demographic characteristics, and symptoms of mental distress in divorce. *Journal of Marriage and the Family, 44,* 87-101.

Kressel, K. (1980). Patterns of coping with divorce and some implications for clinical practice. *Family Relations, 29*(2), 234-240.

Kressel, L., Jaffe, K., Tuchman, B., Watson, C., & Deutsch, M. (1980). A typology of divorcing couples: Implications for mediation and the divorce process. *Family Process, 19,* 101-116.

Kurdek, L. (1981). An integrative perspective on children's divorce adjustment. *American Psychologist, 36*(8), 856-866.

Kurdek, L. (1989). Children's adjustment. In M. Textor (Ed.), *The divorce and divorce therapy handbook* (pp. 77-102). Northvale, NJ: Jason Aronson.

Kurdek, L. A., & Sinclair, R. J. (1986). Adolescents' views on issues related to divorce. *Journal of Adolescent Research, 1*(4), 373-387.

Leahey, M. (1984). Findings from research on divorce: Implications for professionals' skill development. *American Journal of Orthopsychiatry, 54*(2), 298-317.

Leslie, L., & Grady, K. (1985). Changes in mothers' social networks and social support following divorce. *Journal of Marriage and the Family, 47,* 663-673.

Long, N., & Forehand, R. (1987). The effects of parental divorce and parental conflict on children: An overview. *Developmental and Behavioral Pediatrics, 8*(5), 292-296.

Lowery, C. (1989). Psychotherapy with children of divorced families. In M. Textor (Ed.), *The divorce and divorce therapy handbook* (pp. 225-241). Northvale, NJ: Jason Aronson.

Lowery, C. R., & Settle, S. A. (1985). Effects of divorce on children: Differential impact of custody and visitation and custody patterns. *Family Relations, 34,* 455-463.

Maccoby, E., Depner, C., & Mnookin, R. (1990). Coparenting in the second year after divorce. *Journal of Marriage and the Family, 52,* 141-155.

MacKinnon, C. (1988/1989). Sibling interaction in married and divorced families: Influence of position, socioeconomic status, and play context. *Journal of Divorce, 12*(2/3), 221-234.

Martin, T., & Bumpass, L. (1989). Recent trends in marital disruption. *Demography, 26*(1), 37-51.

Masheter, C. (1991). Postdivorce relationships between ex-spouses: The roles of attachment and interpersonal conflict. *Journal of Marriage and the Family, 53,* 103-110.

Matthews, S., & Sprey, J. (1984). The impact of divorce on grandparenthood: An exploratory study. *Gerontologist, 24*(1), 41-47.

McCubbin, H., & Patterson, J. (1983a). Family adaptation to crisis. In H. I. McCubbin, A. Cauble, & J. Patterson (Eds.), *Family stress, coping, and social support* (pp. 26-47). Springfield, IL: Charles C. Thomas.

McCubbin, H., & Patterson, J. (1983b). The family stress process: The Double ABCX model of adjustment and adaptation. In H. McCubbin, M. Sussman, & J. Patterson (Eds.), *Social stress and the family: Advances and developments in family stress theory and research* (pp. 7-37). New York: Haworth Press.

McLoughlin, D., & Whitfield, R. (1984). Adolescents and their experience of parental divorce. *Journal of Adolescence, 7*(2), 155-170.

Melichar, J., & Chiriboga, D. (1988). Significance of time in adjustment to marital separation. *American Journal of Orthopsychiatry, 58*(2), 221-227.

Menaghan, E., & Lieberman, M. (1986). Changes in depression following divorce: A panel study. *Journal of Marriage and the Family, 48,* 319-328.

Milardo, R. (1987). Changes in social networks of women and men following divorce. *Journal of Family Issues, 8*(1), 78-96.

Mitchell, A. K. (1983). Adolescents' experiences of parental separation and divorce. *Journal of Adolescence, 6,* 175-187.

Moreland, J., Schwebel, A., Fine, M., & Vess, J. (1982). Postdivorce family therapy. *Professional Psychology, 13*(5), 639-646.

Musty, T. (1983). Divorce in medical practice: Helping patients through the process. *Arizona Medicine, 40*(6), 392-397.

National Center for Health Statistics. (1991). Births, marriages, divorces, and deaths for April, 1991. *Monthly Vital Statistics Report 40,* No. 4, Department of Health & Human Services. Hyattsville, MD: Public Health Service.

Needle, R., Su, S., & Doherty, W. (1990). Divorce, remarriage, and adolescent substance use: A prospective longitudinal study. *Journal of Marriage and the Family, 52,* 157-169.

Nichols, W. (1986). Sibling subsystem therapy in family system reorganization. *Journal of Divorce, 9*(3), 13-31.

Nichols, W. (1989). Problems and needs of children. In M. Textor (Ed.), *The divorce and divorce therapy handbook* (pp. 61-76). Northvale, NJ: Jason Aronson.

Norton, A., & Glick, P. (1986). One-parent families: A social and economic profile. *Family Relations, 35,* 9-11.

Norton, A. J. & Moorman, J. E. (1987). Current trends in marriage and divorce among American women. *Journal of Marriage and the Family, 49,* 3-14.

Parish, T., & Dostal, J. (1980). Evaluations of self and parent figures by children from intact, divorced, and reconstituted families. *Journal of Youth and Adolescence, 9,* 347-351.

Patten-Seward, P. (1984). Assessing student emotional behavior after parental separation or divorce, *Journal of Student Health, 54*(4), 152-153.

Patterson, G. (1982). *Coercive family process.* Eugene, OR: Castalia.

Peck, J., & Manocherian, J. (1988). Divorce in the changing family life cycle. In B. Carter & M. McGoldrick (Eds.), *The changing family life cycle: A framework for family therapy* (pp. 335-369). New York: Gardner Press.

Pedro-Carroll, J., Cowen, E., Hightower, A., & Guare, J. (1986). Preventive intervention with latency-aged children of divorce: A replication study. *American Journal of Community Psychology, 14*(3), 277-290.

Peterson, G. W., Leigh, G. K., & Day, R. D. (1984). Family stress theory and the impact of divorce on children. *Journal of Divorce, 7*(3), 1-20.

Pettit, E., & Bloom, B. (1984). Whose decision was it? The effects of initiator status on adjustment to marital disruption. *Journal of Marriage and the Family, 46,* 587-595.

Power, R. (1987). Group work with emotionally attached or ambivalent spouses in the process of separating, separated, or recently divorced. *Journal of Divorce, 10*(1/2), 229-240.

Price-Bonham, S., & Balswick, J. (1980). The non-institutions: divorce, desertion, and remarriage. *Journal of Marriage and the Family, 42,* 959-972.

Rands, M. (1988). Changes in social networks following marital separation and divorce. In R. Milardo (Ed.), *Families and Social Networks* (pp. 127-146). Beverly Hills: Sage.

Rice, D. (1989). Marital therapy and the divorcing family. In M. Textor (Ed.), *The divorce and divorce therapy handbook* (pp. 151-176). Northvale, NJ: Jason Aronson.

Riessman, C., & Gerstel, N. (1985). Marital disruption and health: Do males or females have greater risks? *Social Science and Medicine, 20*(6), 627-636.

Rodgers, R. (1987). Postmarital reorganization of family relationships: A propositional theory. In D. Perlman & S. Duck (Eds.), *Intimate relationships: Development, dynamics, and deterioration* (pp. 239-268). Beverly Hills: Sage.

Rowling, L. (1983). Children and divorce: What we can do to help them. *Australian Journal of Sex, Marriage, and Family, 4*(2), 95-102.

Saayman, G., & Saayman, R. (1988/1989). The adversial legal process and divorce: Negative effects upon psychological adjustment of children. *Journal of Divorce, 12*(2/3), 329-348.

Salts, C. (1989). Group therapy for divorced adults. In M. Textor (Ed.), *The divorce and divorce therapy handbook* (pp. 285-300). Northvale, NJ: Jason Aronson.

Schwartzberg, A. Z. (1981). Divorce and children and adolescents: An overview. *Adolescent Psychiatry, 9,* 119-132.

Schwebel, A., Moreland, J., Steinkohl, R., Lentz, S., & Stewart, J. (1982). Research-based interventions with divorced families. *The Personnel and Guidance Journal, 60,* 523-528.

Seltzer, J. (1991). Relationships between fathers and children who live apart: The father's role after separation. *Journal of Marriage and the Family, 53,* 79-101.

Seltzer, J., Schaeffer, N., & Charng, H. (1989). Family ties after divorce: The relationship between visiting and paying child support. *Journal of Marriage and the Family, 51,* 1013-1032.

Shaw, D., & Emery, R. (1987). Parental conflict and other correlates of adjustment of school-age children whose parents have separated. *Journal of Abnormal Child Psychology, 15*(2), 269-281.

Smith, J., Mercy, J., & Conn, J. (1988). Marital status and the risk of suicide. *American Journal of Public Health, 78,* 78-80.

Solnit, A. J. (1983). Children's and parents' reactions to divorce. *Psychiatric Hospital, 14*(3), 133-139.

Spanier, G., & Thompson, L. (1984). *Parting: The aftermath of separation and divorce.* Beverly Hills: Sage.

Sprenkle, D. (1989). The clinical practice of divorce therapy. In M. Textor (Ed.), *The divorce and divorce therapy handbook* (pp. 171-195). Northvale, NJ: Jason Aronson.

Stolberg, A., Camplair, C., Currier, K., & Wells, M. (1987). Individual, familial, and environmental determinants of children's post-divorce adjustment and maladjustment. *Journal of Divorce, 11*(1), 51-70.

Stolberg, A., & Garrison, K. (1985). Evaluating a primary prevention program for children of divorce. *American Journal of Community Psychology, 13*(2), 111-124.

Stolberg, A., & Walsh, P. (1988). A review of treatment methods for children of divorce. In S. Wolchik & P. Karoly (Eds.), *Children of divorce.* New York: Gardner Press.

Storm, C., Sheehan, R., & Sprenkle, D. (1983). The structure of separated women's communication with their nonprofessional and professional networks. *Journal of Marital and Family Therapy, 9*(4), 423-429.

Tepp, A. V. (1983). Divorced fathers: Predictors of continued parental involvement. *American Journal of Psychiatry, 140*(11), 1465-1469.

Thompson, L., & Spanier, G. (1983). The end of marriage and acceptance of marital termination. *Journal of Marriage and the Family, 45,* 103-114.

Thompson, L., & Walker, A. (1982). The dyad as a unit of analysis: Conceptual and methodological issues. *Journal of Marriage and the Family, 44,* 999-1008.

Thurnber, M., Fenn, C., Melichar, J., & Chiriboga, D. (1983). Sociodemographic perspectives on reasons for divorce. *Journal of Divorce, 6*(4), 25-35.

Tolsdorf, C. (1981). Social networks and families of divorce: A study of structure-context interactions. *International Journal of Family Therapy, 3*(4), 275-280.

Tschann, J., Johnston, J., Kline, M., & Wallerstein, J. (1989). Family process and children's functioning after divorce. *Journal of Marriage and the Family, 51,* 431-444.

Tschann, J., Johnston, J., & Wallerstein, J. (1989). Resources, stressors and attachment as predictors of adult adjustment after divorce: A longitudinal study. *Journal of Marriage and the Family, 51,* 1033-1046.

Vogelsang, J. (1982). Working with the separated and divorced. *Journal of Religion and Health, 21*(4), 325-330.

Wallerstein, J. (1984). Children of divorce: A preliminary report of a ten-year follow-up of young children. *American Journal of Orthopsychiatry, 54*(3), 444-458.

Wallerstein, J. (1986). Women after divorce: Preliminary report from a 10-year follow-up. *American Journal of Orthopsychiatry, 56,* 65-77.

Wallerstein, J., & Blakeslee, S. (1989). *Second chances: Men, women, and children a decade after divorce.* New York: Ticknor & Fields.

Wallerstein, J., & Corbin, S. (1989). Daughters of divorce: Report from a 10-year follow-up. *American Journal of Orthopsychiatry, 59*(4), 593-604.

Wallerstein, J., & Kelly, J. (1980). *Surviving the breakup: How children and parents cope with divorce.* New York: Basic Books.

Warren, N. J., Ilgen, E., Bourgondien, M., Konanc, J., Grew, R., & Amara, I. (1987). Children of divorce: The question of clinically significant problems. *Journal of Divorce, 10*(1/2), 87-106.

Webster-Stratton, C. (1989). The relationship of marital support, conflict, and divorce to parent perceptions, behaviors, and childhood conduct problems. *Journal of Marriage and the Family, 51,* 417-430.

Wertlieb, O., Budman, S., Demby, A., & Randall, M. (1984). Marital separation and health: Stress and intervention. *Journal of Human Stress, 10*(1), 18-26.

Westman, J. C. (1983). The impact of divorce on teenagers. *Clinical Pediatrics, 22*(10), 692-697.

White, L. (1990). Determinants of divorce: A review of research in the eighties. *Journal of Marriage and the Family, 52,* 904-912.

White, L. K., Brinkerhoff, D. B., & Booth, A. (1985). The effect of marital disruption on child's attachment to parents. *Journal of Family Issues, 6*(1), 5-22.

White, S., & Mika, K. (1983). Family divorce and separation: Theory and research. *Marriage and Family Review, 6*(1/2), 175-192.

Wilson, H., & Kneisl C. (1988). *Psychiatric nursing* (3rd ed.). Menlo Park, CA: Addison-Wesley.

Woody, J., Colley, P., Schlegelmilch, J., Maginn, P., & Balsanek, J. (1984). Child adjustment to parental stress following divorce. *Social Casework, 65*(7), 405-414.

Wylder, J. (1982). Including the divorced father in family therapy. *Social Work, 27,* 479-482.

Young, D. M. (1989). Group intervention for children of divorce. In M. Textor (Ed.), *The divorce and divorce therapy handbook* (pp. 267-284). Northvale, NJ: Jason Aronson.

Zaslow, M. (1988). Sex differences in children's response to parental divorce: 1. Research methodology and postdivorce family forms. *American Journal of Orthopsychiatry, 58*(3), 355-378.

Zaslow, M. (1989). Sex differences in children's response to parental divorce: 2. Samples, variables, ages, and sources. *American Journal of Orthopsychiatry, 59*(1), 118-141.

Chapter 8

Families' Responses to the Loss of a Child

Sara Rich Wheeler
Margaret M. Pike

To better understand the impact of a child's death on a family and the family's journey through grief when a child dies, one needs to have a definition of systems, family, and its purposes, plus a theoretic framework for understanding grief. When a family member dies, whether during pregnancy, shortly after, or in childhood, unique problems arise with which the family must cope and move on to acquire a new status quo.

The Family as a System

A system is a composite of interrelated and interdependent parts. The parts exist in a state of balance, and when change takes place within one part, compensatory change occurs within the others (Brill, 1990). The family is considered a system made up of intimate and specialized relationships. The family's functions are to nurture the young, meet physical and emotional needs, and expose members to the culture.

Rando (1984) states that all families have their own distinct and characteristic styles. The variables include (1) communication patterns; (2) boundaries between individual family members and also between the family as a whole and the rest of the world; (3) role flexibility within the family subsystem; (4) alliances within the family; and (5) family rules.

Communication patterns within a family may be open or closed or somewhere along the continuum, especially in expressing feelings. Boundaries address how independent and separate the family members' identities are from one another. Family roles may be flexible to rigid. Subsystems are the special relationships that exist between two or more family members. Family rules govern the family members' behaviors, which are acceptable or prohibited.

Families today face problems unique to the time we live in as we approach the twenty-first century. Life spans continue to lengthen; thus families may have to care for their older members (e.g., parents, grandparents). A mobile population often leaves extended family many hundreds of miles away from each other. More and more the family may be defined as a single-parent family and usually headed by the mother. Other outside influences are substance abuse (e.g., alcohol, drugs), changes in healthcare delivery and payment, economic depression, and denial of death, especially as it relates to children.

It would seem that there is enough stress for a family just to survive and maintain a day-to-day balance, without a catastrophic event to truly upset the status quo. The death of a loved one, especially a child, means not only the loss, but the reality of the loss of one of its purposes: to nurture the young. To endure the pain of loss and separation and move toward developing a "new" normal and living life again without the child is one of the biggest challenges any one person or family could ever have in a lifetime.

How does one fully understand the loss of a child and its impact on the family? Many variables must be considered (Rando, 1984; Sanders, 1989):

- Structure of the family
- Communication patterns
- Coping styles
- Previous experiences with loss
- Ages of the family members
- Age of the child who died
- Type of death (expected, unexpected)
- The particular meaning the loss holds for each family member
- Religious, spiritual, and cultural beliefs about death
- Financial resources of the family
- Support systems
- Personality types of family members

Grief Process and Mourning

Mourning is an emotion that results from the universal experience of loss. Davidson (1984) states that the word *mourning* means the way in which mourners adapt from what *was* to what *is:* "Mourning is a process that takes you on the journey from where you were before the loss to where you will be as you struggle to adapt to change in your life."

In the psychoanalytic approach of Deutsch (1937), Freud (1957), Furman (1974), and Wolfenstein (1966), mourning is viewed as a painful struggle. Decathexis of what was lost is an acknowledgment of the reality of the loss and letting go of what was lost. It is accomplished in a piecemeal way and serves as an important defense mechanism. Painful as it is to endure, mourning serves an invaluable and adaptive function (Wolfenstein, 1966).

Bowlby (1980), Davidson (1984), Klaus and Kennell (1982), Parkes (1987), and Sugar (1968) describe attachment theory, loss, and subsequent grief as a normal response to the breaking of emotional and physical bonds. The process of mourning begins with a perceived loss of a valued object where there is an attachment or bond. The response to loss of a valued object is grief. The process of mourning is viewed as normal, similar to the psychoanalytic views of grief. The differences arise in the *process* of mourning. The process in attachment theory is one of actively moving away from the valued object and moving on with one's life, not forgetting, but being able to establish new attachments and bonds.

Davidson (1984) based his research on the works of Bowlby and Parkes. He studied 1200 adult mourners over a 10-year period. Thirty women in his study had experienced the loss of a baby. The grief process he identified is as follows:

Shock and numbness: The feeling of being stunned, interrupted by outbursts of emotion or feelings of panic or distress, predominates. Difficulty in making decisions occurs, and normal functioning is impeded. This phase predominates during the first 2 weeks after a loss. Parents may feel out of control or in a dreamlike, unreal state.

Searching and yearning: The feelings expressed are usually anger, guilt, ambiguity about life, and a profound sense of sadness. There is a yearning for what could have been and a searching for the answer. "Why?" This phase is present at the time of the loss and peaks sometime between 2 weeks and 4 months after the loss. Parents may experience aching arms, hear the sound of a baby or child crying, or have disturbing dreams or insomnia. They may be preoccupied with thoughts of anger, guilt, and self-blame.

Disorganization: Feelings of depression, guilt, and disorganization abound. This occurs when the mourner turns from testing what is real to an awareness of the reality. This phase peaks at 4 to 6 months and slowly subsides over a year. Parents may feel that they will never get over the loss or that they are losing their mind; they may become physically ill.

Reorganization: This stage is identified when the mourner is better able to function at home and work with an increase in self-confidence. The mourner has the ability to cope with new challenges and has placed the loss in perspective. This phase is present in the beginning when parents laugh and later on when they begin to enjoy the simple pleasures of life without feeling guilty. It begins to peak sometime after the first year and slowly subsides as parents begin to move on with their lives. Parents usually express they will never forget their baby or child, but have resumed their life with a "new normal." Reorganization usually is resolved around 24 months. However, there is no time table for grief.

Lindemann (1944) from his research of 101 survivors who lost a relative through a sudden, unexpected disaster, illness, or in the armed services, identified grief symptomatology. His work has formed the cornerstone in understanding normal grief response. His six points follow:

- Somatic distress
- Preoccupation with the image of the deceased
- Guilt
- Hostile reactions
- Inability to initiate and maintain organized patterns of activity
- Appearance of traits of the deceased

In the course of normal grief reactions, some of the bereaved try to avoid the intense feelings of grief and necessary emotions. Morbid or complicated grief responses are an exaggeration of normal grief. Examples of complicated responses to grief are (1) a delay or postponement of response and (2) distorted reactions. Examples of distorted reactions are overactivity without a sense of loss, development of symptoms of the deceased's illness or recognized medical disease, change in relationships with family and friends, furious hostility against specific persons, absence of feelings and emotions, lack of decisiveness and initiative, protracted self-punitive behavior, and agitated depression with preoccupation of worthlessness, self-blame, and need for self-punishment. Survivors with the need for self-punishment are at risk for suicidal attempts.

TASKS OF MOURNERS

Worden's (1991) model has four tasks of mourning that must be accomplished for successful recovery from grief:

- Accepting the loss
- Working through the pain
- Adjusting to the environment
- Moving on

Accepting the reality of the loss occurs when the parents/family come to grips with the reality of the loss. Their child has died, and their life has changed. Seeing, holding, touching, and memorializing are all ways the bereaved can perceptually confirm their child's death. It is important for the bereaved to tell their story about the events, the experiences, and the feelings surrounding the loss to cognitively and emotionally come to terms with the death. Caregivers should use the words "dead" and "died" rather than "lost" or "gone" to assist the bereaved in accepting the reality. This requires interfaces with the first two initial phases of grief.

Working through the pain of grief means the mourner must feel and express the intense emotions of grief. Not all parents/families experience the same intensity of pain, but to experience the death of a child and not experience some feelings of grief is unlikely.

In the case of perinatal loss, society in general tends to minimize the death of a baby because they have not developed a relationship or attachment as the parents have. Mother, father, and siblings often develop images and feel relationship to an unborn baby, regardless of the number of weeks of gestation. Often society equates the number of years of life and visibility of a relationship to how much mourning is appropriate.

Families who experience a loss may suppress or deny their feelings because it seems, on the surface, to be more socially acceptable. The nurse can be instrumental in preparing the family for reactions they may receive from others once they leave the hospital or clinic setting. If a supportive social network is not available and even if it is, a support group can help the parents work through their pain by nonjudgmental sharing of feelings (National Bereavement Support Groups). To deny the pain of grief will lead sooner or later to physical and emotional illness. Unfortunately, it is more acceptable in our society to be treated for physical problems than emotional ones. When no physical reasons for illness can be found, *complicated bereavement* may be the source.

Being able to adjust to the environment after the loss means learning how to accommodate to the changes the loss has brought to their lives. The loss of a child means not being able to fulfill the role of a mother, father, older sibling, or grandparent. The bereaved must cope with issues such as deciding what to do about the nursery and clothes, going back to work, parenting other children, getting pregnant again, and learning how to cope with insensitive family members and friends.

Detachment must occur for the parents to adapt to their loss. Over time, the bereaved have the opportunity to change their view on how the event of the loss has affected their lives. This does not mean they have forgotten about their child. It means that as the weeks and months go by, they have an opportunity to develop a new perspective, different feelings, and various ways of coping.

Moving on with life, or reorganization, means to love and live again. Being able to once more enjoy things that previously gave pleasure, being able to nurture oneself and others, developing new interests, and reestablishing relationships are all signs of "moving on." For some families, the birth of a subsequent child is necessary for them to be able to move on with their lives. Bereaved parents never forget their precious child; their memories become bittersweet.

Bittersweet grief is the term Kowalski (1986) uses to describe the grief parents feel after they have moved through the grief process. This type of grief does not go away, but rather is a holding-on to memories. Parents have said it is a painful, sad grief mixed with wonderful memories of their child. This grief can be triggered at anniversary dates, birthdays, change of season, or with other simple objects or events that stimulate their memories.

ANTICIPATORY GRIEF

Anticipatory grief has been defined as the anticipation of a future loss (Fulton & Gottesman, 1980; Siegel & Weinstein, 1983). These researchers found that advanced warning and the opportunity to experience some anticipatory grief before the death can help facilitate the bereavement process after the death. Other researchers believe that anticipatory grief is impossible (Parkes & Weiss, 1983; Silverman, 1974).

Rando (1986) believes the term is a misnomer.

Anticipatory grief is the phenomenon encompassing the processes of mourning, coping, interaction, planning, and psychosocial reorganization that are stimulated and begun in part in response to the awareness of the impending loss of a loved one (death) and the recognition of associated losses in the past, present, and future. . . . The truly therapeutic experience of anticipatory grief mandates a delicate balance among the mutually conflicting demands of simultaneously holding onto, letting go of, and drawing closer to the dying patient.

Anticipatory grief is stimulated by the reality of life situations families find themselves in. For example, parent(s) whose child is in ICU, NICU or hospice or has a debilitating disease will experience anticipatory grief. There is an alteration in relationships, a change in life-style, and a very real threat to changes in their hopes and dreams for the future with their loved one. Grief responses will occur for what has already been lost, as well as for those losses that occur daily as a result of progressive debilitation, increasing dependency, uncertainties of what the future might bring, loss of control, and so on.

An important task for families facing the dying and ultimate death of their loved one is to balance the physical and emotional demands of caring for their child, coping with the stress this brings, and preventing detachment from the child before death.

The family who has a terminally ill member has several tasks (Futterman, 1972). The family needs to cope with the terminal illness, but also it needs to take care of itself. Cohen and Cohen (1981) identified family coping tasks:

- Denying versus accepting the illness
- Establishing relationships with caregivers
- Meeting the needs of the dying person
- Regulating affect
- Negotiating extrafamilial relationships
- Coping with the after-death phase

During the illness and/or hospitalization the family begins to experience how the present illness foreshadows the absence of their loved one in the future (Rando, 1986a). Going home and finding the child's room empty, attending social functions without the loved one, and dining at a table with an empty chair all portray to the family glimpses of what their life will be like without their child.

In anticipatory grief there should be continued involvement of family members with their loved one. Parents still need to direct their attention, energy, and care-taking activities toward the dying child. Parents, as well as other family members and friends, fluctuate between hope for a miracle and a concrete awareness of the reality of their impending loss. They may not, in some sense, believe that their child will die, but find themselves thinking about what kind of monument they would like, how they will act at the funeral, or what clothes they will wear. The family should be involved in maximizing the quality of their loved one's life, take time to resolve any interpersonal issues (unfinished business), and help their child in the actual dying process. Many families will feel closer to their loved one at the time of his or her death than ever before (Weiss, 1988).

There should not be detachment of the family to their loved one before the death. Premature detachment is an issue of complicated anticipatory grieving. Families may feel that "getting over" the pain of loss will be made much easier if they take a step backward, away from their loved one. This can leave the dying family member feeling alone and isolated and very aware of his or her own mortality.

Professionals can help families by involving them in their loved one's care, providing privacy for resolving issues of unfinished business, answering questions, and preparing them for the inevitability of the dying experience.

SUDDEN VERSUS ANTICIPATED LOSS

The sudden and unexpected death of a child is very difficult for parents. There is not time to anticipate the loss. Because most children's deaths are sudden and unexpected, such as in the case of pregnancy loss, SIDS, or accidents, parents may experience a delayed grief response. Immediately they are asked to make decisions regarding organ donation, autopsy, and funeral arrangement—matters they might never before have thought of in relation to their family. The physical and emotional trauma felt by families in this instance may have a debilitating effect, which may prolong their grief (Miles & Perry, 1985; Parkes & Weiss, 1983; Rando, 1984; Raphael, 1984; Sanders, 1989).

Rando (1986a) identified the following characteristics of the death that will influence the parents' grief response:

- The situation surrounding the death
- The timeliness of the death
- The parent's perception of the preventability of the death
- Whether the death was sudden, unexpected, or anticipated
- The length of illness before death
- The amount of the parent's anticipatory grief and involvement with the child

Research varies in opinions regarding the grief responses of families when the death is anticipated versus when it is sudden and unexpected. Some researchers have found no correlation with anticipating of loss and the subsequent grief response (Schwab, Chalmers, Conroy, Farris, & Markush, 1975). Others have determined a definite qualitative difference between the types of losses (Rando, 1983; Sanders, 1982-1983). Families who experienced chronic, long-term illness and sudden deaths had more difficult adjustments to their loss than those families whose loss was anticipated over a shorter time. Unanticipated bereavement can lead to "an inability to believe that anything can work out well" and so to a kind of low-level clinical depression in people who before their loss were quite different. (Weiss, 1988).

Follow-up after a loss is important for determining families' well-being and needs for referral or support.

The Grief of Parents

Though the process of mourning for all bereaved people has similarities, parents have unique issues to deal with in the death of a child. The reality of the loss violates one of the basic laws of nature: parents should precede their children in death. Another issue parents must face is how to continue to function in the role of parent. Coping with one's grief and parenting surviving children can be a most difficult task for bereaved parents. However, many parents have stated it has been their surviving children who have pulled them through (Scrimshaw & March, 1984). For parents who are parents without a child, the physical and emotional feelings of grief, wanting and needing to be a parent, and lack of support from society can make them feel isolated and alone (Knapp & Peppers, 1980; Limbo & Wheeler, 1986).

Rando (1986a) describes a number of reactions of bereaved parents:

The avoidance phase: Parents may be confused and dazed, unable to comprehend what has happened. There is a desire to avoid the terrible acknowledgement that their child is dead.

The confrontation phase: This is a time of intense emotions, where the perception of the loss is the most acute. It is a time defined as "angry sadness." Extreme emotions are felt: fear and anxiety, anger, guilt, separation and longing, depression, and obsession. During this phase, parents search for meaning, experience grief attacks, identify with the deceased child, neglect other relationships, and experience physiologic manifestations. Parents may experience aching arms, wake in the night to a child crying, feel their dead child needs them, and have disturbing dreams that reveal their feelings of vulnerability, loss, and uncertainty (Knapp & Peppers, 1980; Miles, 1985).

The reestablishment phase: The physical, emotional, and social responses to grief gradually decline as the parent begins to reenter and become involved in everyday life.

CHRONIC SORROW

The death of a child is a devastating event for parents. However, a child with special problems such as mental retardation, a genetic disorder, or chronic illness can be, for some families, just as devastating (Drotar, 1975; Fraley, 1981; Hayes and Knox, 1984; Johnson, 1979; and Zamerowski, 1982.

Drotar (1975), Hayes and Knox (1984), and Zamerowski (1982) used crisis and stress theory to describe the grief that parents experience after learning that their child is impaired either at birth or as the child grows and develops. Progress through these stages is a series of ups and downs with many stages coexisting. Their work also was based on the prior works of Bowlby (1980) and Kübler-Ross (1983).

Shock is the beginning reaction to personal and family crisis. Families are usually stunned. They may experience a feeling of numbness during which they are aware of, but do not acknowledge, the loss. This stage may be characterized by "going through the motions" of life; flat, little, or no affect; inappropriate responses to the situation; or total immobilization — inability to deal with the situation.

In actuality, parents may experience periodic sorrow triggered by stressor events such as the initial diagnosis; hospitalizations; developmental delays; younger sibling surpassing the child developmentally; decision-making about child placement outside the home; the child having behavioral, emotional, or health problems; starting school; puberty; and the child's twenty-first birthday (Wikler, 1981). All of these events that may trigger chronic sorrow are discrepancy between the reality of the child's abilities and the parents expectation of "normal" — what they hope their child could or should achieve (Wikler, 1981).

Fraley's (1981) study of mothers and fathers identified feelings of helplessness, frustration, and depression when their child experienced events considered to be situationally stressful.

The parents also expressed a greater degree of feelings of helplessness, frustration, sadness, and fear for their child's future when their child experienced developmental milestones in adolescence and adulthood.

Chronic sorrow is a natural response of families when a child is disabled, has a chronic illness, or is physically or mentally handicapped (Fraley, 1981). Parents' reactions, responses, and adaptations to their child who has a disability, handicap, or chronic or terminal illness depend on (1) how they deal with crises in their lives, (2) their philosophic view of life, and (3) how they view their abilities to cope (Heisler, 1972). Other factors to consider follow (Zamerowski, 1982):

- Nature, severity, and prognosis of the handicap
- Previous parental coping mechanisms
- Available support systems
- Familiarity with support systems
- Previously held attitudes
- Desire for pregnancy and parenting
- Birth order of the child
- Marital status
- Socioeconomic level
- Ethnicity
- Religion
- Family dynamics
- The professional's attitude

In most instances, fathers do not have the opportunity to be as involved with parenting a child with special problems; they may be more focused on financial concerns (Price-Bonham & Addison, 1978). The father's most powerful influence on the child may be his support of the mother in her ability to cope and her childcare attitudes and behaviors (Bristol & Gallagher, 1986). Meyer (1986) identified that it may be the father who sets the pattern for the child's acceptance or rejection in the family. Fathers appear to have a more steady approach to acceptance and coping with their child's special problem than mothers. Mothers, on the other hand, report significantly poorer emotional and physical health; more symptoms of depression, moodiness, and fatigue; lower self-esteem; and more restrictions on their personal development.

In Fraley's (1990) study, mothers reported a higher frequency for both chronic sorrow and feelings of being burdened, overwhelmed, embarrassed or self-conscious in public, feeling very old, fearing life in 20 to 30 years, feeling concerned about what other people are saying about them, and resenting other people whose children are not handicapped.

Nurses supporting families whose child has special problems should recognize the differences in coping between mothers and fathers. Mothers need opportunities to express their feelings of sadness, weakness, and joys, as well as to receive praise, recognition, and feedback on their abilities to cope.

Both mothers and fathers need to be listened to for accurate perceptions of their needs and coping strategies. This will enable the healthcare professional to develop individualized approaches, strategies, and program planning that meets the family's needs, not just one individual's.

Referrals to support groups, state and national organizations, respite care, and individual and family counseling can be beneficial in meeting these families' needs.

Grief and the Marital Relationship

After a death of a significant person, the mourner is a different person. Thus in the parental relationship the partners are not the same people they were. Schiff (1977) states in her book *The Bereaved Parent* that it is difficult to throw a lifeline to your partner when you yourself are drowning. Parents need to recognize that grief will impact on their relationship. Parents who have usually reacted in one way during a crisis will have a tendency to respond in a similar fashion when a loss occurs (Knapp & Peppers, 1980; Limbo & Wheeler, 1986). Typically, women are allowed to grieve openly, share their feelings more readily, and expect everyone to feel the same way they do. Men, on the other hand, get a very clear message from society. Be strong, take care of your partner and family, and keep your feelings to yourself.

A couple's sexual relationship may be tremendously affected with the loss of a baby or child. Some couples may feel this is one way or the only way to offer comfort and support to each other. Others may feel they should not have any enjoyment in life. Still others may be obsessed to become pregnant again or that sex brings about pregnancy and they couldn't handle a pregnancy at this time.

It is important for parents to be able to communicate with each other in even the most intimate of matters in their relationship. They must let each other know what they are feeling and what they need and expect from each other. Parents must be helped not to blame each other about the death, learn how to express their anger in positive ways, and recognize they will grieve at different times in different ways.

Sibling Grief

Children's responses to loss and their subsequent grief vary with their age, experiences with prior losses, relationship with the deceased, personality, perceptions surrounding the loss, the particular meaning the loss has to them, and, most important, their family's response to the loss (see box on p. 150).

Although children may not understand the concept of death because of their age, they do develop perceptions as to what the loss means to them. Parents should consider this concept in making the decision to tell their surviving children about the loss of the sibling. Parents may feel their children are too young to understand what death means. Parents need help in realizing that children can perceive the differences in their parents' behavior. So even though

---

Children's Responses to Death

Birth to 2 years

Lacks conception of death
Can experience a sense of loss and grief
These experiences lay a foundation for developing a conception of loss and grief

2 to 5 years

Denies death as a normal process
Sees death as reversible
Has unlimited faith in his or her ability to make things happen
May react with anger of displaced anger
Gives responses that may differ little from those of his or her parents

5 to 8 years

Sees death as final; does not see it will happen to him or her
Sees death as scary
Seeks to isolate what causes death and what death means
Feels the vulnerability that accompanies death
May take on more "adult-like" caregiver roles in the family or become "self-reliant"

8 to 12 years

Views death as final and inevitable
May be unable to accept the finality of the loss
Realizes the possibilities of his or her own death; may develop fears of own mortality
Develops affective responses to death, as well as the defenses to handle his or her
    feelings (i.e., denial, avoidance, displacement, and reaction formation)
May create stories or jokes about death to hide fears
Experiences egocentric and magical thinking
Is aware of what this death will mean for his or her future

Adolescents

Understanding surrounding death resembles that of adulthood
Must face personal implications of death
Demonstrates risk-taking behaviors
Seriously seeks the meaning of life
More anxious about the future

Note: Modified from *The Anatomy of Bereavement* by B. Raphael, 1984, London: Hutchinson; and from *How Do We Tell the Children? Helping Children Understand and Cope When Someone Dies* by D. Schaefer and C. Lyons, 1986, New York: Newmarket.

---

parents verbally hide the loss from them, they cannot hide their grief. They may be able to hide their tears, but they cannot hide their emotions at having to cope with life, dealing with their surviving children and their inability to continue with their old patterns of living. Parents who keep their grief from their children may leave the false impression that "the loss of a child in our family really doesn't matter."

Visible Responses of Children to Death

Sadness	Bed wetting
Crying	Nightmares
Loss of appetite	Upsurge of aggressiveness
Withdrawn behaviors	Stuttering
Irritability	Running away
Health problems	Difficulty in school performance
Talking about the deceased	Death phobias
Depression	Sudden outbursts of anger
Separation anxiety	Acting out
Anxiety attacks	Suicide attempts

Note: Modified from *The Seasons of Grief: Helping your Children Grow through Loss* by D.A. Gaffney, 1988, New York: American Library; from *On Children and Death* by E. Kübler-Ross, 1983, New York: Macmillan; and from *Unspoken Grief: Coping with Childhood Sibling Loss* by H. Rosen, 1986, Lexington, MA: Lexington Books.

Grief brings about crisis and change. Until the family system evolves into its "new normal" (i.e., old family rituals are revived or new patterns of family living are developed), the children will be sensitive to the changes in the family system (see box above).

Rosen (1984-1985, 1986) studied 159 children in a 17-state area. Of those who were personally interviewed, the majority (76%) stated they had been unable to share their feelings with anyone at the time and for a long time afterward. This result did not correlate with the age, their sibling's age, social class, family size, or place in the family. Other responses of note were (1) a feeling of responsibility to comfort one or both parents, and (2) a feeling of responsibility to make up to the parents for the loss they had experienced.

Children at any age may feel responsible for the death. Their capacity of "magical thinking" can make them believe their thoughts, feelings, or behaviors toward their loved one might have caused the death. Children may feel guilty for being alive, being well, having wished their sibling dead at some time, or feeling "special" because of their sick sibling (Rosen, 1984-1985). Parents should anticipate these feelings, whether they are verbalized or not. When appropriate, children should be reassured that nothing they said, felt, or did caused the death.

Libby's son, aged 3, asked his mother if he killed his baby sister, who was stillborn. He remembered that he had bumped his mother's abdomen one time when she was pregnant.

In a situation where a sibling was responsible for the death of a sibling, referral for family therapy is very appropriate. Coping with the loss of a child is difficult under the best of circumstances. It would be very easy for the members of the family to develop complicated mourning because of feelings of guilt, blame, and anger directed at the surviving child or themselves.

Once children realize death is irreversible and permanent, they may wonder if their parents may die. The underlying question to this thought is, "Who will take care of me?" This question must be answered honestly by the parents. Parents need to consider who would provide for their children should they not be able to do so and should tell their children who would care for them. Older children may contemplate their own mortality as well.

As children grow older, they will have more experiences with loss and grief. As their cognitive thought evolves from the concrete to the abstract, their questions about surrounding death, grief, and the meaning of life will become more complex. For example:

Eric is the surviving twin whose brother was stillborn. At age 5, he asked for the first time, "Was I born alone?" At age 7, while riding in an airplane in a cloud bank, he asked his next questions: "Do you think Scott looks like me? What do you think he likes to do in heaven? Do you think he likes to play the same things that I like?"

Parents are usually taken by surprise when questions are asked. The questions usually come at a time when the parent least expects them and feels the least prepared to answer.

Parents should explain death in concrete terms rather than the abstract. Schaefer and Lyons (1986) encourage parents to use words like "dead," "stopped working," and "wore out" when explaining death to children. Children have a hard time in deciphering parents' messages about death when words like "passed away," "lost," or "went to sleep" are used.

Involving children at the time of loss, including them in funeral planning, and having them attend the funeral are issues many parents struggle with. Asking a child at any age whether he or she wants to be present, be involved, or attend the funeral takes the burden of decision making off the parents' shoulders. The children's participation in these activities can be beneficial to the family over time. It allows the family to come from the same frame of reference in explaining the death, funeral, and burial. The child's experience with death and funeral activities and the child's understanding of death may affect how the child reacts at funeral activities and his or her subsequent grief response (Gaffney, 1988). There are reports that children who do not attend or participate in funeral activities have a more difficult time accepting the death (Bowlby, 1980; Furman, 1974; Grollman, 1967). There is general agreement that children should not be forced to attend the funeral (Gardener, 1983; Wessel, 1976).

Children do not grieve on the same timetable as their parents. Children who can talk about their experiences and express their feelings usually do better after a loss (Black & Urbanowicz, 1987). The greatest predictor of how well the children will do after a loss is the mental state of the mother (Elizur & Kauffman, 1982).

A Model for Providing Care

Swanson-Kauffman (1986) offers a model of caring for women and their families experiencing miscarriage. This model is easily adapted for families who have experienced the loss of a child at any age. Bereaved families need care, support, and understanding from the professionals when a loss is anticipated, at the time of death, and after. The following are the concepts in her caring model:

Being with: The healthcare professional should help and accept the family's expression of feelings, emotions, and experiences before, during, and after the loss of their child. This gives the professional the opportunity to understand their grief and their perceptions of the experience and to lay the foundation for a one-to-one helping relationship that meets the family at the point of their need.

Knowing: In sharing the experience of loss and grief with a family, the healthcare professional conveys to the family that he or she, on a personal level, understands the family's grief and many dimensions of what they have lost in the death of their child. Families need to feel that on both a verbal and a nonverbal level the people caring for them are human beings who understand their pain.

Doing for: Bereaved families need care in concrete ways—providing a quiet, private area, offering food and beverages, caring for their loved one in life or death with respect and dignity, anticipating their physical comfort needs, and bending rules when necessary.

Enabling: The death of a loved one places the family in crisis. Family members have a difficult time making decisions, knowing what they can and cannot ask for, and understanding how the healthcare system works. The professional, in offering information, anticipatory guidance, and choices, enables the family. Enabling (1) helps families to feel more in control of their situation and experience an increase in their self-esteem and (2) creates an environment where the family feels they can participate in rather than react to.

Maintaining belief: Grief leaves families feeling overwhelmed, inadequate, and unprepared and that they won't be able to "make it." It is important for the healthcare professional to offer support by sharing with the family his or her observation of the family's strength, courage, and ability to handle their grief and situations they may encounter. The professional is not offering false hope, but rather a belief in the ability of the family's human spirit.

Counseling Principles and Techniques

Worden (1991) offers ten counseling principles and procedures to help people during their grief.

1. Help the survivor to identify and express feelings. The feelings of anger, guilt, and sadness seem overwhelming to the bereaved. The expression of these feelings may be difficult for the caregiver providing support but is necessary for positive grief reorganization.

2. Assist the survivor in living without the deceased. Adjusting to life without the loved one is painful and difficult. Survivors need information

on adequate nutrition, exercise, fluid intake, and rest in making this adjustment.

3. Facilitate emotional withdrawal from the deceased. Survivors must make many decisions after the loss of a loved one (e.g., what to do with their room and clothes; what headstone to select; when to return to work and to social activities).

4. Provide time to grieve. Healthcare professionals are responsible for creating a physical and emotional environment where the bereaved can feel comfortable in expressing their emotions. It is difficult for healthcare professionals to be at the side of survivors who have strong outbursts of emotions, such as anger, overwhelming crying, or screaming in the pain of loss, or no response at all. The professional must accept the responses for what they are and not interfere with the overt expressions of grief. The use of touch, handing of tissues, defensiveness in the face of anger, and presuming no response means no grief prevents the expression of emotion in the experience of grief. The professional understands that grief takes time to heal. For some it may be several months, and for others it may be several years. Parents will say, "You never get over it; you just learn to live with the fact that your child has died."

5. Interpret "normal behavior." The public is vastly underinformed about grief and grief process. It is the responsibility of the professional to provide information, both verbal and written, on grief and grief process to survivors, their family, and friends. As the professional listens to the content of grief as it is related by the survivor, it is important to point out the process of grief. This enables the survivor to understand his or her own processes, as well as lays the groundwork for understanding when referral for therapy is necessary.

6. Allow for individual differences. No one grieves in the same way at the same time in a family system. And yet, the expectation is that everyone should. Grief responses are based on age, experiences with prior losses, relationship with the deceased, personality, perceptions surrounding the loss, the particular meaning the loss has to them, and, most important, other family members' responses to the loss.

7. Provide continuing support. Continuing support for the bereaved should be offered through follow-up after discharge. In no instance should bereaved parents be left without follow-up support services (Rando, 1986b). These services can be provided through telephone follow-up from a professional at various intervals for as long as a year after a loss. Referral to a parent or sibling support group is not adequate continuing support. Only about 10% of families who are referred to a support group will attend (Limbo & Wheeler, 1989).

8. Examine defenses and coping styles. In the case of a child's death, Worden recommends additional understanding and intervention modification that go beyond the ten principles.

9. Viewing the body. Making the decision to see their loved one who has

died is sometimes difficult for family members. They may not be sure what death is really like, how their child will look, if they will be able to emotionally stay in control and if they can get through it (Miles & Perry, 1985).

10. Sensitive interventions by healthcare professionals. Professionals can help the family in making decisions and planning for the funeral by providing information on why they might want to make a particular decision, offering anticipatory guidance, being physically supportive with their presence, and sharing what other families have done in a similar situation.

Preparing the family before viewing for how their child will look and feel gives the family the opportunity to emotionally ready themselves. This will help them feel a little more in control of the situation. Some families may want to hold or cradle their loved one. This should be offered as an option, as well.

Providing the family with special memories of their child, such as pictures, lock of hair, footprints, handprints, current weight and height, and articles used in caring for their child can be helpful in the days that follow (Limbo & Wheeler, 1986).

Many families appreciate the involvement of a member from pastoral care or their clergy to be with them during or after a loss. The spiritual support that a member of the clergy can provide can be very comforting. The family may want their loved one baptized, a blessing or prayer offered, or just the presence of the clergy.

A multitude of decisions must be made: What funeral home to use? How involved do they want to be during the funeral preparations (i.e., dressing, bathing)? Special mementos in the casket? What clothing should be worn? Type of casket? Sturdiness of the vault? Cremation or burial? Flowers? Where the services should be held? What the services should entail? Who will perform the services? Who should be notified of the death? Writing the obituary? Where the burial will be? Pallbearers? Music? Special memories they would like to make? . . . the list goes on and on. For the bereaved, making it through the funeral takes all the energy and strength they can gather (Sanders, 1989).

Information about the death should be handled carefully. When a loved one dies, the perception of the family is that everyone should be aware of their loss and be sensitive to their needs. Marking charts and patients' rooms and sending memos to other professionals involved with the family help to ensure that no one responds to the family in an insensitive manner.

Maintaining confidentiality of situations or issues surrounding the loss demonstrates respect for the deceased and the family. Choosing words carefully, such as "died by suicide" rather than "committed suicide," "baby" versus "fetus," and "miscarriage" versus "spontaneous abortion" and using the deceased's name when talking with the family communicate an understanding of the family's feelings. The use of eye contact, not giving false assurances, and offering honest appraisals of situations help in the development of a trusting relationship with the family.

The cause of death should be clarified. At the time of the loss, the family may not have fully comprehended the information given to them by the physician. Usually once the words "I'm sorry, but your child is dead" are spoken, little else is heard. Sending an autopsy report in the mail is a cold, impersonal way for healthcare personnel to end a relationship with the family. A grief conference is an excellent way to demonstrate to the parents and family that they are cared about after their loved one has died (Limbo, Wheeler, & Gensch, 1988).

A grief conference is held 4 to 6 weeks after the loss of the child or when the autopsy report has been received by the physician. The family does not receive a copy of the autopsy through the mail, but at the grief conference. The conference is an opportunity for the parents to ask questions, to receive information about the death of their child from those who cared for him or her at the time, as well as to review the events surrounding the time of the loss. The conference also provides an opportunity for the professionals to assess how the family is doing and to convey their feelings of empathy to the family. The family can decide on who they would like to attend the conference with them, that is, other family members, physicians involved with the child's care, nurses, and anyone the family deems important.

Parents appreciate being remembered by their healthcare providers. Follow-up in the form of a sympathy card, inclusion in the hospital's monthly memorial services, invitation to join a support group, and follow-up phone calls assure the family that neither their child nor they have been forgotten.

Complicated Versus Uncomplicated Bereavement

Grief varies in its intensity, length, and manifestation in individuals and families. It has been speculated that about 30% of all major losses may require professional help (Raphael, 1984). These particular individuals and their families can be at risk for physical and mental health problems.

The healthcare professional caring for the bereaved should observe for the content of their grief, as well as their process. The course of grief can be rocky and fraught with pitfalls. The bereaved can easily become "stuck" or fixated in their grief. The expressions of anger, guilt, and self-blame that persist over time, long past the predominance, the searching, and yearning phase of grief, is fairly easy to distinguish. Expressions of suicidal thoughts are not unusual; however, if one of the bereaved has a plan, immediate referral is required. Sometimes the bereaved have a difficult time in "letting go" of their loved one. This prolongs their grief and delays their ability to return to living life without their child and to experience much satisfaction in life. These individuals or families may become overinvolved in bereavement groups or "causes," which keep them from having balance in their or their family's lives. "When the emotions of grief are unduly inhibited, blocked, or suppressed or when the normal process is blocked, partial, or absent then the normal bereavement response may not occur" (Raphael, 1984).

In a study of families 7 to 9 years after the loss of a child through cancer, McClowry, Davies, May, Kulenkamp, and Martinson (1987) found that families integrated their loss in one of three distinct ways:

1. Getting over it: Their child's death was accepted matter-of-factly, as either God's will or death is something we all have to face — it happens. These individuals felt the death did not have any effect on their current life.
2. Filling the emptiness: Individuals and families reported doing things to keep busy or to fill the emptiness. They became involved in support groups or church and felt they needed to have some good come from the experience. Eventually they moved on and redirected their lives once the emptiness was filled. Others became more involved with work, a few increased their food or alcohol intake, and some became pregnant or adopted other children.
3. Keeping the connection: These individuals or families described an ongoing sense of loss. They did not want to forget. Their experiences of loss and grief became integrated into their lives over time as the pain of grief lessened and they began to focus their energy on other things.

When to Refer

Sometimes the bereaved need more help than support of family and friends, a support group, or even grief counseling. What they may need is a referral for therapy and perhaps medication (see box on p. 158).

When the need for referral has been identified, the professional should not hesitate. In most instances the individual or family has considered seeking professional help. Usually they are tired of feeling the same way day after day and are grateful someone was really listening and understood their feelings. Some may think the professional believes they are "crazy." It is important for the professional's response to be based on his or her knowledge of grief and the grief process. This helps the bereaved understand the "why" behind the referral.

In making the referral, the professional may want to consider the therapist's area of expertise, knowledge of bereavement, type of therapies used, and sensitivity to loss during pregnancy or shortly after.

A courtesy call should be made to the professional to whom the nurse has referred the individual or family. During the call, the nurse may want to tell the professional what his or her role has been with the family. The professional may or may not want to know the nurse's perceptions of the individual or family who has been referred.

Unfortunately, some individuals or families will not agree or want to be referred for further help. This can be a difficult situation for the professional working with them. It is the individual or family's responsibility to make the phone call to the therapist. Should they choose not to make that call, the professional is not responsible for their actions. However, in any further contact with the family, the professional should not engage in discussion regarding the issues for which the referral was originally made. For example, "I don't feel comfortable in discussing your in-laws and your frustrations with them. I believe you need further help in this area, which I am not qualified to give."

Reasons for Referral

- Continuing expressions of anger, guilt, or self-blame, directed at self, partner, surviving children, physician, hospital, grandparents, extended family, friends, or person(s) held accountable for the death
- Unresolved issues with family members
- Increased use of alcohol or drugs
- Overinvolvement in work, home, church, school, family, or friends by either partner or children
- Prolonged lack of sexual activity
- Overprotection of surviving children
- Parental roles taken on by surviving children
- Incongruency between thoughts/feelings and behavior, which leaves the professional confused
- Feelings, tone of voice, and what will be spoken by the bereaved predictable by the professional
- Physical illness over a long period with no clear diagnosis
- Inability to express grief
- Expression of suicidal thoughts with a plan
- Diagnosable mental illness

Note. From *Resolve Through Sharing Parent Support Group Guide* by R.K. Limbo and S.R. Wheeler, 1989, LaCrosse, WI: Lutheran Hospital; from "Symptomatology and Management of Acute Grief" by E. Lindemann, 1944, *American Journal of Psychiatry, 101,* pp. 141-148; from *Grief, Dying and Death* by T.A. Rando, 1984, Champaign, IL: Research Press; from *Parental Loss of a Child* by T.A. Rando (Ed.), 1986, Champaign, IL: Research Press; from *Unspoken Grief: Coping with Childhood Sibling Loss* by H. Rosen, 1986, Lexington, MA: Lexington Books; and from *Grief the Mourning After: Dealing With Adult Bereavement* by C. M. Sanders, 1989, New York: Wiley Interscience.

• • •

This chapter has provided the mental health professional with an overview of grief process, factors influencing grief when a child dies, and strategies in caring for the bereaved.

REFERENCES

Black, D., & Urbanowicz, M.A. (1987). Family intervention with bereaved children. *Journal of Child Psychology and Psychiatry, 28*(3), 467-476.

Bowlby, J. (1980). *Loss* (Vol. 3). New York: Basic Books.

Brill, N. (1990). *Working with people: The helping process* (4th ed.). New York: Longman.

Bristol, M., & Gallagher, J. (1986). Research on fathers of young handicapped children. In J. Gallagher and P. Vietze (Eds.), *Families of handicapped persons* (pp. 81-100). Baltimore: Paul H. Brookes.

Cohen, M.S., & Cohen, E.K. (1981). Behavioral family systems interventions in terminal care. In H.J. Sebel (Ed.), *Behavior therapy in terminal care: A humanistic approach.* Cambridge, MA: Ballinger.

Davidson, G.W. (1984). *Understanding mourning.* Minneapolis: Ausburg.

Deutsch, H. (1937). The absence of grief. *Psychoanalytic Quarterly, 6,* 12-22.

Drotar, B. (1975). The adaptation of parents to the birth of an infant with a congenital malformation: A hypothetical model. *Pediatrics, 56,* 7109-7117.

Elizur, E., & Kauffman, M. (1982). Factors influencing the severity of childhood bereavement reactions. *American Journal of Orthopsychiatry, 53,* 668-676.

Fraley, A.M. (1981). *Chronic sorrow in parents of disabled children.* Unpublished master's thesis. Montana State University, Bozeman, MT.

Fraley, A.M. (1986). Chronic sorrow in parents of premature children. *Children's Health Care, 15*(2), 114-118.

Freud, S. (1957). Mourning and melancholia. In E. Strachy (Ed.), *Complete Works of Sigmund Freud* (Vol. 14). London: Hogarth Press. (Original work published in 1917).

Fulton, R., & Fulton, J. (1971). Anticipatory grief. *Omega, 2,* 91-100.

Fulton, R., & Gottesman, D.J. (1980). Anticipatory grief: A psychosocial concept reconsidered. *British Journal of Psychiatry, 137,* 45-54.

Furman, E. (1974). A child's parent dies: Studies in childhood bereavement. New Haven, CT: Yale University.

Futterman, E.H., Hoffman, I., & Sabshin, M. (1972). *Parental anticipatory mourning.* New York: Columbia University.

Gaffney, D.A. (1988). *The seasons of grief: Helping your children grow through loss.* New York: New American Library.

Gardener, R.A. (1983). Children's reactions to parental death. In J.E. Schowalter, P.R. Patterson, M. Tallmer, A.H. Kutscher, S.V. Gullow, and D. Peretz (Eds.). *The child and death.* New York: Columbia University.

Grollman, E. (1967). *Explaining death to children.* Boston: Beacon.

Hayes, V.E., & Knox, J.E. (Eds). (1984). The expression of stress in parents of children hospitalized with long-term disability. *Journal of Advanced Nursing, 9,* 333-341.

Heisler, V. (1972). *Handicapped child in family: guide for parents.* New York: Grune & Stratton.

Hymovich, D.P. (1981). Assessing the impact of chronic childhood illness on the family and parent coping. *Image: Journal of Nursing Scholarship, 1313,* 71-74.

Johnson, S.H. (1979). *High-risk parenting: Nursing assessment and strategies for the family at-risk* (1st ed.). Philadelphia: J.B. Lippincott.

Kazak, A., & Marvin, R. (1984). Differences, difficulties and adaptation: Stress and social networks in families with a handicapped child. *Family Relations, 36,* 67-77.

Klaus, M., & Kennell, J. (1982). *Parent-child bonding* (2nd ed.), St. Louis: Mosby–Year Book.

Knapp, R., & Peppers, L. (1980). *Motherhood and mourning.* New York: Praeger.

Kowalski, K. (1986). *Infant death: Parental grief* (Cassette Recording). Baltimore: American Journal of Maternal Child Nursing. (National Convention).

Kübler-Ross, E. (1983). *On children and death.* New York: Macmillan.

Lawson, B. (1977). Chronic illness in the school-aged child: Effects on the total family. *American Journal of Maternal Child Nursing, 2*(1), 49-56.

Limbo, R.K., & Wheeler, S.R. (1986). When a baby dies: A handbook for healing and helping. LaCrosse, WI: Lutheran Hospital.

Limbo, R.K., & Wheeler, S.R. (1989). *Resolve through sharing: Parent support group guide.* LaCrosse, WI: Lutheran Hospital.

Limbo, R.K., Wheeler, S.R., & Gensch, B. (1988). Results of sharing counselor manner. *Resolve Through Sharing.* LaCrosse, WI: Lutheran Hospital.

Lindemann, E. (1944). Symptomatology and management of acute grief. *American Journal of Psychiatry, 101,* 141-148.

McClowry, S.G., Davies, E.B., May, K.A., Kulenkamp, E.J., & Martinson, I.M. (1987).

The empty space phenomenon: The process of grief in the bereaved family. *Death Studies, II,* 361-374.

Meyer, D. (1986). Fathers of handicapped children. In R. Fewell and P. Vadasy (Eds.), *Family of handicapped children* (pp. 35-73). Austin, TX: PRO-ED.

Miles, M.S. (1985). Emotional symptoms and physical health in bereaved parents. *Nursing Research, 34*(2), 76-81.

Miles, M.S., & Perry, K. (1985). Parental responses to sudden accidental death of a child. *Critical Care Quarterly, 8*(1), 73-84.

Parkes, C.M. (1987). Bereavement as a psychosocial transition: Processes of adaptation and change. *Journal of Social Issues, 44*(3), 53-65.

Parkes, C.M., & Weiss, R.S. (1983). Recovery from bereavement. New York: Basic Books.

Price-Bonham, S., & Addison, S. (1978). Families and mentally retarded children: Emphasis on the father. *The Family Coordination, 27,* 221-230.

Rando, T.A. (1983). Investigation of grief and adaptation in parents whose children have died from cancer. *Journal of Pediatric Oncology, 8,* 3-20.

Rando, T.A. (1984). *Grief, dying and death.* Champaign, IL: Research Press.

Rando, T.A. (Ed.). (1986a). *Parental loss of a child.* Champaign, IL: Research Press.

Rando, T.A. (1986b). A comprehensive analysis of anticipatory grief: Perspectives, processes, promises, and problems. In Rando, T.A. (Ed.), *Loss and anticipatory grief.* Lexington, MA: Lexington Books.

Raphael, B. (1984). *The anatomy of bereavement.* London: Hutchinson.

Rosen, H. (1984-1985). Prohibitions against mourning in childhood sibling loss. *Omega, 15*(4), 307-317.

Rosen, H. (1986). *Unspoken grief: Coping with childhood sibling loss.* Lexington, MA: Lexington Books.

Sanders, C.M. (1982-1983). Effects of sudden vs. chronic illness death on bereavement outcome. *Omega, 13*(3), 227-266.

Sanders, C.M. (1989). *Grief the mourning after: Dealing with adult bereavement.* New York: Wiley Interscience.

Schaefer, D., & Lyons, C. (1986). *How do we tell the children? Helping children understand and cope when someone dies.* New York: Newmarket.

Schiff, H.S. (1977). *The bereaved parent.* New York: Crown.

Schwab, J.J., Chalmers, J.M., Conroy, S.J., Farris, S.J., & Markush, R.E. (1975). Studies on grief: A preliminary report. In B. Schoenberg, I. Berger, A. Kutscher, D. Peretz, and A.C. Carr (Eds.), *Bereavement: Its psychosocial aspects.* New York: Columbia University.

Schilling, R., Kirkham, M., Snow, W., & Schinke, S. (1986). Single mothers with handicapped children: Different from their married counterparts? *Family Relations, 35,* 69-77.

Scrimshaw, S.C.M., & March, D.M.S. (1984). I had a baby sister but she only lasted a day. *Journal of the American Medical Association, 25*(16), 732-733.

Siegel, K., & Weinstein, L. (1983). Anticipatory grief reconsidered. *Journal of Psychosocial Oncology, 1,* 61-73.

Silverman, P. (1974). Anticipatory grief from the perspective of widowhood. In B. Schoenberg, A. Carr, A. Kutcher, D. Peretz, and I. Goldberg (Eds.), *Anticipatory grief* (pp. 320-330). New York: Columbia University Press.

Sugar, M. (1968). Normal adolescent mourning. *American Journal of Psychotherapy, 22,* 258-269.

Swanson-Kauffman, K.M. (1986). Caring in the instance of unexpected early pregnancy loss. *Topics in Clinical Nursing, 8*(2), 37-46.

Thomas, R.B. (1987). Family adaptation to a child with a chronic condition. In M.H. Rose and R.B. Thomas (Eds.), *Children with chronic conditions: Nursing in a family and community context* (pp. 29-54). Orlando: Grune & Stratton.

Weiss, Robert S. (1988). Is it possible to prepare for trauma? *Journal of Palliative Care, 4*(1), 70-73.

Wessel, M.A. (1976). *The child and the funeral.* In V.R. Pine (Ed.), Acute grief and the funeral. Springfield, IL: Charles C. Thomas.

Wheeler, S.R., & Pike, M.M. (1990). *Grief resource manual.* Indianapolis: Grief Ltd.

Wikler, L. (1981). Chronic stresses of families of mentally retarded children. *Family Relations, 30,* 281-288.

Wikler, L., Wasow, M., & Hatfield, E. (1981). Chronic sorrow revisited: Parent vs. professional depiction of the adjustment of parents of mentally retarded children. *American Journal of Orthopsychiatry, 51,* 63-70.

Wolfenstein, M. (1966). How is mourning possible. *Psychoanalytic Study of the Child, 21,* 93-123.

Worden, J.W. (1982). *Grief counseling and grief therapy: A handbook for the mental health practitioner.* New York: Springer.

Zamerowski, S.T. (1982). Helping family to cope with handicapped children. *Topics in Clinical Nursing, 1,* 41-56.

Chapter 9

Grief and Loss

J. Sherry O'Grady-Cocozza

This chapter invites the nurse to approach a family's grief and loss experience as a life-cycle event wherein the nurse comes to them as an open-minded student. The family is the exquisite, whole, adequate, and wise teacher. The family's experience presents an opportunity for nurses to gather information, resources, skills, and comfort with the issues surrounding grief and loss and apply them to themselves, their own family of origin, and the families with which they work.

Grief and loss, especially propelled by a death, is one of our most powerful emotions. The acuteness of such a crisis can temporarily limit a family's ready access to their own resolution abilities. The goal of nursing intervention, when used to aid a family through a loss, is to help them once again gain access to inner resources (that is, their healing and problem-solving abilities). It is merely to make way for the "inner guide" housed within that particular family and mobilize their own strengths and systems. The goal is to empower the family itself.

Nurses will succeed if they can approach every family, not as an expert in grief and grieving, but as a curious and compassionate student who invites that family to tell and show about itself. The power is always within the family, not external to the family — as if it were in the nurse. It was in the sixteenth century Galileo noted, "You cannot teach a man anything. You can only help him to find it within himself."

Nurses must have knowledge of the concepts of grief, mourning, and bereavement, as well as family systems and theory so that they are better able to identify the life force and strengths of the family unit.

Martha Rogers (1970), a renowned nursing leader, developed a conceptual model of human beings. She had five assumptions, three of which are noted here. (1) "Man is a unified whole, possessing his own integrity and manifesting characteristics that are more than and different from the sum of his parts," (2) "Man and environment are continuously exchanging matter and energy with one another," and (3) "Pattern and organization identify man and reflect his innovative wholeness."

The framework Rogers developed for nursing embodies the highest respect for the capacity within human beings. How much greater is this capacity within the family of a human being?

Systems theory assumes that all important people in the family unit play a part in the way family members function in relation to each other and in the way symptoms erupt. There is a continuum between what is inside each family member and what lies between them. If a relationship in a family emotional system is changed due to death or some other significant loss, then the entire family system is changed.

The structural concepts of families and the changes within such families further shifted the unit of diagnosis and treatment from a single person to a process between people. Both systems theory and structural theories support the assumption that the family is more than a collection of individuals. It is an emotional unit, based on many influences, such as its structure, patterns, scripts, generational history, culture, race, religion, context, and the relationships. The family unit has a life process of its own that is greater than any one part or individual. Structural theoretic concepts are chiefly attributed to the works of Minuchin (1974) and Haley (1971), whereas systems thinking was greatly advanced by Bowen as it applies to the family.

Such theorists as Bowen (1978), Ackerman (1958), and Toman (1969), applying family theory, have considered the impact of loss, grief, and bereavement on the nuclear and extended family system. Walsh and McGoldrick (1991) recently published a landmark book in which they and their coauthors integrate and advance family theory, death and loss research, and the diversity and value of family reactions to loss. Their focus on cultural influences, legacies, and the history of loss in the family can add much breadth to the reader's thinking.

Life-Cycle Losses

Numerous losses are experienced within the family life cycle. Walsh and McGoldrick (1991) note:

All change in life, including desired change such as marriage or retirement, requires loss. We must give up or alter certain relationships, roles, plans and possibilities in order to have others. . . . All losses require mourning in order to get what we need from the experience or relationship in order to move on.

All types of loss disrupt the family equilibrium. In fact, the equilibrium of the unit is disturbed by either the addition or the loss of a member.

Bowen (1978) notes losses can be physical, as in a member's leaving home for college or marriage. They can be functional, as in a member's becoming incapacitated due to a long-term illness or injury, which can change his or her role and function within the family. Third, losses can be emotional, as in the absence of a light-hearted person.

Boss (1991) wrote of ambiguous loss. Such a loss is that which is never officially documented or ritualized, as occurs with missing persons, runaways, or those with mental disturbances that render the person psychologically absent though physically present.

Loss—whether it be through death, separation, divorce, physical or mental disability, emancipation, job disruption, financial loss, retirement, or unmet dreams and expectations as in infertility—starts a wave of disruption that will either accelerate or retard the family's movement to the next life-cycle stage. The ability to mourn the loss adequately determines the particular outcome.

Jackson (1965) used a few simple definitions when referring to the terms *grief, mourning,* and *bereavement.* These definitions are implied when such terms are used throughout this chapter.

Grief is an intense emotion that floods life when a person's inner security system is shattered by an acute loss.

Mourning is the process by which the powerful emotion is slowly and painfully brought under control.

Bereavement is the period in which mourning takes place, frequently of 1-year duration.

Bowlby (1980) adds to these definitions by stipulating that one who experiences grief expresses it in more or less overt ways. He goes on to add that mourning is always to some degree culturally determined.

Death or threatened death will be the focus of attention in this chapter. Many of the principles can be applied to other significant losses in the family's life cycle. How the family adapts to reestablish its equilibrium after the shock wave of death or significant loss depends on numerous factors. All the factors noted should be viewed with attention to those losses which are "anticipated losses" and those which are "unanticipated." Significant loss is never easy, but some we have been preparing a lifetime to "be with" and deal with, such as the death of an aged parent, the separation and individuation of children, the changes in life-styles (single to married), the retirement from one's life work, and so on. However, when loss occurs that is untimely, premature, or totally unanticipated, it adds a serious component of complexity to the grieving process.

Herz (1980) summarized the following factors as most significantly affecting the degree of disruption created by the loss: (1) the timing of the death or serious illness in the family life cycle, (2) the nature of the loss, (3) the openness of the family system, and (4) the family position of the person dying or who died. Viorst (1986) adds to these factors, which will affect the outcome of mourning, such factors as the individual members' inner strengths and outer supports and their own history of love, loss, and death. Parkes' study (1975) noted all of these factors but also included the nature of the attachment (that is, the strength, security, and ambivalence toward the person deceased). Each family and each member within that family will differ in the time it takes to grieve a loss. The variables just noted not only affect the length of time of the grieving process, but also affect the "smoothness" with which one moves through it.

The nurse, when exploring her or his own family's responses to loss or those of a family with whom she or he is working, needs to stand back and observe the whole picture of what this loss means, the factors that are affecting the response to this loss, and the most helpful resources that will aid the family to come to terms with this loss and proceed to the next stage of family and relational development.

The Family Mourning Process

Because many diverse cultures, creeds, and centuries exist, so too do as many ways to mourn exist. It is essential that we as nurses open our minds and hearts to see and join with families "as they are," rather than teaching them how "they should be." We must drop any preconceived ideas that there is a right and wrong way to mourn. If we have a "should," we must realize that it is "our" should and belongs to our family, our culture, our history. It is not "theirs."

The use of language to refer to concepts can greatly affect the way we feel and behave toward them. The terms *normal* and *pathologic* fit well into a medical model system and can help identify diseased conditions. Do they fit, however, when referring to a family within its total historic, cultural, and socioeconomic context?

The terms *uncomplicated* and *complicated mourning* are used when referring to a bereaved family's expression and resolution of grief. Webster's Dictionary (1982) defines complicated as "made up of parts intricately involved; hard to untangle, solve, understand, analyze," and so on.

It is the factors, not necessarily the families, that make mourning complicated or not. As nurses, we cannot change these factors (that is, anticipated or unanticipated loss, timely or untimely loss, violent or dignified loss, and so on). What we do have control over, however, is our own openness to the meaning of this particular loss, to this particular family, with their particular history and style. What we can control is our own open or closed communication system that we represent and model to this family. We can encourage a family's openness to each other in sharing the facts and realities and grief surrounding the loss if we can genuinely invite it.

Minuchin (1975) studied the relationship of certain family organizations and the formation of psychosomatic illness in children. The loss of important persons creates disorganizing events within the family. This emotional stress can impair the emotional and social functioning of that family unit. This type of impaired functioning can be carried over into what Bowen (1972) calls "the multi-generational transmission process," when problems surrounding bereavement can be transmitted to the spouse, who transmits them to the children, and then on to the children's children.

Coleman and Stanton (1972) have proposed that unresolved earlier losses for the parents and grandparents of addicts contribute significantly to the creation of a symptom or illness. In addicts, the individual boundaries often become so diffuse and the generational boundaries are so blurred that the only allowable separation the addict can have is through death.

The function of the symptom within the family is an important dynamic to understand. The symptoms exhibited in one or more members of the family are worked out and arranged with the collaboration of its members. There is a continuum between what is inside each family member and what lies between them. If a relationship in a family emotional system is changed due to death or another significant loss, then the entire family system is changed.

Numerous longitudinal and short-term studies have associated bereavement with high morbidity and mortality rates for remaining close survivors.

Reports in the literature have sought to identify whether real or threatened loss is a precipitating factor in a variety of disorders. Studies have been completed on individuals with cancer, tuberculosis, leukemia, lymphoma, disseminated lupus erythematosus, and psychoneuroses.

Parkes (1964) has performed a well-known study of bereavement and its effects on the physical and mental health of a widowed population. He compared the medical records of widows during bereavement with records on the same patients during the period before bereavement. His findings included (1) medical office consultations increased by 63% during the first 6 months after bereavement; the highest were for psychiatric and chronic somatic conditions, (2) consultation rates for non-psychiatric symptoms increased by half in both elder and younger widows, and (3) higher rates for patients over 64 years of age supported the contention that aged patients in particular tend to express their reactions in somatic symptoms.

Clayton et al. (1968) conducted a study on "normal bereavement." They identified a variable for which Parkes failed to control. It was possible that the women in Parkes' study had become ill during their husband's illness and perhaps only in the first 6-month period after bereavement did they have time to attend to their complaints.

There are more studies on widowhood. Jacobs and Douglas (1979) related the process of grief to several postulated pathogenic mechanisms that lead to illness and death among widowed persons. Their study concluded that the process of grief appears to serve as a bridge between conjugal loss and the illness and death that may arise after it. Grief thereby becomes a mediating process that requires intensive empirical attention.

Rees and Lutkins (1967) studied the "mortality of bereavement" and found that the risk of a bereaved relative dying within 1 year of a bereavement was twice as high if the first relative died in the hospital than if he or she died at home. The risk of the bereaved relative's dying was even greater when the first relative died at sites other than the home or the hospital.

The type of death and the age at which a significant family member's death is experienced by the other members also hold important considerations, because these factors relate to mortality rate and physical and/or social dysfunction of the family.

Rudestam (1977) examined the impact of a young person's suicide on his or her surviving parents and family. He concluded that the painful adaptation period of grief, guilt reactions, denial mechanisms, psychosomatic disorder, and family communication patterns carried with them significant impairment of the surviving members of the family.

Sanders (1979-80) used the Grief Experience Inventory (GEI) and the

MMPI to assess bereavement reactions. She noted a significantly higher bereavement intensity and incidence of physiologic symptoms in parents surviving a child's death.

Through her study of grandparents' deaths, Walsh (1978) raises the possibility that this factor may contribute to the development of schizophrenia.

Black (1978), in her study of the "bereaved child," notes that bereaved children are more likely than children from intact homes to develop psychiatric disorders both in childhood and in adult life. Children most at risk are those bereaved at 3 to 5 years of age and in early adolescence.

The vast amount of literature and studies clearly demonstrate that unresolved mourning can lead to many social, physical, and emotional dysfunctions. Studies indicate that families who have not adequately mourned earlier losses are more or less unable to successfully prepare for, face, and work through subsequent losses. Loss at an early age can make it even harder to negotiate future losses. Much of psychiatric illness is an expression of pathologic mourning.

The quantity and quality of evidence relating object loss to somatic symptom formation, disease occurrences, and mortality rates strongly suggest that emotional and physical states of close relatives—in particular nuclear family members—may be highly related to bereavement.

In this chapter, we are inviting the nurse to consider these findings and implement their usefulness in a preventive mode when possible and intervention mode when necessary. These studies and findings can aid our understanding of factors that put certain families or members at high risk for illness, mortality, or dysfunction. They do not make the families or members inadequate, inappropriate, or incapable of working with and through these factors.

If the term *dysfunctional* is used to refer to a family or mourning process, consider the common definition of the term. Numerous dictionaries define dysfunctional as abnormal, impaired, or incomplete functioning; bad, ill, and so on. The way the term is defined can affect the way the family or mourning process is viewed.

Mosby's Dictionary (1990) defines dysfunctional as "unable to function normally." The prefix "dys" is a Greek derivative. One of the interpretations of dys is "painful." Reframe the term dysfunctional as "functioning painfully." The degree of pain while functioning is dependent on the variables that make it complicated or uncomplicated.

Viewing the family in this context can help the nurse assess when a family is stuck from proceeding in their family system and when they are moving on (that is, when they are observing, listening, and using their own resolution abilities and following their own inner guide, as opposed to being so pained that they are blocked from accessing their normal functioning).

Byng-Hall (1971) noted that the rules for dying and grieving are encoded in family mythology and legends about death in the family. What looks pathologic or "wrong" to one person or group may not only be customary, but may be necessary to another person's or group of persons' resolution. Walsh and

McGoldrick (1991) write, "Grief is a very personal matter—whether they should be more expressive or less so. Every family must find its own way."

One can readily see the implications for present and future generations regarding the successful or unsuccessful resolutions of mourning. Unresolved grief can block generations of family members from shifting to an appropriate new stage of its development.

A family that can acknowledge the dying or death of a loved one can talk openly about the deceased; share experiences surrounding the member and the event; reorganize the family structure and roles; over time, show renewed energy in present and new relationships; respect their own and each others' mourning responses; share appropriate rituals and ceremonies in the service of grief; address any secrets about the death or loss as fact and be receptive to resources and tools useful to the acceptance of such facts. This is a family that is moving on. The family members may then complete the mourning process, no matter what factors surround the loss, as in uncomplicated or complicated bereavement.

A family that denies the death or loss or inappropriately replaces the member through another person; that is closed, blocked, or intolerant of their own or each others' responses; that is isolated, avoidant, or limited in having and or sharing rituals; that is intent to protect others from the truth or ashamed of the events or person or that is cut off from their history or different family members or resources is most often a family who is stuck or will get stuck in moving on. This leads to incomplete mourning, whether it be uncomplicated or complicated bereavement.

The nurse is often in the position of observing and being with the family whether they are moving on or stuck. She or he can best service the family by recognizing, validating, and supporting those choices the family makes for itself and its loved one or by helping to remove what blocks or barriers limit the family to access its strengths and problem-solving ability. This role is quite different than thinking it is our responsibility to tell them what to do to grieve healthfully.

Accessing the Strengths

If we approach our lives and healing from the depths of ourselves, any experience has within it the power to transform and heal (Moss, 1985).

One must have an intrinsic or developed experience that healing is from within, not outside, the family. With this understanding the primary goal of any therapeutic nursing intervention is to help the family know and use their own strength and resources to mourn together and then move on. This process is empowering the family.

Kübler-Ross (1969) made a monumental impact by not only identifying the stages of grief, but also addressing ways to help dying patients. She stressed the "art of listening," of letting patients share their fears and desires for what they perceive the rest of their days will be like and reinforcing their hope and present meaningful existence. A colleague, Tom Nolan (1972), wrote, "The primary emphasis in intervention with the dying is not so much on what can be said to him, but what he is saying to us." LeShan (1967), a noted therapist in this field, notes the importance of helping the patient to find ways to act and react to his or her situation so that he or she may take some semblance of control, which enhances the strength of the whole person.

These very same principles are the key principles to apply not only to the patient, but to the family as a whole system. The following is a summary of interventions from a number of different theorists and clinicians. (Kübler-Ross, 1969; Bowen, 1978, 1991.)

1. Use open and factual terminology and information. If the nurse masks terms through vague or inaccurate language, he or she not only models poorly, but inadvertently advises the family that he or she — as well as they — need protection from the facts. Direct words such as death, dying, cancer, and AIDS can serve to open communications and prevent mystification.

2. Establish at least one open relationship within the family. Bowen (1978) used to seek out the family member who showed the highest level of differentiation to influence change. As nurses, however, we often are dealing with the weakest (dying) physically or neediest (next of kin). We see that as great opportunity. While acknowledging the vulnerability of the dying patient or most grief-stricken loved one, we encourage that member to "teach" the other family members how to meet their needs. We encourage the identified member to verbalize his or her needs and actually tell his or her loved ones how they could best help in the most specific, concrete ways possible. Feelings of helplessness on both sides can thus be interrupted. Rarely do family members not want to help. They just do not always know how. But it is they who teach each other what to do. It may be that we just need to encourage them.

3. Respect the grief stage the family and individual members are in. Hope is always maintained, but as Dr. Kübler-Ross (1969) noted, "It just narrows." The family members and dying person can be in conflicting stages. It is not uncommon for the ill person to be ready to detach and leave this world before the family members are ready to let him or her go.

    However, we have seen the opposite as true when working with a person with AIDS and their family members. The family — often worn, exhausted, and so pained by the intense suffering of the person dying — is more ready to allow the loved one to be released from suffering. However, the patient, often young and dealing with untimely and premature death, fights hard and willfully to hold on to every ounce of life left.

    The nurse can help the family members accept their own stage of grief, and paradoxically there often is an improved respect and tolerance for the others.

4. Elicit and support the use of family rituals and customs. Amber-Black (1991) notes that one of the most important interventions a therapist can make with a family is to help them stay in control of their mourning rituals. As nurses, we can advocate for the family to be with the dying or deceased family

member as they need to be. Support the family members in their need to take time, if they are in shock or highly anxious, and discover what is in their best interest at the time of death or after the death. It may be to remain with or hold their loved one longer, to wail and lament loudly, or perhaps to take charge of a religious ceremony and personalize its music or readings. If given the time and support, they will tell you what is in their best interest.

5. Support as much family connectedness as possible. The whole remains greater than the sum of its parts. As a family engages in the mourning process together they enable and empower themselves and each other.

   The resources within our work settings are rich. The hospice nurse, as well as the hospice movement, has brought the ill and dying person back to the family. They have done and are continuing to do a commendable job of caring for the family on its own territory and letting the family be the teacher. These nurses have much to teach the rest of nurses. Whatever your work setting, use hospice nurses for the family issues, as well as issues for yourself. They are a treasured resource.

6. Allow "caring encounters" between yourself and the family. Objectivity and distance are not necessarily therapeutic when dealing with grief and loss. Montgomery (1991), in an award-winning dissertation entitled "Caring vs. Curing," documented an insightful and original study to validate and identify subjective and sometimes invisible ways in which nurses, therapists, and caregivers participate in a client's healing. She found that most of the psychiatric nurses knew the only time they really made a difference was when they were willing to get involved. Montgomery notes, "It's not what we do, it's what we allow ourselves to become part of. In caring, the helper never becomes the focus of the experience. . . . True caring means being willing to step into the background, empowering the patient to heal himself." She identified the phenomena of expanded consciousness through caring. Montgomery states, "In a caring encounter, the participants experience union at a level beyond the ego, at the level of spirit." She concludes, "Connecting at this level allows us to become deeply involved with, and even love, our clients without succumbing to destructive types of overinvolvement."

   Gaining access to this expanded consciousness between ourselves and the families we become involved with is beyond ourselves or the family members. We are able to tap into a greater source from which comes wisdom and self-renewal.

   Remember, we teach the very thing we need to learn. As one helps the families one works with to seek out the clergy, the supervisor, the physician, the social worker, friends, and other support systems, the same resources are available to the nurse. Appreciation and acceptance of one's own grief process will enable the nurse to identify the resources needed. One group of nurses began their own support group, and it continues today—years later. What they had been providing so well for other families, they finally gave to themselves. This contributes to a nurse's ability to pull more out of an abundance for herself or himself, as well as the families she or he services.

The realization that we are all on the same life journey, that we are all mortal beings, can bring us as professionals in humble union with the families with whom we work. Walsh and McGoldrick (1991) so aptly state:

> Death and loss blur the boundaries between "us" and "them"—clinical experts and distressed families—since we are all vulnerable. In order to help families with loss, we as clinicians and family therapy as a field must face the inescapable fact of death, the inevitability of loss in life, and the terror of our own mortality.

We must be willing to do within our own family what we ask and encourage others to do within theirs. We too enter the process of loss and grief with our legacies, scripts, culture, socioeconomic factors, and family history. We too have numerous resources within ourselves, our personal families, our community, and our professional family.

We can actively attempt to improve our relationship with our nuclear and extended family members. We can seek out our own history and genograms.

We can take time to be quiet within ourselves in relaxation, meditation, and yoga, as well as be with others in entertainment and friendship.

We can open closed communication systems.

We can employ psychotherapy and/or spiritual counseling. We can learn as much as possible about our cultural and religious heritage, aware of the legacies we wittingly or unwittingly will hand down.

One little girl brought home this point one Halloween. At age 6 she had a tremendous fear of a television program her older brother liked to watch, "The Incredible Hulk." When this character would transform into a rather grotesque, super-strong, muscular being, she would shriek and cry in fear. She hated that show and, in particular, that part of the transformation, yet she somehow felt compelled to watch it despite her mother's attempts to remove her from the television area. At age 7, that cute, darling little girl chose to be the "Incredible Hulk" for Halloween. She mastered her fear by becoming the feared object.

Our choice to confront our own feelings of terror around separation, loss, abandonment, and death can enable us to "be with" ourselves, our own families, and the families we are privileged to service not so much as "experts" but as the "beginners" we truly are.

In the course of helping others, "we really do go beyond identification with all that would define us as the 'other.' We really do meet behind our separateness. And for however long that lasts, such meeting is what helps . . . helps at the level of being . . . is help itself. We are sharing the experience of unity. We are walking each other home" (Dass, 1985).

REFERENCES

Ackerman, N. (1958). *The psychodynamics of family life.* New York: Basic Books.

Ackerman, N. (1962). Adolescent problems: A symptom of family disorder. *Family Process, 1*(2), 203-13.

Ackerman, N. (1982). Selected papers. In D. Block & R. Simon (Eds.), *The strength of family therapy.* New York: Brunner & Mazel.

Amber-Black, E. (1991). Rituals and the healing process. In F. Walsh & M. McGoldrick (Eds.), *Living beyond loss* (pp. 207-223). New York: W.W. Norton.

Bacon, C., Renneker, R., & Cutter, M. (1952). A psychosomatic survey of cancer of the breast. *Psychosomatic Medicine, 14,* 453-467.

Barry, H. Jr. (1965). Significance of maternal bereavement before age of eight in psychiatric patients. In R. Fulton (Ed.), *Death and identity.* New York: John Wiley & Sons.

Black, D. (1978). The bereaved Child. *Journal of Child Psychology and Psychiatry in Allied Disciplines, 19*(3), 287-292.

Boss, P. (1991). Ambiguous loss. In F. Walsh & M. McGoldrick (Eds.), *Living beyond loss* (pp. 164-175). New York: W.W. Norton.

Bowen, M. (1971). The use of family theory in clinical practice. In J. Haley (Ed.), *Changing families.* New York: Grune & Stratton.

Bowen, M. (1973). Alcoholism and the family systems. *The Family, 1,* 1.

Bowen, M. (1978). *Family therapy in clinical practice.* New York: Jason Aronson.

Bowlby, J. (1980). *Attachment and loss.* New York: Basic Books.

Brom, O., Freeman, S., & Scotch, N. (1970). *The dying patient.* New York: Russell Sage Foundation.

Byng-Hall, J. (1971). Family scripts and loss. In F. Walsh and M. McGoldrick (Eds.), *Living beyond loss* (pp. 130-143). New York: W.W. Norton.

Carter, E., & McGoldrick, M. (1980). *The family life cycle: A framework for family therapy.* New York: Garden Press.

Clayton, P., DeMarais, L., & Winokier, G. (1968). A Study of Normal Bereavement. *The American Journal of Psychiatry, 125*(2), 1977.

Coleman, S.B., & Stanton, M.D. (1978). The role of death in the addict family. *Journal of Marriage & Family Counseling, 4,* 79-91.

Dass, R., & Gorman, P. (1985). *How can I help.* New York: Knopf.

Day, C. (1952). Pneuma, psyche and soma. *Lancet, 2,* 691-702.

Dongen, C. (1991). Survivors of a family member's suicide: Implications for practice. *The Nurse Practitioner, 16, 7,* 31-39.

Elizur, E., & Kauffman, M. (1982). Factors influencing the severity of childhood bereavement reactions. *American Journal of Orthopsychiatry, 53,*668-677.

Engel, G. (1964). Grief and grieving. *The American Journal of Nursing, 64*(9), 93-98.

Evans, E. (1956). *A psychological study of cancer.* New York: Dodd Mead.

Freud, S. (1917). Mourning and melancholia. In J. Strochey (Ed.), *The standard edition of complete Psychological Works of Sigmund Freud.* New York: W.W. Norton.

Fulton, R. (1972). *Death, grief and bereavement,* Minneapolis: University of Minnesota: Center for Death Education and Research.

Green, W. Jr. (1954). Psychological factors and reticuloendothelial diseases: I. Preliminary observations on a group of males with lymphomas and leukemias. *Psychosomatic Medicine, 16,* 220-239.

Green, W. Jr., & Swisher, S. (1956). Psychological factors and reticuloendothelia diseases: II. Observations on a group of women with lymphomas and leukemias. *Psychosomatic Medicine, 18,* 284-303.

Green, W. Jr., & Miller, G. (1958). Psychological factor and reticuloendothelial disease. *Psychosomatic Medicine, 20,* 124-143.

Haley, J. (1971). *Changing families.* New York: Grune & Stratton.

Haley, J., & Madanes, C. (1977). Dimensions of family therapy. *Journal of Nervous and Mental Diseases, 165,* 88-98.

Harper, N. (1990). *Seven choices.* New York: Clarkson N. Potter.

Herz, F. (1980). The impact of death and serious illness on the family life cycle. In E. A. Carter & M. McGoldrick (Eds.), *The family life cycle: A framework for family therapy.* New York: Gardner Press.

Hollingshead, A.B. (1957). Two factor index of social position. Privately printed. New Haven, Conn.

Hollingshead, A.B. (1985). Factors associated with prevalence of mental illness. Readings in social psychology. New York: Holt, Rinehart & Winston.

Jackson, E. (1965). *Telling a child about death.* New York: Channel Press.

Jacobs, S., & Douglas, L. (1979). Grief: A mediating process between a loss and illness. *Comprehensive Psychiatry, 20*(2), 165-176.

Jacobs, S., & Kim, K. (1990). Psychiatric complications of bereavement. *Psychiatric Annals, 20*(6), 314-317.

Kastenbaum, R. (1972). *The psychology of death.* New York: Springer.

Knight, A. (1966). Emotional problems in catastrophic illness: Impact on families. In *Proceedings of the Symposium Catastrophic Illness.* New York: Cancer Care Inc. of the National Cancer Foundation.

Kowal, S.J. (1955). Emotions as a cause of cancer. *Psychoanalytic Review, 42*(3), 217.

Kübler-Ross, E. (1969). *On death and dying.* New York: Macmillan.

Kübler-Ross, E. (1983). *On children and death.* New York: Macmillan.

Kutsher, A., & Goldberg, M. (Eds.). (1973). *Caring for the dying patient and his family.* New York: Health Science Publishers.

LeShan, L. (1961). A basic psychological orientation apparently associated with malignant disease. *Psychiatric Quarterly, 35,* 314-329.

LeShan, L. (1967). The world of the patient in severe pain of long duration. *Journal of Chronic Diseases, 7,* 10-16.

Lindemann, E. (1944). Symptomatology and management of acute grief. *American Journal of Psychiatry, 101,* 141-148.

McClary, A.R., Meyer, E. & Weitzman, E.L. (1955). Observations on the role of mechanism of depression in some patients with disseminated lupus erythematosus. *Psychosomatic Medicine, 17,* 242-245.

McGoldrick, M., Hines, P., & Lee, E. (1986). Mourning rituals. *The Family Therapy Networker,* Nov-Dec., 28-36.

Minuchin, S. (1974). *Families and family therapy.* Cambridge: Howard University Press.

Minuchin, S. (1975). A conceptual model of psychosomatic illness in children. *Archives of General Psychiatry, 32,* 319-340.

Minuchin, S., & Fishman, H.C. (1981). *Family therapy techniques.* Boston: Harvard University Press.

Montgomery, C.L. (1991). Caring vs. curing. *Common Boundary, 9,* 37-40.

Mosby's dictionary. (1990). Medical, Nursing and Allied Health, (3rd ed.), St Louis, Mosby–Year Book.

Moss, R. (1985). *How shall I live.* Berkeley, Calif: Celestial Arts.

Nolan, T. (1972). The Crisis of Grief and Death. *Sisters Today, 5,* 555.

Nolan, T. (1984). Thanatological counseling of adults and their families. In S. Lego (Ed.). *The American handbook of psychiatric nursing.* Philadelphia: J.B. Lippincott.

Nolan, T., O'Grady-Cocozza, S., & Pipchick, M. (1973). *Thanatology: A study of life process.* Unpublished paper. New York: New York University.

Osterwis, M., Solomon, F., & Green, M. (Eds.) (1984). *Bereavement: Reactions, consequences and care.* Washington, D.C.: National Academy Press.

Parkes, C.M. (1964). Effects of bereavement on physical and mental health — a study of the medical records of widows. *British Medical Journal, 2,* 274-279.

Parkes, C.M. (1975). Determinants of outcome following bereavement. *Omega, 6,* 303-323.

Parkes, C.M. (1987). Bereavement as a psychosocial transition: Processes of adaptation and change. *Journal of Social Issues, 44*(3), 53-65.

Parkes, C.M., & Weiss, R.S. (1983). *Recovery from bereavement.* New York: Basic Books.

Paul, N. (1972). The role of mourning: Empathy in conjoint marital therapy. In G. Zuk & I. Boszormenyi-Nagy (Eds.), *Family therapy and disturbed families* (pp. 186-205). Palo Alto, Calif: Science and Behavioral Books.

Quint, J. (1967). *The nurse and the dying patient.* New York: Macmillan.

Rees, W.D., & Lutkins, S. (1967). Mortality of bereavement. *British Medical Journal, 4,* 13-16.

Rogers, M. (1970). *An introduction to the theoretical basis of nursing.* Philadelphia: F.A. Davis.

Rudestam, K.E. (1977). *The impact of suicide among the young. Essence, 1*(4), 221-114.

Sanders, C.M. (1979-80). A comparison of adult bereavement in death of a spouse, child and parent. *Omega, 10*(4), 303-320.

Sanders, C.M. (1982-83). Effects of sudden vs. chronic illness death on bereavement outcome. *Omega, 13*(3), 227-266.

Schiff, H.H. (1977). *The bereaved parent.* New York: Penguin.

Schmale, A., & Iker, E. (1966). The affect of hopelessness and the development of cancer. *Psychosomatic Medicine, 28*(5), 714-720.

Schoenberg, B., Carr, A., Peretz, D., & Kutscher, A. (Eds.) (1971). *Loss and grief: Psychological management in medical practice.* New York: Columbia University Press.

Schultz, S.J. (1984). *Family systems therapy.* New York: Jason Aronson.

Schultz, S.J. (1991). *Science of Mind,* Oct., 77.

Shapiro, R. (1980). Psychodynamically oriented family therapy. In P. Sholevar, et al. (Eds.), *Emotional disorders in children and adolescents.* New York: Medical and Scientific Books.

Shoor, M., & Speed, M. (1965). Death, delinquency and the mourning process. In R. Fulton (Ed.), *Death and identity.* New York: John Wiley & Sons.

Shore, M. (1990). Love, guilt and resolution. The family in serious and terminal illness. *Families, 1,* 29-36.

Sims, A. (1978). Hypotheses linking neuroses with premature mortality. *Psychological Medicine, 8*(2), 255-263.

Sowell, R., Bramlett, M., Gueldner, S., Gritzmacher, D., & Martin, G. (1991). The lived experience of survival and bereavement following the death of a lover from AIDS. *Image, 23*(2), 89-94.

Stanton, M.D. (1980). Family therapy: Systems approaches. In G.P. Sholevar, R.N. Benson, & B.J. Blinder (Eds.), *Emotional disorders in children and adolescents.* New York: Medical and Scientific Books.

Steele, D. (1980). *Overcoming your grief.* Madison, Wis.: The Center for Grief Counseling and Education.

Toman, W. (1969). *Family constellation.* New York: Springer.

Viorst, J. (1986). *Necessary losses.* New York: Fawcett Gold Medal.

Volkar, E. (1965). Bereavement and mental health. In R. Fulton (Ed.), *Death and identity.* John Wiley & Sons.

Walsh, F. (1978). Concurrent grandparent death and birth in schizophrenic offspring: an intriguing finding. *Family Process, 17*(4), 457-463.

Walsh, F. (1979-80). A comparison of adult bereavement in the death of a spouse, child and parent. *Omega, 10*(4), 303-320.

Walsh, F. (1989). The family in later life. In B. Carter & M. McGoldrick (Eds.), *The changing family life cycle* (2nd ed.), Boston: Allyn & Bacon.

Walsh, F., & McGoldrick, M. (1991). *Living beyond loss.* New York: W.W. Norton.

Websters' New World Dictionary (1982). New York: Simon & Schuster.

Worden, J.W. (1991). *Grief counseling and grief therapy.* New York: Springer.

Chapter 10

Decision Making Within the Elderly Family

Joan L. Fopma-Loy

"Mother wants to stay in her home, but I'm worried about her. What should I do?" "I need some help taking care of my husband, but I don't know where to turn." "I can't keep taking on all of the responsibility for Dad, but my brother and sister won't help." "It seems like a nursing home is the only answer, but what kind of answer is that?" As health care decision making increases in importance and complexity, questions and comments similar to these will increasingly be addressed to nurses working with families with elderly members. What factors account for this increased emphasis on health care decision making of and for the elderly? What role does the family have in health care decision making? What barriers do families face in the decision-making process? How can family psychiatric nurses facilitate family decision making regarding health care for the elderly? Nurses unable to answer these questions will be ill prepared to assist families in resolving the dilemmas they encounter in the decision-making process. In addressing these questions, this chapter provides psychiatric nurses with the knowledge necessary to assist families with the ambiguities and complexities inherent in health care decision making for the elderly.

Factors Accounting for the Increased Emphasis on Health Care Decision Making for the Elderly

DEMOGRAPHIC FACTORS PLAY A MAJOR ROLE IN THE INCREASING IMPORTANCE OF HEALTH CARE FOR OLDER ADULTS

The United States is an aging society. Whereas in 1980, 26 million people, or 11% of the population, were over the age of 65, in 2030 this age group will total 59 million and comprise 19% of the population (Davis, 1986). Of even greater significance are the projected increases in the numbers and proportions of the "frail-old." Currently, one quarter of the population is 75 years old or older; by

2030 this age group will account for one third of the aged. Whereas now 1 in 16 persons in the United States is over the age of 85 years, by 2030, 1 in 11 persons in the United States will be 85 years or older (Clemen-Stone et al., 1987). Furthermore, the female population 85 years old and older will triple between 1980 and 2030 (Davis, 1986). These projections serve to illustrate that the "frail-old" is the fastest growing segment of the United States population.

The rising proportions of the "frail-old," primarily the result of increased longevity and the projected increase in the absolute numbers of the elderly resulting from the aging of the post–World War II baby boomers, will intensify the already growing pandemic of chronic mental and physical illnesses and associated conditions (Clark, 1985; Kramer, 1986). The majority of the elderly suffer from at least one chronic health problem. Most of the elderly are still able to function independently; however, with increased age the need for assistance grows. The high functional dependency rates of the "old-old" were validated by the 1982 National Long Term Care Survey, which reported that 3 times as many persons 85 years old and older report needs for help with activities of daily living as do persons in the 65- to 74-year-old age group (Kane & Kane, 1987). Furthermore, although only about 5% of the elderly are in nursing homes at any one time, those persons who reach the age of 65 years have a 50% chance of spending some time in such a facility and one in four elderly will be in a nursing home at the time of death (Block, 1988).

Estimates indicate that currently approximately 6.6 million elderly need some type of long-term care; about 5.2 million of these persons reside in noninstitutional settings (Kingson et al., 1986). It is projected that the numbers of elderly needing long-term care will continue to increase even if the average age of onset of disabling conditions is postponed. Projections indicate that the total elderly population in need of long-term care will be 9 million by the year 2000, 12.9 million by 2020, and nearly 19 million by 2040 (Kingson et al., 1986).

Thus needs for long-term care will steadily increase. Families currently provide the majority of the long-term care to the elderly. Many of these caregivers, however, are themselves in poor health or have numerous competing demands. One third of spouse caregivers are 75 years old or older, and nearly half of these persons reported their own health as fair or poor. Of child caregivers, 60% are aged 45 to 64 years; about half of all child caregivers are working (Shanas & Nostrand, 1988). Of interest, women can now expect to spend greater periods of time caring for elderly parents than for dependent children (United States House Select Committee on Aging, 1987).

The capacity of families to continue to provide such difficult care over even longer periods will be affected by a number of social trends. First, as indicated, demands for long-term care will increase. Demands will be intensified not only by demographic trends, but also by prospective payment systems, which have increased the acuity of care provided in hospitals, thereby increasing reliance on family caregiving. Prospective payment systems have also led to a proliferation of extended care alternatives, subsequently increasing the need for families to negotiate linkages with extended care (Fischer & Eustis, 1988). Second, changes in family structure will affect family caregiving. Divorce and the increased childbearing of single women have increased the prevalence of single-parent families, which may complicate caregiving. According to Brody, divorce may also bring remarriage, increasing the complexity of kinship structures and challenging family members' conceptions of filial responsibility and loyalty (Kingson et al., 1986). In many cases, single adult children are returning to their parents' homes, creating three and four generational households. Thus caregivers may experience the stresses of caring for the very young and the very old in one household. Increased labor force participation of women may also decrease the ability of families to meet the caregiver role. Finally, baby boom families are having fewer children or no children at all. It is uncertain whether the "baby bust" children will be able to support the caregiving needs of their parents (Kingson et al., 1986). Women of the baby boom generation electing to remain childless will have to rely on other relatives or friends, thereby increasing caregiving demands of those family members who may also have other caregiving responsibilities.

Role of the Family in Health Care Decision Making

Families play two major roles in the provision of health care to their elderly members: that of direct care providers and that of indirect care providers (Sussman, 1976). In their direct caregiving role, families provide "hands on" care. The indirect role, which has been described as case management (Seltzer et al., 1987); according to Lowy, care management (Seltzer et al., 1987); or managerial (Fischer & Eustis, 1988) has been suggested to be an emerging form of family caregiving (Fischer & Eustis, 1988) and, according to Lowy, the most important care-providing function of a family with an elderly member (Seltzer et al., 1987). In the indirect role, families function as planners, supervisors, and mediators of care (Fischer & Eustis, 1988). Although those in the formal service sector also can and do fulfill these functions, "the history and continuity of a family member's interest in an elderly relative enhances the family's potential to serve as a case manager" (Seltzer et al., 1987). The impact of the previously described demographic and social factors on health care delivery systems has been such that the importance of the indirect caregiving role of the family has increased dramatically.

Barriers to Health Care Decision Making

In the optimal decision-making process, persons judiciously identify options, weigh the gains and losses associated with each choice, and freely select the alternative having the most benefits and the fewest negative consequences (Janis & Mann, 1977). Barriers to health care decision making for the elderly often, however, lead to less than optimal processes and outcomes. First, families may not understand health conditions of the elderly member and the anticipated outcomes of these conditions. This lack of understanding, as well as a lack of knowledge of health care services, may contribute to a perception that no options exist or that all options are undesirable (Coulton et al., 1988).

Investigations of family caregivers have indicated that caregivers have received little information useful to them in this role (Kane & Kane, 1987) and consequently experience difficulty making and acting on decisions related to relocation; coping with feelings of entrapment, frustration, and guilt; and dealing with feelings and level of involvement of the care receiver and other family caregivers (Hartford & Parsons, 1982). A lack of time for planning and a lack of common goals in the family have also been noted as constituting significant barriers to effective decision making (Coulton et al., 1988). Thus it appears that although families will be required to assume greater responsibility for management of health care of elderly members, a lack of the time and information necessary for planning, as well as family issues and dynamics, may inhibit the effectiveness of families and of their decisions.

Facilitating Family Decisions: Minimizing Barriers to Effective Decision Making

Given the barriers to optimal decision making encountered by families, nurses may best facilitate family functioning in this area through providing anticipatory guidance, education, and family therapy. Because interventions must be based on the specific needs and resources of the care receiver and the family, a comprehensive assessment must first be conducted. A comprehensive assessment such as that described should be conducted with any family with an elderly member. This is true even if the family presents with problems seemingly unrelated to the needs of the older adult(s) in the family system. In fact, families may often neglect to provide information regarding the elderly member unless questioned directly, not realizing the relationship between problems of other members and those of the older adults in the family. The elements of such an assessment will be presented initially and will be followed by guidelines for intervention.

ASSESSMENT

Functional assessment of the care receiver. The initial dilemma often faced by families is determining the degree of impairment of the older adult and the outcome of this impairment. Functional assessment, or the objective measurement of physical health, activities of daily living, psychologic status, and social status, can answer questions regarding the source(s) of the impaired status of the care receiver and ensure that care and management decisions are applicable and effective. In evaluating functional limitations, the nurse should pay particular attention to sensory impairments, fall-related injury potential, pressure sore risk, and adverse effects of medications (Matteson & McConnell, 1988). Furthermore, the environment must be evaluated to determine if loss of function is related to environmental constraints (physical or social), rather than caused by the effect of disease processes. Many geriatric assessment tools, scales of functional status, cognitive and affective status measures, measures of social functioning, and multidimensional instruments are currently available. Matteson and McConnell (1988) and Kane and Kane (1981) present examples and descriptions of such instruments.

Family assessment. Family assessment is a second crucial component of the assessment process and enables the nurse to define the demands and nature of the support network available to the older adult and to delineate sources of family conflict that may be impeding effective functioning (Matteson & McConnell, 1988). Wright and Leahy's (1984) adaptation of the Calgary Family Assessment model provides a method by which the nurse can systematically assess the structure, development, and functioning of the family. A brief description of each of these components, as well as special considerations regarding application of this framework to assessment of the aging family, follows.

Every family has both an internal and external structure. Components of the assessment of the internal structure include family composition, rank order, subsystems, and boundaries. Culture, religion, social class status and mobility, environment, and extended family are subcategories of the external structure. In relation to structure, it is important to recognize the complexity and diversity of late life families. Elicitation of the elder's perceptions of members of the family are crucial to the identification of all decision makers and support systems (Matteson & McConnell, 1988). Assessment of the environment (home and larger community of the elder and the family) should be carefully attended to when assessing external structure. When the family is considering caring for the elderly relative in their home several important factors related to the environment must be considered. First, the proximity of the home to the elder's former neighborhood and favorite activities should be assessed. With regard to the home environment, the adequacy of the physical space and privacy for all generations must be determined. The presence of physical barriers, such as steps and uneven floors, and the costs of removing such barriers must also be considered. The degree of financial dependency of the older adult and the adequacy of the family income for taking care of the relative in the home are also important to determine. Finally, family values, especially with regard to aging and treatment of the old and sick, should be a component of the assessment of family structure. Genograms and ecomaps are useful tools for assessing the internal and external family structure. Matteson and McConnell (1988) recommend that a genogram constructed with the aging family consists of a minimum of three generations for the older person, including the following: (1) spouse, siblings, cousins; (2) offspring of the older person's generation; and (3) grandchildren.

Developmental assessment of the family is critical to determining the ability of the family to cope with the needs of the care receiver, as well as other concurrent demands. The family as a system confronts major adaptational changes in late life, with illness being a frequently encountered stressor necessitating family support, adjustment to loss, reorientation, and reorganization (Walsh, 1980). According to Carter and McGoldrick (1980), anxiety in a family is both vertical and horizontal. The system's vertical flow refers to patterns of relating and functioning transmitted through the generations and therefore includes family expectations, taboos, and attitudes. All families must also cope with the changes and transitions engendered by the family life cycle. Anxiety produced by these stressors is considered the horizontal flow in the system. For example, within the late life family, developmental tasks of the elderly interact with those of the child and grandchild generations. A lack of fit in these developmental strivings of the generations results in greater stress (Walsh, 1980). The primary factor determining a family's ability to manage life transitions is the amount of anxiety caused by stress on the horizontal and vertical axes at the point at which they intersect (Carter & McGoldrick, 1980). Therefore as the ability of members to cope depends on the nature of the family system and the system's ability and methods of adjusting to changes, both current stressors and transgenerational issues and patterns must be assessed to accurately determine the potential difficulty caused by the transition.

Diagnostic questions that need to be addressed include the following (Simon, 1980): Where is this family in the family life cycle? Is the family encountering any situations that are not phases of a cycle per se but are influencing family life (such as bereavement)? How is the life cycle creating disturbance for this family? What are the major life-cycle issues related to the present problem, and how is the family dealing or not dealing with them? Did the difficulties originate in the transition to or during the current life-cycle phase, or are the problems more long-standing and related to difficulties negotiating earlier transitions? Where in the family system is the key issue that has precipitated or contributes to the presenting problem? Is the current life-cycle transition the basic problem, or has it triggered more serious problems based upon extant family structure weaknesses?

Family functional assessment refers to the assessment of the family's behavior in relation to one another and comprises instrumental and expressive subcategories (Wright & Leahy, 1984). Instrumental functioning of the family refers to the family's activities of daily living, whereas expressive functioning refers to the manner in which the activities of daily living are carried out. Instrumental activities of daily living not only will be greater in number and frequency in the family with an elderly member in need of long-term care, but will also take on greater significance. Family members should be questioned regarding the quality and character of their current day-to-day life, as well as their preferred patterns of daily living. It is important to determine the extent to which caregiving responsibilities are being shared among members, as well as the degree to which these responsibilities are affecting role enactment outside of the family. For example, have or will family members have to give up a job, schooling, or social activities as the result of caregiving demands? It is critical that the nurse note the extent to which the care receiver is included in family problem solving and decision making because studies suggest that the outcome of long-term care is more likely to be positive when the care receiver participates at his or her level of capability (Block, 1988). Although all but the most confused elderly have the potential for involvement, elderly members are often perceived as having limited decision-making abilities and are excluded from health care decisions. It is also important that the nurse elicit each family member's perspective of the problem, as well as the family's attempted solutions. This information is vital, because it allows the nurse to identify any successful solutions, as well as solutions that may be exacerbating the problem or creating new problems. In addition, the nurse will not discount clients by offering solutions that have already been attempted if such information is gathered (Herr & Weakland, 1979). Finally, each family member's goals and desires are elicited as part of the assessment of the expressive functioning of the family. Of special import are the care receiver's desires in relation to aggressiveness of care, living wills, and place of residence (Matteson & McConnell, 1988).

Conflicts between the desires of the care receiver and the family with regard to living arrangements are not uncommon, with the most typical situation being the elder member indicating a wish to continue living independently and the family verbalizing concern regarding this arrangement. Several fundamental issues must be further explored with the family in this event (Matteson & McConnell, 1988). First, the care receiver should be questioned further regarding his or her desires. The reasons for the person's choice, the perceptions of problems and advantages in living alone, and the anticipated difficulties of relocation should be explored. Second, the client's functional status and the means by which needs could be met are reviewed. Finally, safety factors must be considered. Are there any home adaptations that could be made to increase safety? Does the client exhibit cognitive impairments that affect judgment and insight and thus could affect safety? An independent living assessment, such as that exhibited by Matteson and McConnell (1988), could be useful in such a disposition determination.

When family members express a desire to assume or continue in a caregiving role, it is important to evaluate for the presence of high-risk indicators and perceptions of family members regarding care provision (Kosberg, 1988). This will enable the nurse to determine if the family is overburdened or incompetent to provide nonabusive care. Two instruments, the High-Risk Placement Worksheet (HRPW) (Kosberg, 1988) and the Cost of Care Index (CCI) (Kosberg & Cairl, 1986), may aid the nurse in obtaining or synthesizing this important data. The HRPW provides a means of systematically identifying quantitative and qualitative characteristics of the care receiver, major care-giver, and family system hypothesized to be related to elder abuse. The instrument also contains questions addressing the quality of relationships and preferred and ideal placement location. The CCI is a tool developed to assess the potential and actual consequences of providing care. Problem areas identified in the six dimensions, which include personal and social restrictions, physical health, emotional health, value, care receiver as provocateur, and economic costs, may increase the family's awareness of the need to consider alternatives and can also provide a focus for nursing intervention.

ANTICIPATORY GUIDANCE

Nurses are in an optimal position to provide anticipatory guidance to families and thus minimize or eliminate the obstacle of insufficient time for planning. Analysis of the assessment data will facilitate the discussion of anticipated needs and potential problems in meeting those needs. Because the family's ability to anticipate future needs is likely to be impaired by a lack of information, families should be educated regarding the prognosis and the effects of the available therapeutic options (Matteson & McConnell, 1988). Financial planning guidance is also crucial. Education regarding the extent of coverage provided by public and private insurance is needed by families with members in need of long-term care services. Nurses must be aware of knowledgeable resource persons in the community so that they can refer families appropriately.

In some instances, it may be determined that the care receiver is likely to require institutional care at some point in the future. Providing anticipatory guidance for such a relocation should be a primary focus of nursing intervention in that numerous studies support that the effect of relocation varies with the degree of voluntary choice, the predictability and degree of change encountered in the new environment, and the amount of control exercised by the care receiver (Johnson & Grant, 1985). Anticipatory guidance enables the older adult to exercise increased choice and control and increases the predictability of the new environment, thereby decreasing the negative effects associated with institutional relocation. Anticipatory guidance will also assist the family in the process of adjustment.

Such anticipatory guidance to prospective residents and families may take a variety of forms. Community information programs can introduce families to institutional offerings and accessing of services. Other programs may be more specifically oriented toward decision making and preparation for institutionalization. Kasmarik and Lester (1984) suggest that the family's preparation for such a relocation comprises the following phases: (1) acknowledgment of inability to provide continued care; (2) acceptance of family limitations and resolution of guilt; (3) development of more realistic goals and plans; and (4) admission to the institution. Group sessions for families in the various phases of adjustment process and preadmission groups for residents assist families in making and adjusting to the decision for institutional care (Kasmarik & Lester, 1984).

EDUCATION

Once families are able to anticipate future needs, they require further education to maximize effective decision making. At this point families may still experience difficulty in making decisions because they lack information in a variety of areas, including health care conditions and outcomes, normal aging and family development, caregiving skills, and health care services.

A lack of understanding of health conditions and outcomes is problematic for several reasons. First, this lack of understanding may lead to misconceptions about the extent to which the care receiver can control symptoms. Such misconceptions may increase the stress experienced by caregivers and care receivers and may lead to inappropriate decisions. The nurse should teach the family about the nature of the impairment, the expected symptoms, behaviors both within and outside of the care receiver's control, and factors that exacerbate or diminish the impact of the impairment (Matteson & McConnell, 1988). Ineffective family coping may also be related to a lack of understanding of normal aging and family development. Families may be inappropriately attributing symptoms exhibited by the care receiver to normal aging, which may lead them to delay or avoid beneficial treatment. Inability to make decisions may be considered an inevitable component of aging, leading to extrusion of the elderly member from important family decisions. Ineffective family coping manifested by role confusion among members of different generations may indicate a need for education regarding normal developmental tasks of all family members, and the stresses caused by a lack of complementarity of these tasks.

Caregiver stress, of an emotional, physical, or financial nature, may also be a factor contributing to or sustaining ineffective family coping. Emotional and physical strain may be diminished by teaching caregiving skills, such as proper lifting and transfer techniques, use of appropriate cueing techniques, and therapeutic management of disturbing behaviors. Teaching of coping skills and providing guidance in development of social support networks also assist in reducing caregiver stress.

One of the major barriers to decision making is a lack of knowledge and consequent inability to judge health care services. As indicated previously, the case management function of the family is becoming increasingly important. One aspect of case management is the planning role, which is becoming more salient and complicated. Features of the family's planning role include making arrangements for long-term care services and negotiating these arrangements over time as the care receiver's condition or family situations change (Fischer & Eustis, 1988). One of the most difficult aspects of making arrangements is locating and selecting these services. Nurses can assist families with this process by providing them with general considerations and guidelines for selecting home health services, day care services, and nursing homes.

Selecting home health services. Selection of an appropriate home health agency begins with a definition of the services needed, information provided by the previously described assessment process. The extent of coverage provided by the individual's health insurance must be determined in order that families understand the available options and their costs. Families must then identify the available home health services in their community. This information may be obtained by contacting the state or city health department, the state department of aging and social services, or local information and referral services. The National Home Caring Council will provide families with lists of accredited home care services organized by state. The National Association for Home Care will also help families contact their state agency, which will help families locate a home care agency.

Once families have identified agencies in their geographic area, the following questions can be used to evaluate the quality of those home health agencies contacted (Friedman, 1986; National Association for Home Care):

- **Licensure/Accreditation**   Is the agency certified or licensed where this is required? Is the agency approved or accredited by the state or other voluntary accrediting organization? Is it Medicare certified?

- **Services** What types of services are provided directly by the agency? What services are contracted out to other providers? What are the hours of operation—does the agency provide 24-hour care and weekend coverage? What provisions are made for emergency services? How soon will an assessment and plan of treatment be done? Does the evaluation include consultation with the family, the physician, and other health professionals? Is the plan of care written out and understandable? Does the plan of care include specific duties, who is to perform the duties, and the duration of time? Can the client and family review the plan? Will the same person be providing care regularly? Who supervises the care providers, and what are their qualifications? How often are supervisory visits made? Will special equipment be needed for the services to be provided? Is this equipment provided by the agency?

- **Personnel** What are the credentials and qualifications of the executive director and the director of nursing/clinical services? How many homemaker/home health aides are employed? Are the home health aides screened? Do they receive at least 40 hours of training? Do they receive continuing inservice education? Do professionals assume responsibility for care? Does the agency have written personnel policies and a description of basic benefits and a wage scale for each position?

- **Eligibility and Billing** Is there a written statement indicating who is eligible and under what conditions? If an individual does not meet eligibility requirements, will the agency try to locate appropriate agencies or services? Does the agency charge using an hourly or flat rate for services? Are there any minimum hour or day requirements? Are there charges for overtime, travel, special services, and equipment? How frequently are clients billed? Does the agency bill Medicare or private insurers directly? What are the limits on public and/or private insurance reimbursement for needed services? What plans or arrangements are made if reimbursement sources are exhausted?

- **Miscellaneous** How is the agency funded? Is the board of directors or advisory committee representative of the community? Is a list of these persons available? Does the agency issue an annual report and make this report available to the community?

The family should also ask for at least three client references and three professional references (physicians, hospital discharge planners, health care professionals). The following questions should be asked of these references (National Association for Home Care):

- **Client References** What is your opinion regarding the quality of services provided by the agency? Were services delivered as promised? How did the agency respond to emergencies? Was financial information supplied by the agency accurate? Did you have any problems with billing? Would you use the agency again?

- **Professional References** What is your relationship to the agency? Do you regularly refer clients to the agency? What is your opinion regarding the quality of services provided by the agency? Have you received any feedback from clients, especially those with similar circumstances or needs?

When contacting agencies, families are also likely to be asked to provide information regarding the potential client. Families may be asked to describe the care receiver's current condition, ambulatory status, the type of care currently provided and the provider of that care, special requirements of the client, and special equipment currently in use.

Selecting an adult day care facility. Adult day care facilities provide a structured combination of health, social, and supportive services in a structured setting. These programs enable frail and functionally impaired elderly to continue living in their homes and communities. The following guidelines will facilitate the family's selection of an appropriate day care facility (National Council on the Aging, 1984).

Families should first obtain a list of adult day care facilities in their community. When contacting these facilities, families should inquire as to the target population of the facility to determine the appropriateness of the setting for the care receiver. If the person is appropriate for enrollment, the family should visit the facility to evaluate the quality of the organization. Following are a number of considerations that will aid families in evaluating the quality of the adult day care facility:

- **Accreditation/Licensure** Is the agency certified or licensed where required? Is the facility approved or accredited by the state or other standard-setting organization?
- **Services** Is an initial written assessment completed before admission? Does the assessment include personal interviews and a home visit? Is there an individual plan of care for each participant, including functional assessment, goals and objectives of care, activities to meet goals, recommendations for therapy and referrals, and time limits and provisions for renewal? Do the client and the family have the opportunity to contribute to the plan? Is the plan reviewed at least semiannually? Does the facility provide personal care? Are social, leisure, physical, and educational activities, health education/counseling, and contacts with other health professionals provided? Does the facility provide or arrange for family support and individual/group counseling? Does the agency assist participants and their families in learning of and using community resources? Does the agency provide or contract for transportation?
- **Activities** Are there a variety of activities emphasizing different levels of involvement (small and large group, active and spectator, intergenerational)? Do activities emphasize participants' abilities and competences? Are participants permitted to refuse to participate? Is a monthly calendar of activities posted? Are participants regularly involved in planning and evaluating activities?
- **Personnel** Does the director have a degree in health and human services or a related field and at least 2 years of supervised experience? Is there a qualified social service director (minimum of bachelor's degree)? Is there

a registered nurse or licensed practical/vocational nurse with RN supervision who has experience in gerontologic nursing? Is there a qualified activities director? Are licensed therapists (physical, occupational) available? Are there consultants available (legal, financial management)? Is there a minimum of one staff member for every eight participants? If there is a high percentage of severely impaired participants, is there one staff member for every five participants? Are there at least two persons at the facility at all times participants are in attendance? What is the extent of orientation provided to the staff and volunteers? Is there regular inservice training?

- **Dietary** Is a minimum of one midday meal provided? Is a monthly menu posted and/or distributed? Are modified diets available? Are snacks offered? Are fluids available to participants as needed?
- **Physical/Architectural** Is the facility comfortable, attractive, and barrier free? Is there at least 40 square feet of space per participant? Are there a minimum of two restrooms with sufficient toilets (at least 1 per 10 participants)? Is there adequate space for activities? Is there space for special therapies, a rest area, and an area for isolation of participants with contagious illnesses? Are there closets or lockers for personal possessions? Is a telephone available to participants? Does the facility have adequate, glare-free lighting? Does the furniture promote independent functioning? Is there outside space?
- **Safety/Security** Are there at least two well-identified exits? Are there alarm/warning systems at the exits? Are surfaces nonskid and free of underfoot hazards? Are there handrails at stairs and ramps and in restrooms? Is the food handling, storage, and preparation sanitary? Are medications in a locked storage area? Do participants sign in and out at the site? Are there written procedures for handling emergencies? Are there regularly scheduled fire drills and posted fire procedures? Are there written agreements with participants and families for emergency medical situations? Are emergency first aid kits accessible? Is at least one full time staff member trained in CPR and first aid present at all times?
- **Finances/Billing** How are participants billed? Are written, clear statements of costs provided? What are the limits on public and/or private insurance reimbursement?

Selecting a nursing home. Although institutionalization should be predicated on knowledgeable judgments, many families make decisions regarding admission without the benefit of information and guidance that could assist them in this important process. In fact, results of one study indicated that 76% of nursing home admissions may be inappropriate (Smallegan, 1981). It is important to note, however, that families do not "dump" their elderly members into nursing homes. Conversely, a decision to admit a family member is usually made after much stress and sacrifice. It is imperative that nurses working with late life families communicate that nursing home placement is appropriate in certain instances and, in fact, the family may have no alternative.

When such a situation exists, the family should first obtain a list of facilities within the desired area. Then families must determine which nursing homes have the appropriate certification (Medicare, Medicaid) and are within the family's price range. After narrowing the list to approximately six homes, the family should arrange appointments with the administrators of each of these facilities, focusing on the criteria for selection that follow. After narrowing the list further after these interviews, the family should visit two or three facilities unannounced, preferably during the serving of meals (Ohio Commission on Aging).

The following guidelines can assist families in selecting the highest quality institution appropriate for their elderly member (Kasmarik & Lester, 1984; Ohio Commission on Aging):

- **Accreditation/Licensure**   Does the facility have a current license from the state department of health? Does the administrator have a current state license? Is the facility Medicare and Medicaid certified? Does the facility belong to any professional association? Are inspection reports available for review? Is there a history of serious violations from state reports?
- **Policies/Programs**   Is required resident rights information posted? Are civil rights observed? Is resident and/or relative permission obtained before relocation? Does the facility have a residents' council? Are there programs for family members and programs to help new residents adjust?
- **Finances/Billing**   Are written, clear statements of basic costs provided? When are extra costs incurred? Is a deposit required? Are refunds on advanced payments given if the client should leave? Are monthly bills itemized? Will the administrator provide an estimated total monthly cost? Does the facility assist with applications for third party reimbursement? Are provisions made for personal trust accounts? Does the facility provide adequate safeguards for money and valuables? Is compensation made for lost or stolen items? Are there procedures for residents to draw money from personal accounts? Is there a regular accounting of individual funds held by the home? How can purchases be made for items not provided by the facility?
- **Medical Personnel**   Is a private physician allowed? Is there a medical director? What is his or her geriatric expertise? Is his or her name and phone number available to residents and families? How often are residents examined by the staff physician (should be at least every 30 days for 3 months and then at regular intervals)? Is there a thorough examination on admission? Are provisions made for other medical services, such as a dentist, podiatrist, and ophthalmologist?
- **Nursing Personnel**   Is there an RN or LPN/LVN on duty day and night, 7 days a week? How many RNs, LPNs/LVNs, and aides are on duty each shift? What is the number of residents per nurse and per aide? What are the qualifications, training, and experience in gerontological nursing of the nursing staff? What is the extent of the training provided to the aides? What is the frequency of inservice education for staff? What is the turnover

rate? How many nursing staff have been employed longer than 2 years? Are nurses aides paid more than minimum wage? Is the focus of nursing care restorative? Are medications handled properly and supervised by a qualified pharmacist? Is prompt care provided to incontinent residents?

- **Other Personnel**   Is there a full time program of physical therapy directed by a qualified physical therapist? Are occupational and speech therapy available? Is there a licensed social worker? What are the qualifications of the activities staff? Are mental health services available?

- **Treatment Planning**   Is there a current, written plan of care for each resident? Are residents and families involved in treatment planning? Is the plan of care implemented? How are emergencies and readmission to acute care hospitals handled?

- **Activities**   Are there a variety of meaningful activities, including group and individual, daytime and evening? Are there activities for those inactive or confined to beds? Are events and activities posted? Is an on-site library or library services available? Are field trips scheduled, and how many participants are included? Are materials for activities available? Are these free of charge? Do residents use the activity materials? Are radios, TVs, newspapers, and magazines available? Are barbers and beauticians available? Are there planned religious programs? Is voting encouraged? Do volunteers from the community visit regularly? Is there a recreational relationship with another nursing home, school, or agency?

- **Dietary**   Is there a full-time dietician or a consulting dietician? Are menus prepared a week or more in advance? Is the meal plan adhered to? Are meals varied, well balanced, appetizing, and served at normal temperatures and times? Are meals served at appropriate intervals with 14 hours or less between the evening meal and breakfast? Are religious dietary laws, special likes and dislikes accomodated? Are snacks provided? Is the dining room accessible to those in wheelchairs? Do residents dine alone or in groups? Are residents allowed adequate time to eat? Are adequate utensils provided? Do those who need assistance with feeding get help promptly?

- **Location**   Is the facility near a hospital, family, friends? Is it in a pleasant setting?

- **Cleanliness**   Is the facility clean and free from unpleasant odors or heavily scented sprays? Are linens sufficient and clean? Are food, dishwashing, and garbage areas separate?

- **Safety**   Are there smoke and heat detectors and a recently checked sprinkler system? Are emergency exits clearly marked? Are fire drills conducted? What are the smoking regulations, and are they observed? Are disaster plans posted? Is the facility free of underfoot hazards that could cause falls? Are doorway thresholds flat? Are there nonskid floor coverings? Are there nonslip surfaces in bathtubs and showers? Is the lighting adequate and free from glare? Are there ramps for wheelchairs? Are halls wide enough to permit two chairs to pass? Are there grab bars in halls, bathrooms, and elevators? Are there call bells at the bedside and in bathrooms?

- **Comfort and Familiarity** Are the atmosphere and furniture comfortable? Is there adequate closet and drawer space? Is there room for wheelchairs in the bedrooms? Can residents decorate their own rooms? Are there any limits on personal belongings? Are there lounge and outdoor areas? Is there color coding to assist residents with orientation?
- **Social Environment** Are residents treated with dignity and respect? Does the staff encourage independence? Are the residents encouraged but not forced to participate in activities? Do residents wear their own clothes? Is attention paid to resident grooming? Does staff respond quickly to resident calls? Is privacy respected? Is there a privacy room? Are there public phones or phones where privacy is guaranteed? Are there extensive visiting hours?
- **General Observations** Are the residents alert? Are a large percentage of residents restrained or in geri-chairs? What is the quality of interactions between staff and residents, staff and visitors, and among staff?

FAMILY THERAPY

The stresses of adjusting to the aging of one or more family members are numerous and are intensified when the member has long-term care needs. In some cases providing anticipatory guidance and education may be sufficient to enable the family to cope effectively. It is possible, however, that the life-cycle transition being experienced by the family is creating problems with decision making that necessitate the use of family therapy in conjunction with the other nursing interventions previously described. The foci of family therapy will obviously depend on the needs of the client family and those factors that contribute to or sustain their problems. Although any discussion of clinical-theoretic models of practice is beyond the scope of this chapter, a brief description of more commonly occurring issues and interactional patterns will assist nurses in conducting therapy with families with aging members in need of long-term care services.

The primary task to be resolved between adult children and their aging parents is the establishment of an appropriate level of independence for the elderly members within the family system (Cube, 1985). Resolution of this task may be complicated by the chronic illness(es) of elderly parents, a situation that may trigger or exacerbate dependency issues of the child and/or parent (Walsh, 1980). Resolution of such dependency issues depends first on the adult child's achievement of filial maturity (Blenkner, 1965). An adult child who has achieved filial maturity recognizes that he or she cannot always depend on a parent for sustenance and takes responsibility for what he or she should appropriately do for that parent. In addition, the aging parent must be willing to allow himself or herself to be appropriately dependent when necessary. In other words, "not only must the adult child have the capacity to permit the parent to be dependent, but the parent must have the capacity to be appropriately dependent so as to permit the adult child to be dependable" (Brody, 1985). Role inversion, or the assumption of a parental role by the adult children, is not an outcome of this process when a system comprises relatively healthy individuals. Role inversion may occur, however, if the adult child is unable to achieve appropriate filial maturity because of his or her physical, emotional, or social situation, for example, when an adult child is confronting demands relating to his or her own aging (Walsh, 1980). The achievement of filial maturity may also be compromised by a lack of fit between the developmental needs of children and aging parents. This may occur, for instance, if an adult child is individuating at the time parents are manifesting increasing dependency needs (Walsh, 1980). If, in fact, a "parental child" is set up in the family system, the aging parent may become overly dependent, with the adult child responding by becoming overly responsible. This may result in a vicious cycle in which the parent becomes increasingly helpless with concomitant escalating neediness and subsequent increasing caregiver burden and resentment (Walsh, 1980).

Similar situations may occur when a spouse is the primary caregiver. Caregiving may be growth promoting in that it forces the caretaking spouse to confront his or her own concerns related to dependence. If this triggers anxiety-provoking feelings of vulnerability and needs to be taken care of, however, the caregiver may focus on the spouse's illness to avoid dealing with these issues. The caregiving spouse may consequently foster underfunctioning of the dependent wife or husband to meet his or her own needs to appear strong and independent (Walsh, 1980).

Families with aging members may also exhibit interactional patterns manifested by families in other developmental stages (Herr & Weakland, 1979). Older adults may be extruded from the family system or scapegoated for all of the troubles and dissatisfactions in the system as a way for the family to avoid dealing with other system issues. Long-standing dyadic alliances and persisting symbiotic relationships may also be manifested. Any of these patterns are likely to significantly impair the family's capacity for optimal decision making.

To function successfully, later life families must have the capacity to modify structure, roles, and responses as developmental needs and challenges change (Walsh, 1980). The nurse-therapist must assist the family to examine the adaptiveness of patterns that were functional in earlier stages and to explore new alternatives. In conducting therapy, the nurse assists the family to mobilize and utilize their resources in a new way. To be effective in this role, the nurse must be willing to experience the family nonjudgmentally, be knowledgeable regarding and skilled in the use of a clinical-theoretic model of practice, have a sense of self in relation to his or her family of origin, and be cognizant of the interaction of his or her own family life cycle with that of the client family (Simon, 1980).

•   •   •

Families will be called on increasingly to make decisions regarding health care within their roles as direct and indirect care providers. Currently, families are forced to grapple with complex questions and dilemmas without the benefit of professional support and assistance, often with tragic results. Family psychiatric nurses are challenged to obtain the knowledge and expertise necessary in order that they may enable families as health care decision makers.

REFERENCES

Blenkner, M. (1965). Social work and family relationships in later life with some thoughts on filial maturity. In E. Shanas & G. Streib (Eds.), *Social structure and the family: Generational relations.* Englewood Cliffs, NJ: Prentice Hall.

Block, J. A. (1988). Evaluating the patient's capacity to make decisions. In R. E. Dunkle & M. L. Wykle (Eds.). *Decision making in long term care: Factors in planning* (pp. 31-39). New York: Springer Publishing.

Brody, E. M. (1985). Parent care as a normative family stress. *Gerontologist, 25,* 19-29.

Carter, E. A., & McGoldrick, M. (1980). The family life cycle and family therapy: An overview. In E. A. Carter & M. McGoldrick (Eds.). *The family life cycle: A framework for family therapy* (pp. 3-20). New York: Gardner Press.

Clark, P. G. (1985). The social allocation of health care resources: Ethical dilemmas in age-group competition. *Gerontologist, 25,* 119-125.

Clemen-Stone, S., Eigsti, D. G., & McGuire, S. L. (1987). *Comprehensive family and community health nursing.* New York: McGraw-Hill.

Cobe, G. M. (1985). The family of the aged: Issues in treatment. *Psychiatric Annals, 15,* 343-347.

Coulton, C. J., Dunkle, R. E., Chow, J. C., Haug, M., & Vielhaber, D. P. (1988). Dimensions of post-hospital care decision-making: A factor analytic study. *Gerontologist, 28,* 218-223.

Davis, K. (1986). Paying the health bills of an aging population. In A. Pifer & L. Bronte (Eds.), *Our aging society: Paradox and promise* (pp. 299-318). New York: WW Norton.

Fischer, L. R., & Eustis, N. N. (1988). DRGs and family care for the elderly: A case study. *Gerontologist, 28,* 383-389.

Friedman, J. A. (1986). *Home health care: A complete guide for patients and their families.* New York: WW Norton.

Hartford, M., & Parsons, R. (1982). Groups with relatives of dependent adults. *Gerontologist, 22,* 394-398.

Herr, J. J., & Weakland, J. H. (1979). *Counseling elders and their families: Practical techniques for applied gerontology.* New York: Springer Publishing.

Janis, I., & Mann, L. (1977). *Decision-making.* New York: Free Press.

Johnson, C. L., & Grant, L. A. (1985). *The nursing home in American society.* Baltimore: Johns Hopkins University Press.

Kane, R. A., & Kane, R. L. (1981). *Assessing the elderly: A practical guide to measurement.* Lexington, Mass: Lexington Books.

Kane, R. A., & Kane R. L. (1987). *Long-term care: Principles, programs, and policies.* New York: Springer Publishing.

Kasmarik, P. E., & Lester, V. C. (1984). A hard decision: When institutionalization is the best answer. In B. A. Hall (Ed.), *Mental health and the elderly* (pp. 165-184). Orlando, FL: Grune & Stratton.

Kingson, E. R., Hirshorn, B. A., & Cornman, J. M. (1986). *Ties that bind: The interdependence of generations.* Washington, DC: Seven Locks Press.

Kosberg, J. I. (1988). Preventing elder abuse: Identification of high risk factors prior to placement decisions. *Gerontologist, 28,* 43-50.

Kosberg, J. I., & Cairl, R. E. (1986). The cost of care index: A case management tool for screening informal care providers. *Gerontologist, 26,* 273-277.

Kramer, M. (1986). Target populations for psychiatric–mental health nursing 1980-2005. In *Psychiatric mental health nursing: Proceedings of two conferences on future directions* (Pub. No. ADM 86-1449, pp. 4-42). Rockville, MD: U.S. Dept. of Health and Human Services.

Matteson, M. A., & McConnell, E. S. (1988). *Gerontological nursing: Concepts and practice*. Philadelphia: WB Saunders.

National Association for Home Care. (1987). *How to select a home care agency* (Available from National Association for Home Care, 519 C Street, NE Stanton Park, Washington, DC 20002).

National Council on the Aging, Inc. (1989). *Standards for adult day care* (Available from National Council on the Aging, Inc., 600 Maryland Ave. SW, West Wing 100, Washington, DC 20024).

Ohio Commission on Aging. (1989). *How to select an Ohio nursing home* (Available from Ohio Commission on Aging Nursing Home Ombudsman program, 50 W. Broad Street, Ninth Floor, Columbus, OH 43215).

Seltzer, M. M., Irvy, J., & Litchfield, L. C. (1987). Family members as case managers: Partnership between the formal and informal support networks. *Gerontologist, 27,* 722-728.

Shanas, E., & Nostrand, J. F. (1988). The family, the elderly, and long-term care. In R. E. Dunkle & M. L. Wykle (Eds.). *Decision making in long term care: Factors in planning* (pp. 71-84). New York: Springer Publishing.

Simon, R. M. (1980). Family life cycle issues in the therapy system. In E. A. Carter & M. McGoldrick (Eds.), *The family life cycle: A framework for family therapy* (pp. 329-340). New York: Gardner Press.

Smallegan, M. (1981). Decision making for nursing home admission: A preliminary study. *Journal of Gerontological Nursing, 7,* 280-285.

Sussman, M. B. (1976). The family life of older people. In R. H. Binstock & E. Shanas (Eds.), *Handbook of aging and the social sciences* (pp. 218-243). New York: Van Nostrand Reinhold.

United States House of Representatives Select Committee on Aging. (1987). *Exploding the myths: Caregiving in America*. Washington, DC: United States Government Printing Office.

Walsh, F. (1980). The family in later life. In E. A. Carter & M. McGoldrick (Eds.), *The family life cycle: A framework for family therapy* (pp. 197-217). New York: Gardner Press.

Wright, L. M., & Leahey, M. (1984). *Nurses and families: A guide to family assessment and intervention*. Philadelphia: FA Davis.

Unit III

Family Vulnerabilities

Chapter 11

Homeless Families

Ann Ottney Cain

Families are now the fastest growing segment of the homeless population (Long, 1988). The profile of homelessness in the United States is changing. We formerly associated the homeless with hobos and skid-row drunks. In the late 1970s and the early 1980s when mental institutions were emptied faster as part of deinstitutionalization, a new homeless population was turned loose in our country. These changes in the composition of the homeless have been accompanied by changes in public awareness. We began to see homeless people roaming our city streets, bedded down on hot-air grates, and huddled in doorways or sleeping in cardboard boxes for some protection from the weather. At the local, state, and national levels, the magnitude of the problems of homelessness has been forcibly brought to our attention through widespread media coverage that dramatically emphasizes the tragic lives of homeless people. Over the last few years, it has finally dawned on our nation's consciousness that we are truly facing an enormous problem.

Now our perceptions of homelessness must shift again as we come to grips with the startling fact that families with children are the fastest growing homeless group. They must attract our urgent attention, because of the clear danger that homelessness poses to the successful development of children and families (Long, 1988).

Estimates of the number of homeless people vary widely. They range from 250,000 to 2.5 million, with projected increases of 10% to 40% annually. In 1980, families were estimated to be less than 10% of this total population. In 1986 that figure increased to 34% and has continued to increase dramatically. Many experts believe that we are seeing only the beginnings of this trend (Anderson, 1987).

Characteristics of Families Becoming Homeless

Homeless families are everywhere in America. They are in cities, suburbs, towns, and rural areas. They sleep in temporary shelters, welfare hotels and motels, campgrounds, cars, and abandoned houses; under viaducts; and on the streets.

Those who are homeless have many problems besides a lack of a permanent place to live. They also lack money and therefore are short of food, medical care, clothing, educational opportunities, a job that pays enough to live on, and other necessary resources. They are also under much stress, suffer from low self-esteem, and are ignored by others who are afraid of having to respond to their many needs.

There are numerous reasons that families become homeless (Long, 1988). Some of these are the following:

- The job market may change, during which time people who once had a secure income lose their housing when they are laid off or a factory closes.
- People raising children alone have difficulty earning enough to support their households.
- Public assistance allowances have remained at a low level, while rental costs have risen sharply. There is a real shortage of low-cost housing in the United States.
- Parents may have medical conditions, mental disturbances, or substance abuse problems.
- Domestic conflict and spouse or child abuse may have been precipitating factors.
- Adolescent rebellion or rejection of adolescents by their parents can lead to homelessness.
- Fires or arson may have destroyed the housing.
- Buildings may be emptied because they are no longer safe to live in.
- A landlord may abandon a building, and therefore its services and structural integrity may no longer be maintained.
- Rental buildings may be converted to cooperative or condominium status that lower-income persons cannot afford to buy.
- Rents may rise sharply in an inexpensive housing area, and families cannot afford to stay.
- Unexpected crises may cause families to fall behind in their utility bills, rent, and other legitimate expenditures.
- Low-skilled workers may be in decreased demand. People are not trained and cannot find jobs. This does not mean that they do not *want* to work.

Families usually do not become homeless overnight. They may lose their home, move from place to place, and end up staying with family members and friends until they wear out their welcome. Few families go directly from their homes to a shelter—they turn to shelters as a *last* resort. Many homeless families go uncounted because they are among the "hidden homeless," those who double up with relatives or friends for as long as possible. When family members are all crowded together in inadequate space, tension can build and disagreements and cutoffs can occur. Also, landlords may evict families for breaking the lease when they have extra people living in rental properties. Once their supports are exhausted, families become homeless and live any place they can find space. If they are fortunate enough to find shelters, they often find that they can stay only a few nights or a few weeks at most. Shelter space is too scarce to continuously provide for all who need it. Consequently, finding a place to sleep is a constant, ongoing problem. Even if they find jobs, they are usually low paying, and it is unlikely that such families can come up with enough money for the first and the last month's rent that would enable them to rent an apartment.

These families, and especially single-parent families, usually live with the fear that their children will be taken away. If their children are placed in foster care, it eases their current burden but places them in a real bind because they may have very little chance of recovering their children in the future. If the family is not intact, social services will not provide enough money for the parent to get a place to live that is large enough for the children, and child welfare will not release the children unless the parent has adequate living space. This catch-22 produces even greater feelings of failure and loss.

When families become homeless, even though they may have gotten there by many different routes, they become more alike. Homelessness is a manifestation of severe poverty and a lack of any type of permanent residence and usually includes a disaffiliation from family and friends. Problems among homeless families are very similar. Living in crowded shelters, hotels, or motels undermines their self-esteem, partly because of their inability to provide a protected space for themselves and their children. Children are especially sensitive to the many moves involved in becoming homeless, to not knowing where they will sleep from one night to the next, to being crowded together in one room with their parents and siblings, to living in dangerous places, and to being afraid. They may develop behavior problems, their schooling may be disrupted, and—if it is not—they may be teased at school by their peers and teachers. Some children refuse to tell where they live or make up an imaginary place so that they do not have to admit that they are homeless.

In some parts of this country, the service system for homeless families excludes male parents from two-parent families. Some shelters allow only women and children, and financial aid is sometimes available only to single-parent families. When this happens, men may either leave the family or try to play some parenting or spousal role without being visible to these authorities (Long, 1988).

Members of homeless families respond in many different ways to their homelessness. Their moods may vary at different times, but the range includes becoming fighters, becoming street-wise, staying naive, and feeling determined, frustrated, hopeless, anxious, angry, fearful, and confused about why this is happening to them. It is very difficult for them to break the cycle of homelessness once they are in it.

Special Problems of Homeless Families

The experience of homelessness is very unsettling, and it has a profound effect on families. Many problems of homeless families have already been listed. Homeless parents are under an enormous strain while trying to figure out how to make it possible for their families to survive. They experience pervasive feelings of powerlessness, failure, and depression.

Children in homeless families suffer numerous emotional disturbances because of their experiences of loss. These disturbances can become deep-seated fear and can affect how such children relate to other people. They do not have a home and personal possessions that can provide them with a sense of identity and safety. Depression may be evident in the child as he or she shows a lack of interest in his or her surroundings and a lack of energy to interact with other people. Or such depression may be masked by overactivity as the child tries to adjust to continually changing surroundings. Anxiety may be evident in temper tantrums, panic attacks, or physical symptoms. There can be serious lags in children's mental and physical development and in their educational progress. The lack of security and consistency can lead to many difficulties in various areas of their lives. The homeless child may become socially isolated and feel rejected by his or her peers. This kind of rejection can have a devastating effect on self-esteem and overall functioning. As Valerie Mascitti of the New York Advocates for Children commented in her testimony before the Select Committee on Children, Youth, and Families in the U.S. House of Representatives on February 24th, 1987:

The children do learn lessons in the hotels and shelters. They learn, often firsthand, about drug abuse, about physical abuse, about alcohol abuse, and prostitution. They learn to accept mental abuse, and then how to give back all of those abuses. For these children, there is no light at the end of the tunnel, no way out, no American dream.

School experiences and friendship systems for the children in homeless families also present very special problems. Schools provide children with an important social context and offer positive adult role models through contact with teachers and administrators. Schools may be reluctant to accept children from homeless families because they may be out of step with their classmates, and they may require special resources to help them catch up. They move frequently and often miss a great deal of school, disrupting their educational experiences. Friendship and interaction with peers is a very important part of growing up. Being homeless tends to disrupt the usual exchange of peers. Children often lose friends as they move from place to place, and because of the circumstances of being homeless, they may have difficulty making new friends. Peers who know of their homelessness may be very cruel. Peers' parents may discourage their children from making friends with children from homeless families, because of fear that they will be a bad influence. And homeless children themselves may be reluctant to form new friendships, because they are afraid of being embarrassed. All of these experiences have a great impact on the homeless child's adjustment to life.

Deinstitutionalization of mentally ill persons, coupled with inadequate community-based care programs, is one of the major reasons for homelessness. Among homeless persons, a large percentage — usually estimated at between 35% and 50% — suffer from mental illness. With the development of new medicines and with the court decisions that clarified the civil rights of the mentally ill person, the doors of state hospitals have been opened and a new philosophy of community treatment has emerged. Today, usually the only individuals hospitalized for long periods are those who are considered a danger to themselves or to others. How many of these mentally ill adults are part of homeless families has not yet been determined. It is important to distinguish between a serious mental or emotional disturbance and the psychologic distress that often accompanies homelessness. For example, depression is very common among homeless persons of all ages because of the dismal conditions they live in and because of their low self-esteem. These people are not mentally ill per se, but instead are reacting legitimately to their situation in life. There are, however, severe mental and emotional disorders that keep a person from dealing effectively with life. Mental illnesses such as schizophrenia, mood disorders, personality disorders, and anxiety-related disturbances all occur in adults in homeless families. This is particularly true when people have been living under great stress for a considerable period. Unfortunately, this can go on indefinitely with little or no intervention that would allow the person to receive the kind of support or treatment that is needed to prevent or shorten an episode of mental illness.

Substance abuse is another special problem of homeless families. It has been reported that 20% to 50% of homeless persons have problems with substance abuse (National Institute of Mental Health, 1986). Some families who become homeless had this problem *before* they became homeless. Others develop it or it becomes worse because of what happens *after* they become homeless. Alcohol or some other drug may be used to help a person forget that he or she is living in such a desperate condition. Although drinking and drug use may temporarily numb feelings, it creates long-term problems for any family. One aspect of this problem is that concentrations of homeless people in family shelters are fertile ground for those who push drugs. Anytime that you have a collection of disillusioned people who have little hope for the future, they are prey to this type of exploitation.

Large numbers of homeless persons suffer from acute and chronic health problems. The incidence of disease and disability is considerably higher than for many other groups. Physical problems are particularly concentrated in the following areas: musculoskeletal defects, diseases of the nervous system, visual and auditory problems, and cardiovascular disease. In addition to these, the homeless life-style precipitates other medical problems such as tuberculosis, hepatitis, skin diseases, malnutrition, pneumonia, dental problems, cirrhosis, and ulcerated sores, especially on the legs and feet. Homeless persons usually seek medical treatment only when they are experiencing great pain. It is particularly difficult for them to follow through on conditions that require long-term treatment and repeated out-patient visits. In addition to this, illnesses often go untended because many homeless persons are afraid of hospitals, are uninsured, and are perceived to be undesirable patients (National Institute of Mental Health, 1986).

The poverty and poor health of homeless persons signal a critical need for appropriate medical care, even though treating transient people is extremely difficult. Homeless persons will accept care *if* it is offered in a non-threatening manner, *if* the relationship between the medical treatment and feeling better is made clear, and *if* the health services are available near where such persons are presently located.

It is clear that homeless families face all the usual problems of family life, and in addition to those, they must cope with the very special problems of their situation of homelessness.

The Influence of the Family

Before continuing to focus specifically on homeless families, we must develop a concept of what is important in all families and recognize the influence of the family on the ongoing development and life-style of every individual. Developing a systems perspective is very useful.

Every family functions as a system, and knowledge of the family as a system is essential to the assessment process. Every family develops systematic ways of being a family. These include communicating, problem solving, meeting family members' needs for affection and intimacy, resolving conflict, and dealing with loss and change (Cain, 1980).

The family is a system, and the action of each individual family member has an effect on the family as a whole. There is always interaction or dynamic movement between parts, and all parts are interdependent. If one family member is not functioning, it affects all of the other family members. If there is a change in one member of the family, there is a change in the whole system. This is a very important concept—it means that if one family member can be helped to change, the entire family system will change in some way.

A system is greater than the sum of its parts. The family is greater than the sum of its individual family members; it is a larger whole when operating as a unit.

In any family system, members compensate for each other. If one member is underfunctioning in certain areas, another member will compensate by overfunctioning in those areas. Family members consistently deal with each other in specific, reciprocal ways. With enough observation of these mutual patterns of interaction, they can be predicted within the family system. These patterns are reproduced over time and over generations.

The same elements may be part of more than one system. The family is a member of other larger systems and also has subsystems of its own. Systems function at all levels of efficiency from optimal functioning to total dysfunction or failure. The functioning of any system is partly dependent on the functioning of the larger systems of which it is a part and also on the functioning of its subsystems. The nuclear family is a part of the larger extended family system, and both are part of still larger systems such as school, work, church, community, state, nation, and world. Each of these larger systems has an effect on the family and how it functions, as do its subsystems. Examples of subsystems in the family would be different combinations of members, such as dyads, triangles, and members in stereotyped roles or in intense relationships, such as those who are extremely close or extremely conflictual with each other. Minuchin (1974) has described the spousal, parental, and sibling subsystems and has pointed out that subsystems can be formed by generation, gender, interests, or function. These subsystems affect the structure and function of the family as a whole.

The concept of open and closed systems is useful in viewing any family; however, there is no true open or closed system when applied to families. All family systems are open to some degree, but some family systems are more open and some are more closed than others. A family with a greater degree of openness is capable of taking in more messages from its environment and can adapt to what it hears, rather than distorting the information because it cannot handle change. Some families tend to shut out or distort almost all information coming from the environment to avoid upsetting their system's equilibrium. This type of family is more of a closed system — it is similar to a locked safe where nothing can get in. A more open system is able to take in outside information, respond to it flexibly, and still maintain its equilibrium (Cain, 1977).

It is important to consider the characteristics of a healthy, well-functioning family. Knowledge of what such a family is like is very important background information for one to have before he or she attempts to work with individuals and families who are experiencing the emotional difficulties that homeless families are.

Well-functioning families foster the following maturation processes in the family environment:

* Adequate socialization and competence in establishing personal relationships with others
* Development of a sense of identity and self-worth in each family member
* Provision of opportunities for self-expression and self-discipline
* Encouragement of independence and self-sufficiency
* Emancipation of each child, in varying degrees, from parental controls at appropriate stages of development

In dysfunctional families, one or more of these processes are absent or distorted (Thorman, 1965). However, in a well-functioning family, goals and purposes are achieved with minimal confusion and conflict. Role expectations are explicit and clearly defined. Family members help each other deal with their responsibilities and complement one another in their roles. A dysfunctional family lacks these abilities, and its goals and purposes are confused.

A family undergoes many changes during its lifetime, and a well-functioning family can accommodate itself to these changing situations and new experiences. It is flexible, adjusts to fluid conditions and a variety of demands, and is capable of change. In contrast, a dysfunctional family develops stereotyped mechanisms of defense against change and becomes rigid and closed in its functioning (Thorman, 1965).

Thinking is an important part of problem solving, and more of this is seen in well-functioning families. There is more thinking, and they are less dictated by their feelings. There is more of an integration of thinking and feeling. In dysfunctional families, there is little thinking and problem solving, and these families function at a very high feeling level.

Few research studies have been conducted with well-functioning families.

One, by Lewis et al. (1976), found that no single quality was demonstrated by optimally functioning families and not demonstrated by less functional families. There was a mixture of variables that accounted for the impressive differences in style and patterning among the well-functioning families. Some of these included a positive attitude about human encounters, a respect for their own and other's views, a capacity to tolerate individual differences, a problem-solving approach, high levels of initiative and constructive reaching out, a strong parental relationship in which leadership was shared, clear ego boundaries between family members, separateness with closeness but no pull toward family oneness, open expression of both positive and negative feelings, a perception of the family as competent, high degrees of spontaneity, and frequent use of humor and wit.

Homeless families are experiencing the same kind of life-cycle changes that all families go through. A systems perspective takes into account the impact of critical events and the disruption that they can cause in a family, as well as the family's approach and response to those events. The family can be seen as a system that has a life cycle (predictable stages) of its own, as well as each individual member with developmental stages of his or her own. It is important to develop an understanding of the relationships, interconnections, and mutual influence of both the individual and family life-cycle stages on one another.

Life-cycle events are stressors that pose adaptive challenges for both individuals and families. Major life changes stress the entire family system, not just the individual members who are most directly affected. These changes can be a stimulus for either successful adaptation or for dysfunction.

Carter and McGoldrick (1980) have identified the following sequential stages of family life: the unattached young adult, marriage of the new couple, reproduction and rearing of children, launching children and moving on, and the family in later life. They have included special issues with which families must deal, such as death, serious illness, separation, divorce, single parenting, remarriage, and women's roles in families. They emphasize that some periods in the family life-cycle are more critical than are others and merit special attention. It is important to realize that these times in family life are not completely negative or crisis-filled. New, pleasant, and rewarding aspects of one's self or others may be discovered during these periods. Families often discover strengths that they never knew they had. Certainly homelessness would be a special type of crisis and would require the family to use all the strengths that they have developed and to develop new strengths to deal with this very insecure time in their lives.

Some family theories emphasize the uncovering and working through of past losses and conflicts in the family of origin, particularly if these seem to be impairing present relationships. The three-generational family life-cycle model offers a way of taking into account the timing of symptoms and their relationship with both past and current events that have caused disruption in the family. It is important to ask the question, "Why is this happening now?" and to look closely at the life-cycle issues and how they are associated with the specific timing of symptoms in families and family members.

Useful Interventions with All Families

Meaningful assessment data can be collected by taking a three-generational family history. It provides factual information about the overall behavior of the family and is a way of discovering how the family system has functioned over time and how it is functioning now. It is important to get a factual picture and an accurate description of events so that the family situation can be accurately assessed. Transferring this information to a family diagram illustrates the extended family system and is an extremely useful tool in teaching families about family systems and how they function. It assists the family to think broadly in terms of the total family system (Bowen, 1978).

The family history includes dates for all events in the history of the family and includes questions about members of the family on the maternal and paternal sides, ages of family members, sibling positions, education, occupations, divorces and remarriages, deaths, adoptions, births, abortions, family ground rules, family decision making, family secrets, past and current living locations, family crises, type and amount of contact of family members, major family concerns, and so on.

The family time line is a useful tool for assessment of temporal patterns, particularly in clarifying and ordering information that is relevant to the presenting problems and to problem resolution. This entails asking the family to construct a time line indicating the dates of significant events (births, deaths, losses, moves, relationships, and so on) so that you can see how each event fits into the overall picture of the family.

Toman's description of the basic sibling positions (1976), which are based on the genders and age ranks of all the members of the nuclear family, is very useful in reconstructing individual positions and patterns of behavior in a family over time. Sibling positions are viewed as roles that a person has learned in his or her own family and that he or she tends to assume in future situations outside the family. Sibling positions imply certain behavior trends, personality traits, and social inclinations. These patterns are frequently duplicated through generations and are an interesting and valuable source of information about the family.

There are eight basic sibling positions, plus the positions of the only child and twins. They are oldest brother of brother(s), youngest brother of brother(s), oldest brother of sister(s), youngest brother of sister(s), oldest sister of sister(s), youngest sister of sister(s), oldest sister of brother(s), and the youngest sister of brother(s). Knowledge of a person's sibling position can be very helpful in understanding his or her functioning. All of this information is important in providing a comprehensive family assessment and in planning future interventions with the family. Reassessments should be frequent, and evaluations of interventions should be ongoing.

The following specific interventions will be helpful to all families (Cain & Irving, 1984):

• Be objective and do not take sides with any family member.

- Use the "how, who, where, when" style of questioning to gain facts in the situation. Avoid the use of "why?" It cuts off communication.
- Recognize that the family member expressing symptoms is communicating "something" about the family as a whole. He or she is the family "symptom-bearer."
- Give attention to both the verbal and nonverbal messages of all family members.
- Relate family life-cycle events to the current and past functioning of the family.
- When appropriate, teach about sibling position profiles and how they may operate in the family.
- Assist family members to improve their communication and decision-making skills.
- When possible, defuse intense feelings of each family member so that his or her thinking is clearer. Acknowledge that feelings are helpful in identifying problems but that thinking is the necessary component for solving problems.
- Support family members in their efforts toward change, realizing that this is a time of high anxiety for all involved.
- Refuse to keep "secrets." Keep communication open and available to all family members.
- Encourage a sense of humor in family members, and encourage them not to take themselves too seriously.
- Identify and emphasize the areas of family strength. Be aware of, but do not over-focus on, family weaknesses.
- Assist family members to define their own principles and values, which may be different from those of other family members. It is important to help family members to realize that it is okay to think separately and to be different from each other. This does not destroy closeness but will eventually lead to more satisfying family relationships.

These interventions are useful when working with any family and therefore are important when working with homeless families.

Useful Interventions Specific to Homeless Families

Certain approaches are useful to all professionals working with homeless families, and others are specific to the psychiatric nursing specialist. A discussion of the overall approaches will be presented first.

Setting a tone of mutual respect is very helpful in building and maintaining positive relationships with homeless families. This includes giving each family member your full attention when talking with him or her. Distrust is often very evident in homeless families, and it is important to work to overcome this. Work to build a trusting relationship with each family member. This includes being reliable, doing what you say you will do, being consistent, and not promising too much. If tempers are running high, keep your cool so that your self-control will enable the others to regain their control. Do all that you can to strengthen the role of the parents, to help the parents appreciate their children, and to encourage the parents to have some positive activity apart from their children (Long, 1988). Encourage the family members to maintain contact with their extended families. Assist them in bridging any cutoffs and in keeping communication open.

Developing observational, listening, and interviewing skills is very important in working with homeless families. Observation of families includes looking at more than the individual members. It requires observing how the family members relate to each other, both verbally and nonverbally. This helps us determine how the family deals with their problems. Experienced, objective observers are able to put their own feelings aside temporarily to see behavior as broadly as possible. Listening involves paying attention to more than another person's words; it involves paying attention to their tone of voice and their gestures, which often tell us more about what they really mean than the content of their words do. When one is conducting an interview, questions can be very useful in helping to guide the conversation. Appropriate questions give the interviewee the opportunity to tell you what he or she knows or thinks about a situation. It is very helpful in determining another person's knowledge and experience, and it lets the other person know that you are interested in what he or she is thinking or feeling.

Much of what has already been described in terms of problems and experiences of homeless families helps us understand their behavior better. They are a very oppressed group, and it is difficult to assist them in their efforts to break the cycle of homelessness. It is important to help them to select useful activities and goals for each family member and to develop realistic expectations for what they can do, so that they are not eternally disappointed in themselves and their accomplishments. Homeless families are likely to have to work through the processes of denial of the difficulty of their situation, of feeling abandoned, of anger at their circumstances, of depression, and of fantasy–wish fulfillment. As a result of all these factors, such families can become extra demanding at times. It is important to express clearly what is required in each situation and to stress the limitations imposed by the social service organizations so that sympathy for the family does not blur the need to require the family to take care of the tasks and to follow the rules that are part of the structure of society. This kind of limit setting is extremely helpful in working with homeless families.

Another kind of limit setting involves setting limits for yourself as a professional. The extremely needy quality of some homeless families can tempt professionals to make very heroic efforts. These extraordinary efforts in the family's behalf make the professional look and feel good, but they usually do not help the family mobilize its own resources to solve its own problems, and in the long run, homeless families must eventually find their own way. If professionals overfunction continually in this way, they eventually suffer from compassion-fatigue, and they are less helpful to others from this burned-out position. The most useful position for professionals is to present themselves to homeless families as colleagues in working together to find the best solutions to the existing problems (Long, 1988).

Other important approaches for all professionals working with homeless families include locating existing resources or creating new resources whenever possible, making appropriate and timely referrals, and functioning as an effective advocate when it is needed.

Professionals who work with homeless families tend to experience considerable stress. The extreme needs that family members have and the inability of the professional to meet those needs can lead to much frustration. It is important to recognize this and to take steps to reduce the personal stress involved in working with homeless families whenever possible. Professionals need to work to keep their focus clear, to keep from becoming overly involved, and also to keep from inappropriately distancing themselves from homeless families. Maintaining a reasonable balance will produce the most effective functioning.

There are specific areas in which a psychiatric nursing specialist can function while working with homeless families. Assessment is a very important way to evaluate the family's functioning. Observation and analysis of the family structure are essential to a complete assessment. All of the previous suggestions made in terms of assessment can be used very effectively with homeless families. The history taker asks many questions, and the more she or he learns about the family, the more the family learns about itself. This assists the homeless family to think broadly in terms of the family system, and many patterns can be traced through the generations. Once these patterns have been identified, family members can plan ways of changing their own behavior if they desire change (Cain, 1980). This kind of family history data can emphasize the widespread potential for homelessness even among people who have had years of reasonably secure living.

The psychiatric nurse specialist has an excellent background for providing case management services and for membership on multidisciplinary teams. Because homeless families often have complex needs and require the services of a number of agencies, case management is of crucial importance in breaking the cycle of homelessness. Case managers assess family needs and develop a plan of services to meet those needs. The case manager provides essential guidance and acts as a liaison in the securing of necessary services. These services include advocacy for benefits, medical and psychiatric assistance, job training and employment, educational and financial counseling, and referrals for permanent housing. Once these services have been obtained, the case manager maintains contact with the family to reassess needs periodically and to monitor the quality of services. The presence of a skilled, empathetic case manager in the life of a homeless family helps to counteract the feelings of powerlessness the family so often experiences. Case management promotes a humane approach to the problems of homeless families, encourages and facilitates independence, and helps to minimize the length and the number of episodes of homelessness for the family.

The use of multidisciplinary teams for case assessment, planning, and coordination can be very effective when working with homeless families. The philosophy underlying the use of multidisciplinary teams is that many families have multiple problems that require the skills of a broad range of professional disciplines and/or agencies. The team can include, but is not limited to, a social worker, a psychiatrist, a pediatrician, a psychiatric or public health nurse, an attorney, and a school principal. By providing consultation and expertise from many disciplines, these teams identify the range of needs present among parents and children; develop a concrete, coordinated plan of action; and through the use of existing public/private resources, oversee proper implementation of that plan (Gallagher, 1986).

The psychiatric nurse specialist can provide direct care for members of homeless families through individual, group, and family therapy. Child psychiatric nurse specialists are prepared to work specifically with children in homeless families. Some of homeless family members have previously been diagnosed as having mental illnesses. Others, with no previous history of mental illness, have experienced a profound change in their life situation and have been unable to cope. They lack the skills and stamina necessary to cope with all that is required of them. Both of these groups have many varied and complex mental health needs that can be addressed effectively by psychiatric nurse specialists using many of the therapeutic interventions suggested earlier in this chapter. These specialists can also function on mobile mental health treatment teams that seek out homeless persons in need of mental health service but who are too disorganized to seek it out for themselves via the traditional health care delivery system.

Mental health services are needed by all homeless or near-homeless families because of the traumatic psychologic effects produced by the experience of homelessness. Not to have a home of one's own is a profoundly depersonalizing experience. A home—as well as a family, friends, and work—is part of one's self-definition. Being homeless puts one visibly at the bottom of society, and there is no escape from the starkness of that reality. The status of homelessness cuts one off from a previous life-style, from the resources necessary to parent one's children adequately, and from comforting everyday routines. This extreme disruption causes psychologic trauma, depression, and hopelessness.

Consultation with the staff members of homeless shelters is another area in which psychiatric nurse specialists can use their expertise. Shelter staff members are usually not well prepared to deal with mentally ill persons or with persons who are experiencing severe emotional problems. These staff members struggle with maintaining a safe environment, setting limits, establishing trust, maintaining consistency, managing aggressive or violent behavior, and working with residents who are highly stressed and often depressed. Shelter staff members are often extremely motivated to learn more about each of these, because they deal with all of this on a daily basis and have not had adequate mental health consultation available to them. Psychiatric nurse specialists are well prepared to provide consultation and teaching in all of these areas, and it is vital to staff in homeless facilities that they do so.

In Baltimore I participated in a Mental Health Association project entitled "The Homeless Connection." This provided mental health consultation to each of the city shelters on a regular basis by volunteer psychiatrists, psychologists, psychiatric nurse specialists, and psychiatric social workers. This was extremely effective, and shelter staffs were very receptive. It is the type of homeless project that could be duplicated in any of our cities, and it would provide a much-needed service.

Providing care for homeless persons in psychiatric emergency room settings requires the psychiatric nurse specialist to be highly skilled and motivated. It takes a blend of mental health and public health skills to provide any kind of comprehensive service, and this is very difficult to accomplish in a milieu constructed for crisis intervention. Staff members are seldom trained to meet the needs of the multiproblem homeless patient. Because homeless persons are at risk for such a variety of medical health problems related to their living situation, medical treatment of nonemergency problems needs to be integrated into the care given at the time of a psychiatric emergency visit. This places a greater burden on psychiatric emergency staff, and consequently, the comprehensive needs of homeless persons are often not adequately met in emergency settings (National Institute of Mental Health, 1986).

The unstable life-style of homeless families places them at high risk for malnutrition. Accessibility to food remains a critical issue for these families. Soup kitchens evolved in response to the awareness that homeless persons were hungry and unable to provide food for themselves. Soup kitchens have proliferated in recent years, but because they have access only to certain commodities of food, they are limited in the types of meals they can provide. Some soup kitchens provide only food, whereas others have evolved into multiservice programs that may include nursing clinics; clothing exchanges; counseling departments for personal, job, and spiritual counseling; and shower facilities to meet the many needs of homeless persons. The psychiatric nurse specialist's role in these programs can be multi-faceted and depends on the services offered. Clinically, the nurse is confronted with a population having special nutritional needs, in addition to all the other needs previously mentioned in this chapter. Education about nutrition can help homeless persons increase their awareness of the nutritional impact of available food and can promote more positive self-care (National Institute of Mental Health, 1986).

The psychiatric nurse specialist can participate effectively in community self-help groups. Sometimes the professional working with the homeless family often does things *for* the family in need, rather than enabling family members to do things on their own. The family who receives this kind of help does not develop the skills, knowledge, or confidence that is required to solve the problem again the next time it arises. It is much more helpful to accept the right of the family to manage its own life and to enter into a partnership with the family around its goals to help the members achieve such goals as best they can. Self-help groups operate on a similar set of assumptions (Long, 1988):

- People who have been through an experience can be helpful to others who have a similar problem or experience such as homelessness.
- "Credentials," rather than being based on education or social status, consist of having been through the experience oneself.

- Everyone with relevant experience has something of value to contribute, and solutions arrived at by those who have been through the problem are more valid than are suggestions offered by outsiders.
- Mutual support from those who have been through the experience helps one to deal with the lack of self-esteem connected with being homeless.
- Role models within the group encourage participants to see that the problem can be overcome or at least confronted in a way that can be self-enhancing, rather than demoralizing.
- The role of helping others in the group reinforces the coping skills of the person who is doing the helping.
- Taking control of one's life puts the family member in a strong, rather than a weak, position and tends to help solve the problem of lack of motivation.

The role of psychiatric nurse specialists in a self-help group is a supportive one. They may help the group stay on a topic it has chosen. They may facilitate the exploration of ideas and problems that the group is interested in. They may help the group to get more information or to express its feelings and opinions to the proper people. Psychiatric nurse specialists do not take over the group, but instead support the group in setting its own direction and goals.

There are many knowledge gaps in our understandings about the characteristics, needs, strengths, and service delivery imperatives in relation to homeless individuals and families. These can be addressed by nursing research and can be investigated from a nursing perspective. Dr. Judith Maurin, in her paper "Knowledge Gaps Which Can Be Addressed Through Nursing Research" (National Institute of Mental Health, 1986) has identified five categories of nursing research within which important questions about homeless persons and families can be framed. These categories are research that (1) generates knowledge about health and health promotion in homeless individuals and families, (2) generates knowledge about the influence of social and physical environments on health of homeless individuals and families, (3) addresses the care of homeless persons who are acutely or chronically ill, disabled, or dying, as well as the care of their families, (4) studies therapeutic actions that minimize the negative effects of illness by enhancing the abilities of homeless individuals and families to respond to actual or potential health problems, and (5) generates knowledge about systems that effectively and efficiently deliver health care to homeless individuals and families. Dr. Maurin emphasized the contributions that nurse researchers could make through their unique perspective but commented that the many complex problems of homeless persons could best be understood by interdisciplinary research teams. The psychiatric nurse specialist is prepared to conduct individual research or to participate in interdisciplinary research. The research role needs to be expanded to fill in these gaps in knowledge.

Prevention of Homelessness

It is unfortunate that at present most programs for homeless persons are designed to respond to emergencies rather than to prevent them. Fewer resources would be required to prevent a family from being homeless than those needed to shelter a family and to rehouse them later. Despite this fact, the federal government has chosen to cut back its programs for subsidized housing, rental assistance, job training and employment, food stamps, and other benefits that would help prevent homelessness for many families. Almost any program or service designed to reduce poverty or to assist the poor will simultaneously reduce the likelihood that families will become homeless. The existing programs should be expanded and new programs should be established to provide employment, income, and benefits for those who need them and to prevent eviction and to assist with relocation of families who are losing their homes. When costs are measured in terms of human suffering and destructiveness to family life, it is clear that "an ounce of prevention is worth a pound of cure."

Early identification is an important aspect of prevention. The basic task in preventing homelessness is to identify those families that are at risk, *before* they become homeless (Long, 1988). Informal, as well as official, helping networks need to be involved in identifying potential homelessness and in working to reach those families who are not yet known to social agencies. Church congregations, parent-teacher associations, and various community clubs should be provided information about where families with difficulties can be referred. Printed brochures outlining ways to get help should be made easily available, and self-referral should be encouraged. It is estimated that there are up to 14 million Americans who are in danger of becoming homeless. These people are one paycheck away from homelessness.

Appropriate referrals are another vital ingredient in preventing homelessness. If access to resources can be made as barrier-free as possible, families will be more likely to seek assistance. What is needed to establish eligibility must be clearly spelled out for families so that they do not find the process so threatening. Families can get lost between the initial referral and the agency to which they are being sent. The referring professional needs to work carefully to make sure that the referral is timely and appropriate.

Emergency financial assistance can contribute greatly to the prevention of homelessness. A one-time payment of an overdue utility bill or a late rent payment can make it possible for many families to stay in their homes. This kind of assistance needs to be accompanied by counseling to determine whether it is a one-time emergency or if the family will need continuing financial help. Most states have grants to pay for fuel, back rent, and utility bills for families who have received eviction notices. These grants are sometimes not fully used, and they need to be publicized more widely as an important resource for people on the brink of homelessness.

The need for case management and/or multidisciplinary teams has already been discussed. This kind of coordination of services for homeless or near-homeless individuals and families is vital to ensure that the needy can properly use the services that are currently available to them.

Counseling for family problems is another important area of prevention. A wide range of family problems can lead to fragmentation of a family and eventually to homelessness. Early intervention in family conflicts, in domestic violence situations, and in other emotional problems may assist the family in staying together during and after these difficult times.

The decline in low-cost, affordable housing is one of the most urgent problems, and this must be addressed in any discussion of prevention of homelessness. There is a critical need for such resources as transitional housing, state rental subsidies, and permanent low-cost housing. Construction of new, affordable housing or the rehabilitation of dilapidated or abandoned housing may be the only way to stem the tide of homelessness (Long, 1988). All of the shelters, all of the specialized services, all of the food stamps and other subsidies, and all of the newly-mounted concern about homeless persons will not provide the answer for prevention unless an adequate supply of low-cost housing and a rental assistance program are developed to meet the permanent housing needs of homeless or potentially homeless individuals and families. The current shelter system is a Band-Aid and in no way a permanent solution to homelessness.

Legislation passed by the 99th Congress (1988) included an amendment to the Omnibus Drug Bill (H.R. 5582), which listed several considerations for the homeless. It included the following provisions:

- Extending eligibility for food stamps to homeless individuals
- Allowing homeless individuals who qualify for food stamps to use them to purchase prepared meals at soup kitchens
- Requiring the Health and Human Services (HHS) Secretary to devise a method of making Supplemental Security Income (SSI) payments to homeless individuals
- Amending the Job Training Partnership Act to include homeless persons as a targeted group for employment training
- Extending Medicaid health coverage to otherwise eligible homeless individuals
- Requiring the HHS Secretary, with the Secretary of Agriculture, to develop a system allowing individuals to apply for SSI and food stamps before discharge or release from a public institution, such as a mental hospital or prison

These are encouraging provisions that will positively assist homeless individuals and families.

Professionals who work with homeless families need support and encouragement in what they are doing. It is easy to become discouraged by the general lack of adequate resources, to be puzzled by some of the behavior of family members, and to feel powerless to change the situation (Long, 1988). Anyone who works with homeless persons for very long recognizes that the existing resources of emergency shelters, transitional housing, affordable permanent housing, physical and mental health care, and case management services are all inadequate to serve the increasing numbers of homeless individuals and families. Despite this fact, we must work with what we have, persist in fighting for more, and continue to work to resolve the devastating social problem of homelessness.

REFERENCES

Anderson, D. (Nov./Dec., 1987). When the bough breaks. *The Family Therapy Networker, 11*(6), 18-29.

Baumann, D., & Grigsby, C. (1988). *Understanding the homeless: from research to action.* Austin, TX: Hogg Foundation for Mental Health.

Bennett, G. (1989). Substance abuse: a significant factor in the plight of the homeless. *Addictions nursing network, 1,*(1) 2.

Bowen, M. (1978). *Family therapy in clinical practice.* New York: Jason Aronson.

Brickner, P., et al. (1990). *Under the safety net.* New York: W.W. Norton.

Cain, A. (1976). The therapist's role in family systems therapy. *The Family, 3,* 65-72.

Cain, A. (1977). Families and family therapy. In L. Robinson, (Ed.), *Psychiatric nursing as a human experience.* Philadelphia: W.B. Saunders.

Cain, A. (1980). Assessment of family structure. In J. Miller & E. Janosik (Eds.), *Family focused care.* New York: McGraw-Hill.

Cain, A., & Irving, J. (1984). Family work in inpatient settings. In J. Howe, E.J. Dickensen, D.A. Jones, & M.J. Snider (Eds.), *The handbook of nursing.* New York: John Wiley & Sons.

Carter, E., & McGoldrick, M. (1980). *The family life cycle.* New York: Gardner Press.

Damrosch, S., et al. (1988). On behalf of homeless families. *American Journal of Maternal Child Nursing, 13*(4), 259-263.

Gallagher, E. (1986). *No place like home.* Boston: Massachusetts Committee for Children & Youth.

Knapp, P. (1989). *The search for shelter program workbook.* Washington, D.C.: American Institute of Architects.

Lewis, J., et al. (1976). *No single thread: Psychological health in family system.* New York: Brunner/Mazel.

Libonati, C. (1986). *Assessing the needs of homeless and chronically mentally ill women.* Unpublished seminar paper. Baltimore: University of Maryland, School of Nursing.

Long, L. (1988). *Helping homeless families: A training curriculum.* Bethesda, MD: National Institute of Mental Health.

Maurin, J. (1986). *Knowledge gaps which can be addressed through nursing research.* Bethesda, MD: National Institute of Mental Health.

Minuchin, S. (1974). *Families and family therapy.* Cambridge, MA: Harvard University Press.

The National Alliance to End Homelessness. (1991). *What you can do to help the homeless.* New York: Simon & Shuster/A Fireside Book.

National Institute of Mental Health. (1986). *The role of nurses in meeting the health/mental health needs of the homeless: Proceedings of March 6-7, 1986 workshop.* Bethesda, MD.

Selling, L. (November-December, 1988). Out on the streets — nurses bring hope to the homeless. *California nursing review,* 10-36.

Sullivan, P., & Damrosch, S. (1987). Homeless women and children. In R. Bingham, et al. (Eds.), *The homeless in contemporary society.* Newbury Park, CA: Sage Publications.

Thorman, G. (1965). *Family therapy: A handbook.* Beverly Hills, CA: Western Psychological Services.

Toman, W. (1976). *Family constellation.* New York: Springer.

Chapter 12

Stress in Rural Families

Kathryn R. Puskar
Donna Martsolf

This chapter discusses the stresses and mental health problems of adolescents and their families who live in a rural community, presents a model of care for rural mental health using a psychiatric nurse team, and suggests some guidelines for psychiatric nursing assessment and prevention/intervention.

Rural Health Issues

According to Hassinger (1982), 27% of the population in the United States resides in areas that the United States Census Bureau classifies as rural. A difference exists between rural and urban populations in relation to health care needs (Kenkel, 1986). To meet the health care needs of the large population of rural Americans, we must identify the characteristics of this population. Rural America has a unique set of problems that affect the health service process. Cordes (1985) suggests that the single most important characteristic that distinguishes rural from urban areas is low population density. This factor has an important effect on at least three areas of rural life (Cordes, 1985):

- Communication and transportation patterns
- One's sense of community insofar as networks and interactions with family, friends, and neighbors
- The existence, or lack thereof, of specialized services and complex organizations and institutions

Bachrach (1977), Templeman et al. (1989), and Kenkel (1986) add to this list of problems in rural areas: poverty, high unemployment, and occupational stress related to mining, farming, and ranching. Kenkel exemplifies the importance of occupational stress in rural living by citing a study in which farm manager ranked twelfth out of 130 stress-related occupations.

Flaskerud and Kuiz (1984) cite several studies that indicate that rural areas are also affected by the problem of few human service agencies and inadequate mental health resources. The President's Commission on Mental Health

213

addressed this issue in 1978 when a special task panel was appointed to study problems in the provision of rural mental health care. Both poverty and low population density contribute to the shortage of mental health services. Segal (cited in Farie & Cowen, 1986) points out that "rural school district revenues are limited by low incomes and small industrial tax bases." In addition, the low population density leads to a lower amount of government aid to the rural school district. This shortage of public money results in a severe limitation to the mental health services that can be provided to children within the context of the school. A further deterrent to adequate mental health services in rural areas is the isolation experienced by the professional who lives and works in rural areas. Those professionals who live in more urban areas must travel great distances to provide service in more rural areas (Farie & Cowen, 1986).

A second issue related to the adequacy of mental health resources in rural areas deals with the level of public knowledge of the availability of such services. In a study conducted in rural Tennessee (Linn & Husaini, 1985) 75% of the respondents were unaware of the mental health services available in their community. Cordes (1985) indicates that knowing such services are present in a community has great value in reducing anxiety.

A third issue in evaluating the adequacy of rural mental health resources is the belief that psychologic dysfunction and the resultant need for services is great in rural areas. Kenkel (1986) cites several studies that support the idea that there is a clear link between poverty and psychologic dysfunction. A comparison made between rural and urban populations indicates that rural populations have a higher percentage of persons living in poverty. Flaskerud and Kuiz (1984) state that although there is no consistent empiric evidence supporting the claim that rates of mental illness are higher in rural areas, the literature continues to suggest this trend. However, Flaskerud and Kuiz do not indicate which types of mental illness are related to rural living and suggest that the rate of mental illness is not helpful in determining needs for mental health services in rural areas.

Rural Adolescents

Among rural adolescent populations, one of the major mental health concerns is a trend of increasing alcohol use and abuse. In a study of rural adolescents aged 13 to 18 years conducted by Gibbons et al. (1986), 83% of the respondents indicated that they had used alcohol. This is slightly lower than national figures that indicate that 93% of students use alcohol (Johnston et al, cited in Gibbons et al, 1986). Gibbons et al. suggest that "rural youth may be 'catching up' to their urban peers." In addition, the data in the study indicate that rural youth begin drinking at an earlier age than their urban counterparts. Fifty-seven percent had had their first drink by age 12. Gibbons et al. indicate that these findings are similar to those of other studies of rural youth. Sarvela and McClendon, in a 1987 study of rural adolescents in northern Michigan, further clarify the problem of rural adolescent alcohol abuse. The researchers reported that this population is highly prone to abusive drinking. Data were compared with national studies and seem to indicate that rural adolescents, when compared with their urban peers, demonstrate a higher prevalence of alcohol misuse.

Several of the characteristics of rural areas further intensify the problem of adolescent alcohol misuse in these areas. Gibbons' study indicated that time spent at parties and dances and with friends affects how often and how much students drink and whether they are heavy drinkers. In a discussion of the study's results, Gibbons indicates that rural adolescents are faced with the problem of limited recreational opportunities.

Kenkel (1986) adds that community denial is one way that the general population copes with community problems. The rural community sometimes deals with existing problems, such as adolescent alcohol abuse, by ignoring them or refusing to acknowledge their presence. In exemplifying this coping strategy, Kenkel states:

For example, in the case of teenage alcohol abuse, sheriffs do not enforce the laws against selling liquor to minors. The newspaper editor omits the drunk driving arrests from the listing of weekly arrests. Parents allow alcohol at parties for their teenagers.

Forrest (1988) states that depression and related suicide ideas are common among rural adolescents. Forrest cites a recent study (Rosenberg, 1986, cited in Forrest) of 2200 15- to 19-year-olds that was conducted in a rural area of southwestern Minnesota. Although the national average for adolescent suicide attempts is 2 out of every 1000, Rosenberg found that 3 out of 100 adolescents in the rural sample had attempted suicide in a 1-month period. These results were corroborated in several other rural areas. Forrest goes on to state that depressed rural students view drinking as a passive method for dealing with stress. In addition, Forrest indicated that a major roadblock to provision of assistance to these adolescents occurs because rural adolescents believe that confidentiality will not be maintained in their community health care settings.

Models of Care for Rural Mental Health

The literature suggests that there have been at least three models of care used to provide effective general and mental health care in rural areas: (1) Government-sponsored programs, (2) natural caregivers, and (3) prevention programs. Rosenblatt and Moscovice (cited in Cordes, 1985) deal with the first of these:

During the past 10 to 15 years many resources—primarily at the federal level—have gone into various health and medical care policies and programs which are particularly important to rural areas. Examples include the development of mid-level health practitioners, a rapid increase in the number of general and family practitioners, and the following specific programs: Rural Health Services Clinic Act; National Health Services Corps; Community Health Centers; Rural Health Initiative, and migrant Health Centers.

However, as Cordes suggests, recent changes in spending by the Federal government will have a great effect on these programs.

Hassinger (1982) suggests that the second important model of care in rural areas is the social network of family, friends, and neighbors. These groups:

- Provide various alternatives to professional treatment, including home treatment and treatment by lay professionals, faith healers, and untrained midwives
- Offer support that might otherwise be sought from professional sources
- Serve to delay the seeking of professional services because of the process of "network review"

Hassinger also suggests that primary groups and social networks of family, friends, and neighbors are more important in rural than urban areas.

Kenkel (1986) states that natural caregivers are individuals who—without formal positions or roles—provide guidance, support, and assistance to community members. This support is highly valued in the community and is given free of charge. Kenkel goes on to suggest that rural people rarely turn to professional mental health agencies for advice on how to cope. Instead, they use family, clergy, a family doctor, or natural caregivers.

One of the most significant sources of natural caregiving in rural areas is the family. The rural family has many strengths when compared with its urban counterpart but is also experiencing many changes and stresses. Cordes (1985) compared rural and urban populations and suggested that, although the two groups are beginning to show a merging in the area of values, three major differences still exist: (1) morality, (2) religion, and (3) political philosophy. These differences in values reflect themselves in family life. Rural people are more opposed to teenagers having access to contraception and favor greater difficulty in obtaining a divorce. Characteristics that are important to rural residents are independence, honesty, religiosity, and ethnocentricity (Forrest, 1988).

Gotts and Purnell (1986) report the findings of their study, which indicated that the rural father is present in the family more often than is his urban counterpart. In addition, the rural mother is employed full-time outside the home less commonly than is the urban mother. Shoffner (1986) cites several studies that indicate that traditional sex-role attitudes are more prevalent in rural than urban areas. Traditional values have been demonstrated in rural women's dissatisfaction with working outside the home. In further describing the rural family, Gotts and Purnell state that the rural parents in their study indicated less often than did urban parents that they had specific problems as parents. Shoffner also indicated that rural men are not supportive of their wives' working and do not view positively taking on increased family responsibilities. However, Shoffner's study of 525 rural mothers showed that 75% of the mothers had at least one and, in 25% of the cases, all of her relatives living in the immediate area. Thus, child care and rearing responsibilities can be shared by female family members.

Gotts and Purnell (1986) also indicated a close relationship between the rural family and the school. According to this study, rural families are more likely to be called on by the school for volunteer help. In addition, a larger percentage of rural than urban parents attended at least some school-sponsored activities. Gotts and Purnell (1986) conclude that the urban family structure is experiencing greater stress than is the rural. The rural parents in their study did not rely as heavily on formal and professional assistance in child rearing. This study did point out one exception to this general conclusion. When very isolated rural families were examined, it was noted that the parents had lower education and received much less support for child rearing from extended family and neighbors. These families tended to use older children for child care and experienced more stress in their parenting roles than did their urban or less isolated rural peers.

Forrest (1988) states that there is some evidence that the traditional close-knit relationships in rural families are beginning to disappear, however. Several sources of stress on the rural family are apparent. The first of these is mentioned by Forrest, who suggests that financial worries in rural areas affect the whole family structure. In addition, Kenkel (1986) discussed the problem of rural farm families who have to work together on the farm. Citing a 1979 study, Kenkel reported that 75% of farm families indicated the presence of family stress related to the farming occupation.

The third model or care commonly used in rural settings is that of prevention programs. Kenkel (1986) states that, unlike their urban colleagues, rural mental health practitioners have heeded the call in the past 20 years for primary prevention as a vital component of mental health services. Because rural areas have fewer resources and personnel to deal with mental health issues in adolescents, mental health prevention programs aimed at large groups of students are an important alternative to treating the most troubled few. According to Kenkel, these programs have shown themselves to be both cost-effective and efficacious. In part, their effectiveness in rural areas is related to the stigma attached to mental illness by rural residents. This stigma often causes reluctance to enter sickness-oriented treatment programs. However, the focus on prevention and health fits well with rural values. Prevention in rural areas focuses on the generalist role of the mental health practitioner.

Kenkel (1986) offers a word of caution for prevention programs that teach coping skills. When these programs are based on liberal, humanistic values, the program is likely to be rejected by the community. The values of individual rights and choice may conflict with "traditional moralistic and religious values present in many rural communities" (Kenkel, p. 467). The prevention program that uses parents as teachers might be better accepted by the rural community.

Gibbons et al. (1986) argue that the idea of prevention should be used to deal with adolescent alcohol abuse in rural areas. Gibbons et al. draw the following conclusion: "Due to the frequent lack of financial resources and few treatment services in rural areas, the school must play an important role in addressing prevention issues. Consequently, an educational approach, based in the school, offers the most potential for prevention" (p. 899).

In a study of patterns of alcohol use among rural adolescents, Gibbons et al.

(1986) suggest the following applications of the study's findings:

- Because the study's findings link beginning alcohol use in rural areas with junior high–age students, prevention programs should be aimed at those in lower grades
- Prevention programs should present alternative ways than alcohol use for adolescents (especially males) to achieve their "rite of passage" into adulthood
- Because alcohol abuse is evident in rural areas, educating students in rural areas about the nature and effects of alcohol and the responsible use of the drug is important.

Gibbons et al. also suggest that urban prevention programs need to be adapted to address the special problems in rural areas.

Recently, at least one child psychiatrist has begun to question current approaches to rural child and adolescent mental health services. Along with several colleagues, Petti (Benswanger, Sonis, Fialkov, & Petti, 1984; Petti, Benswanger, & Fialkov, 1987; Petti & Leviton, 1986; Woodward & Frank, 1988) has suggested that new approaches are needed to provide accessible mental health services to rural adolescents who, as a group, may be especially at risk of developing psychiatric disorders. Petti and Leviton (1986) suggest that attempts made by the federal government to address health personnel shortages in rural areas have met with failure. They suggest instead a set of four essential elements for adequate rural youth mental health services:

- Funding of demonstration projects that would deliver both direct and indirect services, train staff, and evaluate outcomes
- Training or upgrading the level of training of mental health workers specific to the needs of rural youth
- Creation of support systems at state and local levels to facilitate the recruitment and retention of core mental health professionals in rural areas
- Commitment of academic institutions to research concerning mental health and related issues of rural areas.

Petti et al. (1987) and Benswanger et al. (1984) describe two training programs that are aimed at preparing child psychiatrists for rural practice or at providing continuing education of rural mental health practitioners. Petti et al. suggest that the program designed to use fourth-year psychiatric residents as consultants to rural mental health care facilities has had some positive effects on interesting the residents in rural practice settings and preparing them for these settings. However, only one half of these residents went on to maintain at least a part-time working relationship in a rural environment after their practicum. Petti et al. concede that the program has been only partially successful in increasing the number of child psychiatrists in rural areas.

Benswanger et al. (1984) describe a second program that is aimed at retaining mental health professionals of many disciplines (psychiatry, psychology, social work, nursing, and mental health administration) in the rural setting.

This program is aimed at decreasing the professional isolation and stagnation felt by those who practice in rural areas. Four courses are offered in the university setting. The courses are designed to meet the continuing education needs as expressed by mental health professionals who are already practicing in rural areas. In this way the educational resources of the urban university are extended to a network of rural mental health agencies.

Several articles written by nurses deal with the issue of provision of nursing services in rural areas. Although not aimed specifically at the issue of rural mental health nursing, these articles cite similar problems in the training, recruitment, and retention of nurses in rural areas (Biegel, 1983; Stuart-Burchardt, 1982; Thobaden & Weingard, 1983). Thobaden and Weingard suggest that rural nursing carries with it certain difficulties. Among these are the effects of isolation and the necessity of traveling long distances. To combat these problems, Thobaden and Weingard and Biegel suggest that rural clinical and preceptor nursing programs are essential. Biegel says, "It is evident from this study and the literature that the mentor/preceptor concept is even *more* appropriate for a *rural* newcomer, who will provide the professional and personal nourishment necessary for success" (p. 46).

Stuart-Burchardt (1982) adds that retaining nurses in rural settings could be facilitated if rural nursing was viewed as a nursing specialty similar to medical, surgical or pediatric nursing. Stuart-Burchardt goes on to argue that few student nurses consider rural nursing as a career option because they are rarely exposed to this type of nursing during their educational experience. It is the responsibility of nursing education programs to orient students to the opportunity of rural nursing, according to Stuart-Burchardt.

In both the study conducted by Biegel (1983) and that done by Thobaden and Weingard (1983), nurses were asked to indicate why they chose to work in rural areas. In both studies, growing up in a rural community, the husband's job being located in a rural area, and liking the area and rural setting were among the most frequent responses. These findings would seem to be important in the recruitment of rural nursing students who might be more willing to return to the rural setting for practice.

Psychiatric Nurse Team in a Rural Area

In a pilot project conducted by Puskar and Lamb (1989), a preventive mental health program for adolescents was initiated in a rural area. The project used the services of two nurses prepared at the doctoral level and one doctoral nursing student with a master's degree. The project staff gained easy entry into a rural high school in southwestern Pennsylvania. Initial entry was made through a meeting with the school superintendent and the director of counseling services. Subsequent meetings with the high school principal and school nurse were held to coordinate various aspects of the project. The school nurse served as liaison between the project staff and the school district throughout the duration of the project.

The program consisted of two phases. In Phase I, 69 students aged 16 to 18 years in the junior level health class were administered a series of paper and pencil instruments. The testing was conducted in two 45-minute sessions and took 3 days to complete. The tests were designed to measure anger, stressful events, problems, ways of coping, levels of depression, and suicide ideation. Suicide ideation was present in 15.9% of subjects and depression in 14.1%. Descriptive statistics revealed the most frequent life event listed was breaking up with a boyfriend/girlfriend; most frequent problems were related to adjustment to school; and most common stress situations related to family. Coping methods were delineated with a few gender differences noted. The most common method of coping was self-control.

At the conclusion of the testing phase, the instruments were scored by computer. These scores were then reviewed by the nurses on the project staff. Students who scored above the score of 77 (determined to be clinically depressed on the Reynolds Adolescent Depression Scale) or exhibiting suicidal ideation (with a score of 41 or above as determined by the Suicide Ideation Questionnaire) were contacted by the project staff. These students were then interviewed individually and were referred to the appropriate mental health services in the community. Parents of these students were also contacted by phone to review the results of the screening.

Six of the students involved in the initial screening were chosen to participate in Phase II of the project. These students were those who scored above the mean on the Reynolds and the Suicide Ideation Questionnaire and yet their scores did not place them in the at-risk group. The group was conducted according to the protocol for the Adolescent Coping Skills Group as developed by the project staff. This 10-session group was designed according to a cognitive approach that is aimed at teaching adolescents mental health concepts related to stress and various coping skills. The group also provided opportunity for the adolescents to practice various coping techniques within the context of the group.

Role of Nurse in Rural Areas

Nurses are in a key position to provide services to rural families because of the lack of services, transportation problems, and the issue of access. Several issues related to provision of mental health services in rural areas became apparent to the psychiatric nurse team in the course of running this group and have implications for the role of nurses in general in rural areas. The first of these is the lack of mental health services in the area and the reluctance of the rural population to use the few available services. In the screening phase of this project, 11 students and their families were contacted because their scores were significantly high on the screening measures of depression or suicide ideation. Of these students, only two students went on to seek treatment. All students agreed to see the nurse team.

Transportation was a second important issue in the second phase of the project. Because the group met during the activities period at the end of the school day, transportation after school had to be arranged for group members.

In many cases, the distance from the school to the students' homes precluded asking their parents to come for them. Therefore, the group members rode the elementary school bus home after the group meeting. As a result, the group time was severely curtailed. Geography also played a part in the ability of the nurse researchers to reach the school for screening and for leading the group in Phase II of the project. The nurse research assistant drove 70 miles one way to screen the students and to lead the group.

A third issue is related to the specialized needs that adolescents from rural families exhibit. In the group it became apparent that these students did not have access to many recreational activities. Although students mentioned hunting and fishing as possible recreational outlets, they also indicated that most social activities centered around the use of alcohol. This was confirmed by a conversation with the high school guidance counselor, who stated that there has always been a "drinking problem" in this high school because of its proximity to the border of West Virginia 7 miles away. The problem of alcohol use in this school was dramatized when, in the third week of Phase II of the project, a student in the junior class was killed while riding with a classmate who was driving under the influence. In discussing this incident, the group members explained that alcohol use was partially condoned by parents who supplied the alcohol for some of the parties.

Finally, in working with this rural population, the nurse team observed the influence of the family. There was little difficulty calling students' families during the day to obtain permission to enter the study. The nurse confirmed that few of the students' mothers worked outside the home. In addition, in only two cases did the parents of students who wished to participate refuse to grant them permission to do so. However, it should be noted that approximately 30 students themselves refused to participate in the study. When the nurse team talked with some of these students about their reasons for refusal, many of them indicated a fear of reprisal in the community for their answers to the questions about their stresses and coping methods.

In summary, the nurses who led the Coping Skills Group were able to verify experientially several generalizations made by Stuart-Burchardt (1982) and Biegel (1983) about the provision of nursing care to rural clients. Stuart-Burchardt makes the following generalizations about rural nursing:

- The rural nurse functions more independently than does the urban nurse.
- The rural nurse functions to the fullest extent allowed under the Nurse Practice Act.
- The rural nurse cannot be "professionally detached" and has to be prepared to become involved with people and give of herself.

Biegel suggests that the rural nurse must be a generalist; flexible, versatile, and adaptable; resourceful and able to deal with crises; culture conscious; able to use a holistic approach; people-, family-, and community-oriented, self-reliant and independent. Each of these characteristics was necessary for the effective use of the Coping Skills Group as a nursing intervention in a rural setting.

• • •

In conclusion, this chapter highlights several mental health problems and issues for rural families with adolescents. A model of care that uses a psychiatric nurse team collaborating with the school nurse and guidance counselors in a rural high school is described. Issues of transportation difficulties and inadequate supply of mental health professionals are identified as characteristic of rural communities. Psychiatric nurses who function in rural settings must incorporate flexibility, adaptability, a tolerance of lack of resources, and independence into their assessment, prevention, and intervention activities.

REFERENCES

Bachrach, L.L. (1977). Deinstitutionalization of mental health services in rural areas. *Hospital and Community Psychiatry, 28,* 669-672.

Benswanger, E.G., Sonis, M., Fialkov, M.J., & Petti, T.A. (1984). Continuing education as a link between urban and rural mental health professionals. *Hospital and Community Psychiatry, 35,* 617-619.

Biegel, A. (1983). Toward a definition of rural nursing. *Home Healthcare Nurse,* (Sept/Oct), 45-46.

Cordes, S.M. (1985). Biopsychosocial imperatives for the rural perspective. *Social Science Medicine, 21*(12), 1373-1379.

Farie, A.M., & Cowen, E.L. (1986). The development and implementation of a rural consortium program to provide early, preventive school mental health services. *Community Mental Health Journal, 22*(2), 94-103.

Flaskerud, J.H. & Kuiz, F.J. (1984). Determining the need for mental health services in rural areas. *American Journal of Community Psychology, 12*(4), 497-509.

Forrest, S. (1988). Suicide and the rural adolescent. *Adolescence, 22*(90), 341-347.

Gibbons, G., Wylie, M.L., Echterling, L., & French, J. (1986). Patterns of alcohol use among rural and small-town adolescents. *Adolescence, 21*(84), 887-900.

Gotts, E.E. & Purnell, R.F. (1986). Families and schools in rural Appalachia. *American Journal of Community Psychology, 14*(5), 499-519.

Hassinger, E.W. (1982). *Rural health organization: Social networks and regionalization.* Ames, Iowa: Iowa State University Press.

Kenkel, M.B. (1986). Stress-coping-support in rural communities: A model for primary prevention. *American Journal of Community Psychology, 14*(5), 457-477.

Lamb, J., & Puskar, K. (1991). School-based adolescents mental health project: Survey of anger, depression, and suicide in adolescence. *Journal of Child and Adolescent Psychiatric-Mental Health Nursing, 4* (3), 101-104.

Linn, J.G. & Husaini, B.A. (1985). Chronic medical problems, coping resources, and depression: A longitudinal study of rural Tennesseans. *American Journal of Community Psychology, 13*(6), 773-742.

Petti, T.A., Benswanger, E.G., & Fialkov, M.J. (1987). Training child psychiatrists in rural public mental health. *Hospital and Community Psychiatry, 38*(4), 398-401.

Petti, T.A., & Leviton, L.C. (1986). Re-thinking rural mental health services for children and adolescents. *Journal of Public Health Policy,* (Spring), 58-77.

President's Commission on Mental Health. *Report to the President,* (1978). (Vol 1). Washington, D.C.: U.S. Government Printing Office, Stock NO. 040-000-00390-8.

Puskar, K., & Lamb, J. (1991). Life events, problems, stress, and coping methods of adolescents. *Issues in Mental Health Nursing, 12* (3), 267-281.

Puskar, K., & Lamb, J. (1989). Promotion of coping in suicidal and nonsuicidal adolescents. University of Pittsburgh Research Development Fund.

Rosenblatt, R.A., & Moscovice, I.S. (1982). *Rural health care.* New York: Wiley.

Sarvela, P.D., & McClendon, E.J. (1987). Early adolescent alcohol abuse in rural northern Michigan. *Community Mental Health Journal, 23*(3), 183-191.

Shoffner, S.M. (1986). Child care in rural areas: Needs, attitudes, and preferences. *American Journal of Community Psychology, 14*(5), 521-539.

Stuart-Burchardt, S. (1982). Rural nursing. *American Journal of Nursing,* (April), 616-618.

Templeman, T., Condon, S., Starr, D., & Hazard, C. (1989). Stressful life events in rural settings. *Journal of Rural Community Psychology, 10,* (1), 41-53.

Thobaden, M., & Weingard, M. (1983). Rural nursing. *Home Healthcare Nurse,* (Nov/Dec), 9-13.

Woodward, J., & Frank, B. (1988). Rural adolescent loneliness and coping strategies. *Adolescence, 23*(91), 559-565.

Chapter 13

Family Abuse

Barbara Parker

Family violence refers to a range of behaviors occurring between family members and includes the physical and emotional abuse of children, child neglect, spouse battering, marital rape, and elder abuse. Conceptualizing abuse within families involves several different issues. Although each family is unique, certain characteristics appear to be common to most violent families. Furthermore, regardless of the type of abuse occurring within a family, all members—including the extended family—are affected. Steinmetz and Straus (1974) noted that "any social pattern as widespread and enduring as violence must have fundamental and enduring causes." Family violence, though often unnoted, is at the core of many family disturbances. Violence may be the "family secret," and is often perpetuated through generations (Millor, 1981; Parker & Schumacher, 1979; Perry et al., 1983).

Although numerous research studies and theories have been postulated on the causes, treatment, and prevention of family violence, the field has more questions unanswered than answered. Hotaling and Straus (1980) noted that "the family is the training ground for violence" and ponder why the social group designated to provide love and support is also the most violent group to which most people belong. They point out that behaviors that would be unacceptable between strangers, co-workers, or friends are frequently tolerated within families.

Feminist authors note that the majority of victims of family violence are the most vulnerable and powerless family members: women, children, and elderly persons (Dobash & Dobash, 1988; Campbell & Humphreys, 1984). They postulate that the root of the violence is the abuser's need for power and control that is acted out by violent behavior.

Violence and abuse are generally believed to be caused by an interaction of personality and demographic, situational, and societal factors that have an impact on a family. Many of the unique characteristics of the family as a social group—time spent together, emotional involvement, privacy, and in-depth knowledge of each other—can facilitate both intimacy and violence. Indeed, a given family can be both loving and supportive, as well as violent.

One issue to confront is the terminology used to describe people who have experienced violence. Traditionally the term *victim* has been used, along with discussions of *syndromes*. These labels serve to distance the nurse from the person who has experienced abuse, because we search for differences between ourselves and the survivors to decrease our feelings of vulnerability. Therefore in this chapter the term *survivor* will be used in an attempt to emphasize that the person who has experienced abuse has many strengths and coping strategies that can be incorporated into the plan of care.

This chapter begins with a discussion of several factors common to violent families, regardless of the specific type of abuse. In the second section, specific issues about child abuse, wife abuse, and abuse of elderly persons are discussed. The third section includes guidelines for psychiatric nurses in the treatment of violent families and strategies for the prevention of family violence.

Societal Influence on Family Violence

Any attempt to understand violence in American families must consider the influence of society on the family. The United States has a higher level of violence in comparison with other Western nations (Bersani & Chen, 1988), and many believe that societal willingness to tolerate violence sets the stage for family violence. Societal norms are sometimes used to justify violence to maintain the family system. For example, in a number of families the husband's use of violence is considered legitimate if the wife is having an extramarital affair (Elbow, 1977). These authors cite the following as factors serving to justify such violence: historical attitudes toward women, children, and elderly persons; economic discrimination; the nonresponsiveness of the criminal justice system; and the belief in women and children as property (Campbell & Humphreys, 1984; Chapman & Gates, 1978, Dobash & Dobash, 1988).

Characteristics of Families that are Violent

Several themes are common to violent families. These include multigenerational abuse, social isolation, the use and abuse of power, and alcohol and drug use and abuse.

MULTIGENERATIONAL TRANSMISSION PROCESS

The multigenerational transmission process refers to the prevalent finding that family violence is perpetuated through generations by a cycle of violence. Although several theories have been postulated about this phenomenon, the most enduring is that of social learning theory, where violence is viewed as a learned behavior.

Social learning postulates that a child learns to be violent in the family setting in which a violent parent has been a role model. In this perspective, violence and victimization are learned behaviors by exposure to violence in childhood. This exposure teaches both the means and the approval of violence. Children who witness violence not only learn specific aggressive behaviors, but also acquire the belief that violence is a legitimate way to solve problems within a family. When frustrated or angry as an adult, the individual relies on this learned behavior and responds with violence.

Social learning theory was first applied to child abuse when researchers noted that many child abusers were themselves abused as children (Kempe & Helfer, 1980). A number of authors have also examined the multigenerational process with wife abuse by noting the incidence of violence in the family of both the survivors and the abusers. An extensive literature review conducted by Hotaling and Sugerman (1986) identified the witnessing of parental violence during childhood or adolescence as one of the strongest risk factors for the abuse of a spouse in adulthood, especially for men. The case is less persuasive that women learn to be victims of wife abuse from childhood experiences with violence.

To date, there is limited empirical evidence of intergenerational transmission of violence in the abuse of elderly persons. Pillemer and Suitor (1988), however, postulate that abuse of elderly persons could be the result of formerly abused children displaying both retaliatory and imitative behavior or modeling behavior observed between their parents and grandparents.

Many treatment modalities, especially cognitive approaches, are based on the social learning model that violent reactions can be unlearned and replaced with constructive responses to conflict.

SOCIAL ISOLATION

Some authors have noted that violent families are also socially isolated, because particular types of violence are considered to be aberrant or illegitimate and become a "family secret." Exposure of such violence can result in formal or informal sanctions from other family members, neighbors, the police, or the judicial system; therefore the abuser often purposefully keeps the family isolated (Becker & Coleman, 1988; Okun, 1986). Social isolation has been found to be a factor in abuse of elderly persons (Phillips, 1983; Pillemer, 1985), wife abuse (Landenburger, 1988), and child abuse (Campbell & Humphreys, 1984; JAMA, 1985).

THE USE AND ABUSE OF POWER

An additional commonality within the various forms of family violence is the use and abuse of power. In virtually all forms of family violence, the abuser has some form of power or control over the victim. For example, with the sexual abuse of children, the abuser is usually a male in an authority position victimizing a young female in a subordinate position (Finkelhor, 1983; Walsh & Liddy, 1989). A recent study of sexual abuse of patients by caregivers (Newbern, 1989) also noted the power disparity between the violator and the child victim.

Power issues appear to be a central factor with wife abuse. Many authors have noted that wife abuse is controlling behavior that creates and maintains an imbalance of power within the relationship. Although wife abusers will justify the use of violence for trivial events, such as not having a meal ready or not keeping the house tidy, many authors have noted that the violence is related to the husband's need for total domination of his wife. For example, Schechter (1982) interviewed a number of wife abusers and survivors and found that for many women their moves toward self-assertion through jobs or school infuriated their husbands. The women's success or recognition was perceived as threatening to their husbands who used abuse in an attempt to regain control over their wives.

In a cross-cultural analysis, Levinson (1988) found that wife beating was found more often in societies worldwide where husbands had more economic and decision-making power than did wives. Wife beating was more likely to be totally absent where women had their own economic resources and/or forms of solidarity with other women.

ALCOHOL AND DRUG USE

The relationship between alcohol and drug use and family violence has been studied extensively. Victims of violence frequently report concurrent substance abuse by the abuser. Most researchers, however, deny that substance abuse is a direct causative factor in violence, because it does not meet the criteria of stability, consensus, and consistency. That is, people who abuse alcohol are not consistently violent and people who are violent are not always intoxicated. Instead, it has been suggested that rather than acting violent because one is drunk, the person uses alcohol as a means of deviance disavowal (Berk et al., 1983).

Recently Lenord and Jacob (1988) conducted an extensive literature review of the relationship between alcohol abuse and family violence. They concluded that some evidence implicated alcohol use and alcoholism in marital violence, although the evidence related to child abuse was much weaker. In addition, with marital violence, confounding variables such as the stress of alcoholism on the family system or familial expectations that drinking will increase aggressive behavior have not been adequately controlled in research studies.

Child Abuse

The earliest form of family violence that was recognized within the health professional literature was physical abuse to children. Although violence to children was considered a social problem in the previous century, it was not until the 1940's that it was first identified as a medical problem, indeed a unique "syndrome." In 1962, the classic article by C. Henry Kempe and his associates, "The Battered Child Syndrome," first brought sustained interest to the problem of physical abuse to children. By the end of the 1960's, every state had enacted legislation mandating the report of suspected child abuse and neglect (JAMA, 1985). Under current regulations, nurses and any other professionals providing services to children are required to report suspected incidents of child abuse and neglect.

There are many forms of abuse to children, including physical abuse or battering, emotional abuse, sexual abuse, and neglect. Although research on the many forms of child abuse has been extensive, there is still much that is unknown on the causes, treatment, or prevention of child abuse.

The theoretic framework on the causes of child abuse that has been the most enduring is known as the Helfer and Kempe (1976) model of child abuse and neglect. The model incorporates both psychologic and social factors, thus providing for a more comprehensive approach than traditional medical models. The model hypothesizes that three factors are present in child abusing families: (1) a special parent, (2) a special child, and (3) stress.

A special parent refers to characteristics in the caregiver that generate a proneness to use violence as a way to alleviate stress or communicate displeasure. The adult may be immature (in fact may be an adolescent), have unrealistic expectations of the child (Egeland et al., 1980; Fesbach, 1980), or have been abused himself or herself as a child (Burgess, 1984). Numerous studies have suggested intergenerational transmission of violence (Disbrow et al., 1977; Perry et al., 1983; Straus, 1980), and indeed this appears to place a parent at risk for abusing his or her own children. However, other controlled studies (Starr, 1982) examining parental punishment history and current child abuse found no difference between abusive and nonabusive parents. Simply experiencing abuse as a child does not totally determine an adult's later behaviors. Many people who were abused as children are able to avoid violence with their own children. Straus (1980) suggests that key factors may be the age at which the child was abused and which parent was abusive. Experiencing abuse from a father at age 4 may be a totally different experience than experiencing abuse from one's mother as an adolescent.

A special child refers to characteristics of the child that place him or her at increased risk for abuse. In most child-abusing families, abuse is directed to one "special child" (Millor, 1981). The characteristics of special children include the presence of handicaps (Nesbit & Karagianis, 1982), learning disabilities, aggressive behaviors, hyperactivity, or chronic health problems (Lynch, 1975; Sherrod et al., 1984). Additional features include children who are unwanted or unplanned or who may remind the parent of a disliked relative or an unhappy time of his or her life. This is not to imply that some children "deserve to be abused," but rather that each child brings certain characteristics to the parent-child interaction that interrelate with the parent's own characteristics (Millor, 1981).

Stress is a subjective phenomenon that is defined by the family and may or may not be apparent to the nurse. Some known stressors include unemployment (Steinberg et al., 1981) poverty (Straus, 1980; Zuravin, 1989), health problems of other family members, or marital discord. Other authors have questioned the direct relationship between stress and increasing rates of child abuse (Pagelow, 1984; Straus, 1980) and note that the presence of resources and other mediating factors must also be considered when indicating stress as a causal factor in child abuse. Egeland et al. (1980) found that a high level of stress alone did not differentiate between abusing and nonabusing mothers but that mothers who were both highly stressed and abusive were often unaware of the difficulties and demands of being a parent. Seagull (1987) also found that parents of abused children tended to perceive their children more negatively and derived little emotional satisfaction from the child.

These three factors seem to work together to set the stage for potential physical abuse or neglect. However, to date, research has not indicated any factors that are present in all abusing parents and absent in all nonabusing parents (Starr, 1988).

SEXUAL ABUSE OF CHILDREN AND ADOLESCENTS

Sexual abuse is defined as the involvement of children and adolescents in sexual activities they do not fully comprehend and to which they do not freely consent (Feinauer, 1989). Sexual abuse results in both long-term and short-term problems. Short-term physical signs and symptoms include sexually transmitted disease or infection, vaginal or rectal bleeding, itching, soreness, recurrent urinary tract infections, or pregnancy. The presence of any of these signs and symptoms in a child or adolescent should cue the nurse to further assess for sexual abuse, even if such abuse is not readily disclosed by the child. Short-term emotional indicators include behavioral changes, difficulty sleeping, school problems, or chronic fears or unhappiness.

The long-term effects of sexual abuse as a child include sexual problems, difficulty trusting others, anxiety and panic attacks, depression, and substance abuse. A recent study by Feinauer (1989) of adult women who had been sexually abused as children found that these women experienced more emotional distress and long-term effects when the perpetrator was a person who was known and trusted by them. Feinauer found that the kinship relationship between the victim and the abuser was less important in creating distress than the emotional bond the victim felt toward the perpetrator. Thus a critical factor seems to be the violation of the child's trust, as well as the physical trauma.

NURSING ASSESSMENT OF CHILD ABUSE

Nursing assessment of actual or potential child abuse begins with a thorough history and physical examination. Gathering a history of child abuse can be a stressful experience for both the nurse and the family. It is therefore essential that the nurse first examine her or his own values and past experiences to maintain a therapeutic and nonjudgmental clinical approach.

In obtaining a history it is important to establish an honest, trusting environment that is not intended to punish or shame either the child or the parent (Campbell & Humphreys, 1984). If the nurse recognizes that most abusive parents are genuinely embarrassed about their behavior and would like assistance in developing alternative approaches to discipline, an environment can be established that will facilitate honesty and sharing. The setting for the interview needs to be quiet, private, and uninterrupted.

In general the initial interview should be conducted by separating the child and the adult(s). This decision, however, is dependent on the child's age and other extenuating circumstances. The nurse should honestly state the purpose of the interview, type of questions being asked, and the subsequent physical examination. The approach needs to be calm and supportive, because both the child and the family will be affected by uneasiness.

The interview with the parent(s) can begin with a discussion of the problem that first brought the child to a health care facility. During this discussion, pay particular attention to the parents' understanding of the problem, discrepancies in the stories, and the parents' emotional responses. The interview can then be expanded to discussions of how the parents "discipline" the child, or how often they spank the child. The initial interview is not the time to directly confront the abuser, because measures must be taken to thoroughly document and report the abuse to ensure the child's safety.

When the nurse suspects child abuse, she or he must report such suspicions to protective services. An investigation by the state protective service agency is legally mandated and also serves to reinforce to the family the seriousness of the problem. When protective services are involved, the nurse should explain to families precisely what will happen in an investigation and the time involved. In addition, the psychiatric practitioner should maintain frequent contact with the assigned worker to ensure a comprehensive, consistent approach. Nurses who work with violent families need to know exactly how protective services work in the community in which they practice. It is extremely valuable to personally know the professionals at the agency to remain informed about the policies and reporting protocols and ensure successful coordination and continuity.

Long-term therapy of child-abusing families is a complex process, beyond the scope of an overview chapter on all forms of family violence. Psychiatric nurse practitioners who wish to engage in long-term therapy with such families should receive advanced training in courses specifically devoted to this topic.

Wife Abuse

Domestic violence between adults is generally referred to as spouse abuse, regardless of the marital status of the couple. A distinction that needs to be clearly differentiated, however, is that the problem is abuse of women. Although some authors have contended that husband abuse is as prevalent as wife abuse (Steinmetz & Lucca, 1988), numerous other authors (Campbell & Humphreys, 1984; Dobash & Dobash, 1988; Stark & Flitcraft, 1988) have argued that husband abuse and wife abuse are not comparable. Studies of "husband abuse" do not examine the important issues of self-defense, resulting injuries, provocation, and differences in physical strength. Therefore in this chapter the focus is on wife abuse.

The experience of being abused by a partner in an intimate relationship has profound effects on the woman's health, children, career, and perceptions of herself. Wife abuse also includes the emotional degradation and intimidation that almost always accompanies physical abuse and the sexual abuse (or marital rape) that is part of the violence in about half the cases of female battering (Campbell, 1989b). The violence is part of a system of coercive control that may also include financial coercion, threats against children and other family members, and destruction of property (Schecter, 1982). Wife abuse is the most widespread form of family violence, with at least one in every six wives being hit by a husband sometime during their relationship and at least 1.6 million women each year being severely and repeatedly beaten by her spouse (Straus & Gelles, 1986).

Women can be abused by their partners at any point in the relationship; however, there do seem to be times that are particularly dangerous. For example, most survivors of abuse report that their partners were not violent while they were dating. The violence generally begins after the couple are living together or become legally married or the woman becomes pregnant. Although there are currently no controlled studies documenting that pregnancy places women at increased risk for abuse, there is nursing research documenting the incidence of wife abuse during pregnancy and the effect on maternal and infant health.

Bullock et al. (1989) interviewed 593 women in the postpartum setting and reported that the women experienced blows to the abdomen, breasts, and genitals and sexual assault during their pregnancies. In addition, Bullock et al. found that the battered women were four times more likely to deliver a low-birth-weight baby than were women who did not experience abuse during their pregnancies.

Recent findings from a prospective prenatal study being conducted by McFarlane and Parker (McFarlane et al., 1992) has documented the incidence of abuse both before and during pregnancy. In this sample of over 700 Hispanic, black, and white prenatal patients, the rate of abuse was 25% in the year preceding pregnancy and 16% during pregnancy. This study also documented a significant relationship between experiencing abuse and entering prenatal care later in the pregnancy.

THE EXPERIENCE OF ABUSE FOR THE SURVIVOR

The experience of abuse has been described by Landenburger (1988), who conducted a series of interviews with abused women. Landenburger identified four stages of a violent relationship and the differing themes involved in each stage of entrapment.

In the *binding* or initial stage of the relationship, the focus is on establishing the relationship and possibly a family. In this phase the woman copes by attempting to ignore or minimize warning signals of potential or actual violent incidents. As problems occur, the woman tries to change her behavior to "make things right." As these attempts prove futile, she begins to question her own abilities as a wife or mother and wonders why she is unable to stop the violence. She may think about leaving the abuser but still believes that she can somehow stop the violence.

The second stage of the process, *enduring,* continues the process of self-blame and acceptance of responsibility for the abuse. She may begin to hide the signs of abuse, lose hope, and feel worthless as a person. This stage can last anywhere from months to years.

The third stage, *disengaging,* often begins as the woman begins to realize that she is not alone in her problem and she begins to identify with other women. She may seek help as she begins to gain enough confidence in herself to think about leaving the relationship.

In the *recovering* phase the woman gradually becomes more independent. She may have residual feelings of guilt or may grieve the loss of her partner or the relationship. Campbell (1989b) found that women leaving an abusive relationship experienced stress and grief over their decision to leave their partners. She also noted that a normal marriage takes as long as 4 years to dissolve and usually includes attempted reconciliations. However, when survivors of abuse experience grief over the termination of the relationship or attempt a reconciliation, they are labeled as pathologic or masochistic.

Although not all women experience these phases sequentially, or even remain in a violent relationship beyond the binding stage (Parker & Schumacher, 1977), this conceptualization of the process is useful in understanding the phenomena and developing interventions. Counseling the abused woman should take into account the stage in which she is and her perception of and hopes for the relationship.

Hoff's recent study (1990) of 9 battered women and 131 social network members over a 2-year period also add insight to the abuse process, which Hoff labels as going from victim to survivor. Hoff describes the "complex interactional process between . . . personal, cultural and political-economic factors" that contributes to women's feeling entrapped in a violent relationship. Hoff also describes how the women in her study were successful crisis managers in their day-to-day lives, but that "the system" continually defined the battering problem as a personal one, thus contributing to the women's attempts to solve it on a private level.

ASSESSMENT OF THE ABUSED WOMAN

Nursing assessment of women who have experienced abuse must be conducted privately and with assurances of confidentiality. Many women feel ashamed or responsible for the violence, and assessment must be approached in a nonjudgmental, gentle manner. At the same time, the nurse should be direct in her or his questions, because it is unfair to expect the woman to respond to indirect or oblique communication.

If abuse is revealed, the nurse's first response is critical. It is important that an abused woman realize that she is not alone; important affirmation can be given with a statement about the frequency of wife abuse. The extent of the abuse and what forms are being used need to be elicited and described in the record. Careful documentation using a body map is necessary for potential legal actions, which are frequently child custody suits as well as criminal action related to the violence.

The kinds of responses to the violence the woman has experienced are also obviously a critical area for a mental health assessment. It is important that these responses be interpreted to the woman as normal within the circumstances. Signs of posttraumatic stress disorder, depression, and low self-esteem need to be assessed and recorded. Attribution about the abuse is also an important issue. One nursing study (Campbell, 1989b) revealed that women who blamed the abuse on an unchanging personality characteristic within themselves had a lower level of self-esteem and increased depression. Therefore the nurse must carefully assess the woman's beliefs about the abuse and the responsibility regarding the abuse. Because many wife abusers find an excuse for the violence, the woman may be unnecessarily accepting the blame for the abuser's actions.

A common response is for the woman to report the violence but attempt to minimize the frequency or severity of its occurrence. This may take the form of blaming herself, blaming alcohol use by herself or her partner, or asserting that the violence was a temporary aberration caused by family difficulties or unemployment. Kelly (1988) notes that "forgetting" or minimizing are effective coping strategies, especially if sexual abuse is involved. She points out that if the woman believes that others will not define her problem as seriously as she does, minimizing the event in her own mind will make her feel less alienated from others.

Several authors have studied racial and ethnic minority women and observed some characteristics that differ from the assessment of abuse with white women. One characteristic of both black and Hispanic women is an increased reluctance to report abuse, especially if the nurse or therapist is from a different cultural group.

Torres (1991) reported that Hispanic women were more tolerant toward abuse than were white women in her study and that acts such as hitting or verbal abuse had to occur more frequently with Hispanic women before they would seek services for the violence. In addition, Torres found that Hispanic-American women were more sensitive to perceived criticisms of themselves, as well as their family, culture, and male relatives (including their husbands). White (1985) notes that for black women, a sense of racial loyalty may make it more difficult to report violence, especially if they believe the information will be used to perpetuate racist views about black men.

INTERVENTIONS WITH SURVIVORS OF WIFE ABUSE

This section focuses on intervention strategies designed for work with only the survivor of abuse; strategies for working with the entire family are delineated later in the chapter.

The most important consideration in the initial assessment of the survivor of wife abuse is to determine the woman's safety (Parker et al., 1990). Violence usually escalates over time in both frequency and severity, and assessment must carefully determine the woman's current safety.

A related concern is the need to advise the woman that the interview itself is not necessarily providing documentation of the abuse. This may be especially important for women with language difficulties or others who do not understand the official system of reporting abuse. In working with abused women, the nurse must be aware of state reporting procedures and be available to assist the woman in filing a report if she so requests.

Intervening with survivors of wife abuse can be a difficult experience for the psychiatric nurse practitioner. As noted in the Campbell study (1989a), women who are abused have as much difficulty terminating a relationship as women who have not experienced abuse. This means that often the woman will remain in the relationship, especially if her partner is remorseful or promises to change his behavior. The practitioner needs to remember that the woman wants only the violence to end, not necessarily the relationship. Women who remain in violent relationships require as much, if not more, support and counseling.

Interventions with survivors of abuse include assistance in objectively evaluating the relationship and its inherent strengths and limitations. Because the woman may be in a state of intense confusion or feeling conflicting loyalties, it is important for the nurse to have extensive skills in problem solving and decision making. The woman may be in crisis with feelings of disequilibrium, fear, and helplessness.

For an abused woman, intervention strategies entail first making sure she has the information she needs, such as that assault of a wife is illegal and the state and local laws and ordinances. She also needs to be aware of the local battered woman's shelter(s) that are available for advice, support, and group participation, even if she does not intend to enter the shelter at the time. There is now a national hotline for shelters, where any woman can call and get information about abuse, including the number of the nearest shelter (1-800-333-SAFE).

Mutual goal setting is particularly important when working with abused women. Nurses can easily become frustrated if they impose their goals on the woman, who may not be ready for drastic action. It is hoped that the nurse and client have time to develop a long-term relationship within which they can work through the normal denial and minimization that takes place when the woman's primary attachment relationship is threatened. The nurse and client together can then explore and expand on all the options about which the woman has thought and devise others. Dealing with an abusive situation is a recovering process, detailed by Landenburger (1989), which takes time and ongoing support. The nurse, whether in a short or extended intervention situation, can help the client mobilize both natural and system support so that her economic, as well as emotional, needs are addressed.

One approach is for the nurse and the survivor to jointly brainstorm various options. The options include remaining in the home and seeking help for herself and/or her spouse, remaining in the home and attempting to anticipate the violent attacks and protect herself and her children, or leaving the relationship either temporarily or permanently. When a complete list has been generated, the nurse and client can jointly determine the positive and negative consequences of each option and select the best alternative. If the woman decides to remain in the relationship, intervention can focus on methods of recognizing imminent violence and ways of protecting herself and her children.

If (and when) the woman decides the situation is not going to change, she may be ready to make long-term decisions. At this point, the practitioner can assist the woman with practical alternatives such as a list of shelters for abused women and information on local police protection and available legal resources. For example, in many states an abused woman can obtain a restraining order from the police or have police protection while she is removing her belongings from the home. Once again, it is critical for the psychiatric practitioner to be aware of the local laws and services.

At this point the practitioner and woman will be making such decisions as when she should leave, where she will go, and which possessions she should take. In making these decisions, the nurse needs to be cognizant of the beginning evidence that the most dangerous time for a woman in a violent relationship is after she has left the abuser. Women appear to be at higher risk for homicide after leaving a relationship than while enduring the violence (Hart, 1988). Plans to leave therefore need to be carefully made to avoid last-minute crisis decisions. Information on the potential for homicide using the Danger Assessment (Campbell, 1986a) might also be considered.

Often the plan for leaving a violent relationship includes the use of a shelter for battered women. Shelters are available in every state and are an important source of temporary housing and counseling. However, in planning to use a shelter the psychiatric nurse needs to also be aware of shelter limitations. Most shelters for abused women are over-crowded and have "waiting lists." This means the woman cannot wait until the next crisis and expect to find space in a shelter. She needs to contact the shelter before leaving and place her name on the waiting list. If her home is too dangerous, she might need to make temporary arrangements with a friend or relative or a homeless shelter while calling the shelter daily to determine space availability.

Most shelters offer nonshelter group counseling, which is highly recommended for women who have survived abuse. Survivors of abuse with a long-term relationship with a psychiatric nurse should also be encouraged to maintain this affiliation while in a shelter or receiving shelter counseling. Women who have left a violent relationship require a variety of services and multiple sources of support. Therapeutic long-term relationships should therefore be maintained whenever possible.

Abuse of Elderly Persons

Abuse of elderly persons includes direct physical assaults, neglect, financial abuse, psychologic abuse, or acts that violate elderly persons' right to self-determination. Although the phenomenon of abuse of elderly persons has been known for decades, it is the area of family violence that has been researched the least. Authors of review articles on abuse of elderly persons (Hudson & Johnson, 1987; Pillemer & Suitor, 1988; Yin, 1985) note that there is no reliable estimate of the prevalence of abuse of elderly persons, and the causes of maltreatment are generally unidentified. Thus developing assessment techniques and effective interventions is extremely difficult. This chapter will focus on caretaker abuse of elderly persons, although one must be recognize that abuse of elderly persons is often spouse abuse.

Physical abuse of elderly persons includes acts of both commission and omission. Abuse of elderly persons frequently involves a type of benign neglect, because family members may withhold needed personal or medical care. A cross-sectional survey of health professionals indicated that passive neglect (inattention or isolation) was by far the most common form of abuse of elderly persons (Hickey & Douglass, 1981). Examples include leaving nonambulatory elderly persons unattended for long periods or without needed services. Frequently this form of abuse occurs in families where the needs of such persons exceed the capacity of the families' resources, such as families where all the adults are working or there are small children.

Active physical abuse includes direct blows or shoving the elderly person, tying the person to a chair when the caretaker must leave the home or is otherwise occupied, or the misuse of medications. Frequently elderly persons are over-sedated in an attempt to make them more passive and manageable (Pollick, 1987).

Financial abuse includes both direct theft and the misuse of the person's financial assets or property. Children may visit the elderly parent to steal monthly Social Security checks and physically or psychologically abuse the parent when he or she objects. Families with an elderly relative in the home may rely on Social Security to provide for all the family members and keep the elderly person home even when institutionalization is indicated.

Psychologic abuse includes verbal assaults and threats, provocation of fear, and isolation of the elderly person, either physically or emotionally (Beck & Ferguson, 1981). This includes treating elderly persons in a manner that diminishes their personal identity or dignity. Psychologic abuse may be the result of the stress of caregiving, expressed in the form of emotional outbursts toward the elderly person. Psychologic abuse is particularly complex, because it generally involves the interaction of parties who have established patterns of interactions over many years.

DOCUMENTING ELDER ABUSE

Documenting abuse of elderly persons is complicated by several factors. Because many frail elderly persons are also subject to falls, bruises from abuse may at times be difficult to differentiate. In addition, because elderly persons may be forgetful due to decreased cerebral circulation, obtaining a history may be difficult. Complicating these conditions is the fear of many elderly persons that reporting abuse may lead to retaliatory violence or an unwanted placement in a nursing home. Agencies may also be reluctant to report suspected abuse due to a lack of knowledge in identifying or dealing with the problem (Pollick, 1987).

Recent research on the abuse of elderly persons has focused on the influence of stress on caregivers, especially those caring for frail or impaired persons. Bunting (1989) identified that caregivers experience stress from restrictions on time and freedom, economic burdens including curtailment of employment, and adjusting to the changing roles and capabilities of the elderly person. These stressors are then often perpetuated by inadequate support systems for the caregivers. Frequently the elderly person's needs compete with the available family resources of attention, time, energy, and money, and the caretaker feels torn between the needs of his or her children and his or her parents. If this stressful situation is compounded by a family history of violence as a means of problem solving, abuse of the elderly person can occur.

Steinmetz (1988) conducted extensive interviews with 104 caregivers of elderly kin. She found that 23% reported using physically abusive methods at some time to control the elder. Seven significant variables were identified in predicting physical abuse: stress resulting from caring for a mobile but senile elderly person, stress from emotional dependency, total mobility dependency, elderly persons who were verbally abusive, elderly persons who refused to eat or take medications, elderly persons who called the police, and elderly persons who invaded the caretakers' privacy. Steinmetz notes that a confounding aspect of abuse of elderly parents by adult children is that it is not always possible to separate the victim from the perpetrator. Her sample described "caring, thoughtful, loving children who felt duty bound to care for their elderly parent" and who felt overburdened and overstressed by the elderly parent who hit or slapped them, threw food or refused to eat, was verbally abusive, or manipulated the caretaker through the use of guilt. The current lack of community support facilities, such as adult daycare and respite services, further compounds the problem.

Treatment Guidelines with Violent Families

Although there is some literature on the causes and effects of violence on families, the literature available on specific treatment guidelines for psychiatric practitioners is limited. Compounding this lack of information is the need for research studies evaluating the merits of various approaches. Indeed, the issue of family versus individual therapy with violent families is controversial, and there is a diversity of opinions among service providers about which services and treatment approaches are the most effective.

Most of the literature on family therapy with violent families suggests the use of a cognitive-behavioral-educational approach. This approach postulates that because the use of violence is a learned behavior, one can similarly learn to become nonviolent (Adams, 1988). In addition, because family violence affects all members, optimal treatment approaches include services specifically developed for each family member. The primary objective in all approaches is to stop the violence and replace it with behaviors that facilitate the growth of all family members.

Nurses working with families that have experienced violence or abuse must be aware that whenever one type of abuse is encountered, there must be a high index of suspicion for other kinds of violence occurring either to the same person or another family member. Incest victims' mothers are frequently being physically abused by the same man, and the victims' siblings may also be experiencing sexual and physical abuse. The children of battered women are also at high risk for physical abuse. A young man who has been sexually assaulted may attack a younger child. The list of possibilities is unfortunately long, but they all need to be considered.

Families can be treated in therapy as a unit, or family members can attend groups developed for each family member. For example, in one model for the treatment of wife abuse (Weidman, 1986), three separate groups are available: a men's group, a women's group, and a children's group.

TREATMENT APPROACHES FOR WIFE ABUSERS

In the men's group the focus is on resocialization, cognitive restructuring of irrational belief systems, and skills training (that is, conflict resolution). The objectives are to explore and understand feelings preceding and leading to violence, sex-role stereotypes, and attitudes about and expectations within relationships.

Other approaches in working with violent men (Cook & Frantz-Cook, 1984) include teaching the abusers how to know when they are getting upset by learning to read their body cues. This approach acknowledges that abusive men may need help in identifying cues to the buildup of violence. The abuser is taught to pay attention to his body's response to different feelings. For example, the therapist might describe that some people know they are angry because they get pains in their neck or their stomach feels tight. The abusive men are given assignments to learn more about themselves and their body responses to anger. If they find tension building up, decisive actions are taken to avoid violence, such as a predetermined "time-out."

In addition to finding other ways to deal with their anger, abusive men often need to reevaluate their values and beliefs about the role and status of women and their expectations of relationships. Abusive men have been found to have higher levels of hostility toward women than maritally satisfied, nonviolent men (Maiuro & Eberle, 1989). Therefore determining the abuser's attitudes toward women and women's roles in relationships is an important consideration in therapy sessions.

Edleson (1984) describes a program in which interpersonal skills are taught. This includes skills in conflict resolution in defusing stressful situations without resorting to the use of violence. Additional objectives in group therapy for abusive men are reducing social isolation and dependency on the partner for meeting all social needs, providing positive role models, and increasing self-esteem as the members share coping strategies and support each other (Sedlak, 1988).

TREATMENT APPROACHES FOR SURVIVORS OF WIFE ABUSE

Treatment groups for abused women are designed to enable the women to feel less isolated by exposure to others with similar experiences and the provision of social support. In addition, survivors of abuse can learn assertiveness skills and reduce self-blame by recognizing the part that social forces have played in their victimization (Humphreys & Campbell, 1988).

Campbell (1986a) describes a nurse-led "survivor group" for battered women based on models from "rap groups" of Vietnam veterans. In this survivor group, as in many groups for survivors of wife abuse, a frequent topic was the women's feelings of being controlled by their partner. A second theme expressed was the damage to their self-esteem that followed the abuse and the psychologic pain they endured. Strategies to end the violence, including the advantages and disadvantages of leaving the relationship, are also a common theme. This topic often includes the effect of the ongoing violence on the children and economic considerations. Appropriate nursing interventions in these discussions include the recognition that decisions to terminate any relationship are difficult and that each woman needs to carefully assess the advantages and disadvantages of each option.

TREATMENT GUIDELINES FOR CHILDREN IN WIFE-ABUSING FAMILIES

Comprehensive family approaches with wife-abusing families must include therapy with the children. Children respond to abuse in a variety of manners, ranging from hiding in fear to attempts to protect their mother. Older children are sometimes inadvertently hurt when they attempt to stop the abuser or protect their mother. For this reason, special children's groups are important. It is often advisable to separate children by ages so that preadolescents have a separate group from adolescents. These sessions include discussions and exploration of how the children are affected by the violence, along with assurances that they are not responsible for the violence. Such issues as guilt, embarrassment, anger, shame, and feeling different from their friends may also be addressed.

WORKING WITH THE COUPLE

In some situations, couple counseling is indicated. Couple counseling is appropriate when both parties are motivated to maintain the relationship while ending the violence.

In the initial visit with a violent family the most important consideration is to develop a plan to prevent future violence. This plan is based on the premise that each person is responsible for his or her own behavior and that any form of violence is unacceptable. Developing the plan includes identifying cues that indicate when anger is escalating and possibly leading to violence. With the abuser, the previously mentioned body cues may be taught. The woman is also asked to identify signs that violence may be imminent. For some couples this will involve increased arguments or disagreements. For others, the husband may begin drinking, watching television, being short-tempered with the children, or reporting problems at work. It is important that the therapist convey the message that the woman is not responsible for the violence but that her observations can assist in her safety. The man's responsibility is to control his anger; the woman's responsibility is to protect herself.

The next part of the violence avoidance plan is to determine what each person will do if either believes that violence is imminent. Some therapists believe that the abuser must leave the home for a predetermined time, with a minimum of 2 hours. Others advocate that the plan be individualized, with predetermined people for both the husband and wife to contact (Weidman, 1986). In either approach, if children are involved, the plan needs to include arrangements for their safety.

The plan must be mutually agreed on, with both individuals agreeing to follow it, despite its possible inconveniences. In addition, it is of critical importance that the woman be informed of local shelters and available services if the plan fails. This information is given not to imply that failure is expected, but rather to establish the consequences of future abuse and to reiterate that violence is not acceptable. Some therapists recommend that both parties be forewarned that therapy will terminate if future violence occurs.

Later therapeutic interventions in couple counseling include assessment of current and past family stressors, communication patterns, values, and beliefs. Potential areas for exploration include financial and social family resources, religious beliefs and possible differences, indications of substance abuse or infidelity, and issues related to conflicts over the children.

Exploring behavior patterns within the family of origin may be fruitful. Was violence present in either family of origin? What was the symbolic meaning of violence within each partner's family of origin? What types of discipline were taught in the family of origin, and what are the couple's current beliefs regarding discipline?

Couple counseling can be an effective treatment modality in ending wife abuse when both partners are highly motivated to end the violence and develop more healthful communication patterns.

Preventive Approaches for Psychiatric Nurses

The prevention of family violence is a critical goal for all nurses who work with families. Prevention encompasses working with families to eliminate ongoing violence and primary prevention.

PRIMARY PREVENTION

Primary prevention refers to an activity that stops a problem before it occurs. Primary prevention of abuse includes strengthening individuals and families so they can cope more effectively with multiple life stressors and competing demands. This might take the form of anticipatory guidance while working with families in the hospital or community. For example, respite care is needed for families with severely ill or incapacitated family members. Planning in advance for relief from responsibility will prevent strained relationships and potential violence or abuse.

In addition, psychiatric nurses can conduct programs in the schools, workplace, or community. Strategies such as nurse-developed educational programs in high school parenting classes or childbirth education classes can be used to ease the expected stress of child rearing. These classes could include topics such as normal child development and expectations, basic skills of infant care, and means of disciplining children that do not involve physical punishment. Additional educational strategies include teaching family members that conflict resolution does not have to mean that one party must win while the other loses and respect for individual differences among family members.

Nurses can also be involved in elementary and middle schools teaching family life and sex education courses. Sexual abuse of children can be prevented or detected when children are taught about inappropriate sexual contact and what they should do if it occurs.

The findings from nursing research can also be used effectively in prevention. For example, one nurse researcher testified before the Michigan House and Senate Judiciary Committees on the consequences of marital rape. The study findings were released to the media, and the nurse researcher became known in the state capital because her testimony was so graphic and compelling. The bill to eliminate "spousal immunity" in rape prosecution was passed unanimously in the Michigan House and Senate (Campbell, 1989a).

SECONDARY PREVENTION

Secondary prevention of family violence involves the identification of families at risk or those who are beginning to use violence. Early indicators of families at risk include violence in the family of origin of either partner, communication problems, excessive family stress such as an unplanned pregnancy or unemployment, or inadequate family resources.

• • •

Family violence is a complex process involving the interaction of social, personal, and family forces. Psychiatric nurses intervening with violent families will be both challenged and rewarded. Although interventions may be difficult, strategies to end the cycle of violence are worth the effort.

REFERENCES

Adams, D. (1988). Treatment models of men who batter. In K. Yllo & M. Bograd (Eds.), *Feminist perspectives on wife abuse.* Newbury Park, Calif: Sage.

Beck, C., & Ferguson, D. (1981). Aged abuse. *Journal of Gerontological Nursing, 7*(6), 333-336.

Becker, J.V., & Coleman, E.M. (1988). Incest. In V.B. Van Hasselt, R. Morrison, A.S. Bellack, & M. Herson (Eds.), *Handbook of family violence.* New York: Plenum.

Berk, R., Berk, S., Loseke, D., & Rauma, D. (1983). Mutual combat and other family violence myths. In D. Finkelhor, R. Gelles, G. Hotaling, & M. Straus (Eds.), *The dark side of families: current family violence research.* Newbury Park, Calif: Sage.

Bersani, C., & Chen, H. (1988). Sociological perspectives on family violence. In V. Van Hasselt, R. Morrison, A. Bellack, & M. Hersen (Eds.), *Handbook of family violence.* New York: Plenum.

Bullock, L., McFarlane, J., Bateman, L., & Miller, V. (1989). The prevalence and characteristics of battered women in a primary care setting. *The Nurse Practitioner, 14*(6), 47-52.

Bunting, S. (1989). Stress on caregivers of the elderly. *Advances in Nursing Science, 11*(2), 63-72.

Burgess, A. (1984). Intrafamilial sexual abuse. In J. Campbell, & J. Humphries (Eds.), *Nursing care of victims of family violence.* Reston, Va: Reston.

Campbell, J. (1986b). Nursing assessment for risk of homicide with battered women. *Advances in Nursing Science, 8*(4), 36-51.

Campbell, J. (1986a). A survivor group for battered women. *Advances in Nursing Science, 8*(2), 13-20.

Campbell, J. (1989a). Nursing research helps change law. *American Journal of Nursing, 84,* 947.

Campbell, J. (1989b). A test of two explanatory models of women's responses to battering. *Nursing Research, 38*(1), 18-24.

Campbell, J., & Humphreys, J. (1984). *Nursing care of victims of family violence.* Reston, Va: Prentice-Hall.

Chapman, J., & Gates, M. (Eds.) (1978). *The victimization of women.* Newbury Park, Calif: Sage.

Cook, D., & Frantz-Cook, A. (1984). A systematic approach to wife battering. *Journal of Marital and Family Therapy, 10*(1), 83-93.

Council on Scientific Affairs, American Medical Association (1985). AMA diagnostic and treatment guidelines concerning child abuse and neglect. *JAMA, 254*(6), 796-800.

Disbrow, M., Doerr, H., & Caufield, C. (1977). Measuring the components of parents' potential for child abuse and neglect. *Child Abuse and Neglect, 1,* 279-296.

Dobash, R.E., & Dobash, R.P. (1988). Research as social action: The struggle for battered women. In K. Yllo & M. Bogard (Eds.), *Feminist perspectives on wife abuse.* Newbury Park, Calif: Sage.

Edleson, J. (1984). Working with men who batter. *Social Work, 29,* 237-242.

Egeland, B., Breitenbucher, M., & Rosenberg, D. (1980). Prospective study of the significance of life stress in the etiology of child abuse. *Journal of Consulting and Clinical Psychology, 48,* 195-205.

Elbow, M. (1977). Theoretical considerations of violent marriages. *Social Casework, 58,* 515-526.

Feinauer, L. (1989). Comparison of long-term effects of child abuse by type of abuse and by relationship of the offender to the victim. *American Journal of Family Therapy, 17*(1), 48-56.

Fesbach, S. (1980). Child abuse and the dynamics of human aggression and violence. In G. Gerber, C. Ross, & E. Zeigler (Eds.), *Child abuse: An agenda for action.* New York: Oxford University Press.

Finkelhor, D. (1983). Common features of family violence. In D. Finkelhor, R. Gelles, G. Hotaling, & M. Straus (Eds.), *The dark side of families: Current family violence research.* Newbury Park, Calif: Sage.

Hart, B. (1988). Beyond the "duty to warn": A therapist's "duty to protect" battered women and children. In K. Yllo & M. Bograd (Eds.), *Feminist perspectives on wife abuse.* Newbury Park, Calif: Sage Publications.

Helfer, R., & Kempe, C.H. (1976). *Child abuse and neglect.* Cambridge, Mass: Harper & Row.

Herrenkohl, E., & Herrenkohl, R. (1979). Perspectives on the intergenerational transmission of violence. In D. Finkelhor, R. Gelles, G. Hotaling, & M. Straus (Eds.), *The dark side of families: Current family violence research.* Newbury Park, Calif: Sage.

Hickey, T., & Douglass, R.L. (1981). Mistreatment of the elderly in the domestic setting: An exploratory study. *American Journal of Public Health, 71,* 500-507.

Hoff, L.A. (1990). *Battered women as survivors.* London: Routledge.

Hotaling, G.T., & Straus, M. (1980). *The social causes of husband-wife violence.* Minneapolis: University of Minnesota Press.

Hotaling, G.T., & Sugerman, D. (1986). An analysis of risk markers in husband to wife violence: The current state of knowledge. *Violence and Victims, 1,* 101-124.

Hudson, M., & Johnson, T. (1987). Elder neglect and abuse: A review of the literature. In C. Eisdorfer (Ed.), *Annual review of gerontology.* New York: Springer.

Humphreys, J., & Campbell, J. (1988). Abusive behavior in families. In C. Gilliss, B. Highley, B. Roberts, & I. Martinson (Eds.), *Toward a science of family nursing.* Menlo Park, Calif: Addison-Wesley.

Journal of the American Medical Association (1985). AMA diagnostic and treatment guidelines concerning child abuse and neglect. *JAMA, 254*(6), 796-800.

Kelly, L. (1988). How women define their experiences of violence. In K. Yllo & M. Bograd (Eds.) *Feminist perspectives on wife abuse.* Newbury Park: Sage.

Kempe, C., Silverman, F., & Stelle, B. (1962). The battered child syndrome. *JAMA, 181,* 17-24.

Kempe, C.H., Helfer, R. (1980). *The battered child.* Chicago: University of Chicago Press.

Landenburger, K. (1988). Conflicting realities of women in abusive relationships. *Communicating Nursing Research, 21,* 15-20.

Landenburger, K. (1989). A process of entrapment in and recovery from an abusive relationship. *Issues in Mental Health Nursing, 10,* 209-227.

Leonard, K., & Jacob, T. (1988). Alcohol, alcoholism, and family violence. In V. Van Hasselt, R. Morrison, A. Bellack, & M. Hersen (Eds.), *Handbook of family violence.* New York: Plenum.

Levinson, D. (1988). Family violence in cross-cultural perspective. In V. Van Hasselt, R. Morrison, A. Bellack, & M. Hersen (Eds.), *Handbook of family violence.* New York: Plenum.

Lynch, M. (1975). Ill-health and child abuse. *Lancet, 2,* 317-319.

Maiuro, R., Eberle, J. (1989). New developments in research on aggression: An international report. *Violence and Victims, 4*(1), 3-15.

McFarlane, J., Parker, B., Soeken, K., and Bullock, L. (1992). Assessing for abuse during pregnancy: Severity and frequency of injuries and associated entry into prenatal care. *JAMA, 267* (23), 3176-3178.

Millor, G. (1981). A theoretical framework for nursing research in child abuse and neglect. *Nursing Research, 30,* 78-84.

Okun, L.E. (1986). *Woman abuse: Facts replacing myths.* Albany, New York: State University of New York Press.

Nesbit, W., & Karagianis, L. (1982). Child abuse: Exceptionality as a risk factor. *Alberta Journal of Educational Research, 28,* 69-76.

Newbern, V. (1989). Sexual victimization of children and adolescent patients. *Image, 21*(1), 10-14.

Pagelow, M. (1984). *Family violence.* New York: Praeger.

Parker, B. (1979). Communicating with battered women. *Topics in Clinical Nursing, 1*(3), 49-53.

Parker, B., & Schumacher, D. (1977). The battered wife syndrome and violence in the nuclear family of origin: A controlled pilot study. *American Journal of Public Health, 67*(8), 760-761.

Parker, B., Ulrich, Y., Bullock, L., Campbell, D., Campbell, J., King, C., Landenburger, K., McFarlane, J., Ryan, J., Sherdian, D., & Torres, S. (1989). A protocol for safety: Research on the abuse of women. *Nursing Research, 39,* 248-250.

Perry, M., Wells, E., & Doran, L. (1983). Parent characteristics in abusing and non-abusing families. *Journal of Clinical Child Psychology, 12,* 329-336.

Phillips, L. (1983). Abuse and neglect of the frail elderly at home: An exploration of theoretical relationships. *Journal of Advanced Nursing, 8,* 379-392.

Pillemer, K. (1985). Social isolation and elder abuse. *Response to the victimization of women and children, 8*(5), 1-4.

Pillemer, K., & Suitor, J. (1988). Elder abuse. In V. Van Hasselt, R. Morrison, A. Bellack, & M. Hersen (Eds.), *Handbook of family violence.* New York: Plenum.

Pollick, M. (1987). Abuse of the elderly: A review. *Holistic Nursing Practice, 1*(2), 43-53.

Schechter, S. (1982). *Women and male violence.* Boston: South End Press.

Seagull, E. (1987). Child psychologist's role in assessment. In R. Helfer, & R. Kempe (Eds.), *The battered child* (4th Ed.). Chicago: University of Chicago Press.

Sedlak, A. (1988). Prevention of wife abuse. In V. Van Hasselt, R. Morrison, A. Bellack, & M. Hersen (Eds.), *Handbook of family violence.* New York: Plenum.

Sherrod, K., O'Conner, S., Vietze, P., & Altemeier, W. (1984). Child health and maltreatment. *Child Development, 55,* 1174-1183.

Stark, E., & Flitcraft, A. (1988). Violence among intimates: An epidemiological review. In V. Van Hasselt, R. Morrison, A. Bellack, & M. Hersen (Eds.), *Handbook of family violence.* New York: Plenum.

Starr, R. (1982). A research based approach to the prediction of child abuse prediction. In R. Starr Jr. (Ed.), *Child abuse prediction: Policy implications.* Cambridge, Mass: Ballinger.

Starr, R. (1988). Physical abuse of children. In V. Van Hasselt, R. Morrison, A. Bellack, & M. Hersen (Eds.), *Handbook of family violence.* New York: Plenum.

Steinberg, L., Catalano, R., & Dooley, D. (1981). Economic antecedents of child abuse and neglect. *Child Development, 52,* 975-985.

Steinmetz, S. (1988). *Duty bound: Elder abuse and family care,* Newbury Park, Calif: Sage.

Steinmetz, S., & Lucca, J. (1988). Husband battering. In V. Van Hasselt, R. Morrison, A. Bellack, & M. Hersen (Eds.), *Handbook of family violence.* New York: Plenum.

Steinmetz, S., & Straus, M. (1974). Intra-family violence. In S. Steinmetz, & M. Straus (Eds.), *Violence in the family.* New York: Harper & Row.

Straus, M. (1974). Violence research, violence control, and the good society. In S. Steinmetz, & M. Straus (Eds.), *Violence in the family.* New York: Harper & Row.

Straus, M. (1980). Stress and child abuse. In C. Kempe, & R. Helfer (Eds.), *The Battered Child* (3rd ed.). Chicago: University of Chicago.

Straus, M.A., & Gelles, R.J. (1986). Societal change and change in family violence from 1975 to 1985 as revealed by two national surveys. *Journal of Marriage and the Family, 48,* 465-479.

Torres, S. (1987). Hispanic-American battered women: Why consider cultural differences? *Response, 10*(3), 20-21.

Torres, S. (1991). A comparison of wife abuse between two cultures: Perceptions, attitudes, nature and extent. *Issues in Mental Health Nursing, 12*(1), 113-131.

Walsh, D., & Liddy, R. (1989). *Surviving sexual abuse.* Dublin: Attic Press.

Webster-Stratton, C. (1985). Comparison of abusive and non-abusive families with conduct disorder children. *American Journal of Orthopsychiatry, 55,* 59-69.

Weidman, A. (1986). Family therapy with violent couples. *Social Casework, 67,* 211-218.

White, E. (1985). *Chain, chain, change: For black women dealing with physical and emotional abuse,* Seattle: Seal Press.

Yin, P. (1985). *Victimization and the aged.* Springfield, Ill: Charles C. Thomas.

Zuravin, S. (1989). The ecology of child abuse and neglect: Review of the literature and presentation of data. *Violence and Victims, 4*(2), 101-120.

Chapter 14

Intrafamilial Child Sexual Abuse

Charlotte M. Gilbert

Of the estimated 138,000 cases of child sexual abuse that are believed to occur each year in the United States (National Center on Child Abuse and Neglect, 1988), intrafamilial child sexual abuse composes the most studied and reported form of child sexual abuse: no socioeconomic, cultural, or age group is excluded, although prepubertal girls and boys are reportedly victimized most frequently (Brassard, Tyler, & Kehle, 1983; Campbell & Humphries, 1984; Finkelhor, 1986, 1987; Fore & Holmes, 1984; Gordon & O'Keefe, 1985; Justice & Justice, 1979; Mims & Chang, 1984; Patton, 1991). Other forms of incest—such as sibling, mother-child, and other family member incestuous relationships—are considered underreported (Authier, 1983; Finkelhor, 1987; Patton, 1991). Traditionally, the parameters of incest have been limited to members of biologic families: father and child(ren), mother and child(ren), and/or siblings. Incestuous relationships may occur in biologic families of origin (classic: biologic parent-child, siblings) or in families blended by remarriage, cohabitation, foster care, or adoption.

This chapter focuses on incest as a form of child sexual abuse. Although it is recognized that females can molest children, and boys may be victims of incestuous relationships, the most studied and reported form of incest is that between father or stepfather and daughter (Finkelhor, 1987; Gelinas, 1983; Sturkie, 1986). Discussion shall be limited to incestuous relationships (1) involving male parental figures and female children and (2) between siblings. Implications for nursing practice and research are examined.

Definition

Child sexual abuse is defined as sexual interaction between dependent, developmentally immature children and adolescents—who are unable to fully comprehend the activity and give informed consent—and adults or older youths (Justice & Justice, 1979). The power of the adult, even without actual threat or use of physical force, is influential (Authier, 1983). Sexual activity may include the following behaviors: exhibitionism, voyeurism, fondling, oral-genital sex, attempted intercourse, intercourse with or without penetration, exhibition of children sexually, exposing children to pornography, and manipulating children to engage in sexual acts with adults, each other, or animals (Salter, 1988).

Incest as a form of child sexual abuse may be defined as any sexual activity between a child under 18 years of age and parent, stepparent, extended family member, surrogate parent, or sibling (Justice & Justice, 1979; Salter, 1988; Sgroi, 1982); developmentally delayed victims are age exempt (Anderson & Mayes, 1982; Russell, 1986; Vander Mey & Neff, 1986). The crucial psychosocial dynamic in incest is the violation of familial/kinship roles, whether or not the persons are blood related (Finkelhor, 1979; Gelanis, 1983; Gordon & O'Keefe, 1985; Justice & Justice, 1979; Sgroi, 1982; Vander Mey & Neff, 1986).

Historical Influences on Incest

CULTURAL

The taboo against sexual relationships among close family members was originally proposed as a means to promote family harmony, decrease genetically defective offspring, and ensure relationships beyond the nuclear family. Gordon and O'Keefe (1985) suggest that the incest taboo is concerned with a prohibition against the formation of new families through incestuous mating. Based on their review of case records of child abuse in Boston from 1880 to 1960, Gordon and O'Keefe (1985) propose that nonreproductive sex between family members occurs with frequency, and although socially prohibited — much the same as the prohibition against murder, incest occurs with as many violations.

Further challenges to the notion of an incest taboo are presented by Twitchell (1987). The author reports that although incestuous relationships may produce defective children, they may also produce children who are of above average intelligence. It has been found that when individuals are raised together from early childhood, mating and/or reproduction is not likely to occur. Viewed from this perspective, incest avoidance may be a biologically encouraged and a shared value among a group of people at conscious and unconscious levels.

Whether one believes that a taboo or incest aversion exists, the creation of the taboo to control family sexuality has resulted in unintended consequences, namely, a societal prohibition to refrain from the identification and discussion of issues related to family sexuality. Until recently, sexual education and rights were not considered a topic worthy of study or discussion. Generations of children and adults were deprived of knowledge related to their bodies and sexual rights. The taboo implicitly denied sexuality and fostered secrecy about such matters. Thus the sexual taboo, which was created to protect family members, did just the opposite; children who experienced molestation had little knowledge of the travesty that was happening to them and were less disposed to divulge the secret because sexuality was not a matter for discussion.

CHILD BEHAVIOR

Explicit cultural messages to children have included injunctions to obey their elders without question and to be seen and not heard (Campbell & Humphries, 1984). Although these messages might provide respite for the adult, they do little to promote the child's safety from unscrupulous adults. The explicit cultural message to children was to obey and be quiet, which resulted in an implicit message that reinforced not telling, remaining quiet, and most certainly obeying elders who knew more than children. A climate conducive to child sexual abuse was created.

FREUD

Freud is credited for positing therapy as a legitimate intervention in cases that had previously been relegated to anthropologic or moral domains (Vander Mey & Neff, 1986). However, Freud did much to discredit the phenomenon of child sexual abuse as a legitimate area of concern, study, and intervention. In 1896, Freud delivered his famous lecture on hysteria and proposed that the hysteria of his patients (6 men and 12 women) was related to their childhood intrafamilial sexual abuse. Such abuse was perpetrated by an adult family member or an older sibling who had, in turn, been previously abused by adults (Miller, 1986). In 1897, Freud attributed the abuse to hysterical fantasies and subsequently developed a theory of psychosexual development that posited the child as the parental seducer. Thus incest became the product of a psychosexual developmental period during which the child desired to seduce the parent of the opposite gender and sometimes succeeded (Campbell & Humphries, 1984; Finkelhor, 1979; Herman, 1981; Miller, 1986; Russell, 1986; Salter, 1988; Sgroi, 1982; Vander Mey & Neff, 1986). It was not until the mid-1970's that the issue of child sexual abuse was again brought to public attention (Burgess & Holmstrom, 1975; Kempe, 1978; Sgroi, 1975).

KINSEY

A researcher of the 1940s and 1950s, Kinsey is noted for his groundbreaking research in sexuality. He found child sexual abuse to have been an almost universal experience of adult respondents (Finkelhor, 1979). Kinsey chose to minimize this fact and proposed instead that childhood sexual experiences produced no physical harm, were sought out by children, and—if emotional problems did result—they were due more to hysteria on the part of the respondent than to the actual sexual experience (Finkelhor, 1979; Russell, 1986; Salter, 1988).

FEMINIST MOVEMENT

Feminists and victims were able to break the silence about child sexual abuse and legitimize it as an important area of concern and study. Indeed, the feminist movement cast doubt on traditional beliefs about child sexual abuse, such as the child as a seducer of adults and mothers as collusive partners in incest (Finkelhor, 1979; Russell, 1986; Salter, 1988; Twitchell, 1987). Even social anthropologists were not left untouched; they were criticized for attention to the "why" of the incest taboo, rather than on the prevalence and factors associated with its occurrence (Russell, 1986).

Boss and Weiner (1988) suggest that women's experiences and developmental issues have historically not been studied from a woman-centered perspective. They contend that theory, research, and scholarly endeavors about human growth and development were specific to the lives of men and boys. Boss and Weiner state, "A majority of mental health practitioners have been working with the meanings of predominantly male-derived, male-focused ideas about behavior and relationships. They have diagnosed, labeled, and in a clinical sense seen their clients through these lenses, these versions of truth" (p. 239). Scientists who were supposed to be unbiased and dedicated to discovering the truth were unwilling to recognize and expose the problem of incest (Russell, 1986).

Sacrosanct traditional family system theory concepts as related to family violence were also challenged by feminists, that is, the contribution of each family member to family problems. The theoretic framework of family system theory was found to encounter major difficulties when applied in an attempt to explain either family violence or individual responsibility for such (Boss & Weiner, 1988; Dell, 1989).

Explicit cultural messages generated by the feminist movement have challenged traditional ways of viewing female development and sexual experience. As a result, implicit cultural messages are beginning to empower children to refuse inappropriate adult requests and to place ultimate responsibility on the person who committed the sexual abuse—the adult.

ETHNICITY

McGoldrick (1982) studied the family life cycle and ethnicity. The author suggests that ethnic values and identification are retained for many generations after immigration and play a significant role in family life and personal development throughout the life cycle. Values that were functional in another place and time often become dysfunctional when transferred into modern American life: ethnocentrism, clannishness, prejudice, fear, and deep distrust of outsiders.

The explicit cultural message of ethnicity promotes distrust of a new society, whereas the implicit cultural message suggests that trust be placed solely within the family. Both messages place the family at risk by instituting closed boundaries for what may be several generations and creating one of the parameters of an incestuous family: a family cut off from the larger world and one in which needs must be met solely by family members.

LAW

Incest is a crime. The law varies from state to state as to how child sexual abuse is defined and what punishment or discipline is rendered to those who sexually abuse children. In general, child sexual abuse—including incest—is not likely to be reported. Russell (1986) found in a study of 938 female adults who were victimized as children, only 30 survivors reported the abuse and only 7 convictions resulted. Yorker (1988) suggests several reasons for the child's reluctance to seek legal recourse: guilt related to family separation, possible perpetrator incarceration, and an adversarial trial process in which the child is at a disadvantage.

The legal system imparts a potent explicit cultural message to child sexual abuse offenders that promotes offender disinhibition; offenders are not likely to be convicted, and if they are, they are likely to receive reduced sentences (D. Szymanowiski, South Carolina Department of Corrections, personal communication, April 10, 1989). Jackson and Sandberg (1985) studied the attribution of incest blame among rural attorneys and judges and found a gender difference among male and female attorneys; male attorneys attributed more blame to incest victims than did female attorneys. Further, the researchers found that attribution of blame affected offender outcomes in terms of imprisonment, probation, or fines.

The legal system communicates implicit messages to children that foster the child's silence about the abuse. The child may be further victimized by a legal system that is for the most part insensitive to the needs of children or by the reality that offenders are not likely to go to court or receive sentencing.

Dynamics of Child Sexual Abuse

Finkelhor (1986) states that four preconditions are necessary for the occurrence of child sexual abuse. An offender must not only be motivated to sexually abuse, but also must overcome internal inhibitions against sexually abusing the child. In addition, the offender must overcome both external inhibitions against sexual abuse and the resistance of the child. According to Finkelhor, many children at risk for sexual abuse will never experience it, even if the offender has overcome external obstacles to molesting and child resistance has been reduced, as long as the preconditions of molester motivation and the negation of internal inhibitions have not been met.

Sgroi (1982) suggests that the dynamics of sexual abuse form predictable patterns. Although the patterns provide a description of the phases of child sexual abuse in general, they also may be encountered in incest. According to Sgroi, during the engagement phase the adult seeks and gains access to a child. Subsequent phases are characterized by sexual interaction between the adult and child, and secrecy that is maintained by manipulation (affection, bribery, threats, and/or force). The final phase may take one of two directions: the abuse may be disclosed accidently or purposefully, or the sexual abuse may remain forever a secret.

Another perspective on family dynamics is proposed by Gilbert (1988b) who suggests that incestuous family dynamics are similar to those seen in psychosomatic families: enmeshment, overprotection, rigidity, and conflict avoidance (Minuchin et al., 1978). Role boundaries in enmeshed families are diffuse; therefore roles may be interchanged, such as parent-child role reversal. The secret nature of the abuse may be maintained through a form of parental overprotection whereby sexually abused children are discouraged from venturing beyond family environs. Rigid compliance to family norms and boundaries also serves to maintain secrecy of the abuse, since contact between family members and the community is minimal, thus decreasing opportunities for disclosure. The desire to avoid conflict may foster secrecy, denial, and minimization of the abuse among family members, thereby increasing the risk for other family members and generations to experience sexual abuse.

Although families who sexually abuse their children may share similar patterns of behavior, each is unique. They are influenced by a variety of factors, including family composition, history, culture, and coping and problem solving abilities. Thus it is very difficult to attribute a particular set of characteristics by which incestuous families may be identified. Single factor theories, such as incest due to patriarchy or cultural influences, cannot adequately explain the phenomenon because of the multivariate nature of incest (Gelanis, 1983). Thus Finkelhor's idea of preconditions for sexual abuse (1986), Sgroi's phases of sexual abuse (1982) and Gilbert's analogy to psychosomatic family dynamics (1988b) are helpful but — in and of themselves — do not adequately explain the phenomena. Theories of child sexual abuse, including incest, are still evolving.

Characteristics Observed in Incestuous Families

The characteristics of families in which incest has occurred vary (see the box below). One may find families who isolate themselves from the larger world through the creation of rigid boundaries that limit access to the family, or they may be disrespectful of boundaries and limit setting related to generations, roles, and environmental privacy (Schetky & Green, 1988). Families may

---

Characteristics of Families at Risk of Incest

Enmeshment, overprotection, rigidity, and conflict avoidance
Role reversal/parentified child
History of incest in family or in parents' family of origin.
Patriarchal family structure
Rigid or chaotic family structure
Family violence
Alcohol/substance abuse
Sexual estrangement of marital partners
Emotionally and/or physically absent/ill parents
Isolation
Deficient social skills
Low self-esteem
Impaired self-control, especially among adult or teen-aged males who are sexually attracted to female familial children
Indiscreet parental sexual behavior/extramarital affairs
Hostile/paranoid attitude toward outsiders
Lack of anticipatory guidance and education related to familial sexual roles/boundaries

adhere to patriarchal principles, engage in role reversal (child nurtures the parent), or become chaotic as parental responsibilities are negated (Authier, 1983; Finkelhor, 1979; Herman, 1983; Sgroi, 1982).

PARENTIFIED CHILD

Estrangement of marital partners has been identified as a characteristic often seen in incestuous families (Authier, 1983; Gelinis, 1983; Sgroi, 1982). In conjunction with marital estrangement, one may find the parentified child. Gelinis proposes that the parentification of a child is a gradual process whereby the child begins not only to function as a parent, performing tasks such as cooking, cleaning, and nurturing, but also assumes responsibility for those tasks. Over time, the child internalizes the role and develops an identity that includes taking care of others and possibly fulfilling a parent's sexual needs. Eventually, other family members' needs become primary to the exclusion of the child's needs.

The parentified female child becomes an adult who is attracted to men who need caretaking (Gelinis, 1983). Over time, the adult parentified child becomes exhausted from meeting the needs of her husband and family, including her husband's affection and attention needs. To meet family needs, both parents will parentify their child. The child's responsibilities will become more adultlike; the mother will expect the child to assume more adult female caretaking responsibilities, and the father will expect the daughter to meet his nurturant and possible sexual needs. Eventually, another cycle of parentified children is produced.

MOTHER

Many explanations have been voiced to account for maternal behavior in incestuous relationships. Sgroi (1982) states that mothers may be physically or psychologically absent and thus fail to protect, they may ignore seductive behavior between male parent and child, or they may create situations that provide opportunities for participants to engage in sexual behavior. Family dissolution, stigma, and reduced financial circumstances as a result of disclosure are other realities that may result in less effective maternal actions to stop the abuse (Wright, 1991). Elbow and Mayfield (1991) propose that after disclosure, some mothers act calmly and decisively, whereas others display crisis behavior (shock, confusion, and disbelief) that may be interpreted as passivity, weakness, dependency, or collusiveness. In a study of 24 case records of maternal behavior in validated father-daughter incest, Elbow and Mayfield found that only 4 (17%) of the mothers did not believe their daughters and at least 29% of the mothers initiated protective action.

FATHER

Numerous characteristics have been attributed to fathers or male parental figures who have engaged in incest. Fathers and father figures have been described as having the following characteristics: dependency or power needs, impulsiveness, poor judgment, and/or substance abusing (Gelinis, 1983; Salter,

1988; Sgroi, 1982; Ralphing et al., 1967). They are believed to exert power through force, intimidation, apportionment of attention, or belittlement (Sgroi, 1982). Fathers usually deny both their feelings of sexual attraction to their children and the sexual abuse of the same, and through the use of cognitive distortions attribute the desire for sexual interaction to the child (Schetky & Green, 1988).

Although limited and sometimes conflicting, research is providing some knowledge of incestuous male parental behavior. For example, Abel et al. (1981) conducted a study of incest and extrafamilial offenders, in which a plethysmograph (an instrument that measures physiological responses of an organ or limb) was used to assess the penile sexual arousal patterns of each group of offenders. The researchers found no differences in the sexual arousal patterns of the two groups of offenders to children.

Parker and Parker (1986) studied sexually abusing and nonabusing fathers in prisons and mental health centers in relation to their experience with the early socialization of their daughters. They found that fathers who were not present in the home and had not participated in the early socialization (caretaking, nurturing) of their daughters were more likely to sexually abuse them. The researchers concluded that physical and psychologic distance from the female child during the early years may increase the probability of sexual abuse by producing a lower threshold for sexual abuse.

These studies lend some support for Finkelhor's premise (1986) about the preconditions necessary for child sexual abuse. For example, in the Parker and Parker study (1986) an offender may have overcome external inhibitions to sexually abuse a child in that he gained access to a child and he may have reduced the child's resistance, but early paternal-child nurturing may have been a protective factor that prevented the offender from overcoming an internal inhibition and activating the motivation to abuse.

CHILD

To survive the experience of incest, victims reportedly engage in various coping mechanisms. Behavioral symptoms may serve to communicate the child's distress and place the child at risk for developmental problems (Gelinis, 1983; Gilbert, 1988b).

Children who have been sexually abused may repress or dissociate disturbing events or periods of time. Despite the use of denial, repetitive cognitive intrusions occur (Gelinis, 1983; Sgroi, 1982; Justice and Justice, 1979; Ralphing et al., 1967). Burgess et al. (1987) conceptualize these reactions as a cognitive-behavioral information process. According to the authors, the child uses trauma encapsulation, a psychologic process in which a variety of cognitive defenses are employed to help the child control the anxiety of the event, prevent disclosure of the abuse, and maintain a facade of normalcy. The trauma is encapsulated through the defenses of dissociation, avoidant or somatic behaviors, repression, splitting, suppression, or compartmentalization. The child becomes at risk developmentally due to the diversion of psychic energy to maintain cognitive defenses that encapsulate the trauma. The following areas may become compromised: the child's sense of right and wrong, belief about self, body awareness, personal power, and the child's ability to self-comfort and self-protect.

SIBLING INCEST

Sibling incest is believed to occur with considerable frequency, yet it has received the least amount of study (Bank & Kahn, 1982; Finkelhor, 1979; Meiselman, 1978; O'Brien, 1991; Ralphing et al., 1967). It may be defined as sexual interaction between individuals who have one or more parents in common, with brother-sister incest the most common type reported (Finkelhor, 1979; Gilbert, 1989; Loredo, 1982). Sibling incest occurs for many reasons: mutual explorative play that becomes more sexual and compelling, the inability of parents to meet their children's affiliative needs, or the desire to exercise power and control over another (Bank & Kahn, 1982; Gil, 1987). Parents of incestuous siblings have been found to share several common characteristics: physical and/or emotional distance and unavailability to their children; indiscreet parental/extramarital sexual activity; family secrets, such as parents who had been sexually abused themselves as children (Smith & Israel, 1987); and high rates of physical, sexual, and/or substance abuse (O'Brien, 1991). In a study of 170 adolescent sexual offenders, including 50 adolescent sibling incest offenders, O'Brien found that the sibling incest offenders were more likely to have experienced prior sexual victimization, possessed greater social skills deficits, committed more sexual crimes over a longer time period involving more intrusive sexual behavior (penetration), and were least likely to be adjudicated for their offenses. The latter finding may not be conclusive. In a case record review of families in which sibling incest had occurred, Gilbert (1992) found that both sibling incest offenders and victims were at risk of emotional, behavioral, and legal problems, as well as removal from the home.

Effects of Abuse

FAMILY

Incest has an impact both on the family as a unit and on each member individually and has implications for present and future family functioning. On disclosure of incest, families are disrupted by agency intervention, possible removal of family members, legal implications, emotional sequelae, and financial strain (Hubbard, 1989; Wright, 1991). The response of family members contributes to the reaction and adjustment of the victim(s) to the abuse (Authier, 1983).

Family reactions to incest vary. Because incest is a crime, abusers may react defensively to protect themselves, become hostile toward the child or anyone who supports the child, exploit power to control the child and other family members, or undermine the credibility of the allegation (Sgroi, 1982). If the incest remains undisclosed and untreated, incestuous role modeling places the family at risk for intergenerational repetition of incest. For example, the survivor of incest may sexually victimize others or align with a significant other who may sexually victimize their child(ren). The original incest perpetrator may continue to victimize other generations of children within and external to the family (Abel et al., 1988).

CHILD

Finkelhor and Browne (1986) conceptualize the effects of child sexual abuse within four categories of traumagenic dynamics. These categories include traumatic sexualization, stigmatization, betrayal, and powerlessness. Traumatic sexualization is defined as a process that occurs when a child's sexuality (sexual feelings and attitudes) are shaped in an inappropriate developmental and interpersonal manner. When children who have experienced sexual abuse realize that someone on whom they are dependent has caused them harm, they experience the dynamic of betrayal. The dynamic of powerlessness/ disempowerment is experienced when the child is rendered powerless; his or her will, desires, and sense of efficacy are contravened. Stigmatization results when negative connotations about the abuse are communicated to the child and become incorporated into the child's self-image.

The child who survives an incestuous experience may experience initial and/or long-term consequences (Anderson, 1981; Browne & Finkelhor, 1986; Brunngraber, 1986; Gold, 1986; Gomes-Schwartz et al., 1985; Sgroi, 1982). Human responses to incest are dependent on the interplay of numerous factors: the level of personality development before incest; current age and developmental stage of the child; coping mechanisms; cognitive ability and stage of development; duration and frequency of the abuse; the degree of coercion and physical trauma; the relationship between the child, the perpetrator, and other family members; the child's self-esteem; familial and institutional response to disclosure; and access to therapeutic intervention (Brunngraber, 1986; Schetky & Green, 1988). Behaviors that may be observed in children who have been sexually abused include changes in self-concept resulting in decreased self-esteem, feelings of guilt and shame, isolation, family loyalty conflicts, vulnerability and helplessness, questions about body integrity, issues of power and control, anger and hostility, fear, anxiety, depression and suicide, and loss and grief (Adams-Tucker, 1985; Anderson, 1981; Brassard et al., 1983; Brunngraber, 1986; Burgess & Holmstrom, 1975; Gilbert, 1988b; Lamb, 1986; Oates et al., 1985; Sgroi, 1982; Sturkie, 1986).

In incestuous relationships, additional threats to the achievement of developmental tasks are related to trust and parent-child roles. Perhaps the most crucial and potentially long-lasting effect of incest is related to the developmental issue of trust. Families are expected to provide children with nurturance, protection, care, and role modeling. The experience of incest either negates the ability of the family to provide the latter or promotes the exploitation of members to receive some form of protection, nurturance, or care. The betrayal of basic trust between child and family member interferes with the child's sense of safety in relationships with others in the present and possibly into the future.

Children who have experienced incest are often thrust into role reversal within the family constellation: the child becomes the caretaker of adults and other siblings. Gelinis (1983) proposed that a child who has reversed roles becomes an adult who has not had the benefit of childhood. Subsequently, parts of the child's personality are hyperdeveloped (caretaking and sense of responsibility) at the expense of other parts (self-system, social skills, personal talents, and self-esteem). Because of a paucity of knowledge related to the balance of obligation and entitlement in relationships, such children—as adults—may enter into relationships that are exploitative of themselves and their children.

MOTHER

Mothers are often blamed for the incest. Mothers may have been aware of the incest and encouraged it, may have known about the incest and failed to stop it, or may have been forced to choose between the child or the offender (Justice & Justice, 1979; Sgroi, 1982). Gelinis (1983) proposed that the mother shares responsibility for the sexual abuse only if she actively participated or knowingly allowed the abuse to continue. For example, in families where fathers are dominant, there may be no family member who is strong enough to resist him when he is sexually interested in his daughter. Perhaps the most glaring omission from a discussion of culpability is ownership for the responsibility for the incest. Ultimately, the responsibility for incest rests with the offender.

OFFENDER

The effects of incest disclosure for the offender are considerable (Schetky & Green, 1988). Offenders may become depressed or suicidal after disclosure of incest (Ralphing et al., 1967). This may be due to stigmatization, community outrage, legal and family problems, and/or personal remorse for the abuse. Perhaps the greatest impediment to progress with offenders is their persistent use of the coping mechanisms of denial and cognative distortion, even in the light of evidence to the contrary (Sgroi, 1982). External factors such as the legal system foster offender denial. For example, the admission of abuse places the offender at risk for criminal prosecution and incarceration.

SIBLINGS

Family members other than those directly involved in the incest—such as siblings, the other parent, and extended family members—may not know about the incest, may misinterpret it, or may treat the victim as a scapegoat. They may be angry with the victim for the special position that the victim may have enjoyed within the family. On disclosure, family members may be overwhelmed by stigma and disruption and project their wrath on the child who experienced the sexual abuse or the agencies that intervene. When more than one sibling is involved in incest, victims may be unaware that other siblings have been victimized, or they may be aware of other victimized siblings but be unwilling or afraid to discuss the matter (Sgroi, 1982).

SIBLING INCEST

Although generally perceived by society as an innocuous activity, especially when the siblings are chronologically comparable, sibling incest is not necessarily without trauma (Cole, 1982; Lieske, 1981; Loredo, 1982; Russell, 1986). There exists the potential for rivalry, unrestrained visciousness, and pregnancy because of the immaturity of the offender (Gelinis, 1983; Meiselman, 1978). Russell cautions that an age difference of less than 5 years between siblings engaged in incest does not imply that consent was involved or that the experience was mutually desired or enjoyed. The dismissal of the seriousness of sibling incest may contribute to the neglect of many cases that are serious and/or decrease support for the victim (O'Brien, 1991; Russell, 1986).

The effects of sibling incest on parents is notable; they must divide their attention and loyalties between their child who has been molested and their child who has offended. Parents may experience emotional turmoil, blaming, and anger toward each other and other family members. If both children live at home, parents may be concerned about the degree of vigilance that must be maintained, as well as how to reestablish normal, trusting bonds between family members (Gil, 1987).

Both sibling incest victims and abusers may suffer severe consequences after disclosure, such as removal from the home, emotional/academic problems, and legal difficulties (Gilbert, 1992). The sexual offense of sibling incest is a crime and is usually indicative of offender psychologic problems (Gil, 1987). As a result of disclosure of incest, the youth may experience probation, detention in a juvenile facility, or a prison sentence. If the youth is going to address psychologic problems and learn to control deviant sexual behavior, therapeutic intervention is required.

Family-Focused Interventions

Incest is a crime. As such, all who have contact with children, including nurses, are required to report cases where children either have been or are suspected of having been sexually abused.

Due to the criminal nature of the act, the law requires the child to testify and witnesses to corroborate the complaint in cases that proceed to court (Kempe, 1978). This requirement often places children at a distinct disadvantage. Because of the secretive nature of adult-child incest, there rarely will be witnesses to the act. Physical evidence of sexual abuse is present in less than 50% of the cases (De Jong, 1985). Children, by virtue of their age and developmental stage, may not be able to testify on their own behalf or may require considerable anticipatory guidance to do so.

The adversarial process of the legal system naturally predisposes family members to divide loyalties, a position that may be doubly difficult for the child. The offender may have also been a source of nurturance for the child, and if the legal system forces the child to testify against the offender the child may suffer from additional guilt and intense family wrath. Children are often pressured to recant their disclosure, especially when informed of the difficulties that the family may encounter: separation of family members, public shame, loss of financial support, or possible severe punishment of the perpetrator (Meiselman, 1978). Sgroi (1982) proposes that the law be used to provide the necessary leverage to ensure that the abuse ceases, including a mandate for offender treatment and monitoring to minimize the risk of recidivism.

It is important that from the moment of initial contact the family as a whole and each member individually be treated humanely and with respect. This is sometimes easier said than done when one considers the multiple agencies that intervene with families and the emotions that surface when members of society, including agency personnel, interface with incestuous families who are also experiencing emotional turmoil.

INTERVENTIONS

No empirical evidence exists to support the superiority of one approach over another, nor is much guidance available for practitioners in their decision making related to the treatment of incestuous families (Finkelhor, 1988; Sgroi, 1982). In part, this is due to the fact that parent-child incest is committed by so many different types of families that there is no one prescription for all families (Meiselman, 1978; Sturkie, 1986).

Family-focused interventions may include victims, mothers, siblings, and offenders in individual, group, dyad, marital, or family therapy. Dependent on the philosophy espoused, reunification of all family members versus concern for mothers and victimized daughters only, criteria for inclusion in therapy and treatment outcomes vary (Herman, 1981; Salter, 1988; Vander Mey & Neff, 1986). Elbow and Mayfield (1991) propose that a blanket policy that separates perpetrator and child initially be reconsidered and replaced by a differential assessment that determines the ability of the family to prevent further abuse. They suggest that the assessment address not only perpetrator and mother characteristics and the extent of the sexual abuse, but also include consideration of the child's age, ability to protect self from further abuse, family receptiveness to family treatment, and the mother's ability to assume a protective and supportive role for her child.

Anderson and Mayes (1982) suggest that regardless of the approach, families in crisis need immediate support, reassurance and hope, and information related to short-term and long-term plans for all family members, including access to self-help groups or individuals who have experienced similar circumstances and who are currently in treatment. Levitt et al. (1991) report the results of a study in which 119 primary caretakers of children who were sexually abused by family members or babysitters reported the services they considered as most helpful: physician evaluation, victim and witness assistance services, guardian ad litem services, and professional counseling services. Almost one third of the respondents indicated the need for long-term counseling and support groups for all family members and resources related to financial assistance.

CHILD

Individual, dyadic, group, and family therapies have been used with child survivors of incest. Once the secret of incest has been disclosed, individual therapy is believed appropriate since the child is able to receive individual attention and assessment and begin the work needed to address issues to the sexual abuse (Meiselman, 1978; Sgroi, 1982; Vander Mey & Neff, 1986). The individual attention also establishes boundaries between family members, which may not be present in incestuous families. A criticism of the individual therapy approach is that it may be viewed initially as replicating the original abuse experience — a situation in which an adult and a child are alone and in which confidentiality may be perceived as secrecy.

Group therapy for victims of incest has special merit (Anderson & Mayes, 1982; Blick & Porter, 1982; Gilbert, 1988c, 1989; Herman, 1981; Meiselman, 1978; Sturkie, 1983; Vander Mey & Neff, 1986). Group therapy provides members with the following opportunities: the secret of abuse becomes less potent since all members share a common history; it is a safe place in which to vent feelings; a sense of belonging results, which may reduce feelings of isolation and loneliness; new behaviors may be acquired; and support is provided. Another benefit of group therapy is its ability to offset what may be perceived as the secretive nature of individual treatment (Vander Mey & Neff, 1986).

Regardless of the approach, the fact remains that a paucity of therapeutic services exist for sexually victimized children. In a follow-up study of 150 children seen at the Sexual Assault Center in Seattle, Washington, Conte and Berliner (1990) found that 15% of the children received no treatment and 23% were treated for 1 month or less. Conte (1991) concludes that most victims of child sexual abuse do not receive adequate intervention.

Mother-daughter dyadic therapy may occur in concordance with child individual therapy. A strong mother-daughter relationship is believed to be the best deterrent against further sexual abuse (Herman, 1981). The goal of dyadic therapy is to strengthen the mother-daughter relationship and resolve issues associated with the abuse, such as anger, rivalry, and failure to protect.

Family therapy is viewed as the end point in treatment if the mother decides that the family is to remain together. The child's safety from continued sexual abuse must be ensured. In the best of situations, the child remains at home with the mother, although children are often placed in foster care when serious doubt exists about the family's ability to protect the child from further abuse (Meiselman, 1978).

MOTHER

Mothers are often forgotten in the crisis after disclosure of the abuse, yet they play a key role in the support of their children (Anderson & Mayes, 1982). Maternal support of a sexually victimized child is a complicated matter. Everson et al. (1989) studied maternal support after disclosure of incest and reported the following findings: the level of maternal support was inversely related to the recency of the mother-offender relationship (that is, mothers who were most supportive of their children had perpetrators who were ex-spouses), and the level of maternal support was more strongly predictive of the child's initial psychologic functioning than were type or length of abuse or the perpetrator's relationship to the child. The researchers also noted a strong association between supportive mothers' reports and the clinical interview of the child but limited agreement between ambivalent and unsupportive mothers and the clinical interview. The researchers suggest that a serious challenge exists as to the validity of maternal reports and research methodologies that rely solely on parental child behavior checklists.

Other postdisclosure issues that mothers may have to consider include financial and emotional insecurity, isolation, and an estranged mother-daughter relationship (Levitt et al., 1991; Wright, 1991). Brunngraber (1986) proposes that the mother's role be strengthened to empower her in protecting the child; she may need financial assistance, a safe temporary residence, and nonblaming support. Self-help groups such as Parents United can provide support and refer the mother to needed services in addition to providing assistance with temporary child-care and housing needs (Herman, 1981).

In combination with such other therapies as individual and crisis, mother-daughter dyadic therapy is considered important to the resolution of mother-daughter estrangement. During dyadic therapy, mothers acknowledge their role as parent and protector of the child and apologize for their inability to fulfill these roles in the past (Anderson & Mayes, 1982). If the marital partners consider reunification important, then marital therapy may be concurrent with other therapies.

OFFENDER

An offender's first concern is usually with legal issues. The offender needs support and information about the court and process of treatment. Because of the punitive nature of the legal system, it is not unusual for offenders to deny or rationalize the abuse rather than accept responsibility for it (Anderson & Mayes, 1982).

The offender who is considered manipulative and neither seeks voluntary treatment nor reveals the full extent of offenses is not considered a good candidate for individual therapy (Meiselman, 1978). Herman (1981) states "Successful engagement of offenders in treatment seems to be directly related to the degree of cooperation between the treatment program and the criminal justice program" (p. 153). Interventions with offenders must be authoritative, supportive, consistent, and nonpunitive with emphasis on positive aspects of the offender (Sgroi, 1982).

Group therapy is espoused as a modality that can provide the offender with both motivation and external control for behavioral change (Herman, 1981; Salter, 1988; Sgroi, 1982; Vander Mey & Neff, 1986). Structured group therapy provides members with peer confrontation, support, and self-control learning opportunities, including cognitive strategies and aversive training. For example, the offender could be taught that whenever he thinks about unacceptable sexual impulses, he would also think about the consequences of such action. In return for behavioral change, the offender receives much group support.

The father is believed to hold the key to releasing much of the child's guilt; therefore the goal of offender therapy is his acceptance of full responsibility for the incestuous behavior, acknowledgement of parenting failure, and apology to the victim and the family. Because offender recidivism is difficult to determine, the reunion of the offender with the family is often based on several conditions, such as continued supervision by the court, active involvement in an appropriate treatment program, acceptance of responsibility for the incestuous relationship, and apology to the daughter (Herman, 1981). Offender charac-teristics considered most consistent with successful offender rehabilitation are nonviolence, admission of responsibility for the abuse, expression of remorse and desire for change, a strong work history, and sobriety (Anderson & Mayes, 1982; Herman, 1981; Meiselman, 1978; Sgroi, 1982).

SIBLINGS

The issues and concerns of nonoffended siblings are usually neglected. Nonoffended siblings are least likely to be involved in treatment (Woodworth, 1991). The siblings may or may not be aware of the incest. Siblings need to be encouraged to express fears, ask questions, and clarify misperceptions, such as the displacement of responsibility for incest onto someone (victim) other than the offender (Anderson & Mayes, 1982).

SIBLING OFFENDERS

Although sibling offenders engage in initial denial, they are reported to eventually acknowledge their offense (Gil, 1987). This is considered a positive sign, because it is very difficult to commence therapeutic intervention with a person in denial. Other factors that may characterize the youthful offender include immaturity, impulsivity, lack of social skills, low self-esteem, sexual confusion/stimulation, and learned behavior such as molestation as a child. Children who have been molested may molest others in an attempt to make sense of the molestation that happened to them or to master their experience. The youth attempts to master the earlier sexual experience through the recreation of sexual abuse, the difference being that in the current situation the youth is in control of the experience. Gil suggests that young male offenders have a difficult time exposing their molestation, except through their molestation of others; thus they need help with both victim and offender issues.

Parents need assistance with their own emotions related to the following: parental failure to protect their children, children involved in the incest, and the multiple systems that have an impact on the family, such as legal, mental health, and social services. To effectively monitor the future behavior of the offender, parents have to learn which situations are a high risk for repeated sexual offenses for the offender. Gil (1987) proposes that there is no guarantee that the offender will not repeat a sexual offense; however, the risk for recidivism is diminished through appropriate therapeutic and legal interven-tion.

FAMILY THERAPY

During the 1960's, family therapy was enthusiastically recommended as the treatment of choice in incestuous families. Meiselman (1978) reported that some difficulties associated with the routine application of this approach included lack of offender cooperation in therapy; potential for intergenerational violation when all members were present, but the problem involved husband and wife; and a philosophy that espoused that all members contribute to and are responsible for resolution of the family problem. Family therapy has therefore been replaced by a more cautious stance reflecting the reality and complexity of therapeutic interventions with incestuous families. It is believed that incest occurs in different types of families, an additional reason to find a singular theoretical approach wanting (Finkelhor, 1979; Meiselman, 1978; Sturkie, 1986).

After or concurrent with later stages of individual therapy, dyadic therapy, or group therapy, family treatment commences if the mother has decided to keep the family intact. Vander Mey and Neff (1986) caution against premature commencement of family treatment; they insist that the offender must be able to accept responsibility for actions and apologize to the victim. Before family counseling, the husband and wife must identify critical issues with which they must deal if the marriage is to survive (Anderson & Mayes, 1982).

Because the family can not return to the status quo of predisclosure behavior, anxiety is inherent in the family system as members initiate behavioral change, address relationship issues, and formulate the rules by which family members will operate, that is, privacy, monitoring offender behavior, and so on. Herman (1981) suggests that self-help groups are an important source of support to families both at this time and after the conclusion of formal therapy.

One of the most important issues related to family treatment and reconstitution, yet the most difficult to document, is recidivism (Finkelhor, 1986; Levitt et al., 1991). Kroth (1979) studied families who participated in Garretto's Child Sexual Abuse Treatment Program in Santa Clara County, California. Although 95% of the couples reported that they would remain together, at the conclusion of therapy 41% of the couples reported reluctance to report future molestation if it recurred as compared with 18% at intake. Levitt et al. (1991) found that 8% of the respondents in a study of families after disclosure of incest indicated that some abuse had recurred. Because reliable long-term data on outcome treatment are difficult to obtain, Meiselman (1978) proposed that the well-being of child and mother become the criteria for successful therapy, as well as lack of paternal domination, a daughter who is comfortable in her father's presence, and parents who relate as marital partners.

Incestuous behavior is never really cured. It must be managed for a lifetime (Herman, 1981; Salter, 1988; Vander Mey & Neff, 1986). It is proposed that the success of a program is not dependent on the total reconstruction of the family but the healthy functioning of whatever segment of the family chooses to stay together (Anderson & Mayes, 1982).

THERAPIST ISSUES

Regardless of the approach, the therapist must be aware of the range of emotions that are encountered in work with incestuous families (Gilbert, 1988c; Sturkie, 1986). Therapists may be uncomfortable with the subject matter, neglect to explore the sexual abuse, and instead treat presenting symptoms (Meiselman, 1978). Therapists who work with incestuous families interface with persons from numerous systems, such as police officers, judges, probation officers, and case workers of social service agencies. Supervision — individual or peer — is recommended to alleviate therapist stress, foster realistic therapeutic goals, and provide a safe place in which the therapist can ventilate emotions and explore options.

Other Interventions

PREVENTION

The prevention of child sexual abuse is one of the fastest growing programs of the child sexual abuse movement (Finkelhor, 1986). It is believed that the vulnerability and abuse of many children could be reduced through education. Prevention programs may be targeted toward child, parent, or professional audiences. Finkelhor questions whether there are groups of children that should be specially targeted, such as children who live in stepfamilies, have disabilities or emotional problems, or have parents who were sexually victimized as children. Prevention programs have yet to address prevention in terms of helping adults resist abusing, especially when the ultimate responsibility for abuse rests with the adult. Other problems associated with prevention programs include learning that may be lost over time (Finkelhor, 1986); children who may become frightened by the presentation (Garbarino, 1987); at-risk group issues that are not addressed, such as sibling incest (Gilbert, 1989); and information related to sexual matters, such as terminology (Finkelhor, 1986).

ANTICIPATORY GUIDANCE

Education of children and parents in the form of anticipatory guidance is a therapeutic intervention that can be used in conjunction with more traditional therapies and/or prevention programs. Gilbert (1989) suggests that many concepts relative to the prevention of intrafamilial incest (parent-child) can also be used for the prevention of sibling incest, because both occur within the family context. Content of such programs could include attention to spousal relationships; values; normal child growth and development, including sexual development; role boundaries; stress reduction; and issues related to parents molested as children, if relevant.

RESEARCH IMPLICATIONS

The study of child sexual abuse, including incest, is of recent origin. Professional efforts have been directed toward intervention rather than research (Finkelhor, 1988). The need exists for short-term and long-term evaluation studies of prevention programs, the development of valid and reliable instruments, and the monitoring of the effects of training on parents and professionals (Finkelhor, 1986), as well as comparative studies to determine cost-effectiveness of differing therapeutic and self-help interventions (Rew, 1989).

A multitude of areas in child sexual abuse, including incest, require nursing attention. Because of the relatively recent interest in child sexual abuse, nursing research has the opportunity to contribute to the field and to its own body of knowledge. We believe that the most expedient approach for nurses to study incest is through use of the nursing metaparadigm (person, health, environment, and nursing) within a nursing conceptual framework. For example, a nursing framework that one could use is that of Roy (Roy & Roberts, 1981). Within that framework, Roy proposes that the role of the nurse is to assist the individual to adapt or cope positively. Numerous human responses to incest could be organized within the four modes of Roy's conceptual framework (physiologic, self-concept, role function, and interdependence), and adaptation could be measured through output in the modes (Gilbert, 1990). Nursing research based on the Roy framework could address the effectiveness of nursing interventions or prevention programs to promote adaptation through measurement of empirical referents in the four modes. The knowledge thus generated by nursing research would have the potential to contribute to nursing science and the body of knowledge on incest.

·   ·   ·

Although the majority of children do not experience incest, current reports indicate that child sexual abuse — including incest — occurs with frequency and is a problem of considerable magnitude. Initial and long-term human responses to incest affect the children involved, their families, and society.

Numerous factors contribute to the creation of a family atmosphere that facilitates incest: parental and family history, cultural and societal factors, gender issues, and marital and parenting difficulties. Once incest has been disclosed, families must interface with numerous agencies, change behaviors, and ensure that the sexual victimization of their child ceases. Although diverse interventions with various family members and the family as a whole are used to promote family health and adaptation, empirical data are lacking to substantiate the superiority of one treatment approach over another.

An opportunity exists for nurses to contribute to the field of child sexual abuse from a nursing perspective. The use of nursing conceptual models and the development of nursing theories of incest could contribute both to nursing research and practice and the field of child sexual abuse.

Child sexual abuse, including incest, is a serious societal problem worthy of nursing's attention. Unlike the children's refrain, "Rain, rain, go away," child sexual abuse will not go away by merely wishing it so. A concerted nursing effort is required to confront, intervene, and advocate for healthy families and the cessation of incest.

REFERENCES

Abel, G.G., Becker, J., Cunningham-Rathner, J., Mittleman, M., & Rouleau, J.L. (1988). Multiple paraphilic diagnoses among sex offenders. *Bulletin of the American Academy of Psychiatry and the Law, 16*(2), 153-168.

Abel, G.G., Becker, J.V., Murphy, W.D., & Flanagan, B. (1981). Identifying dangerous child molesters. In R.B. Stuart (Ed.), *Violent behavior*. New York: Brunner/Mazel.

Adams-Tucker, C. (1985). The unmet needs of sexually abused youth: Referrals from a child protection agency and clinical evaluations. *Journal of the American Academy of Child Psychiatry, 23*(6), 659-667.

Anderson, C., & Mayes, P. (1982). Treating family sexual abuse: The humanistic approach. *Journal of Child Care, 1*(2), 31-46.

Anderson, L.S. (1981). Notes on the linkage between the sexually abused child and the suicidal adolescent. *Adolescence, 4,* 157-162.

Authier, K. (1983). Incest and sexual violence. *Family Therapy Collections: Sexual Issues in Family Therapy, 5,* 101-128.

Bank, S.P., & Kahn, M.D. (1982). *The sibling bond.* New York: Basic Books.

Blick, L.C., & Porter, F.S. (1982). Group therapy with female adolescent incest victims. In S.M. Sgroi (Ed.), *Handbook of clinical intervention in child sexual abuse* (pp. 147-175). Lexington, Ma: D.C. Heath.

Boss, P., & Weiner, J.P. (1988). Rethinking assumptions about women's development and family therapy. In C.J. Falicov (Ed.), *Family transitions: Continuity and change over the life cycle* (pp. 235-251). New York: Guilford Press.

Brassard, M.R., Tyler, A., & Kehle, T.J. (1983). Sexually abused children: Identification and suggestions for intervention. *School Psychology Review, 12*(1), 93-98.

Browne, A., & Finkelhor, D. (1986). Impact of sexual abuse: A review of the research. *Psychological Bulletin, 69*(1), 66-77.

Brunngraber, L.E. (1986). Father-daughter incest: Immediate and long-term effects of sexual abuse. *Advances in Nursing Science, 8*(4), 15-35.

Burgess, A., Hartman, C.R., Wolbert, W.A., & Grant, C.A. (1987). Child molestation: Assessing impact in multiple victims (Part I). *Archives of Psychiatric Nursing, 1*(1), 33-39.

Burgess, A., & Holmstrom, L.L. (1975). Sexual trauma of children and adolescents. *Nursing Clinics of North America, 10,* 551-563.

Campbell, J., & Humphries, J. (1984). *Nursing care of victims of family violence.* Reston, Va: Reston Publishing.

Cole, E. (1982). Sibling incest: The myth of benign sibling incest. *Women and Therapy, 1,* 79-89.

Conte, J.R. (1991). Child sexual abuse: Looking backward and forward. In M.Q. Patton (Ed.), *Family sexual abuse: Frontline research and evaluation* (pp. 3-22). Newbury Park, Ca: Sage Publications.

Conte, J.R., & Berliner, L. (1990). *What happens to sexually abused children after disclosure.* (Available from J.R. Conte, School of Social Work, University of Washington, Seattle, WA 98195).

Dell, P.F. (1989). Violence and the systemic view: The problem of power. *Family Process, 28*(1), 1-14.

De Jong, A.R. (1985). The medical evaluation of sexual abuse in children. *Hospital and Community Psychiatry, 36*(5), 509-512.

Elbow, M., & Mayfield, J. (1991). Mothers of incest victims: Villians, victims, or protectors? *Families in Society: The Journal of Contemporary Human Services, 72*(2), 78-85.

Everson, M.D., Hunter, W.M., Runyon, D.K., Edelson, G.A., & Coulter, M.L. (1989). Maternal support following disclosure of incest. *American Journal of Orthopsychiatry, 59*(2), 197-207.

Finkelhor, D. (1979). *Sexually victimized children.* New York: Free Press.

Finkelhor, D. (1986). *A sourcebook on child sexual abuse.* Newbury Park, Calif: Sage.

Finkelhor, D. (1987). The sexual abuse of children: Current research reviewed. *Psychiatric Annals: The Journal of Continuing Psychiatric Education, 17*(4), 233-238.

Finkelhor, D. (1988). *Stopping family violence: Research for the coming decades.* Newbury Park, Calif: Sage.

Finkelhor, D., & Browne, A. (1986). Initial and long-term effects: A conceptual framework. In D. Finkelhor (Ed.), *A sourcebook on child sexual abuse* (pp. 180-198). Newbury Park, Calif: Sage.

Fore, C.V., & Holmes, S.S. (1984). Sister-sister incest as a manifestation of multigenerational sexual abuse. *Journal of Adolescent Health Care, 7,* 202-204.

Garbarino, J. (1987). Children's response to a sexual abuse prevention program: A study of the spiderman comic. *Child Abuse & Neglect, 11,* 143-148.

Gelinis, D.J. (1983). The persisting negative effects of incest. *Psychiatry, 46,* 312-332.

Gil, E. (1987). *Children who molest: A guide for parents of young sex offenders.* Walnut Creek, Calif: Launch Press.

Gilbert, C.M. (1988a). Children in Women's shelters: A group intervention using art. *Journal of Child and Adolescent Psychiatric Mental Health Services, 1*(1), 7-13.

Gilbert, C.M. (1988b). Psychosomatic symptoms: Implications for child sexual abuse. *Issues in Mental Health Nursing, 9,* 399-408.

Gilbert, C.M. (1988c). Sexual abuse and group therapy. *Journal of Psychosocial Nursing and Mental Health Nursing, 26*(5), 19-23.

Gilbert, C.M. (1989). Sibling incest. *Journal of Child and Adolescent Psychiatric and Mental Health Nursing, 2*(2), 70-73.

Gilbert, C.M. (1990). A structured group nursing intervention for girls who have been sexually abused utilizing Roy's theory of the person as an adaptive system. *Dissertation Abstracts International, 52,* 296.

Gilbert, C.M. (1992). Sibling incest: A descriptive study of family dynamics. *Journal of Child and Adolescent Psychiatric and Mental Health Nursing, 5*(1), 5-9.

Gold, E.R. (1986). Long-term effects of sexual victimization in childhood: An attributional approach. *Journal of Consulting and Clinical Psychology, 54*(4), 471-475.

Gomes-Schwartz, B., Horowitz, J.M., & Sauzier, M. (1985). Severity of emotional distress among sexually abused preschool, school-age, and adolescent children. *Hospital and Community Psychiatry, 36*(5), 503-508.

Gordon, L., & O'Keefe, P. (1985). The normality of incest: Father-daughter incest as a form of family violence. In A. Burgess (Ed.), *Rape and sexual assault: A research handbook* (pp. 70-82). New York: Garland Publishing.

Herman, J.L. (1981). *Father-daughter incest.* Cambridge, Ma: Harvard University Press.

Herman, J.L. (1983). Recognition and treatment of incestuous families. *International Journal of Family Therapy, 5*(2), 81-91.

Hubbard, G.H. (1989). Perceived life changes for children and adolescents following disclosure of father-daughter incest. *Journal of Child and Adolescent Psychiatric and Mental Health Nursing, 2*(2), 78-82.

Jackson, T.L., & Sandberg, G. (1985). Attribution of incest blame among rural attorneys and judges. *Women & Therapy, 4*(3), 39-56.

Justice, B., & Justice, R. (1979). *The broken taboo.* New York: Human Sciences Press.

Kempe, C.H. (1978). Sexual abuse, another hidden pediatric problem: The 1977 C. Anderson Aldrich lecture. *Pediatrics, 62*(3), 382-389.

Kroth, J.A. (1979). *Child sexual abuse: Analysis of a family therapy approach.* Springfield, Ill: Charles C. Thomas.

Lamb, S. (1986). Treating sexually abused children: Issues of blame and responsibility. *American Journal of Orthopsychiatry, 56*(2), 303-307.

Levitt, C.J., Owen, G., & Truchsess, J. (1991). Families after sexual abuse: What helps? What is needed? In M.Q. Patton (Ed.), *Family sexual abuse: Frontline research and evaluation* (pp. 39-56). Newbury Park, Ca: Sage Publications.

Lieske, A.M. (1981). Incest: An overview. *Perspectives in Psychiatric Care, 29*(2), 59-63.

Loredo, C.N. (1982). Sibling incest. In S.M. Sgroi (Ed.), *Handbook of clinical intervention in child sexual abuse* (pp. 177-189). Lexington, Ma: D.C. Heath.

McGoldrick, M. (1982). Ethnicity and family therapy: An overview. In M. McGoldrick, J.K. Pearce, & J. Giordano (Eds.), *Ethnicity and family therapy* (pp. 3-30). New York: Guilford Press.

Meiselman, K.C. (1978). *Incest: A psychological study of causes and effects with treatment recommendations.* San Francisco: Jossey-Bass.

Miller, A. (1986). *Thou shall not be aware: Society's betrayal of the child.* New York: New American Library.

Mims, F.H., & Chang, A.S. (1984). Unwanted sexual experiences of young women. *Journal of Psychosocial Nursing and Mental Health Services, 22*(6), 6-14.

Minuchin, S., Rosman, B.L., & Baker, L. (1978). *Psychosomatic families: Anorexia nervosa in context.* Cambridge, Ma: Harvard University Press.

National Center on Child Abuse and Neglect (1988). *Study findings: Study of national incidence and prevalence of child abuse and neglect* (DHSS Publication No. He 23.1210: In 2/2 88-16506). Washington, D.C.: U.S. Department of Health and Human Services.

Oates, R.K., Forrest, D., & Peacock, A. (1985). Self-esteem of abused children. *Child Abuse and Neglect, 9,* 159-163.

O'Brien, M.J. (1991). Taking sibling incest seriously. In M.Q. Patton (Ed.), *Family sexual abuse: Frontline research and evaluation* (pp. 75-92). Newbury Park, Ca: Sage Publications.

Parker, H., & Parker, S. (1986). Father-daughter sexual abuse: An emerging perspective. *American Journal of Orthopsychiatry, 56,* 531-549.

Patton, M.Q. (Ed.) (1991). *Family sexual abuse: Frontline research and evaluation.* Newbury Park, Ca: Sage Publications.

Ralphing, D.L., Carpenter, B.L., & Davis, A. (1967). Incest: A geneological study. *Archives of General Psychiatry, 16,* 505-511.

Rew, L. (1989). Long-term effects of childhood sexual exploitation. *Issues in Mental Health Nursing, 10,* 22-244.

Roy, C.S., & Roberts, S.L. (1981). *Theory construction in nursing: An adaptation model.* Englewood Cliffs, N.J.: Prentice Hall.

Russell, D.E.H. (1986). *The secret trauma: Incest in the lives of girls and women.* New York: Basic Books.

Salter, A.C. (1988). *Treating child sex offenders and victims: A practical guide.* Newbury Park, Calif: Sage.

Schetky, D.H., & Green, A.H. (1988). *Child sexual abuse: A handbook for health care and legal professionals.* New York: Brunner/Mazel.

Sgroi, S. (1975). Sexual molestation: The last frontier of child abuse. *Children Today,* May-June, 18-21.

Sgroi, S. (1982). *Handbook of clinical intervention in child sexual abuse.* Lexington, Ma: D.C. Heath.

Smith, H., & Israel, E. (1987). Sibling incest: A study of the dynamics of 25 cases. *Child Abuse and Neglect, 11,* 101-108.

Sturkie, K. (1983). Structured group treatment for sexually abused children. *Health and Social Work, 8*(14), 299-308.

Sturkie, K. (1986). Treating incest victims and their families. In B.J. Vander Mey and R.L. Neff (Eds.), *Incest as child abuse* (pp. 126-165). New York: Praeger.

Szymanowiski, D. South Carolina Department of Corrections (personal communication, April 10, 1989).

Thorman, G. (1983). *Incestuous families.* Springfield, Ill: Charles C. Thomas.

Twitchell, J.B. (1987). *Forbidden partners: The incest taboo in modern culture.* New York: Columbia University Press.

Vander Mey, B.J., & Neff, R.L. (1986). *Incest as child abuse: Research and applications.* New York: Praeger.

Woodworth, D.L. (1991). Evaluation of a multiple-family incest treatment program. In M.Q. Patton (Ed.), *Family sexual abuse: Frontline research and evaluation* (pp. 121-134). Newbury Park, Ca: Sage Publications.

Wright, S. (1991). Family effects of offender removal from the home. In M.Q. Patton (Ed.), *Family sexual abuse: Frontline research and evaluation* (pp. 135-146). Newbury Park, Ca: Sage Publications.

Yorker, B.C. (1988). The prosecution of child sexual abuse: Legal issues related to child advocacy. *Journal of Child and Adolescent Psychiatric and Mental Health Nursing, 1*(2), 50-51.

Chapter 15

The Impact of HIV Infection and AIDS on the Family

Patrick E. Kenny

Few issues are as complex as HIV infection and acquired immunodeficiency syndrome (AIDS). With the identification of the first cases in 1981, HIV infection and AIDS have had a profound impact on the medical, social, and political institutions of our time. Perhaps no other disease offers a microcosm of the modern world. The impact and development of moral, ethical, and legal questions have been unparalleled.

The psychologic and social impact on the family may result in psychiatric symptoms frequently seen in life-threatening diseases. These include anxiety, depression, delirium, substance use, suicidal ideation, anger, denial, and other indicators of maladaptive coping.

At present, there is no cure for the HIV infection but prevention is possible. Given the absence of an effective vaccine, prevention of transmission through education and behavioral changes represents the single most important focus for controlling the HIV epidemic.

Infection with HIV leads to a progressive loss of immune function and the development of opportunistic infections and malignancies rarely observed in individuals with an intact immune system. Nearly all organ systems are affected, either directly by the immunodeficiency state or indirectly by the malignant and infectious sequelae of HIV infection. The progression of HIV infection proceeds from the acute initial infection through a symptomatic period to symptoms indicative of AIDS. The ultimate outcome for most individuals infected with HIV is death.

The focus of this chapter is the impact of HIV infection and AIDS on the family and psychosocial concerns for the client and significant and supportive others. Issues related to the treatment modalities and options are also addressed.

Overview

AIDS has an influence on all aspects of society and the family. AIDS has had a significant impact on such societal institutions as relationships, marriage, child bearing, parenting, family dynamics, and estate planning.

Before the identification of HIV and AIDS as a distinct disease entity, the traditional family unit — centered around the institution of marriage — had undergone tremendous changes. The turbulence of the 1960s and 1970s rapidly altered the status quo. Marriage rates declined, divorce rates skyrocketed, nontraditional relationships (both heterosexual and homosexual) increased, and single-parent households became commonplace. Sexual awareness and freedom contributed to these changes. The family unit experienced enormous stress and, in many cases, a disintegration of the support systems that heretofore had enabled the family to adequately cope with life-threatening illnesses.

The AIDS epidemic presents challenges and opportunities for the nurse. HIV infection has a direct impact on all aspects of the individual's life. Nurses in their role of primary caregiver in the health care system interact with all individuals and groups. During the AIDS epidemic, nurses are challenged to create and provide humane delivery systems for the care of clients with HIV infection, their families, and their communities.

Definition(s)

AIDS is a condition in which the immune system, the body's primary defense against disease, is damaged. The damage is caused by a specific type of virus known as retrovirus. Identified as human immunodeficiency virus (HIV), it infects a specialized portion of the immune system called the T-4 lymphocytes and also infects the brain cells and other portions of the immune system.

Unusual and life-threatening diseases are common in people with AIDS, as a result of their compromised immune system. People with AIDS are vulnerable to serious illnesses that normally would be fought off by a healthy immune system. These illnesses are technically termed "opportunistic infections" (OIs) or opportunistic diseases. Many persons with HIV infection have more than one of these diseases. Among the most common diseases are Kaposi's sarcoma, *Pneumocystis carinii* pneumonia (PCP), toxoplasmosis, *Mycobacterium avium,* intracellular mycobacteriosis, esophageal or invasive candidiasis, primary CNS lymphoma, progressive dementia, and progressive multifocal leukoencephalopathy.

HIV is transmitted through three principal routes of infection: sexual contact (semen and vaginal secretions), parenterally (blood-blood contact via shared needles or transfusion of infected blood or blood products), and perinatally (mother to fetus), and possibly through breast milk. HIV has also been isolated in saliva, tears, cerebrospinal fluid, amniotic fluid, and urine. However, studies have implicated *only* blood, semen, vaginal secretions, and possibly breast milk. The virus is *not* viable outside the body. The transmission of HIV has also been associated with specific high-risk behaviors.

Sexual Behaviors

Sexual transmission is a primary factor in the HIV epidemic. Individuals engaging in unprotected sex, with multiple partners, and receptive anal intercourse have the greatest risk of HIV infection. Initial indications in 1981 were that the disease was predominantly occurring in gay/bisexual men and persons using IV drugs. Exposure and response to education have dramatically decreased the number of new cases in these populations, while increases in the heterosexual population have indicated a significant problem — the second wave of infection. Persons who acquire HIV infection via sexual contact with a person of the opposite sex represent a small but growing group of AIDS cases reported to the Centers for Disease Control (CDC). Heterosexual HIV transmission has also been responsible for a high female prevalence of HIV infection in central cities where IV drug use is high. In addition, data from recent studies have suggested that sexually transmitted diseases (STDs) such as genital herpes, syphilis, and gonorrhea may be important in the transmission of HIV infection. Risk behaviors that aid in the transmission of STDs probably aid in HIV transmission (Brandt, 1988).

The role of prostitution in HIV infection has also been implicated, because of the higher rate of STD infection and IV drug use.

There is a higher rate of transmission if intercourse occurs during menses or bleeding occurs during intercourse. Transmission is higher from male to female but does occur from female to male.

Psychoactive Drug Use

Unquestionably, IV drug use is a major factor in HIV infection. This risk behavior accounts for the second largest number of cases reported to the CDC. The prevalence of IV drug use contributes to the disproportionate incidence among women, children, and ethnic/racial minorities. Secondary infection of partners contributes to the epidemic. Investigational studies indicate that *some* substances, such as intravenous cocaine and opiates, alcohol, and marijuana, have immunosuppressive effects and may act as a cofactor.

Epidemiology and Demographics

As of November 1991, statistics indicate there are 199,106 cases of AIDS in the United States (the full syndrome, not simply HIV infection); of these, 196,000 are adult. Heterosexually transmitted cases account for 2500, of which 10.3% are female and three fourths are black or Hispanic. Women with HIV are the fastest growing group. Represented in the statistics is a 9:1 ratio of men to women. Among military statistics, there is a 1:1 ratio of men to women. AIDS represents the fifth leading cause of death for women and is the leading cause of death of black women in New York City. AIDS is now the second leading cause of death in *all* men 25 to 40 years of age in the United States.

Pediatric cases are 3106. It is estimated that 1 or 2 births per 1000 nationwide are HIV positive. In the metropolitan inner cities the number rises to 8 per 1000 births. The CDC estimates that there is a 12% to 45% risk of transmission perinatally if the mother is HIV positive. Breast feeding confers higher risk.

The CDC estimates that there are 1 to 1.5 million infected individuals in the United States. In comparison, the World Health Organization (WHO) estimates that there are 10 million cases of AIDS worldwide and by the year 2000 there will be 40 million.

The impact of the statistics on the individual, family, community, and society is immeasurable. The need for the increased financial resources places significant strain on all aspects of society because of the shift of resources to HIV care. The impact on the health care community will similarly be affected as increasing numbers of individuals with HIV infection are diagnosed, hospitalized, and treated. Not only the acute care setting, but outpatient, hospice, and psychosocial services, will need to adapt to an increasing caseload of clients who are living longer from time of diagnosis as we become more aware of HIV, case finding, and the benefit of early treatment. A thorough assessment must be completed before beginning treatment. The box on p. 272 provides an assessment tool listing pertinent information to obtain.

Treatments

Treatment of the client with AIDS presents a significant challenge to the health care team. The approach must be interdisciplinary to provide comprehensive, compassionate care. It is important that services are coordinated and take into consideration the needs of the client and the client's family — not those of the health care delivery system.

The American Nurses' Association's Code for Nurses (1976) states that, "The nurse must provide services with respect for human dignity and the uniqueness of the client unrestricted by consideration of social or economic status, personal attributes or the nature of the health problem." Pursuant to this, nurses have the obligation to provide competent, comprehensive nursing care while maintaining privacy and confidentiality. Further, nurses must advocate for their clients so that access to services in the institution is unrestricted.

Treatments for those with AIDS have significantly improved since the first case of AIDS was diagnosed. Although there is no standard treatment or "cure," early recognition and diagnosis have assisted in the management of AIDS. Treatment is disease-specific and aimed at symptom relief.

An underlying problem for the treatment of AIDS is the immune system deficiency. Many of the current antibiotics rely on an intact immune system. When the immune system is impaired, antibiotic therapy must continue for longer periods, leading to other problems and complications.

Assessment Tool

Basic information

Name: Allergies:
Room number: Height:
Physicians: Weight:
                                         Diet:
Age: Diagnosis:
Name/Telephone #   Admission:
   of significant other: Current:
Clergy/religious support:
Contributing factors:
Past medical history:

Social history (environmental factors, living arrangements, type of neighborhood, support system(s), and working environment, and conditions):

Health practices (regularity of health care and dental care, breast self-exam (BSE), testicular self-exam (TSE), health insurance and personal self-care practices);

Educational background:

Physiologic adaptation/responses

Patterns of elimination:
Fluid/Food patterns (likes, dislikes, eating times):
Activity/Rest patterns:
Personal hygiene patterns:
Altered lab values:
Attitudes about sexuality/sexual activity:
Past sexual activity history:

Other pertinent information

Drug/Alcohol usage: patterns, preferences, amounts, specific types of drug, alcohol, current usage?

Descriptive summary:

Side effects of any of the treatments must be considered because of the severity and disabling nature of the illness.

TREATMENT ISSUES AND OPTIONS

To date there is no "cure" for AIDS. However, there are effective medications, either in common use or investigational, that offer treatment options for the person living with AIDS (see the box on p. 273).

Medications Used to Treat AIDS

Specific therapies

Zidovudine (AZT) – An antiviral drug that interferes with the life cycle of the virus, delays the onset of opportunistic infections, decreases morbidity, and extends life of the individual. Originally, dosage was 200 mg every 4 hours, which necessitated that the individual take the medication around the clock. Dosage parameters now are 100 mg five times a day, which help accommodate a more normal sleeping schedule. It should be noted that an AZT-resistant state occurs in some cases.

Didanosine (DDI) – The second mode of therapy, it offers some individuals an alternative to AZT and produces an increase in CO-2 cells. In some cases, a 2-week rotation of AZT and DDI is used and occasionally they are used concurrently. DDI *is* toxic and is used cautiously.

Dideodoxycytidine (DDC) – An investigational drug, it does not get into the central nervous system.

Nonspecific therapies

Interferon Alfin – An oncologic agent that has shown promise in controlling Kaposi's sarcoma in some clients. It is a biologic response modifier that is additive with AZT, not synergistic.

Trimethoprim and sulfa methoxezole (Septra) – Used to treat cryptospordosis and PCP. Often used as a preventative in HIV-positive individuals. About 65% of clients on septra develop agranulocytosis and skin eruptions.

Gancyclovir – Used to treat cytomegalovirus (CMV) retinitis.

Sulfadiazine – Used to treat encephalopathy and used prophylactically for toxoplasmosis.

Chloromycetin – Used after CO-2 counts fall below 100.

Pentamioine – Used to treat PCP. Used in its intravenous form, as well as an aerolized form useful for home therapies.

Imreg I – Investigational – appears to slow or prevent the development of *Pseumocystis carinii* pneumonia.

Additional treatments may include chemotherapy and/or radiation therapy for specific diseases (for example, Kaposi's sarcoma).

Cost data from several studies indicate that the costs of providing care for a person with AIDS from time of diagnosis ranges from $67,000 to $200,000. Several factors have an impact on these costs, including the type of infection seen as well as the treatment setting (acute care or critical care unit, hospice, home, or intermediate care facility). Overall, the average length of inpatient hospital stay for clients is 19 days, well above the average 6.5 days for all other patients and well above the DRG authorization of 16 days, again having an impact on the financial resources of the health care institution. Contributing to this dilemma is the lack of community-based facilities available to the person living with AIDS and his or her family.

Physiologic Aspects

Infection with HIV leads to a progressive loss of immune function and the development of opportunistic infections and related signs and symptoms.

HIV is, in essence, a chronic illness. For some individuals the progression from diagnosis to death may be rapid, whereas others experience periods of remission and exacerbation. In general, the time span between becoming HIV positive and developing full-blown AIDS is increasing, because early diagnosis occurs as well as treatment with such life-extending treatments as AZT.

The consequences for the individual, his or her family, and the health care community are significant because the individual may experience more opportunistic infections, multisystem synergistic problems, and side effects of medications.

Physical problems affecting the individual with HIV infection involve the entire person—ventilation, nutrition, elimination, neurologic function, host defenses, energy maintenance, and comfort. All organ systems are affected, but the lung seems to be the most common. Respiratory complications often manifest as dyspnea or dyspnea on exertion (DOE) and nonproductive cough. Nursing has considerable expertise in using interventions to reduce respiratory problems and complications seen in chronic obstructive pulmonary disease (COPD), asthma, and lung cancer and can use these interventions to produce energy conservation and reduce pulmonary dysfunction.

Disabling complications also include alterations in nutrition and elimination. Malnutrition is thought to result from malabsorption, increased basal metabolic rate, and decreased nutrient intake. Contributing factors include anorexia, altered taste sensation, dysphagia, odynophagia, nausea, and vomiting. Opportunistic infections such as cryptosporidia may also play a role. Intervention strategies may include relaxation techniques, decreasing or eliminating mouth pain, and providing bland foods and smaller, more frequent meals.

Diarrhea is a common symptom seen in clients with HIV and is frequently related to parasite infections, bacteria, and side effects of medications. Maintaining oral hydration, preventing skin breakdown, and controlling the diarrhea are priorities in nursing care.

More than 40% of all HIV-infected individuals experience neurologic complications (Levy et al., 1985). This complication presents one of the most challenging for the individual and his or her family and calls for coordination of care and support for and by all concerned.

Persons living with AIDS also experience an increased occurrence of nosocomial infections, evidenced by respiratory infections, recurrent fevers, skin and mucous membrane manifestations, and susceptibility to infection.

Pain control is imperative for these individuals, and a variety of approaches may be used, including pharmacologic and nonpharmacologic interventions (such as therapeutic touch, relaxation techniques, massage therapy, guided imagery, and accupressure).

Persons who are HIV positive incur physical problems that are within the scope of nursing practice. Individualized nursing strategies need to be developed to provide symptom relief to reduce the stress of living with a chronic, physical illness.

AIDS-RELATED DEMENTIA

The major neurologic manifestation is AIDS-related dementia. Approximately 75% of clients show nervous system abnormalities on autopsy.

Early manifestations of AIDS-related dementia include withdrawal, depression, irritability, and apathy (McArthur & McArthur, 1986). As the course of the disease progresses, language difficulties, learning and memory difficulties, and failure to achieve developmental milestones (in children) are common manifestations.

Encephalopathy seen in HIV-positive clients may be due to the presence of an opportunistic infection or the actual presence of the virus in the brain (Price et al., 1988). Neurologic manifestations from HIV infiltration of the brain do not readily respond to treatment and present a special challenge to the treatment team. AZT may reverse symptoms but is not uniformly successful. Psychotic medications may be useful but need to be used cautiously. Nursing interventions must focus on promoting client comfort and delaying the decline of cognitive functioning through memory improvement using techniques from research on Alzheimer's disease. These include mnemonics, rehearsal, exercise, and psychotherapy. Family members and supportive others need to be supported and helped to recognize and anticipate neurologic manifestations and how to respond to the client under those circumstances.

Psychological Aspect of AIDS

AIDS is a condition that has profound psychologic parameters, as does any catastrophic illness. It affects the total population, not just the individual and his or her family. Three groups of individuals can be differentiated, each group having specific psychologic concerns and needs. They are (1) the person with AIDS, (2) the person who is HIV positive, and (3) the worried well.

THE PERSON WITH AIDS

The person with AIDS faces a number of issues, including the following:

- Family issues—Acceptance or nonacceptance of life-style, ability to provide care at home, fear of contagion, education about the illness, acceptance of significant other as primary partner, entitlements, and support services
- Primary partner relationships—Effects of illness on significant other, fear of contagion, visitation rights, legal issues (wills, power of attorney, and shared property), and future planning
- Discrimination—In the delivery of services, in employment, reactions of the community, and ostracism by peer group
- Referrals/future health care planning—Need and availability of nursing home care, availability of housing and loss of housing, availability of treating

physicians and dentists, necessity of frequent hospitalizations, and burial information and resources

- Financial regulations/eligibility—Availability and continuation of private insurance, Medicare coverage and eligibility, eligibility for Social Security disability and necessity of waiting period, medical assistance and related eligibility regulations, limited home care reimbursement, and disability income plans from employer
- Guilt—The person with AIDS (PWA) may experience feelings of guilt related to high-risk behaviors, life-style choices, and so on. It is common to have thoughts of "If only I had . . ." or "I should have . . ." This introjection of feelings and self-condemnation is common
- Loss of self-esteem—The PWA often lacks confidence in self, perceives self as inferior to others, and perceives self as "less than . . ." because of the disease state. PWAs may verbalize low self-esteem by putting themselves down, degrading themselves, exhibiting an inability to form close relationships, and distancing themselves from existing relationships
- Fear of loss of physical attractiveness—This is closely tied to self-esteem in our youth- and beauty-oriented culture. The effects of medications, treatments, and the disease itself are anticipated and feared. Verbalizations often surround the fear of disfigurement and the fear of rejection by others because of physical appearance.
- Increased dependency—Young adults are most commonly affected by AIDS, and these young adults have been in control of their lives. With every hospitalization, control is relinquished to the caregiver who decides when the PWA will eat, sleep, bathe, and so on. As the disease state progresses, control is progressively lost to the health system, family, and significant others. The final decisions about treatments and degree of aggressiveness of treatment in the final stages are all indicative of loss of control. Dependency on others for the activities of daily living (ADL) and other necessities of life is frequent. PWAs often express embarrassment that others have to perform intimate aspects of daily care for them.
- Isolation—The client with AIDS fears being "abandoned" and forgotten by peers, family, and friends. Often these people feel awkward around the PWA—they do not know what to say, may overidentify with the PWA (because of close age and similar life-style and because the diagnosis makes others around the PWA feel vulnerable). The isolation may be physical and real or psychologic as the client becomes distant and isolated or as others isolate him or her.
- Stigmatization—The PWA must deal with the labels used by society in connection with AIDS. There is the specter of a "terminal illness," as well as a sexually transmitted disease. In part, the lack of a "cure" for AIDS produces an intense social reaction that stigmatizes vulnerable individuals. The PWA often internalizes societal condemnation ("I have AIDS because I'm . . .").
- Loss of occupational and financial status—Financial stressors can be severe. As the disease progresses, the ability of the PWA to work on a regular, full-time schedule becomes impaired. The PWA's job may be jeopardized.

Further, the client may lose health care insurance if the job is lost, increasing his or her out-of-pocket costs. The client will no longer be able to maintain his or her home and life-style because of significantly reduced income. The costs of treatment are also exorbitant and may leave the PWA destitute.

- Confusion over options for medical treatment and impact of hospitalization—The PWA is frequently confronted with a variety of confusing options in medical care, starting from time of diagnosis (such as which physician and facility to choose). Further, decisions about treatment selection (surgery, chemotherapy, AZT, and so on) and specific instructions (such as "no code" order) must be made. The PWA needs simple explanations of options and feedback to help him or her make appropriate decisions.

- Psychologic issues—Any chronic, debilitating disease produces psychologic effects that are difficult for the PWA and his or her family to deal with. PWAs are filled with a sense of great loss. They may exhibit symptoms of reactive depression to their losses. They may withdraw socially, neglect ADL, and have a flat, "sad" affect, become unable to sleep, and be agitated or anxious.

- Death and dying issues—It must be remembered that our society is not comfortable with death. We have elaborate rituals to allow us not to acknowledge death as a reality. We rarely use the words "dying" and "death." Death is something that happens to others and not to us and is often equated with punishment and retribution. It will be helpful to remember that PWAs will experience the stages of death and dying (as identified by Dr. Elizabeth Kübler-Ross). These steps are not sequential and irrevocable—they are fluid, and the client will go through various stages in response to many factors. In many cases, PWAs feel they are on an emotional "roller coaster" (anger, denial, depression, and so on). Clients need acknowledgment that this is "normal" and "okay."

To address the complexity of these issues and concerns, one must have a multidisciplinary approach to treatment, including physical, psychologic, and spiritual care. In some cases, inpatient or outpatient psychiatric or psychologic treatment is appropriate, in addition to the needed medical treatments.

PERSONS WHO ARE HIV SEROPOSITIVE

There is a significantly larger, but less-defined, group of people who are HIV-positive. These may be characterized by evidence of immunosuppression without the presence of an opportunistic disease. People in this group show signs of distress related to not knowing what direction the disease will take. This uncertainty leads to anxiety. The person with HIV requires a supportive nonjudgmental environment but generally does not necessarily need psychotherapy. Issues for persons with HIV include the following:

- Feelings of isolation—The person with HIV will have many similar issues to the PWA, but because of the nebulous state of the illness, may be more acutely affected by the sense of isolation imposed by peers and friends who are aware of the person's HIV status. He or she may feel awkward around individuals and unsure in social situations. The person with HIV often looks "healthy" and "normal" but may self-impose isolation because of the feeling that he or she is not "normal."

- Poor social and occupational functioning—The person with HIV may look "healthy" but often experiences debilitating effects of the virus. If these effects are frequently experienced, the lack of energy to perform the usual tasks normally required in day-to-day activities and work and job patterns may be sporadic. Social interaction may be limited because of fear of contagion (infecting others).
- Loss of initiative—The person with HIV may lose the normal sense of initiative or human drives that are pleasurable. The person with HIV may develop a "why bother" attitude that AIDS and death are inevitable. A reluctance to start new friendships, relationships, or jobs; symptoms of moderate depression; a sense of inadequacy; and decreased self-esteem are commonly experienced by the person with HIV.
- Frustration of achievement and productivity needs—This is closely related to feelings of isolation and loss of initiative. The person with HIV will often experience feelings of frustration when unable to meet occupational or social demands. Previously a "productive" member of the community, the person with HIV may feel that he or she cannot "produce" in our producer-consumer society because of lack of energy and malaise. Self-esteem and self-ideal are closely linked to our "role" in society, and this role achievement may be impaired for the person with HIV.

It has been theorized that psychologic distress may contribute to immunosuppression, so stress reduction is a priority. These clients also need education about infection control measures, assistance with establishing of a support system, and exploration of adaptive coping mechanisms.

THE "WORRIED WELL"

This group is composed of those who have high-risk factors and behaviors. Individuals in this category can benefit from therapeutic interventions for depression and anxiety. Some of the critical issues for this group are the following:

- Obsessional thinking about the syndrome—The individual may be obsessed with the feeling that he or she may be infected and will develop the disease or that others with whom he or she has contact have the disease.
- Death and dying and the process of dying—Individuals preoccupied with death may have experienced the death(s) of peers, friends, and loved ones, and this may focus their thinking on death and the frailty of human life.
- Problems in job performance—Anxiety and preoccupation with AIDS may contribute to the development of job-related problems such as inability to meet job requirements.
- Loss of work time and job productivity—Poor attendance, sporadic attendance, and erratic work habits may be related to preoccupation with the AIDS virus and generalized anxiety.

- Strained relationships and friendships — This often occurs in a group of friends who have been affected by the death of one of the group or in cases where the relationships are altered because one friend has withdrawn socially.
- Primary partner relationships — If the individual is not currently in a primary relationship, there may be reluctance to become involved in a committed relationship because of fear of continued commitment and the possibility of loss of one of the partners due to becoming ill.
- Repeat visits to emergency rooms or primary physician's office — Individuals may have vague presenting symptoms (malaise, fever, sore throat, or fatigue) or concern that skin lesions (macula, acne, or moles) may be symptomatic of Kaposi's sarcoma or that allergy or cold symptoms are suggestive of *Pneumocystis carinii.* They become overly aware and concerned about minor symptoms and seek constant reassurance and support.
- Sexual issues — These individuals may not be aware of what sexual activity is considered safer sex and what is not. They may not be familiar with medical and clinical terms used for sexual acts and need education in lay terms that they will understand (that is, street language).
- Grief and the loss of friends who have died or have just been diagnosed — As individuals, we react to loss in our lives the way we have always reacted — our normal way of handling grief. The worried well need to know that it is "okay" to grieve for the loss of friends and for those diagnosed (a real current *and* anticipated loss). In addition, they will experience Kübler-Ross's stages of grief and need to be aware that the feelings they have are normal.
- Family issues (possibly related to life-style) — The worried well may be reticent and experience difficulty in telling family, friends, and loved ones about a life-style they have because of fear of their reactions. This can create greater stress for them in maintaining "secrets" from those loved ones. Family and friends, too, may have fears and anxieties about the life-style, may have difficulties accepting the life-style, and may feel that these individuals are "destined" to get AIDS. Emotional withdrawal, distancing, and estrangement may occur.
- Guilt over life-style and fear of exposure — The worried well individual may feel guilt over the life-style and experience the "if only" or "I should," and he or she may feel that the life-style and its potential exposure/knowledge by other individuals may have an adverse impact on job, family, schooling, and so on, because of societal disapproval of the life-style. This creates increased internal stress to either create elaborate "covers" or change the life-style, if feasible for the individual.

It should be remembered that individuals will vary in their awareness, understanding, and coping abilities. Empathy is imperative in helping all individuals reduce fears of AIDS, and education is necessary to reduce the incidence of the illness.

CLIENT AND FAMILY

The client with HIV and his or her family experience crises at various points during the course of the disease. By using crisis intervention principles, the nurse or therapist can assist the family and client toward stabilization and a greater ability to support the person living with AIDS. The accompanying box lists key strategies to promote psychologic adaptation.

Key Strategies to Promote Psychologic Adaptation

Establish a data base on AIDS.
Assess the biopsychosocial needs of the AIDS client.
Increase self-awareness to avoid stigmatization of the client.
Respect the client's need for privacy and confidentiality.
Help the client replace unhealthful behaviors with healthful coping behaviors.
Help the client to identify and establish support systems.
Establish a support system for caregivers of AIDS clients.

The initial crisis occurs when the client receives the initial diagnosis of HIV seropositivity. Given that clients are aware of the prognosis and course of the disease they often perceive AIDS as an always fatal disease.

The client is in a stage of disequilibrium as he or she attempts to understand and absorb not only the diagnosis itself, but the implication of that diagnosis. The client will experience the stages of resolution of the crisis as identified by Peplau, as well as stages of "death and dying" identified by Kübler-Ross. It is important to remember that the stages are not static, and the client may move up and down the continuum based on many factors. Two points to consider are that the *family* will also experience these stages and that they are frequently not synchronous with those of the client. It should be noted that "family" is used in a broad sense as defined by the client and may include a supportive (significant) other, a person who is not blood-related but is viewed as family, or the client's extended circle of friends.

The client will experience a crisis state with each hospitalization, each new symptom, or each outwardly visible sign or symptom of the presence of the disease (e.g., a Kaposi's lesion).

By using the various sources available within the family structure, the community, and the county, the nurse or therapist will have the best likelihood of successfully supporting the client through the crisis period.

Early in the course of the disease, social support is paramount to set the stage for dealing with future crises. Symptoms such as fever, fatigue, and myalgia may interfere with the client's normal work, home, or social functioning. Not only does this decrease self-esteem, but it separates the client from a source of support. See the accompanying box for a list of national AIDS resources.

In the later stages of the disease, frequent hospitalizations, increasing symptoms, and visible progression of the disease create further psychologic devastation. Depression commonly follows loss of job, role, independence, and

National AIDS Resources

AIDS Hotline
Public Health Service
Atlanta, GA
1-800-342-AIDS

National Gay and Lesbian Task Force
1-800-221-7044

AIDS Action Council
729 Eighth Street, S.E.
Suite 200
Washington, D.C. 20003
(202) 547-3101

American Red Cross
AIDS Education Office
1730 D Street, N.W.
Washington, D.C. 20006
(202) 737-8300

American Association of Physicians for Human Rights
P.O. Box 14366
San Francisco, CA 94114
(415) 558-9353

National Association of People with AIDS
P.O. Box 65472
Washington, D.C. 20035
(202) 483-7979

Lambda Legal Defense and Education Fund
132 West 43rd Street
New York, NY 10036
(212) 944-9488

Computerized AIDS Information Network (CAIN)
c/o J.R. Tellum
8033 Sunset Blvd., Suite 934
Los Angeles, CA 90046
(213) 222-7222

American Friends Service Committee
1501 Cherry Street
Philadelphia, PA 19102
(215) 241-2421

Centers for Disease Control (CDC)
Center for Prevention Services
Technical Information Services
1600 Clifton Road
Atlanta, GA 30333
(Books, Slides, Pamphlets)

financial security. Neurologic complications may further erode the client's self-esteem and may increase the client's social isolation, because friends and family may withdraw psychologically or physically if they are not able to cope with the changes or impending death.

The crisis state may be increased by the social stigma associated with AIDS. This is especially true if the diagnosis and disease have identified the individual as having acquired the virus through high-risk behaviors (such as IV drug abuse or gay/bisexual activity with multiple partners). The client may be forced to disclose such behavior(s) or status to his or her spouse or significant other, friends, employer, and family, creating immense psychologic stress. The client is vulnerable to feelings of rejection and guilt and is subject to discrimination in housing, jobs, and health care. The client may be at risk for losing health care benefits and/or life insurance benefits.

Suicidal ideation is common, and the individual should be thoroughly assessed for the presence of ideation, a plan of action, and the means to carry it out. Attention should also be paid to the lethality of the plan and whether the client has prodromal signs, such as making final plans, giving away possessions, using words that may indicate an intention (for example, saying "goodbye") or other behavioral changes (secretiveness, withdrawal). The client may need both hospitalization in an inpatient mental health setting and psychopharmacology with psychotherapy until the acute crisis is resolved.

It is imperative that the nurse or therapist also deal with her or his own feelings related to the disease, high-risk behaviors, and loss. The client will be watching carefully for *any* sign of rejection, judgmental behavior, or patronization. Autodiagnosis by the nurse or therapist will help prevent a transference issue from arising and inadvertently introducing a stall in the therapy relationship.

Symptom Management: Information for Therapist and Client

The following information will prove helpful in discussions with the client and family. Although the client may have a primary medical caregiver, he or she will often use the nurse as a source of information. Remember to provide any such information in simple, understandable terms, with a copy in writing for the client to refer to, because he or she may not fully absorb the material at the time it is given.

PNEUMOCYSTIS CARINII PNEUMONIA (PCP)

What to Watch For

- Shortness of breath under circumstances that would not normally cause shortness of breath
- Dry cough
- Unexplained fevers higher than 101° F, for more than 24 hours

What to Do

- Record your temperature with a thermometer every 4 hours.
- Drink plenty of fluids.
- Call your doctor if the symptoms become worse or fail to improve over 1 or 2 days.

What Information to Give Your Doctor or Nurse

- Duration or shortness of breath in days or weeks. Is it getting worse, better, or staying the same? What makes it worse? Better?
- Duration of cough. Are you producing any phlegm (sputum)? If so, what color, how much, and when?
- What has your temperature been for the past 24 hours? What have you done or taken for it? Have these measures helped?

What to Expect

What your doctor decides to do will depend on how serious he or she thinks the problem is. The doctor may choose to

- Wait for further developments and keep in touch with you by phone
- Order a chest x-ray examination

What You Might Expect If You Are Admitted to the Hospital

- Further chest x-rays examinations
- A bronchoscopy — insertion of a flexible tube into the bronchial tube to obtain a lung tissue biopsy for PCP; besides an open lung biopsy, this is the only way to make a definite diagnosis of PCP
- Arterial blood gas measurements — removal of a small amount of blood from an artery in the wrist or the groin to determine how well your blood is oxygenated

What You Can Expect If You Do Have PCP

- To have oxygen administered through your nose if the blood gas measurements indicate a low oxygen level, or if you are short of breath
- To receive one of two antibiotics — either trimethoprim sulfasoxazole, a sulfa drug, or pentamidine
- Frequent chest x-ray examinations

Your Responsibilities as a Client

- Communicate fears, needs, and concerns to staff. They care about you and want to help so that they can best meet your needs.
- Understand what is happening to you, what is planned, and what the treatment goals are.
- Continue to take your medicine after discharge from the hospital. PCP has a high recurrence rate; therefore prevention is essential. Unfortunately, the sulfa drugs Bactrim and Septra have a high rate of reactions. If you

develop a rash and/or fever while taking either of these medications, call your doctor.

ORAL CANDIDIASIS (THRUSH)

What to Watch For

- Soreness of mouth or tongue, a "burnt" feeling
- Pain or difficulty in swallowing
- Appearance of white patches on the tongue or back of the mouth that do not come off with a toothbrush

What to Do

- Make an appointment to be seen by your doctor. Unless this problem entirely prevents you from eating, it is not an emergency and can wait a few days for treatment.
- While waiting for an appointment, you can rinse your mouth with a warm saltwater solution (about 1 tsp salt per 8 oz glass) every 2 to 3 hours.

What to Expect

If your doctor thinks that you have candidiasis, you may get a prescription for either nystatin (Mycostatin) suspension or ketoconazole (Nizoral) tablets. It is essential that you take the medication as directed, or it will not work. Do not skip doses!

Your Responsibilities as a Client

Consult your doctor if the problem has not resolved after 2 weeks of medication.

WEIGHT LOSS

What to Watch For

Unexplained weight loss of more than 10 pounds in 1 month that cannot be regained. (In immunocompromised conditions such as cancer and AIDS, weight loss commonly occurs without reason and despite good appetite.)

What to Do

- Weigh yourself without clothes or shoes no more than once a week, and keep a record. Weigh yourself at approximately the same time of day.
- Keep a food intake diary to determine calorie intake whenever you think you are losing weight. (See "Nutrition and Exercise" in this section for more information.)
- Try to eat a diet well balanced in fats, proteins, and carbohydrates.
- If you are losing weight, maintain intake at a minimum of 20 calories per pound of ideal body weight (see "Nutrition and Exercise" in this section for specifics on how to determine this). You can do this by using sauces, gravies, Sustacal, Ensure, Carnation Instant Breakfast, and other liquid nutrient products.

- If eating three large meals a day is difficult, split your total daily intake into six smaller meals.
- If you continue to lose weight, call your doctor.

What Information to Give Your Doctor or Nurse

- How many pounds have you lost over what period of time?
- Approximately how many calories do you consume each day?

What to Expect

If your weight loss has been excessive (more than 20 pounds in 1 month), you may be admitted to the hospital for evaluation and perhaps intravenous feedings.

Your Responsibilities as a Client

- Eat, even when you are not hungry.
- Explore new ways of meeting nutritional needs.
- If you do not feel well enough to cook for yourself and no one else is available, ask your local social service organization for assistance in making arrangements to get help.

DIARRHEA

Immunocompromised clients are particularly prone to intestinal parasites such as amoebae, giardia, and cryptosporidia. There are treatments available for amoebae and giardia, but not for cryptosporidia. Diarrhea may also occur without an identifiable cause.

What to Watch For

- More than six loose stools per day
- Watery, mucoid, or bloody stools
- If stool is bloody, whether the blood comes before, with, or after the bowel movement
- Approximate volume of bowel movements

What to Do

- Call your doctor and describe your stools; a stool specimen for parasites or bacterial culture may be required. Get stool containers from a hospital laboratory. If your doctor is concerned about cryptosporidia, a special container containing a preservative can be obtained. Stool specimens are more easily obtained if plastic wrap is placed across the toilet bowl to prevent the stool from falling into the toilet water.
- If stool cultures are negative but diarrhea persists, try altering your diet—avoid dairy products, spices, coffee, alcohol, and foods high in fat. Drink liquids at room temperature. Avoid fresh fruits and juices high in acid.

What to Expect

- If stools contain amoebae or giardia, you may be given a prescription for metronidazole (Flagyl). Medication that is not completed is not effective; take the entire regimen as directed. Alcohol intake while taking Flagyl may cause an adverse reaction.
- Drugs that delay transit time from food ingestion to elimination may be prescribed (for example, Lomotil).
- There is no known treatment that will eliminate cryptosporidia, but medications can be prescribed to reduce discomfort.

Your Responsibilities as a Client

- Take medication as prescribed.
- Do *not* drink alcohol while taking Flagyl.
- Maintain fluid intake (noncaffeinated) to prevent dehydration. (Chipped ice or popsicles may be easier to tolerate if diarrhea persists.)
- Report symptoms of weakness, dizziness, or excessive weight loss.

DEHYDRATION

This occurs when there is excessive loss of body water due to fevers, sweating, diarrhea, or decreased fluid intake.

What to Watch For

- Dryness of oral mucous membranes and tongue
- Skin on back of hand when pinched (into tent shape) does not return to its place quickly
- The passage of very little (less than 1 cup) or no concentrated urine over a 12-hour period (concentrated urine is dark yellow)
- Inability to take in as much fluid as is being lost in diarrheal stools
- Confusion — difficulty in remembering where you are or behavior that is strange for you
- Dizziness when standing

What to Do

- Control fevers as advised by your physician.
- Increase fluid intake with water, juices, Gatorade, popsicles, ice, and so on.
- Measure the amount of urine passed.
- Call your physician if you start feeling more confused, cannot increase your urine output to at least 1 quart every 12 hours even after increasing fluid intake, or are having difficulty taking in enough liquids.

What Information to Give Your Doctor or Nurse

- What has your temperature been for the past 24 hours?
- Approximately how much fluid have you taken in for the past 48 hours?
- Approximately how much urine have you passed in the past 24 hours?
- Do you have diarrhea, and if so, how severe is it?

- What is your weight today? How does it compare with what it was a week ago?

What to Expect

If your doctor does not think you can manage at home, he or she may admit you to the hospital to give intravenous fluids.

Your Responsibilities as a Client

- Maintain a fluid intake that is at least 1 quart more than your combined urine and stool output.
- Be alert for signs of dehydration.
- Report any concerns to your physician.

FEVERS

Usually fevers are a sign of infection, but an immunocompromised state is often accompanied by nighttime fevers and sweats for which no cause can be found.

What to Watch For

- Temperatures higher than 101° F
- The time of day when the fevers occur
- Night sweats that soak through bed clothes and sheets
- Other signs of infection (sore throat, headache, cough, and so on)

What to Do

- Record temperature every 4 hours (not more often) for 2 to 3 days, and look for a pattern.
- Discuss findings with your doctor — call sooner if other symptoms coincide with fevers.
- Drink plenty of fluids to replace the water you lose through sweating.
- Ask your doctor whether he or she prefers aspirin or acetaminophen (Tylenol) and the preferred method of taking the medication.

What to Expect

- If your doctor suspects an infection, he or she may want to conduct blood or urine cultures, x-rays, examinations, and so on.
- If no cause is found and the fevers are related to the immunocompromised state, you can expect them to recur episodically and last for several days at a time.

Your Responsibilities as a Client

- Rest when you are tired.
- Consult with your doctor as to the best approach to take when fevers occur.
- Maintain fluid intake to compensate for fluid loss through night sweats and increased metabolism. Gatorade may be helpful for restoring electrolyte balance.

FATIGUE

This is a common symptom in those who are immunocompromised that may interfere with life-style, lasting either for an indefinite period or occurring in cycles.

Your Responsibilities as a Client

- Consult with your physician if fatigue prevents you from working or caring for yourself, becomes significantly worse, or is associated with cough, shortness of breath, or a new fever.
- Maintain an exercise program that does not cause excessive fatigue but helps maintain muscle mass.
- Inquire about eligibility for disability (financial assistance) if fatigue prevents you from working.

CHANGES IN MOOD, PERSONALITY, BEHAVIOR, SPEECH, OR MEMORY

When they affect the brain or central nervous system, opportunistic infections may develop slowly and are accompanied by subtle changes in personality or speech. Spouses, significant others, or close friends are often the first to recognize these.

What to Watch For

- Changes in the way you respond to situations, that is, anger for no reason, suspicions of others' behavior, desire to be alone (if it is uncharacteristic of you), difficulty coping with things that are not normally a problem
- Difficulty understanding or forming words
- Difficulty with balance or ability to walk; new weakness of an arm, leg, hand, or foot
- Severe headaches or neck stiffness
- Changes in the way close associates react to you
- Difficulty remembering where you are or recalling important events

What to Do

- Ask those who know you well whether they have noticed any changes in your behavior.
- Discuss any concerns with your physician.
- Don't allow yourself to think that you are going crazy.

What to Expect

If your physician thinks your concerns may be valid, he or she may

- Hospitalize you to evaluate for opportunistic infection
- Allow you to stay home while he or she evaluates your symptoms further
- Recommend that you have someone stay with you to help, if needed

Nursing Care of Client and Family

The concerns and needs of clients with AIDS, their families, and their friends are complex and varied. Many individuals who are HIV positive or have AIDS have weak, inadequate, or no support systems. Given the peak age range of incidence for AIDS (20 to 49 years), many of these individuals are in the younger, most productive years of their lives. Dealing with a chronic, debilitating illness and facing death at a young age create profound psychosocial stress on these individuals and their families.

Nursing has the opportunity and the obligation to use its unique skills, expertise, and ability to provide compassionate, competent care through the roles of case manager, coordinator, educator, and advocate.

• • •

Nursing has a long history of giving compassionate care and support to those in need. Traditionally, nurses have ministered to the unwanted, the sick, and the poor. This history spans the care given during the epidemics of the Middle Ages and includes the exemplary works of Florence Nightingale, Jane Delano, and Clara Maas. Nursing has consistently demonstrated its ability to respond to crises in the past with unique organization and leadership.

Another crisis in health care threatens the general welfare of society. AIDS presents challenges, as well as opportunities, for nursing. The profession is capable of demonstrating its commitment, readiness, and leadership to society and to the person living with AIDS. Nurses' traditional role of client advocate must continue.

The client living with AIDS must attempt to find care in a health care system that is unfamiliar and frightening. The person living with AIDS has no control over his or her life and routines, does not know the medical "jargon," and is often treated as a statistic. The nurse must act to support and protect the client and interpret that unfamiliar world to him or her.

As nurses, we are challenged by every aspect of this disease. We must create and deliver humane care for the client, his or her family and significant and supportive others, and society. As nurses, we can do no less.

REFERENCES

Ader, R. (1981). *Psychoneuroimmunology.* New York: Academic Press.

Allen, J.R., & Curran, J.W. (1988). Prevention of AIDS and HIV infection: Needs and priorities for epidemiologic research. *American Journal of Public Health, 78,* 381-386.

American Nurses' Association (1985). Code for nurses. Kansas City, MO. ANA.

Bakeman, R., McCray, E., Lumb, J.R., Jackson, R.E., & Whitley, P.N. (1987). The incidence of AIDS among blacks and Hispanics. *Journal of National Medical Association, 79,* 921-928.

Bayer, R. (1989). Perinatal transmission of HIV infection: The ethics of prevention. *Clinical Obstetrics and Gynecology, 32,* 497-505.

Belman, A.L., Ultmann, M.H., Horoupian, D., Novick, B., Spiro, A.J., Rubenstein, A.,

Kurtzberg, D., & Cane-Wesson, B. (1985). Neurological complications in infants and children with acquired immunodeficiency syndrome. *Annals of Neurology, 18,* 560-566.

Bloom, D.E., & Carliner, G. (1988). The economic impact of AIDS in the United States. *Science, 239,* 604-610.

Boguslawski, M. (1980). Therapeutic touch: A facilitator of pain relief. *Topics in Clinical Nursing, 2*(1), 27-37.

Brandt A.M. et al. (1988). Compulsory premarital screening for the human immunodeficiency virus. *Journal of the American Medical Society, 258,* 757-762.

Brown, L.S., & Primm, B.J. (1988). Sexual contacts of intravenous drug abusers: Implications for the next spread of the AIDS epidemic. *Journal of the National Medical Association, 80,* 651-656.

Bye, L.L. (1988). *The elements of a comprehensive community AIDS prevention campaign.* (videotape). San Francisco: Communication Technologies.

Centers for Disease Control. (1989). First 10,000 cases of acquired immunodeficiency syndrome — United States. *Morbidity and Mortality Weekly Report, 38,* 561-563.

Centers for Disease Control. (1990, February). *HIV/AIDS surveillance.* Atlanta: Division of HIV/AIDS, CDC.

Chlebowski, R.T. (1985). Significance of altered nutritional status in acquired immune deficiency syndrome (AIDS). *Nutrition and Cancer, 7,* 85-91.

Clark, P.E., & Clark, M.J. (1984). Therapeutic touch: Is there a scientific basis for practice? *Nursing Research, 33,* 37-41.

Coates, T.J., Stall, R.D., Catania, J.A., & Kegeles, S.M. (1988). Behavioral factors in the spread of HIV infection. *AIDS, 2*(1), S239-S246.

Cohen, F.L., & Hardin, S.B. (1989). Fatigue in patients with catastrophic illness. In S.G. Funk, E.M. Tournquist, M.T. Champaigne, L.A. Copp, & R.A. Wiese (Eds.), *Key aspects of comfort* (pp. 208-216). New York: Springer.

Cohen, J.B., Hauer, L.B., & Wofsy, C. (1989). Women and IV drugs: Parenteral and heterosexual transmission of human immunodeficiency virus. *Journal of Drug Issues, 19,* 39-56.

Des Jarlais, D.C., Wish, E., Friedman, S.R., et al. (1987). Intravenous use and the heterosexual transmission of human immunodeficiency virus: Current trends in New York City. *New York State Medical Journal, 20,* 283-286.

DiClemente, R.J., Zorn, J., & Temshok, L. (1986). Adolescents and AIDS: A survey of knowledge, attitudes and belief about AIDS in San Francisco. *American Journal of Public Health, 76,* 1443-1445.

DonLou, J., Wolcott, D., Gottlieb, M., & Landsverk, J. (1985). Psychosocial aspects of AIDS and AIDS-related complex: A pilot study. *Journal of Psychosocial Oncology, 3,* 39-55.

Driscoll, C.E. (1987). Pain management, *Primary Care, 14*(2), 327-252.

Epstein, L.G., Sharer, L.R., Joshi, V.V., Fojas, M.M., Konigsberger, M.R., & Oleske, J.M. (1985). Progressive encephalopathy in children with acquired immune deficiency syndrome. *Annals of Neurology, 17,* 488-496.

Fischl, M.A., Dickerson, G.M., Scott, G.B., Klimas, N., Fletcher, M.A., & Parks, W. (1987). Evaluation of heterosexual partners, children, and household contacts of adults with AIDS. *Journal of the American Medical Association, 257,* 640-644.

Fitzgerald, L. (1988). Exercise and the immune system. *Immunology Today, 9,* 337-339.

Flavin, D.K., Franklin, John E., & Frances, R.J. (1986). The acquired immune deficiency syndrome (AIDS) and suicidal behavior in alcohol dependent homosexual men. *American Journal of Psychiatry, 143*(11), 1440-1443.

Geis, S., Fuller , R., & Ruth, J. (1986). Lovers of AIDS victims: Psychological stress and counseling needs. *Death Studies, 10,* 43-53.

Grady, C. (1989). Ethical issues in providing nursing care to human immunodeficiency virus-infected populations. *Nursing Clinics of North America, 24,* 523-534.

Harris, C.A., Cabradilla, C.D., & Robert-Guroff, M. (September, 1985). HTLV-III infection and AIDS in heterosexual partners of AIDS patients. *Proceedings of the Interscience Conference on Antimicrobial Agents and Chemotherapy.* Minneapolis, Minn.

Haverkos, H.W. (1987). Factors associated with the pathogenesis of AIDS. *Journal of Infectious Disease, 156,* 251-257.

Haverkos, H.W., & Edelman, R. (1988). The epidemiology of acquired immunodeficiency syndrome among heterosexuals. *Journal of the American Medical Association, 260,* 1922-1929.

Holland, J.C., & Tross, S. (1985). The psychosocial and neuropsychiatric sequelae of the acquired immunodeficiency syndrome and related disorders. *Annals of Internal Medicine, 103*(5), 760-764.

Jarvis, R.M., Closen, M.L., Hermann, D.H.J., & Leonard, A.S. (1991). *AIDS law in a nutshell.* St. Paul, Minn: West Publishing.

Keller, S.E., Schleifer, S.J., Bartlett, J.A., & Johnson, R.L. (1988). The sexual behavior of adolescents and risk of AIDS. *Journal of the American Medical Association, 268,* 3586.

Kübler-Ross, E. (1969). *On death and dying.* New York: Macmillan.

Levy, R.M., Bresden, D.E., & Rosenblum, M.L. (1985). Neurological manifestations of the acquired immunodeficiency syndrome (AIDS). Experience at UCSF and review of the literature. *Journal of Neurosurgery, 62,* 475-495.

McArthur, J.H. & McArthur, J. (1986). Neurological manifestations of an acquired immunodeficiency syndrome. *Journal of Neurological Nursing, 18*(5), 242-249.

Miramontes, H., Boland, M.G., & Corless, I.B. (1988). *Nursing and the human immunodeficiency virus: A guide for nursing's response to AIDS.* Kansas City, MO: American Nurses Association.

Nelson, W.J. (1987). Nursing care of acutely ill persons with AIDS. In J.D. Durham, & F.L. Cohen (Eds.), *The person with AIDS: Nursing perspectives* (pp. 95-109). New York: Springer.

Nichols, S.E. (1985). Psychosocial reactions of persons with the acquired immunodeficiency syndrome. *Annals of Internal Medicine. 103*(5), 765-767.

Nyamathi, A., & Van Servellan, G. (1989). Maladaptive coping in the critically ill population with acquired immunodeficiency syndrome: Nursing assessment and treatment. *Heart and Lung, 18*(2), 113-120.

Peplau, H.E. (1952). *Interpersonal relations in nursing.* New York: Putnam.

Presidential Commission on the Human Immunodeficiency Virus Epidemic. (1988). *Report of the presidential commission on the human immunodeficiency virus epidemic.* Washington, D.C.: U.S. Government Printing Office: 0-214-701:QL3.

Price, R.W., Brew, B., Sidtis, J., Rosenblum, M., Sheck, A.C., & Cleary, P. (1988). The brain in AIDS: central nervous system HIV-1 infection and AIDS dementia complex. *Science, 239,* 586-592.

Schmitt, F.A., Bigley, J.W., McKinnis, R., Logue, F.E., Evans, R.W., Drucker, J.L., & The AZT Collaborative Working Group. (1988). Neuropsychological outcome of zidovudine (AZT) treatment of patients with AIDS and AIDS related complex. *The New England Journal of Medicine, 319,* 1573-1578.

Sundwall, D., & Bailey, D. (1988). Meeting the needs of people with AIDS: Local initiatives and federal support. *Public Health Reports, 103,* 293-298.

Trace, L.D. (December 1987). *The total cost of nursing care for patients with AIDS.* New York: National League for Nursing, Publication # 21-2191, 231-248.

U.S. Department of Health and Human Services. (1990). *HIV infection: Prevention and care.* National nursing research agenda – developing knowledge for practice – challenges and opportunities. U.S. Public Health Service.

U.S. Department of Health and Human Services. (1989). Nursing and the HIV epidemic: A national action agenda – Proceedings. U.S. Public Health Services.

Williams, A.B., D'Aquila, R.T., & Williams, A.E. (1987). HIV infection in intravenous drug abusers. *Image, 19,* 179-183.

Williams, L.S. (1986). AIDS risk reduction: A community health education intervention for minority high risk group members. *Health Education Quarterly, 13,* 407-421.

World Health Organization. (1988). *Guidelines for nursing management of people infected with human immunodeficiency virus (HIV), WHO AIDS series 3.* Geneva: World Health Organization.

Chapter 16

Families With Chronically Ill Children

Joan K. Austin

Approximately 10% to 15% of all children under the age of 18 are chronically physically ill (Pless & Perrin, 1985). The onset of a chronic physical condition in a child leads to psychologic, behavioral, and social stress for the child and the family (Stein et al., 1988). How well the child and the family subsequently deal with the stress and adapt to the chronic condition is affected not only by the characteristics of the illness, but by those of the family. Failure to adapt to the condition can lead to psychosocial problems for all family members, especially the child with the chronic condition. Psychiatric mental health nurses are in unique positions to intervene with families of chronically ill children to prevent and/or reduce the incidence of mental health problems often found in these families. In this chapter the impact of chronic childhood conditions on the child and the family are explored, with an emphasis on interventions for psychiatric nurses that facilitate the mental health of all family members.

Mental Health Problems Associated With Chronic Illness Child

According to Robert Massie (1985), a 25-year-old with hemophilia, "The most important thing to remember about a chronic illness is that it is exactly that: chronic. . . . I have never known a moment when I did not have hemophilia, and that fact has pervaded my family life, my education, my experiences with medicine, and my spiritual growth. . . . [Having a chronic illness] becomes melded into one's identity" (p. 14). Living with a chronic illness and the myriad associated stressors places the child at risk for mental health problems. Research strongly supports that children with chronic conditions experience more mental health problems than do children from the general population. In a comprehensive study by Rutter and colleagues on the Isle of Wight the incidence of psychiatric disorder was 17.2% for children with physical disorders and 6.6% for the children in the general population (Rutter et al., 1970). There is also evidence in the literature that some conditions, especially those involving the brain (Breslau, 1985; Rutter et al., 1970), are associated with even higher rates of psychiatric disturbances than are other chronic conditions. For example, in the Isle of Wight study approximately 29% of the children with idiopathic epilepsy were found to have behavior problems compared with approximately 12% of children with other physical disorders (Rutter et al., 1970). In addition, Austin (1989) found behavioral problems in 26% of the children with epilepsy and in only 11% in children with asthma.

Even though the incidence of mental health problems is higher, the patterns of problems are similar to those found in physically healthy children (Achenbach, 1978). In the Isle of Wight study the distribution of neurotic and antisocial behavioral patterns was similar for the general population and the chronically ill children. Mental health problems most commonly associated with chronic physical illness in children are low self-esteem, social maladjustment, anxiety, school avoidance, dependency, somatic symptoms, learning problems, and behavioral problems (Drotar & Bush, 1985; Garrison & McQuiston, 1989).

PARENTS

Parenting a healthy child is not without its problems. Thus it is not surprising that parenting the child with a chronic physical condition has been anecdotally reported to be stressful. Parents are faced with coping with the chronic condition themselves and helping the affected child, as well as the other children in the family, to cope with the condition. Kessler (1977) points out that parents of chronically ill children have problems with discipline because they are confused by their feelings of sympathy, their own frustrations with the condition, uncertainties about what the child can really understand, and the tedium of dealing with a chronically ill child day in and day out. Little research has been carried out to describe the impact of the chronic condition on the parents. The research available indicates that parents are also possible victims of the chronic condition (Austin, 1991). They have been found to be burdened by financial concerns, worries about the health of the child, and stress from realizing that their child is in a compromised position both physically and socially. Parents were also found to have concerns about the child's dealing with the chronic condition at school and about the negative impact of the chronic illness on the child's future.

According to Garrison and McQuiston (1989), siblings and mothers of chronically ill children have increased levels of psychologic distress and adaptation problems. There are also indications that a chronic condition in a child results in strain on the marital relationship (Burr, 1985). Although results from the research are still preliminary, there does not appear to be a strong relationship between the severity of the chronic condition and parental adjustment to the condition (Garrison & McQuiston, 1989). Some children with very debilitating conditions do well emotionally, and some children with very mild chronic conditions experience serious mental health problems.

Although much of the literature focuses on the problems of families whose children are chronically ill, there are some studies that report positive effects on the family. For example, one research study on fathers of chronically ill children indicated a positive effect on the marital relationship (McKeever, 1981).

SIBLINGS

Until recently there has been little research on the impact of a child's chronic condition on other siblings. Taylor (1980) reported that siblings were often given incomplete information by parents to keep them from worrying. Increased anxiety and need for coping were found in the siblings, as well as feelings of social isolation. Siblings frequently reported that they had less time with their parents, had family activity plans disrupted, and had increased chores as a result of the chronic condition in the sibling (Kruger et al., 1980; Pinyerd, 1983; Taylor, 1980). Siblings may also feel that they need to be high achievers to compensate for the parental disappointment caused by the chronically ill sibling (Seligman & Darling, 1989). The limited research available is inconclusive on whether siblings of chronically ill children experience more behavior problems than do other children, with some studies indicating increased mental health problems and some not (Seligman & Darling, 1989). For example, Taylor (1980) found that one third of siblings reported positive effects, such as increased cooperation, self-esteem, empathy, and cognitive mastery.

Theoretic Frameworks

Two frameworks that provide a basis for psychiatric nursing with families of chronically ill children are presented here. The first framework describes phases that family members go through as they adapt to the chronic condition. The second framework, the Double ABCX Model of Family Adaptation and Adjustment (McCubbin & Patterson, 1983) (Fig 16-1), identifies factors both within the family and outside the family that affect how well families adapt to a chronic stressor, such as a chronic illness in a child. Together, these two frameworks—one with a developmental emphasis and the other relevant to any time in the adaptation process—provide a comprehensive framework for developing interventions for families coping with a chronic illness in a child.

STAGES OF ADAPTATION

Our society values healthy, fully functioning individuals who are physically attractive. When children are found to have a chronic physical condition that limits their ability to function fully in their environment, they deviate from these desired social norms. Families of children with chronic conditions are confronted with adapting to having a child who is less than perfect by society's standards. From the literature it appears that, regardless of the type of chronic condition, there are many similarities in this grief process through which families go in their response and subsequent adaptation to the condition

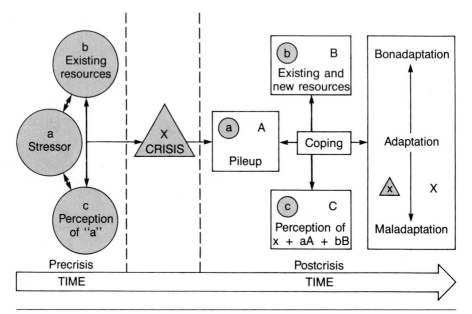

Fig 16-1. Double ABCX Model. (Note: From Family Adaptation to Crisis [pp. 26-47] by H. McCubbin and J. Patterson. In H. McCubbin, A. Cauble, and J. Patterson [Eds.], 1983a, *Family Stress, Coping, and Social Support*, Springfield, IL: Charles C. Thomas.)

(Massie, 1985). Commonly, family members are viewed as experiencing stages in their process of adaptation (Austin, 1979; Shapiro, 1983; Thomas, 1987; Waechter, 1977). Austin (1979) conceptualizes the process of adaptation as occurring in four stages: disbelief, anger, demystification, and conditional acceptance.

Disbelief. Generally, the first reaction experienced by family members is that of disbelief or shock, a common reaction to something that is completely unexpected. Parents have reported that they felt like they were dreaming and expected to wake up at any time and find out that the diagnosis really was not true. In this stage the denial serves to protect family members from experiencing immediately the full impact of having a child with a chronic condition.

Anger. Once the stage of disbelief subsides, family members begin to realize the full impact of the chronic condition on their lives. They find themselves experiencing myriad feelings, including guilt, anger, grief, and anxiety. Often the most pervasive feeling, however, is that of anger. Anger is an expected result of the status quo of the family having been disrupted by the diagnosis of the chronic condition. During this stage the family is faced with helping their child deal with the diagnosis and its ramifications, such as painful medical procedures. It is not uncommon for parents to have somewhat contradictory feelings, such as guilt for having caused the condition, as well as a sense of having no control over the condition. In addition, families experience increased time and financial obligations that cause even further stress. Varying degrees of family disruption are commonly experienced in this stage, and it is not uncommon for family members to become angry with health care professionals — especially when the condition is not well controlled by medical management.

Demystification. This third stage is marked by the active seeking of information about the chronic condition. It is very common for family members to read about the condition or to seek out other families who have experienced the same condition. Learning about the condition provides them with knowledge about what to expect and serves to provide them with a beginning sense of control even if the condition is not controlled. It is during this stage that family members begin to make plans about how they will manage aspects of the condition, as well as maintain the stability of the family. Family members also learn that there are other problems that are worse, a coping mechanism known as downward comparison (Wills, 1981), which helps to put the chronic condition into perspective. During this stage, anxiety lessens as the sense of control increases.

Conditional acceptance. The final stage occurs when the family is able to live fairly comfortably with the condition and its ramifications. Knowing about the condition and developing plans for how to handle events, such as hospitalizations, help the family become more comfortable with the condition and prevent the chronic condition from negatively affecting the family. Family activities adapt to the chronic condition, and the family becomes relatively comfortable with the condition and the ramifications. In this stage the family is able to manage the chronic condition in such a way that the mental health of the family is not negatively affected. It is also in this stage that family members often report the positive effects from having dealt with the chronic condition that are reported in the literature (Seligman & Darling, 1989). For example, some parents report that having dealt with the chronic condition has helped the family to be stronger as a family unit and helped individual members to become more understanding of others with problems (Austin et al., 1984; Austin & McDermott, 1988). In addition, McKeever (1981) found the chronic condition to have a positive effect on 5 of 10 marital relationships, and Taylor (1980) found that siblings of chronically ill children derived increased self-esteem, empathy, and cognitive mastery from having a chronically ill brother or sister.

Even though these four stages are presented as though they are experienced sequentially, this is not always the case. Families are unique and do not all respond similarly. These stages are representative, however, of the process that many families go through in the adjustment to a chronic condition in a child. Many families report that they experience some of the stages over again as the condition changes or as new situations arise. In addition, Olshansky (1962) found that parents of mentally retarded children remained in a stage of chronic sorrow, which should not be considered pathologic. Knowledge of the stages will aid the nurse in anticipating family responses and in preventing mental health problems. Furthermore, the nurse will be better able to recognize when mental health interventions are needed.

DOUBLE ABCX MODEL OF FAMILY ADAPTATION AND ADJUSTMENT

While the stages framework depicts phases that families go through as they adapt, the Double ABCX Model of Family Adaptation and Adjustment (McCubbin & Patterson, 1983) provides a framework to describe factors that influence family adaptation at any given point in the adaptation process. The model is a multivariate one that takes into consideration social variables, as well as family demands and resources in the prediction of family adaptation. The Double ABCX Model is based on Hill's ABCX Model (Hill, 1949), which predicts family crisis from a stressful event. The Double ABCX Model extends Hill's work by applying it to chronic stressors. In the Double ABCX Model there are five major concepts: family demands, family adaptive resources, family definition, coping, and adaptation. The model proposes that family demands interact with family adaptive resources and family definition to produce coping behaviors. These coping behaviors lead to the outcome, adaptation.

Concepts defined by McCubbin and Patterson (1983) and made relevant to chronic illness in a child follow. The concept of *family demands* refers to the accumulation of stressors and strains brought about by the chronic condition in the child, as well as other changes being experienced by the family. *Family adaptive resources* represent the assets available to the family that help them deal with the stressors and strains, such as social support. The concept of *family definition* depicts the meanings or attitudes the family holds about the total situation of the chronic illness and the ramifications of living with it daily in a family member. *Coping* refers to the cognitive and behavioral processes that family members make in an effort to deal with the chronic condition, as well as other stressors and strains. The final concept, *adaptation,* is the outcome or the adequacy of functioning for individual family members, as well as for the family unit.

Desired Mental Health Outcomes

For the family with a chronically ill child, the overall desired mental health outcome is the creation of a family environment that facilitates the optimal development of both the chronically ill child and other family members.

INFANTS

For optimal development, infants need a secure, nurturing environment where they are well cared for. A stable adult who derives satisfaction from interactions with the infant is needed in the environment for proper attachment and bonding to occur. These conditions help the infant learn to trust and to love, which in turn provide a strong foundation for future developmental tasks (Lipsitt, 1983).

EARLY CHILDHOOD

According to Erikson, children between the ages of 1 and 5 years are involved in the nuclear conflicts of autonomy versus shame and doubt, and initiative versus guilt (Freiberg, 1983). During these ages, children need an environment where there are opportunities to do things independently and to feel good about the tasks that they are able to carry out on their own. When children are over-restricted in activities because of a chronic physical condition, they are deprived of feeling competent, which is a basis for later diminished self-esteem (McCollum, 1973).

MIDDLE CHILDHOOD

During this period it is important for children to feel valued by their peers and to be a member of a group. The nuclear conflict during this stage according to Erikson is that of industry versus inferiority (Billingham, 1982). Academic and social success at school are important aspects in the development of industry, because they provide an opportunity for the child to win recognition. When a child has learning problems or misses a large amount of school because of a chronic condition, it can lead to the child's feeling inadequate or inferior (Freiberg, 1983).

During this period the child has the cognitive ability to begin to conceptualize illness (Billingham, 1982). The task for the psychiatric nurse is to help the child develop as positive an attitude toward having the chronic condition as possible. The child should also use coping strategies that emphasize the development of competence and avoid coping strategies of feeling different and withdrawing (Austin, Patterson, & Huberty, 1991).

ADOLESCENCE

The major tasks for children during adolescence are the development of a strong identity and a good body image, the establishment of intimate relationships, the achievement of independence from family, and the commitment to educational and career goals (Billingham, 1982). The chronically ill child also has to incorporate the chronic condition into the accomplishment of these tasks and become self-sufficient in the management of the chronic condition.

Desired outcomes for the adolescent with a chronic condition are many. The adolescent needs to be knowledgeable about the condition and its treatment so that he or she can be completely independent in the management of the condition. In addition, the chronically ill adolescent needs to have a positive attitude toward the condition and be able to identify some positive aspects from having grown up with a chronic health problem. The adolescent should feel good about his or her body and not have the chronic condition be the primary focus for the body image. The chronic condition is thought to be melded into the adolescent's identity much the same as intelligence or athleticism and should not be viewed as an inherently negative attribute, but one that is either neutral or positive.

PARENTS

The parents are partially responsible for creating an environment that is conducive to the optimal development of the chronically ill child. For parents to be able to provide the proper environment for their chronically ill children, they need to be knowledgeable about the condition, its treatment, and the coping processes that healthy families use. The parents need to have a positive attitude toward the chronic condition and convey that attitude to the child. Parents also need to deal successfully with having a child with a chronic condition so that they can in turn help him or her.

Because children with chronic conditions are at risk for poor self-esteem, parents need to be proactive and prevent the development of self-concept problems. Parents should help their children be aware of their feelings and express them appropriately. The parents should enhance their children's self-esteem by focusing on their positive qualities and listening to and valuing their ideas (Brenner, 1984). Parents should provide an atmosphere that fosters independence, initiative, and competence in their children.

Nursing Interventions to Facilitate Mental Health

The overall goal of psychiatric nursing interventions is to help the family successfully adapt to the stress from the chronic condition while facilitating the mental health of the family unit and each individual member. The psychiatric nurse needs to be knowledgeable about the chronic condition and the unique stressors associated with each condition before intervening with families. It is also important for the nurse to be knowledgeable about the side effects of the treatments for the condition. Identification of side effects should be included in the assessment of the family and taken into consideration when planning interventions with the families.

The use of both the stages of adaptation perspective and the Double ABCX Model provides a comprehensive theoretic framework to guide psychiatric nurses as they intervene with families of chronically ill children. In addition, these frameworks facilitate the nurse's using a broad-based approach in intervening with these families. Interventions need to be based on a comprehensive assessment of the child with the chronic condition and the family unit. Strategies for interventions are presented first from the stages perspective and then from the Double ABCX Model.

STAGES OF ADAPTATION

Interventions should take into account the stage of adaptation, because family members have different needs at different times after diagnosis. Generally, there are no time limitations attached to each stage and the times may vary for different conditions, depending on severity. Families who have a child with epilepsy usually report that it takes about 1 year to reach the stage of conditional acceptance. In addition, many of these families report that they experience stages over again as they are confronted with a new problem, such as a change in their child's seizure control.

The psychiatric nurse should keep in mind that family members may go through the stages at different times. For example, with chronic conditions that begin in early childhood, the parents generally will have adapted to the condition before the child or siblings are even aware of the condition. Later, when the child with the chronic condition and the siblings are developmentally able to comprehend the ramifications of the condition, they begin the process of adaptation. Leahey and Wright (1985) caution that all family members should not be expected to go through the stages in the same fashion and that nurses should not specify how the family should grieve. Before any interventions, a comprehensive assessment of stage needs to be carried out so that interventions are appropriate to facilitate movement toward conditional acceptance.

Disbelief. Generally it is not helpful to offer a large amount of specific information about the chronic condition during the disbelief stage. Attempting to teach before the family has come to terms with the diagnosis may further increase their anxiety. For example, parents report that learning about problems that could occur later—such as long-term side effects from medications—not only increased their anxiety but was not something with which they would need to deal at that time. It is important to gear the information given to the needs of the individual family. For some families it is inadvisable to provide too much information, even if it is appropriate, because they may not be ready to believe the diagnosis. Other parents report that they often forgot information that was given to them right after diagnosis because they were so anxious. On the other hand, one should provide information that parents want and need.

The nurse definitely must provide information that is needed before the next visit. For example, parents of children with newly diagnosed epilepsy would need to know about giving the medication, side effects that need to be reported, basic information on seizures, and information about what feelings they may expect to have in relation to the situation. It is very important for the nurse to encourage the parent to call as questions arise.

Sometimes when families are in the stage of disbelief, they do not follow through on needed medical treatments for the child. In this situation, it is important for the nurse not to withhold information. The nurse must be supportive and even acknowledge that it is common to want to deny that all of this is happening, and yet must confront the family with the need to seek medical attention.

Anger. The anger stage can be difficult for the nurse because the nurse may be the object of the family's anger. It is not uncommon for families to become angry with the persons associated with the treatment of the condition or the persons who gave them the diagnosis. The nurse's awareness that this is a difficult period for the family should help her or him to not take the anger personally. Helping the family to express their emotions in an accepting atmosphere can help them work through their feelings.

Family members and the child also are often unnecessarily worried about things that are not mentioned. If the nurse describes common fears that parents have, it often helps parents bring their own fears out in the open. The nurse can then reassure the family about unfounded fears. It is also common during this period for parents to become angry with other families who appear not to have as much to cope with. For example, a mother whose child had multiple handicaps told another father whose child had a well-controlled seizure condition that he could not possibly understand her because he really had no problem at all compared with hers. Nevertheless, it is often helpful for parents to meet with other parents during this stage. Parents often report that it is helpful to talk with someone else who has or is experiencing similar feelings. Families need to know that feelings of anger, guilt, and rejection are not uncommon.

The nurse needs to explore feelings of guilt, anxiety, and rejection with families so they can be dealt with openly. Overindulgence and overprotection of the child with the chronic condition may result from parents' inability to cope successfully with these feelings. Overindulgence may occur because the parents want to make life easier for the child and to compensate for the chronic condition. Regardless of the cause, the child gets the message that he or she is different and more fragile than other children. Nursing educational interventions focusing on appropriate activity limitations and problems resulting from over-restriction and overindulgence should help prevent overprotection and overindulgence. These interventions are especially needed because children with chronic conditions are at risk for dependency and poor self-esteem.

Demystification. The stage of demystification provides the greatest opportunity for the nurse to intervene with the family. During this stage, family members actively seek information about the condition and are also receptive to learning about how other families have coped successfully with chronic conditions in children. During this stage, feelings of anger are fading and the family has more energy to cope. Especially helpful in this stage are interventions that help family members develop a sense of control over the condition. It may also be helpful for the nurse to use downward comparison to assist the family in putting the chronic condition into perspective, by helping them to realize that there are others who have it worse. Many parents report that seeing other children with worse problems helps them to realize that there are positive aspects to their own situation.

Conditional acceptance. Even during this final stage it is important for the nurse to realize that living with a chronic condition in a child involves a certain amount of underlying stress on the family, which makes them more vulnerable to other family crises. During this stage, interventions are usually minimal unless the family is experiencing new situations that require additional coping on the part of the family. When there are new developments in the child's condition that result in changes, the family may reexperience a prior stage, especially the anger stage. Sometimes family members are disconcerted, because they feel that they should be better able to cope or because they remember how sad and angry they felt earlier and do not want to return to those feelings. Primarily the nurse needs to reassure them that a recurrence of earlier feelings is common when families are confronted with new problems and that this recurrence generally does not last long. One strategy for helping the family during this stage is to encourage the family members to use those strategies which were most helpful in the past.

When the nurse helps the family members build on their strengths, it is also a time when the family members can begin to identify how the experience may have even been helpful to them. The nurse could help the parents to reflect on what they have learned and to inform them about the research that has found that all family members can benefit from the experience of living with a chronic condition.

DOUBLE ABCX MODEL

In the Double ABCX Model (see Fig 16-1), the four concepts of family demands, family adaptive resources, family definition, and coping are proposed to influence adaptation. Psychiatric nursing interventions should be focused on each of these four areas to enhance adaptation.

Family demands. The family with a chronically ill child is confronted with increased demands from living with the chronic condition. Each chronic condition has its unique set of stressors with which the family must cope. The stressors from the chronic condition are added to the already existing set of demands experienced by the family from other normative and non-normative transitions. A comprehensive assessment of all family stressors, including identification of which stressors could be controlled by the family, is necessary before interventions to reduce stressors are carried out. Each stressor should be explored to determine what steps could be taken by the family to reduce the stress. The psychiatric nurse going through this task with the family members often helps the family come up with new strategies for coping with an existing problem. This process also provides information to the nurse about how the family handles problems.

It is especially important that the psychiatric nurse address each of the illness-related stressors with the family members to determine whether the concerns are based on accurate information. According to Leahey and Wright (1985), many families have either incorrect or inadequate disease-related information, which can lead to stress. Correction of misinformation, especially that causing unfounded fears, is one way to reduce stress for the family. The nurse should also provide education to the family about the normal stages of adaptation so, for example, the family realizes that the feelings they are experiencing are common and are reassured that they will not always feel so angry. At times, family members need a total break from caregiving to reduce stress. An intervention that is helpful for these families is a total break or a respite from the care of the child. Often the family members feel guilty about wanting to get away, and the nurse needs to give them permission to do so. In these situations the nurse must help them understand that respites are necessary for them to prevent burnout and help them find suitable arrangements for the care of the chronically ill member while they are gone.

Family adaptive resources. Resources of the family include those assets available to the family which help them deal with accumulated stressors from the chronic condition and other events. These include individual, family, and extra-family resources. Resources of individuals include self-esteem and independence. Family resources include stability, role flexibility, shared values, and good communication patterns that help them resolve conflict and solve problems. Extra-family resources include financial and social support.

When family members have a high level of self-esteem and good communication patterns, they feel free to express their feelings openly and are able to resolve conflicts and solve problems as they arise. When families do not have these resources, the psychiatric nurse needs to intervene to establish open communication within the family. A comprehensive assessment to determine which needs of each of the family members are not being met should be carried out. It is especially important to assess needs of siblings, because they often feel left out and may be afraid to say anything because of feelings of guilt for being healthy. Mothers are at risk for depression, because they often add the care of the chronically ill child to other roles. The nurse can help the family members discuss their feelings openly so strategies can be developed to resolve problems. Nurses can also help family members enhance each other's self-esteem by teaching them to listen to and value each other's opinions.

If families do not have medical insurance that covers health care expenses, the nurse can provide information on community services and programs to help them. For example, in most states, funds are available for children with disabilities through the state department of health. The nurse should not only make the family aware of different resources that may be available, but be available to assist and support them as they go through the often frustrating experience of applying for benefits.

Although some families have sufficient social support to help them cope with the situation, others do not. For these families the nurse can provide information on different organizations that have support groups or parent-to-parent programs for families of children with chronic conditions. Many organizations, such as the Epilepsy Foundation of America, have a variety of support programs for families coping with epilepsy. It is important for the psychiatric nurse to be aware of the services available for families through the different organizations and to design support programs for parents if none are available. For example, families who have similar problems could be matched up with the goal of providing both emotional and physical support for each other (for example, respite care).

Family definition. The family definition is the meaning that the family gives to the chronic condition and its effect on the family. Research supports that parents' attitudes toward epilepsy are positively related to parental adjustment (Austin et al., 1984). Thus it is important for the nurse to assess family members' attitudes toward the child's chronic condition.

Some families view anything less than a perfectly healthy child as very negative. It is important for the nurse to explore these feelings to help the parents sort out what needs of theirs are not being met. For example, some parents get their own self-esteem needs met through their children's accomplishments. A chronically ill child would not be able to live up to his or her parents' expectations. The psychiatric nurse could help the parents sort out their needs from their children's needs and help the parents to achieve self-esteem in more appropriate ways.

One source of negative attitudes is inaccurate information leading to unfounded fears. For example, some family members erroneously believe that long-term medication for treatment of a chronic condition can lead to drug addiction or brain damage. The nurse needs to present information with the overall goal that family members' attitudes will be based on accurate information.

It is important to point out to parents that their attitudes are conveyed to the child with the chronic condition. Focusing only on problems gives the child the message that he or she is a problem for the family and leads to poor self-esteem in the child. For some families, merely learning about other families in similar situations who have led successful lives gives them more positive attitudes. For others, introducing them to families who are dealing with a variety of chronic conditions—especially those which are relatively more debilitating—helps them put their own child's condition into perspective. Nurses can also help families explore what they have learned from the condition's presence and to reframe the chronic condition from being totally negative to having some benefit.

Coping. In the Double ABCX Model, coping involves the things family members do to help them deal with stress. Lazarus and Folkman (1984) describe both emotion-focused and problem-focused forms of coping. Emotion-focused coping has as its goal the reduction of emotional distress; problem-focused coping has as its goal the control or alteration of the problem. Nurses must assess what family members are doing to deal with the ramifications of living day to day with a child with a chronic condition and make a judgment about whether the coping strategies used by individual family members are effective in meeting the needs of the family. Nurses need to assess whether family members are using the resources that are available to them. Is the child receiving regular medical care? Are medical procedures being carried out as directed? If not, the nurse needs to determine what is leading to poor care and intervene accordingly. For example, if financial resources are a problem, the nurse can help the family use problem-focused strategies and identify available resources. If the family members are distressed about the condition, the nurse can help them use more emotion-focused coping strategies—such as reframing and finding positive aspects from the situation. Another intervention strategy is to help the family find and use social support.

• • •

In summary, there is both anecdotal and research evidence in the literature that children with chronic physical conditions are more at risk for mental health problems than are children in the general population. Studies also indicate, however, that many children with chronic conditions apparently adapt well to their chronic illness and do not experience serious mental health problems. Furthermore, those children who do exhibit problems are not always the ones who have the most severe disease conditions. Although the consensus of clinical opinion and anecdotal reports is that other family members experience disruption when a child is chronically ill, there is little research available to describe factors that lead to specific problems. There is even less research available on the process of successful family adaptation. Furthermore, research available has major limitations, including the use of retrospective data, lack of longitudinal design, lack of healthy control groups, failure to differentiate among children by severity of disease or extent of disability, failure to consider length of time since onset of illness, and failure to include family system variables (Austin, 1991; Burr, 1985). The state of the current research in nursing does not provide a comprehensive body of knowledge on which to base nursing practice (Austin, 1991). Research with large samples of families that are followed over time is needed to provide an understanding of the factors that lead to both poor and good adaptation in families with chronically ill children.

Working with families with chronically ill children can be quite challenging for the psychiatric nurse. Many complex factors need to be taken into consideration when intervening to facilitate adaptation. The psychiatric nurse needs to be knowledgeable about the chronic condition, signs of both functional and dysfunctional coping, and strategies of intervention to facilitate adaptation. Even though a consistent body of research is not now available, the two theoretic frameworks presented — which are based on the available research and literature in the field — provide a foundation for the psychiatric nurse to use to intervene with families. According to Schilling (1988), all forms of professional interventions depend on a combination of strategies based on research, theory, clinical judgment, and experience. Working with families of chronically ill children, while challenging, can also be quite rewarding. Psychiatric nurses have the opportunity to enhance the lives of all family members.

REFERENCES

Achenbach, T.M. (1978). Psychopathology of childhood: Research problems and issues. *Journal of Clinical and Consulting Psychology, 46,* 759-776.

Austin, J.K. (1979). Stages in a family's reaction to epilepsy in a child. *Indiana State Nurses' Association Bulletin, 5*(5), 1-3. (Available from the National Epilepsy Library, Epilepsy Foundation of America, 4351 Garden City Drive, Suite 406, Landover, MD 20785)

Austin, J.K. (1988). Childhood epilepsy: Child adaptation and family resources. *Journal of Child and Adolescent Psychiatric and Mental Health Nursing, 1*(1), 18-24.

Austin, J.K. (1989). Comparison of child adaptation to epilepsy and asthma. *Journal of Child and Adolescent Psychiatric and Mental Health Nursing, 2*(4), 139-144.

Austin, J.K. (1991). Family adaptation to child's chronic illness. In J.T. Fitzpatrick, R.L. Tauhton, & A.K. Jacox (Eds). *Annual review of nursing research* (pp. 103-120). New York: Springer.

Austin, J.K., McBride, A.B., & Davis, H.W. (1984). Parental attitude and adjustment to childhood epilepsy. *Nursing Research, 33*(2), 92-96.

Austin, J.K., & McDermott, N. (1988). Parental attitude and coping behaviors in families of children with epilepsy. *Journal of Neuroscience Nursing, 20*(3), 174-179.

Austin, J.K., Patterson, J.M., & Huberty, T.J. (1991). Development of the Coping Health Inventory for Children (CHIC). *Journal of Pediatric Nursing, 6*(3), 166-174.

Billingham, K.A. (1982). *Developmental psychology for health care professions.* Boulder, Co: Westview Press.

Brenner, A. (1984). *Helping children cope with stress.* Lexington, Mass: D.C. Heath.

Breslau, N. (1985). Psychiatric disorder of children with physical disabilities. *Journal of the American Academy of Child Psychiatry, 24,* 87-94.

Burr, C.K. (1985). Impact on the family of a chronically ill child. In N. Hobbs, & J.M. Perrin (Eds.), *Issues in the care of children with chronic illness* (pp. 24-40). San Francisco: Josey-Bass.

Drotar, D., & Bush, M. (1985). Mental health issues and services. In N. Hobbs, & J.M. Perrin (Eds.), *Issues in the care of children with chronic illness* (pp. 514-550). San Francisco: Josey-Bass.

Freiberg, K.L. (1983). *Human development: A life span approach* (2nd Ed.). Monterey, Ca: Wadsworth Health Sciences Division.

Garrison, W.T., & McQuiston, S. (1989). *Chronic illness during childhood and adolescence.* Newbury Park: Sage Publications.

Hill, R. (1949). *Families Under Stress.* New York: Harper & Row.

Kessler, J.W. (1977). Parenting the handicapped child. *Pediatric Annals, 6*(10), 654-661.

Kruger, S., Shawver, M., & Jones, L. (1980). Reactions of families to the child with cystic fibrosis. *Image, 12*(3), 67-72.

Lazarus, R.S., & Folkman, S. (1984). *Stress, appraisal, and coping.* New York: Springer.

Leahey, M., & Wright, L.M. (1985). Intervening with families with chronic illness. *Family Systems Medicine, 3*(1), 60-69.

Lipsitt, L.P. (1983). Stress in infancy: Toward understanding the origins of coping behavior. In W. Garmezy, & M. Rutter (Eds.), *Stress, coping and development in children* (pp. 161-180). New York: McGraw-Hill Book Co.

Massie, R.K. (1985). The constant shadow: Reflections on the life of a chronically ill child. In N. Hobbs, & J.M. Perrin (Eds.), *Issues in the care of children with chronic illness* (pp. 13-23). San Francisco: Josey-Bass.

McCollum, A.T. (1981). *The chronically ill child: A guide for parents and professionals.* New Haven: Yale University Press.

McCubbin, H., & Patterson, J. (1983). The family stress process: the Double ABCX Model of Adjustment and Adaptation. In H. McCubbin, M. Sussman, & J. Patterson (Eds.), *Social stress and the family: advances and developments in family stress theory and research.* New York: Haworth Press.

McKeever, P.T. (1981). Fathering the chronically ill child. *American Journal of Maternal Child Nursing, 6,* 124-128.

Olshansky, S. (1962). Chronic sorrow: A response to having a mentally defective child. *Social Casework, 43,* 191-194.

Patterson, J.M. (1988). Chronic illness in children and the impact on families. In C.S. Chilman, E.W. Nunnally, & F.M. Cox (Eds.), *Chronic illness and disability.* Newbury Park, Calif.: Sage.

Pinyerd, B.J. (1981). Siblings of children with myelomeningocele: Examining their perceptions. *Maternal Child Nursing Journal, 12*(1), 61-70.

Pless, I.B., & Perrin, J.M. (1985). Issues common to a variety of illnesses. In N. Hobbs, & J.M. Perrin (Eds.), *Issues in the care of children with chronic illness* (pp. 41-60). San Francisco: Josey-Bass.

Rutter, M., Graham, P., & Yule, W. (1970). A neuropsychiatric study in childhood. *Clinics in Developmental Medicine, 35, 36.*

Rutter, M., Tizard, J., & Whitmore, K. (1970). *Education, health and behavior.* Huntington, New York: Robert E. Krieber.

Schilling, R.F. (1988). Helping families with developmentally disabled members. In C.S. Chilman, E.W. Nunnally, & F.M. Cox (Eds.), *Chronic illness and disability* (pp. 171-192). Newbury Park, Calif.: Sage.

Seligman, M., & Darling, R.B. (1989). *Ordinary families, special children*. New York: The Guilford Press.

Shapiro, J. (1983). Family reactions and coping strategies in response to the physically ill or handicapped child: A review. *Social Science and Medicine, 17,* 913-931.

Stein, R.E.K., Jessop, D.J., & Ireys, H.T. (1988). Prevention of emotional problems in children with chronic illness and their families. In L.A. Bond, & B.M. Wagner (Eds.), *Families in transition: Primary prevention programs that work.* Newbury Park, Calif.: Sage.

Taylor, S.C. (1980). The effect of chronic childhood illnesses upon well siblings. *Maternal Child Nursing, 9*(2), 109-116.

Thomas, R.B. (1987). Family adaptation to a child with a chronic condition. In M.H. Rose, & R.B. Thomas (Eds.), *Children with chronic conditions* (pp. 29-54). Orlando: Grune & Stratton, Inc.

Waechter, E.H. (1977). Bonding problems of infants with congenital anomalies. *Nursing Forum, 16*(3/4), 298-318.

Wills, T.A. (1981). Downward comparison principles in social psychology. *Psychological Bulletin, 90*(2), 245-271.

Chapter 17

Effect of Cancer on the Family

Anne M. Delengowski

When addressing the cancer experience, society often views a disease with few survivors. Too often, society also pictures a disease that affects a certain individual. If one would choose the two most prevalent misconceptions about this disease, these two would certainly rank very high.

Someone always survives the cancer experience, and the family system—however one might define family (which does include the individual with cancer)—is affected by this experience. Lewandowski and Jones (1988) state that the occurrence of cancer affects the entire family system, generating anxiety and altering communication patterns and relationships among its members. Compounding the social issues surrounding these misconceptions is the fact that many health care professionals directly dealing with this disease fail to recognize the reality of these misconceptions. This chapter sheds insight into these realities. It also centers on the realities of survivorship.

Cancer, meaning crab, is often defined as a devastating disease. But most often health care professionals see this definition only as it depicts the physical aspect of this disease, when, in fact, it describes the emotional turmoil it produces on the individual and the family as they attempt to survive the experience.

The cancer experience is not unlike other chronic, potentially life-threatening diseases. Although many people perceive that the beginning of the disease is initiated on diagnosis, the actual process begins before the diagnosis. This prediagnostic phase is the first in the cancer experience. The second begins upon diagnosis. The third phase is experienced during active treatment. The fourth phase may be long-term survival for the client or may end in death. The last phase is the survival of the family after the death of a loved one. These phases divide the course of living with cancer.

Lewandowski and Jones (1988) describe nursing interventions throughout the course of living with cancer, directing efforts toward the described needs of the family. It was noted that the predominant needs throughout the varied course of cancer are the needs for information, for hope, for opportunities to ventilate feelings, and for interventions to be directed toward the client.

Following is a description of each of the phases, as well as the nursing care necessary to ensure long-term survival of the family.

Martocchio (1985) defines the continuum on which families exist during this experience. The potential roles that the family may acquire during this experience include being partners in the care of their loved one, participating in the care, observing the care, or being recipients of care by the health care providers. As one will see as the different phases of the cancer experience progress, the family flows through this continuum from active roles to more passive roles, in an attempt at survival. As a health care professional, one must help the family identify their role and assist in the changes within the continuum.

Prediagnosis Phase

The cancer experience, although many see as beginning upon diagnosis, truly begins when the physical signs begin to herald the onset of a disease process. This could take the nature of a lump in the breast, a continuous cough or simply weight loss, lack of energy, or bruising. These subtle signs often elicit a tremendous amount of fear within the individual. This fear, whether shared with others within the family system or not, begins to take an emotional toll on the individual, which directly affects the rest of the family. This often signifies the beginning of the stress related to the cancer experience.

The period between the onset of symptoms and diagnosis most often depends on the individual's normal reaction to fear. Attempting to ignore the symptoms is not an unusual reaction. If this is the reaction to the symptoms, often a tremendous amount of regret is seen in later phases, if cancer is confirmed. Immediate medical attention also is a response. Even this response often does not give way to immediate answers. The waiting period between the onset of symptoms and the results of tests to verify a diagnosis is often perceived as one of the worst periods in the experience. This period could extend hours or even weeks before a definitive diagnosis is made. The emotions surrounding this phase are most likely the result of fear of the unknown and the clear uncertainty of future.

During the prediagnosis phase, the health care provider must be an avid listener. The process of listening during this phase includes soliciting an accurate assessment of the family. This assessment also includes information about past experiences with health care and with cancer as a disease. The burden of past bad experiences often is excess baggage that impedes successful survivorship. Dispelling misconceptions is most important.

Honesty and openness are important qualities during this initial interaction. Encouraging these qualities within the family group is critical. If these qualities fail to develop early in the experience, fear of the unknown is exacerbated as the experience continues. Fear of the health care professionals' withholding information is a common theme throughout the rest of the phases if trust is not developed and nurtured in this phase. This trust must be validated not only with the health care provider and the individual with cancer, but also with the family.

During this phase, allowing time for discussion is most important. Developing a clear understanding of what brought the individual to seek medical attention is important. Soliciting fears of both the patient and family is critical. All of this information should be kept in a written file for future use by all health care providers.

If the diagnosis is not made at this time, it is important to educate the family on primary prevention.

Diagnosis

After a long waiting period a diagnosis is finally confirmed. One cannot disregard the tremendous amount of energy spent during the prediagnosis phase. From the point of first symptom to the diagnosis can be a very long period, a time spent in fear. Sometimes, the diagnosis becomes somewhat a period of relief, that the unknown is no longer an entity but is replaced by a feeling that maybe something can be done.

After the diagnosis of cancer, most people try to make sense out of the ordeal. Frequently, they initially develop a sense of guilt. This guilt is often experienced by all the recipients of care. It arises as one seeks to find the reason that the cancer developed. Individuals often blame the cancer on past "sins," omissions, or overindulgence.

This guilt is overwhelmingly perceived by parents of children with cancer. Parents often review their past life and how they could have caused the child to develop this horrible disease. This guilt, although not rational, is very real to those experiencing it. These feelings can also be experienced by the siblings of the child with cancer.

Allowing family members to ventilate their fears is crucial to long-term survival. Clearly understanding the existence of these feelings is essential, while at the same time helping those involved to understand that most often these feelings lack validation. Another useful technique is to help the family understand that the past is history. There is nothing that one can do to change the past. It is important to acknowledge the past but to continue on to the future without the burden of the past preventing acceptance of the present.

This phase brings the major task of decision making. The decisions to be made include selection of doctors, health care facilities, as well as treatment modalities. It is important that the family is involved in this process. Martoccio further states that the family's inability to participate or assist the patient in securing competent medical care, follow prescribed treatment regimens, or recognize signs of complications may result in feelings of helplessness and loss of control. It is the health care provider's responsibility to help the family to understand that decisions made out of love are not wrong, and once made, they must continue on with the future.

If the decision is made to establish health care in a facility away from home, many burdens are left with the family. Traveling, lodging and meals are extra financial burdens to the already stressed family system. Child care is a difficulty if the well spouse elects to spend time with the sick partner. Information regarding resources for these difficulties is most helpful.

One phenomenon that often occurs during this phase may be termed the "honeymoon" period. This is a unique time when many social supports become available to the individual and family upon diagnosis. Much attention is directed to all involved. Because the process is new and quite an emotional time, many social supports come to the aid of the family. This period is often short lived. As the novelty of the disease wears off and the time through the treatment phase extends for months, social supports begin to dwindle. People who have served as social supports return to their lives, and the cancer continues to invade the world of the family. Families need to be aware of this phenomenon.

Derdiarian (1987) sums up many of the clinical needs of the client with cancer on diagnosis. The study concludes that persons whose cancer was recently diagnosed may benefit from opportunities to express their informational needs and that this information should be shared with the interdisciplinary team to formulate the basis for care, follow-up, and changes in the informational need over time.

Tringali's study (1986) addresses the needs of family members at three distinct phases in the cancer experience—the initial phase, recurrence, and follow-up. This small but significant study found that the family members valued professionals who answered questions with honesty in all phases.

Treatment Phase

The next phase, the treatment phase, is rarely easy. Many issues must be addressed in this phase, the first being the family's experiences with or perceptions of the disease. Cancer care has changed dramatically in the last decade. Diseases that had no options years ago are now very treatable. Diseases that were treated years ago are treated differently with much greater success. Treatment side effects, which had few antidotes in the past, are now able to be treated effectively. The reality of cancer is that 45% of people diagnosed are alive 5 years after the diagnosis. (Boring, Squires, & Tong, 1991).

Education is one of the most important tasks in this phase. Educating the client and family about the treatment and potential side effects is most important. This information is best directed to the entire family system, both verbally and in written form. The information should be presented honestly and concisely, without overwhelming the individuals involved. Time should be allowed for questions and for interpretation of information. Allowing time for questions by individual members outside of the group is helpful.

Another helpful recommendation during this phase is to establish roles for the family to aid the individual during this time. Powerlessness and loss of control are very often valid problems that occur in this phase, as well as future phases. Not only are these issues for the individual with cancer, but powerlessness and loss of control are strongly felt by family members—for example, the mother who feels that she can no longer nurture her ill child, the role she has played the child's entire life. Individuals with cancer and their families are stripped of their sense of self-worth as it was defined within the family, because the health care system begins to intrude on these roles. This becomes evident in the anger that is often directed toward the health care providers, especially during this phase. The most practical way of overcoming this is to define each member's role within the family before the onset of the illness and define how that role may be helpful within the context of the present situation. Encourage spouses and parents to bring in the individual's favorite foods, allow these individuals to assist in the personal care, and, especially, allow them to plan early discharge needs. In addition to this, health care providers must understand that the side effects of treatment often are devastating to the family members. Parents who watch their beautiful child's hair fall out, the husband who watches his wife lose the physical beauty she once had, and the wife and children who watch their strong husband and father shed many pounds and become so weak that he can no longer independently perform basic needs — these are situations that have a tremendous emotional impact on the family system and must be acknowledged by the health care provider.

Identifying the different family roles within the system necessitates addressing the role that children play. They are often the hidden victims in the tragedy of cancer. Whether the children are the siblings, children or grandchildren, they are affected by this disease no matter what age they are. They sometimes become the recipients of misdirected anger, or become emotionally neglected as one sees them as too young to understand. The result of such treatment is often problems such as acting out or a dramatic change in performance in school. Children are affected by this disease. Their life will be changed as a result of this disease. This change can be one of positive, healthy growth if fostered appropriately. Including children in discussions at an age-appropriate level is helpful. Allowing time for questions in a quiet place is also helpful. Addressing these issues within the school system facilitates open communication if problems begin to arise. Spending quality time with the healthy child reconfirms the child's sense of self-worth.

Finally, understanding in this phase and others that the family and patient may be at different emotional levels is important. The patient, after many lonely hours in the hospital, might have come to a different emotional level than the rest of the family, who have been busier socially. It is important to note the different level at which each individual member is.

It is important to understand that this phase may end in a finite period, or may last a long time. The period of adjustment during this phase has many peaks and valleys. An individual may have an uncomplicated course and go on for long-term survival with limited difficulty. Others may reach the end of what is supposed to be their treatment phase to find that they are not in remission and must proceed with further treatment. These families have difficulty in continuing the course and need a tremendous amount of support and encouragement.

Long-Term Survival

Who are the survivors of cancer? When one is diagnosed with this disease, the survival period begins. Therefore at this point, the cancer patient becomes a survivor. Webster (1986) defines the term *survive* in view of remaining alive or in existence and *survival* as the act of surviving, persisting in society. One is led to believe, therefore, that surviving is in fact an active process. Certainly, the diagnosis of cancer, as society views it, is a critical event in an individual's life. It is at the beginning of this event that the process of survival is initiated, the process of remaining an active member of society, the process of remaining alive.

Hassey-Dow (1990) eloquently describes this process in terms of the enduring seasons of survival. Through this terminology, one sees that this process once again is an active one, but takes on many different and varied forms. Winter, with its gloom, certainly could be an analogy for the diagnosis of this disease. The treatment of the disease at this point certainly entails the destruction of both cancerous cells and normal, healthy cells. It is during this winter that the emotions of both the family and the client with cancer are at a low point. This period most often is finite, and spring or regrowth comes. In the winter sometimes the storms are bad; but with the right equipment, year after year, the winters pass and spring comes. It is so hard, in the middle of a bad winter, to ever imagine the beauty of spring, but it comes. So is it in the life of a client with cancer and the family. Winter passes and spring comes. Hair regrows like the budding of new flowers, and life begins to look pretty again. Strength returns, as does the bright sunshine of future hope.

Spring is the time of renewal and regrowth, and in most cases, spring comes to the life of a cancer patient who is in the process of surviving. Summer, with its warmth and beauty, is the period of long-term survival for the individual with cancer. During the summer, the memories of winter's past are dimmed by the miracle of the new season. Threatening storms do occur during summer, as does the fear of recurrence in the survival period of an individual with cancer. How do we as health care professionals assist individuals during the survival seasons?

If the client does in fact gain remission from the disease, the victory is sweet but not always long lived. Many difficulties arise in the survival period. First is the fear of recurrence. Most individuals with cancer say the fear of recurrence rarely goes away. The fear certainly dims with time. What was a normal cold in the past becomes an overwhelming threat after the diagnosis of cancer. There no longer is a simple headache or backache, but the fear that the cancer has returned. Individuals and their families become not only concerned about these events, but often overprotective, preventing an early return to social normalcy. The time between doctor visits is occupied by fear.

Along with the physical changes and fears accompanying cancer are the very real and valid changes in social lives. Most individuals state that at least one friend becomes distant during the cancer experience and never returns. The friend's fear of his or her own mortality often prevents the friend from remaining close to the individual with cancer. Often adolescents and young adults with cancer experience this difficulty. Best friends before the cancer experience become nonentities during and after the experience. Helping the client and family understand the rationale for this difficulty is helpful. Helping them understand allows them to realize that nothing they did caused the friend's withdrawal. Also, discussing these issues with friends early on might prevent this occurrence. Going to the school of the child to discuss facts about cancer and dispelling fears helps dissipate this problem. Allowing friends to see the cancer patient as a hero sheds a special light on the patient.

Another difficulty during this period is somewhat of a double-edged sword. The need to talk about the experience seems to always be present for the cancer patient, but the family and friends become weary of listening. The individual with cancer becomes frustrated in an attempt to discuss his or her story, while those who went through the experience with the individual want to put the experience behind them and look to the future. Support groups specifically for patients with cancer are helpful during this adjustment time. They allow the individual to fulfill these needs with individuals who have similar histories.

Individuals with cancer also suggest that society fails to see them as individuals first and cancer patients second. Topics of conversation center on the cancer as opposed to normal living. Empowering these individuals to be their own advocates is helpful.

Young persons with cancer often have difficulty readjusting to normal life. The emotional rollercoaster that they have experienced is overwhelming, and they have not had the life experiences to assist in the readjustment to this time. Resocialization to school and the social world can be difficult for a child. This is compounded by the inability of the parents to assist during this time. Once again, support groups can be most helpful, in addition to individual therapy if warranted. Long-term survival to a young child ideally means many years. This means it is most important to recognize problems and address them with realistic answers. Tutoring to assist the child toward the same level of academic achievement as his or her peers allows the child a step forward in becoming adjusted.

With the young adult, other issues surface. The issue of discrimination toward individuals who have had cancer is evident throughout the oncology literature. Discrimination in the workplace and on issues surrounding insurance abound. These issues are important and need to be addressed with the individuals and their family.

Another major issue during the period of survivorship is that of fertility in this age group. Issues of sperm banking and egg banking are being addressed as this age group survives this disease. Consultation with a fertility specialist is important for those who might desire children in the future.

Long-term survival is the expectation of people with cancer, but the quality of this time will depend on the energy spent on preparing the individual and the family for the challenges of this time.

Terminality

As with many chronic illness, this disease may have a terminal phase. The point from the beginning of the onset of the cancer experience until the end might have been a short time or many years. If it was a short period, accommodation by the family will have been very difficult, because the phases probably were short and adjustment nearly impossible. Life to the family in this dilemma is analogous to a rollercoaster ride. The highs are interrupted by tremendous downward slopes, and the ability of the family members to even catch their breath, let alone adjust, is nearly impossible. It is reasonable to suggest that an individual might have terminal cancer on diagnosis. This is feasible in the case of an individual who initially sought diagnosis with an advanced cancer. It is also conceptual that an individual could die during the treatment phase. Cancer treatment, especially in very aggressive diseases, requires potentially life-threatening treatments. The families involved in these scenarios need a great deal of follow-up or referral after the death, because little preparatory time has been spent before the death.

In any case, what does the death of the individual mean? Ideally, by this point, the physician has discussed the issue of code versus no code with the client. An astute physician would have addressed the issue of life support with the individual with cancer when he or she was in a healthier state. This places the decision where it rightfully belongs — to the individual who has the disease. The federal Self-Determination Law requires health care facilities to address the issue of "living wills" or "durable power of attorney" with the patients as they enter the health care facility.

If there is no time for this issue to be addressed with the client, this becomes a major issue for the family. Having to make the decision is sometimes a major difficulty. The family is already under an enormous emotional burden. The illness has placed a tremendous amount of stress on the family. Throughout the treatment phase, family members often becomes cheerleaders to maintain hope and strength for the individual with cancer, but they are then asked to take an entirely different role in deciding the code issue. A great deal of time must be spent with this family to allow them to come to a decision that is comfortable for all individuals involved.

Issues prominent during the terminal phase include the physical and emotional well-being of the individual with cancer. Most work done with families who have terminal loved ones (Hull, 1989) suggest that the major concern of the family is the care of the loved one. It is evident that the care of the family becomes secondary to the care of the individual with cancer.

The care of the person with terminal cancer emphasizes both physical comfort and emotional needs. Although the idea that all people with cancer have pain at the terminal phase is a myth, it is a true fear of people with cancer and their families. Pain management, especially in cancer care, has almost become a science. Once myths were dispelled about the client with cancer becoming addicted to the narcotics, and the fear that the person would not be able to get enough medication to take the pain away, pain management in the client with cancer no longer becomes an insurmountable task. The liberal use of narcotics, with antidotes for the side effects, has made pain management much easier. The advent of technology has allowed health care the ability to use novel approaches to the delivery of these drugs.

Other physical problems during this time include issues surrounding feeding and breathing. Often, gastrointestinal disorders impede the ability of the person with a terminal disease, such as cancer, to eat or drink. Although most often the dying person has little regard for these issues, the family often has difficulty dealing with them, because the ability to eat and drink is so fundamental to life. They feel the person is "starving" to death or is thirsty. Little do they understand that forcing this issues could create even more difficult problems, such as aspiration pneumonia, if the person has difficulty with the gag reflex or if the person vomits with an obstructive disorder. Gentle reassurances about the condition of the person and what could be the consequences of forcing these issues allow the family to have a better understanding of the issues. The most important factor is to allow the family to understand that the person is not uncomfortable.

The dyspnea that often accompanies the terminal phase is another source of distress for families. It is rare that a person with cancer dies suddenly. More often there is a period between the time one is told that there is nothing more that can be done until the ultimate death. This length of this period can vary greatly, but one frequent telltale sign of approaching death is the changes in the breathing pattern. Often shortness of breath may accompany the later stages of advanced cancer because of prior treatment, infection, and/or the cancer itself. The liberal use of oxygen usually assists in the comfort of the individual. But as death approaches, very real changes occur in the patterns of breathing. Cheyne-Stokes respirations, evidenced by patterns of rapid breathing, followed by periods of apnea, occur frequently as death approaches. This breathing pattern, although well known to those who deal with dying persons, can be a frightening sight for families. Secretions in the throat often accompany this pattern of breathing. This also escalates the anxiety of the family as they watch the passing of a loved one. How does one help at this time as one sees the anguish in the faces of the family members?

It is surprising that health care has educational classes to prepare mothers to bring life into the world, but health care clearly shies away from helping to educate the family on how to deal with both the physical and emotional outcomes accompanying the end of life. Clearly, an educated family who is prepared for the physical outcomes of death is more readily able to deal with the changes. Often, the individual who is dying is unconscious by the time most of these changes are occurring, and the family needs to understand that the level of consciousness probably does not allow the individual to feel the sensations of the dying process. It is most often the family who is suffering as they sit and watch. If the family understands that the client is probably not feeling anything, they are probably more willing to sit and hold the client's hands than experience anguish at the passing of time.

The so-called "death rattle" often occurs at the end of life. The family often becomes frustrated by the sounds that appear to be causing distress to the family member. Families need to know that it is unlikely that the secretions are of any discomfort to the client, and attempts at clearing them often create more of a hindrance than a help. The uneducated family becomes frustrated by health care providers who appear to ignore this need of their loved one. The time spent in preparing the family for the physical difficulties associated with the dying process is time well spent, because families are better prepared to deal with what is known.

Giving the family tasks to support comfort allows them less of a sense of powerlessness during this phase. It helps them feel a sense of accomplishment at a time when they feel so out of control. Teaching the family how to assist in small tasks, such as oral care and turning and positioning to support physical comfort, allows the family a sense of worth. Gentle reassurances throughout this phase that the client is physically comfortable or that the health care team will help to make him or her comfortable is extremely supportive during this most difficult time. Also, constant reinforcement of the family's worth is an important task at this phase.

After the physical needs are met, the next important identified factor is the emotional needs. One sees multiple steps as one faces the challenges of helping the family face the task of helping a loved one die a peaceful death. One difficulty is that often the individual's acceptance of his or her death is not consistent with the family's stage of acceptance. This disparity results from many factors. One is the process of the previous phases. If the individual was able to adjust emotionally with the progression of the disease, acceptance is somewhat easier. If the individual becomes tired of dealing with the disease, he or she often concludes that continuing to struggle is too difficult and a peaceful acceptance is attained. On the other hand, the family is not as intimately involved within the process of the physical and emotional trauma of the disease and has difficulty understanding this acceptance. Most often the individual with cancer comes to acceptance more quickly than does the family because of these issues.

This becomes yet another challenge for the caregiver because now she or he must progress at different levels with each party.

Although the client and family are often at different levels of acceptance, the issues are still the same. One such issue is when the person will die. This is one issue to which those in health care at times believe they have the answer, but really do not. Very broad, educated guesses are often able to give the clients and families time to prepare for the job of finishing life's business. It is important that patients and families understand that the answer to "when" death will occur is only an estimate for them to prepare, but the exact time is really not known.

All individuals, no matter what age group they represent, have tasks to complete to prepare for death. Some age groups have more pronounced tasks because their shorter lives may not have allowed them the normal progression of preparing for life's end. Young adults, who are supposed to be at the prime of their life, are one such group who have much unfinished business. For example, the young parent has children to assist to maturation. The "job" of parenting represents a major task with which one must deal before life ends. How one is able to deal with it is a major task, representing a challenge to even the most skilled health care provider. Preparing the well parent for continuing on is part of this task. Emotional preparation of both the well parent and the children is yet another task. Allowing the arena for open, honest communication is an important role for the health care provider. Assisting the client and the family with the knowledge and opportunity to complete this business is important. One such way of dealing with this is with the use of audio or video taping. This allows the dying parent a real opportunity to have a sense of involvement in the child's future. For example, parents may tell children in their own words what their life was about and what the child meant to them. Mothers may tell daughters what they might have told them in the future if they were a part of their lives. If audio or video taping is not feasible, one may allow the dying parent to tell an individual with whom he or she is comfortable, information that the individual can share with the children at a later date. Parents' bequeathing certain important mementos to their children encourages their "touching" the future of their children.

It is most ideal to have the family involved in the client's emotional preparation for death, but often the family have their own needs at this time and are unable to assist in this way. The astute health care provider will be able to assist both the family and client in their needs at different levels. Often if the needs are eminent, two health care providers must assist at this time in order to ensure adjustment.

Needs of the family are multiple. Foremost is the emotional adjustment to the physical loss of a very important part of their lives. It is inconceivable to most people to understand suffering and loss. Some use strong religious beliefs to overcome the fear that accompanies this phase. This is a very strong, effective coping mechanism for support of these survivors. One difficulty with this coping mechanism is that shame can result if anger is directed to the higher being when things are starting to decline. Families need to know that this is a very common feeling. Incorporating the assistance of a religious person certainly helps during this time.

Another task of the family is preparing the children of the family for the reality of death. Much work has been done in this area, and one is referred to the literature because it is not within the focus of this chapter to incorporate all the information necessary to assist in this very important task. It is essential to understand that the children are important within the family and they cannot be excluded from any phase. During this phase, the one that brings the ultimate uncertainty in life, adults feel uncomfortable dealing with children's concerns because there are no exact answers to the "why's" and "what happens next." Most often this is the first time the family has needed to deal with the compelling issue of death of a loved one. Health care providers need to empower the well family members to understand which developmental stage the child is in and how to assist him or her in this phase as well as the future, when the reality of life without the loved one sets in. Written materials and references to support groups are concrete ways of helping, because often during this time the family is dealing with concomitant issues.

Another important task at this phase is preparing the client and family for life after death. One simple but important task is dealing with wills and financial aspects. Although this seems unimportant in this scenario, it represents an important issue in the future. Most clients really want their families to make a smooth transition to the future after their death. Allowing the topic to focus and providing information assist the family with this task.

Another task in which some clients want a part is the funeral and such other arrangements after their death. Some clients are clear about what they want on their death. If this is important, helping the client and family accomplish this is important. Enabling the client to express his or her wishes to the family helps during this time.

One of the most difficult tasks of this phase is being able to instill hope at what appears to be such a hopeless time. Scanlon (1989) describes creating a vision of hope in palliative care. She states that compassionate care fosters a vision of hope. What does one hope for at the end of life? Dying with dignity, being free of physical and emotional discomfort, seeing families to the phase of peaceful acceptance, and discovering that even the end of life can bring quiet joy are all hopes that the client may have. When a health care provider can assist the client and family to this point, a true sense of accomplishment is found.

One area that is often not addressed in the literature is the issue of when the health care provider's family member has cancer. This issue is valid in that it is reasonable to expect that at some point this may be a reality for one who deals with clients with cancer. The health care provider is forced to play two roles during this phase. The first of these two roles is often that of health care provider and director. This individual is often forced into the role of asking questions, synthesizing the information, and arriving at the answer, even if this is not his or her area of expertise. Society sees a nurse as a nurse and a doctor as a doctor, regardless of the specialty. The overwhelming demands of these roles leave little time for the more important role, that of being the loved one. The health care provider is going through the same phases as the other family members but often is not able to deal with the emotional end of the phases, because he or she is too busy within the other role.

The role of director and provider does have advantages and disadvantages. The advantages of this role include that of feeling a real sense of accomplishment in assisting with the care, goal setting, and treatment outcomes. A real sense of accomplishment is felt because the provider has tasks with specific outcomes that assist the loved one. This helps overcome the sense of powerlessness that often is felt by family members of clients with cancer. But these positive aspects are accompanied by negative aspects. Being the first recipient of bad news, as in the role of the director, the care provider/family member has an enormous responsibility to support the others emotionally. Being viewed as the expert, this particular family member may be unable to deal with the emotions that he or she is experiencing.

Another added feeling experienced by these individuals is, at times, a sense of jealousy by other family members. Although most of the time the family wants this member to be the spokesperson, other members resent this role at times when emotions are intense. This likely extends from the other family members' sense of powerlessness and inability to feel as a valued member of the family. Role reversal often occurs, for instance when the provider/family member is a child of a sick parent. The well parent may resent the child's role in the sick parent's illness. Although somewhat irrational, the high stress level produces feelings that otherwise would not exist. This is an enormous burden, as this person tries to close gaps and be supportive and rational at a time that feels chaotic.

It is the role of health care workers to support this colleague in this most difficult period. Allowing him or her to choose the role that feels most comfortable is important. Often it is easier to discuss illness with someone who understands medical terminology than with someone who does not. However, although communicating with the colleague may be easier, one must be careful not to override the needs of each member of the stressed family. Allowing the colleague to ventilate his or her emotions and being supportive of his or her needs is helpful. Identifying the various roles that the person might be assuming is helpful. It allows him or her to see why he or she is feeling so overwhelmed. Most of all, supporting the person's values and commending him or her for the enormous task that he or she has assumed is most helpful.

Family Survival

After all the phases are over, life continues. Life is never easy, and certainly the loss of a loved one is one of life's burdens that is so hard to understand and accept. However, with quality health care, including both physical and emotional care, directed toward both the client and the family, a future is possible. Directing the family members to support groups to enhance their ability to cope with difficult times helps with future holidays, anniversaries, and other difficult periods. Follow-up with families by the health care providers allows the family to recall the experience with others involved. Time does ease the pain, but the period is much different for each individual, and the families need to understand this. Survivors of major battles become heroes; so too are the patients and families that survive the cancer experience.

REFERENCES

Boring, C., Squires, T., & Tong, T. (1991). Cancer statistics. *Ca: A Cancer Journal for Clinicians, 41,* 9-36.

Derdiarian, A. (1987). Informational needs of recently diagnosed cancer patients – Part II. *Cancer Nursing, 10*(3), 156-163.

Gambosi, J., & Ulreick, S. (1990). Recovering from cancer: A nursing intervention program recognizing survivorship. *Oncology Nursing Forum, 17*(2), 215-219.

Hassey-Dow, K. (1990). The enduring seasons in survival. *Oncology Nursing Forum, 17*(4), 511-516.

Hull, M. (1989). Family needs and supportive nursing behaviors during terminal cancer: A review. *Oncology Nursing Forum, 16*(6), 787.

Lewandowski, W., & Jones, S. (1988). The family with cancer: Nursing interventions throughout the course of living with cancer. *Cancer Nursing, 11*(6), 313-321.

Lovejoy, N. (1986). Family response to cancer hospitalization. *Oncology Nursing Forum, 13*(2), 33-37.

Martocchio, B. (1985). Family coping: Helping families help themselves. *Seminars in Oncology Nursing, 1*(4), 292-297.

Scanlon, C. (1989). Creating a vision of hope: The challenge of palliative care. *Oncology Nursing Forum, 16*(4), 491-496.

Tringali, C. (1986). The needs of family members of cancer patient. *Oncology Nursing Forum, 13*(4), 65-70.

Webster's Ninth New Collegiate Dictionary. (1986). Springfield, MA: Merriam-Webster.

Wegmann, J. & Ogrinc, M. (1981). Oncology nursing conflict: A case presentation of holistic care and the family in crisis. *Cancer Nursing*. February, 43-48.

Welch, D. (1981). Planning nursing interventions for the family members of adult cancer patients. *Cancer Nursing*. October, 365-370.

Chapter 18

Depression and Its Effect on the Family

Christine S. Fawcett

Depression is a human condition that is not experienced just by individuals, but also by their families, work colleagues, and sometimes communities. It is a condition that is met and responded to with much dread, self-doubt, pain, and the misunderstanding that it may be limitless; that is, it may continue forever.

Individual Focus

Individuals, primarily women, have been treated separately for this condition for years (Weissman & Klerman, 1987). Treatment has focused on a variety of differing ideas, myths, and beliefs. Among these beliefs are the following:

- Women are the weaker sex.
- Women have regular cycles of loss.
- Women are more sensitive than men.
- Women seek treatment more often than men.

Connected with these myths or ideas is a tendency to isolate the woman and treat her separately from the rest of the family system.

Within the past 15 years, children and adolescents have also been the targets of treatments for their depression. Working against another set of myths (Kelly, 1991), clinicians have begun to acknowledge that children indeed feel and experience depression. Although families are often included in therapy, the child is usually identified as the patient and the focus of treatment.

Elderly members of society have also been identified as being at risk for depression (McCullough, 1991). Among the experiences of elderly depression are the following categories: loss, attack, restraint, and threat. *Loss* refers to loss of a spouse, child, or ability to work. *Attack* alludes to such things as stereotypes of elderly. *Restraint* is associated with restraint of activity. *Threat* is the fear of being cut off from friends, family, and freedom. Each of those categories reflects a disconnection or dysfunction of the elderly member and the family.

However, little has been done to understand the overall family's changes when depression occurs to one or more of its members. This chapter discusses that dilemma.

Family Patterns

Just as depression affects the individual in a multifaceted fashion, a similar effect is seen when observing the family. Family functioning, speed of processing, and ease of handling situations are slowed or at times even halted.

The affect of the family, or the emotional barometer, is lowered. Tearfulness or emotional lability is common. The joy or happiness of the family appears diminished, or even absent. The tempo of the family is uneven, with much focus on feelings of despair and helplessness. Any plans, dreams, or goals of the family appear to be lost. The family's aspiration to remain together or cohesive is overshadowed with doubt. Often this family attempts to disguise this phenomenon. Excuses are made for behaviors or lack of behaviors. Often, too, as with individuals, the thoughts and feelings related to depression appear overwhelming to the family members.

Depression of the family might be most easily seen in the family that is grieving a loss. One stage of the grief is the depressed stage, which allows the processes of the family to become slowed. Verbal communication among members becomes limited. Bowen (1986) notes that the "emotional shock wave" of loss may result in serious depression of one of the members.

Upon making a home visit for a newly referred client, Nora, a public health nurse, was astonished to relate how much the home "felt" like depression. The family members hardly spoke to each other or spoke in very quiet tones; the rooms were barely lighted; an aura of despair appeared.

Role conflict may appear to diminish in families experiencing depression; however, what occurs is movement to a set of stereotyped role behaviors for male and female members. Members also "take over" the responsibilities of those who appear to be more incapacitated by feelings of depression. This takeover is usually done with little verbal disclosure or acknowledgment but with a great deal of covert communication.

Assuming another's role can be burdensome and create anger, resentment, and hostility. Indeed, the emotional tension of the family increases, and much anxiety is experienced by each member. This tension and anxiety are not openly dealt with and may serve as the basis for an ever-increasing conflict.

Coleen's boyfriend, Joe, contacted a therapist when Coleen's behavior dramatically changed about a month after the death of her mother. She was unable to go to work or to concentrate on reading or cooking (her previous interests) and refused to speak with him about anything. She physically would go into another room away from him or any other person.

Joe had handled Coleen's finances since her mother's death and made arrangements for her time off with her employer. He managed all of her activities of daily living for her with the exception of her self-care endeavors. He related to the therapist that he was exhausted, felt neglected, and did not know how much longer he could go on.

Minor problems may escalate to major issues. Former problem-solving abilities begin to be limited, and negotiations between spouses and siblings decrease.

The family begins to live in negativity; that is, they believe that they cannot do something, they will never be able to accomplish a goal; or things will never be good again. Patterns of living together begin to be influenced by a focus on what cannot be done rather than on what their previous goals were.

In many cases, apathy results. The ever-increasing tension serves as a force that prevents individuals from discussing and resolving emotionally laden issues. Those charged issues are referred to again and again and serve to stimulate recurring feelings of high emotionality, high anxiety, and a high degree of helplessness.

Jody and Dan, in their mid-30s, had been married for 15 years and had two children, ages 9 and 6 years. Five years ago Dan was fired from a position he had held for only 3 months. Jody was not working at the time, having given birth to the younger child just a few months before. When Dan lost his job, Jody immediately assumed full-time employment. At this point much tension was felt between the couple, Jody was furious at Dan for taking the job that she believed was "over his head." She was also angry at his "ability" to sit on the couch while she tended to her job, the house, and the children. All former patterns of communication between them stopped; they stopped sleeping together and having sex. Jody paid the bills without consulting Dan. When he did find employment, Jody sought treatment, saying she had a "rotten" marriage. Six years into the depression, this couple appeared for assistance.

The expression of angry feelings is quite common in much human communication. In a family where depression is the theme, however, angry feelings are not worked or processed to resolution. Anger is free-floating and serves as a self-escalator. The intense feelings may be expressed verbally, may be expressed physically as abuse, or may be internalized by individuals.

In spite of the uncomfortable feelings and thoughts that the family is experiencing, these families are also quite resistant to change. They appear to be stuck and may listen to observations and possible interventions to facilitate a change, but are reluctant to modify their behaviors. Some therapists conclude that the family is enjoying the dysfunction. This is usually an incorrect assumption.

The depression is as frightening to leave as it was when it began. Once the patterns begin, the "stuck" quality of the family process seems as though it is bonded with glue or even quicksand.

Effects on Members

Any member of the family may respond to a depressed family system with a variety of reactions. Any of the responses may affect any of the members, without regard to gender or age. None of the effects produces a positive result.

PROBLEMS WITH SELF-ESTEEM

When an individual lives with shame, doubt, and disparagement, the long-term effect on self-esteem is negative. A variety of unhealthy "fixes" to low self-esteem are sometimes used to decrease the pain that this creates.

POWERLESSNESS

Individuals begin to believe that they have no power to complete, fix, or control factors in their lives. This feeling and belief system of powerlessness is self-perpetuating. Somewhere it must be broken, and the individual and family must learn what they *do* have the power to control or handle.

CHRONICITY

Chronicity is also a process that may have much to do with a multigenerational process. If a family believes that depression will always be a part of life and there is no way to control it, it becomes a part of the family theme.

FEARFULNESS

Fearfulness is another symptom of remaining unchanged and stuck in the same self-perpetuating negative patterns. The fear is usually connected to both "what will the future bring" and "will it always be this bad?"

LONELINESS

As an interpersonal phenomenon, this experience is one of dread, shame, and self-doubt. In depressed families, many individuals live collectively in their own isolated loneliness.

VULNERABILITY

This concept brings with it the risk of something worse happening to the individual if he or she changes beliefs. In many instances, depressed families are vulnerable for severe illness or death. In most cases, physical health is lacking.

LACK OF COMPETENCE

As they grow, individuals from depressed families do not believe in themselves, their value, worth, or abilities. Any rewards they receive are negated by them as not being valuable enough.

IMPAIRED SOCIAL ROLE FUNCTION

Connected with lack of competence is an individual's and family's inability to learn how to manuever and interact in society. Often maladaptive behaviors are learned and thought to be correct.

EXAGGERATION OF PAST FAILURES

Because the depressed family processes so much information in a negative fashion, they are constantly reminded of past failures. These failures are reminders to them of how bad things are and are used frequently to reorient themselves and their members. As these stories are related, they usually grow and are expanded — into further negativity.

INDIVIDUAL GROWTH PLATEAU

All members of depressed family systems do not grow and develop their true abilities. Internal mechanisms limit or hold them back from their potentials. Obstacles block their goals; some of the obstacles are of their own construction.

• • •

In addition, many other health disabilities are a consequence of depression. These include but are not limited to suicide, alcoholism, drug abuse, and other addictions.

REFERENCES

Beck, Aaron T. (1967). *Depression: Causes and treatment.* Philadelphia: University of Pennsylvania Press.

Beck, Aaron T. (1988). *Love is never enough.* New York: Harper & Row.

Belenky, M.F., McVicker, B., Goldberger, N.R., & Tarule, J.M. (1986). *Women's ways of knowing.* New York: Basic Books.

Bowen, M. (1986). *Family therapy in clinical practice.* Northvale, NJ: Jason Aronson.

Buckwalter, K.C., & Babich, K.S. (1990). Psychologic and physiologic aspects of depression. *Nursing Clinics of North America, 25,* 4.

Burns, D.C. (1980). *Feeling good: The new mood therapy.* New York: Morrow.

Burns, D.C. (1989). *The feeling good handbook.* New York: Morrow.

George, L.K., Blazer, D.G., Hughes, D.C., & Fowler, N. (1989). Social support and the outcome of major depression. *British Journal of Psychiatry, 154,* 478-485.

Keitner, G.I., & Miller, I.W. (1990). Family functioning and major depression: An overview. *American Journal of Psychiatry, 147,* 9.

Kelly, G.L. (1991). Childhood depression and suicide. *Nursing Clinics of North America, 26,* 3.

Kerr, N.J. (1988). Sign and symptoms of depression and principles of nursing intervention. *Perspectives in Psychiatric Care, 24,* 48-63.

Lin, N., Dean, A., & Ensel, W. (1986). *Social support, life events, and depression.* New York: Academic Press.

Lum, T.L. (1988). An integrated approach to aging and depression. *Archives of Psychiatric Nursing, 2,* 211-217.

McCullough, P.K. (1991). Geriatric depression: Atypical presentations, hidden meaning. *Geriatrics, 46*(10), 72-76.

Mondimore, F.M. (1990). *Depression.* Baltimore: Hopkins Press.

Morin, G.D. (1990). Seasonal affective disorder, the depression of winter: A literature review and description from a nursing perspective. *Archives of Psychiatric Nursing, IV,* 182-187.

Scarf, M. (1980). *Unfinished business: Pressure points in the lives of women.* New York: Doubleday.

Schneidman, E. (1985). *Definition of suicide.* New York: John Wiley & Sons.

Seligman, M.E.P. (1975). *Helplessness.* San Francisco: Freeman.

Styron, W. (1990). *Darkness visible.* New York: Random House.

Tavris, C. (1982). *Anger: The misunderstood emotion.* New York: Touchstone Books.

Viorst, J. (1986). *Necessary losses.* New York: Simon & Schuster.

Weissman, M.M., & Klerman, G.L. (1987). Gender and depression. In R. Formanek & A. Gurian (Eds.), *Women and depression: A lifespan perspective.* New York: Springer.

Chapter 19

Borderline Families

Pamela E. Marcus

This chapter provides an overview of the behavior exhibited by people who are diagnosed with a borderline personality disorder. A review of some concepts of Bowen's family systems theory is presented to provide a context to examine the interactions of borderline families. Family relationships and interactions are examined to determine the impact these have on a person developing a borderline personality disorder. An exploration of early family trauma is considered as it relates to the development of this personality disorder. The response family members demonstrate to the symptoms of borderline personality disorder are considered as they relate to how these behaviors manifest and perpetuate in a predictable fashion. In light of this information, implications for therapeutic interventions are then discussed.

The following is an example of an individual with borderline personality disorder who demonstrates some of the acting out behavior that often brings the patient into the treatment setting.

Case Study

Melissa is a 26-year-old single woman who has been in therapy with a psychiatric clinical specialist for the past 3 years. She has been in a stormy relationship for the last 2 years, which broke up last week. Her initial response to her boyfriend's leaving was to become angry and critical. She would call his house and leave venomous messages on his answering machine, accusing him of leaving her for someone prettier or telling him how much pain she is in due to his leaving. He did not respond to her messages; after a week of calling several times a day, she took an overdose of acetaminophen. She called him shortly after taking the pills to tell him that "she will be out of his life forever, and that she still loves him." He responded by calling an ambulance and met her in the emergency room in a remorseful mood.

Melissa was emotionally labile in the emergency room—one minute full of tears and the next, angry and spitting fire. She was critical of the nursing staff and saw their giving her activated charcoal as a means of poisoning her to "complete the task." She began to scream that she would bring a lawsuit against them for murdering her. The psychiatric team was called to evaluate her and recommended hospitalization.

Diagnostic Criteria for Borderline Personality Disorder

Because of the stigma that has been placed on patients with borderline personality disorder, it is very important that the diagnosis be made after careful consideration. One useful method is to compare the behaviors exhibited by the patient to several criteria, such as those outlined by the *Diagnostic and Statistical Manual of Mental Disorders,* Third Edition, Revised (D.S.M. III-R); Gunderson (1984); and Masterson (1976). These three descriptions of the symptoms exhibited by those with borderline personality disorder are outlined below, as well as how these behaviors are demonstrated by clients frequently encountered by nursing staff.

The D.S.M. III-R states that a person with borderline personality disorder demonstrates a "pervasive pattern of instability of mood, interpersonal relationships, and self image, beginning by early adulthood and present in a variety of contexts." To satisfy the criteria, a person must meet five of the following eight:

- A pattern of unstable and intense interpersonal relationships characterized by alternating between extremes of overidealization and devaluation
- Impulsiveness in at least two areas that are potentially self-damaging
- Affect instability; marked shifts from baseline mood to depression, irritability, or anxiety, usually lasting a few hours and only rarely more than a few days
- Inappropriate, intense anger or lack of control of anger
- Recurrent suicidal threats, gestures, or behavior, or self-mutilating behavior
- Marked and persistent identity disturbance manifested by uncertainty about at least two of the following: (1) self-image, (2) sexual orientation, (3) long-term goals or career choice, (4) type of friends desired, and (5) preferred values
- Chronic feelings of emptiness or boredom
- Frantic efforts to avoid real or imagined abandonment

Gunderson (1984) outlined seven criteria that grew out of a decade of research and his interpretation of the existing empirical and clinical evidence gathered before these criteria. These are listed in approximate order of importance:

- Intense unstable interpersonal relationships
- Manipulative suicide attempts
- Unstable sense of self
- Negative affects
- Ego-dystonic psychotic experiences
- Impulsivity
- Low achievement

Masterson (1976) developed his criteria for borderline personality disorder by studying the concepts of ego-psychology and the role the mother plays during the separation-individuation phase of development (18 to 36 months of age). He outlines six feelings that are tied to feelings of abandonment and against which the client defends during his or her entire life. These six constituent feelings are the following:

- Depression
- Anger and rage
- Fear
- Guilt
- Passivity and helplessness
- Emptiness and void

The client handles the awareness of these feelings by denial of the separation, projection, clinging, and avoidance. These abandonment feelings are so intense that they are split off from the client's awareness but are observable due to the defense mechanisms employed to keep them in check. These defenses block the client's developmental growth from the stages of separation-individuation to autonomy. The client becomes stuck in one of the subphases of the separation-individuation stage. This has ramifications, because it relates to being able to achieve object constancy.

Masterson (1976) points out four consequences of the inability to achieve object constancy:

- The client does not relate to objects (persons) as wholes but as parts.
- The object relationship does not persist through frustration but tends to fluctuate widely.
- The client is unable to evoke the image of the person when he or she is not present.
- The client cannot mourn.

These consequences have important ramifications in the therapeutic relationship, because there will be times of frustration, as well as feelings of abandonment, due to the boundary setting and work that is done within this relationship. Masterson states that there is a persistence of the primitive defense mechanisms, such as splitting. Splitting is when the person sees only a "good" side or a "bad" side to another person. Only one of these opposites is at work at any given time; there is only black or white, but no gray. Therefore the client has a narrow view of the world, because he or she can see only one side to a problem or person.

Gunderson (1984) describes the concept of splitting as the "inability to synthesize contradictory good and bad self or other representations." When splitting is seen on a nursing unit, the client senses the natural rift that may be taking place between staff members and plays on this by picking up on the topic of disagreement and going from staff member to staff member discussing this issue. For example, during a vacation the attendant physician saw one of my clients in my absence. Because of the content of the session, the physician lengthened the session. On my return, the client repeated several times how the physician cared for her more than I did, because he spent more time with her in his sessions than I schedule. Indeed, this client had picked up on an area of professional disagreement; however, this issue was used as a therapeutic tool for the client to learn that there may be different ways to work on the same problem.

The earlier case example of Melissa can be used to look at her behavior in the context of a borderline personality disorder as the Axis II diagnosis. This shows how using the three types of diagnostic criteria helps highlight some of the problem areas and will drive further assessment questions and a nursing care plan.

Assessment

When evaluating Melissa, consider the following behaviors that fit the criteria for a borderline personality disorder. She is reacting to abandonment issues, using the defenses of depression, anger, rage, and fear (of being murdered). Splitting is evident, because she attacks the nurses for carrying out the physician's order to give her the activated charcoal. Clinging is demonstrated by her multiple phone calls to her boyfriend, and when he does not respond, she attempts suicide to exact a saving response from him. The boyfriend hears her call about her overdose and obtains help for her.

In this example, one also begins to get a picture of a chaotic, emotionally intense relationship. Further questions need to be asked about this relationship later, after Melissa is medically stable and able to talk about her problems. In exploring further with her during the next session, questions about her sense of self will be enlightening in terms of further intervention. Questions to ask are How does she see herself? What goals does she have? How does the relationship fit into these goals? Does she have other people who are supportive of her in her life? What is her family like? Is anyone available to provide emotional support? It will be important to determine the status of the relationship with her boyfriend, so that plans can be made depending on whether the psychotherapy will be addressing the loss of the relationship or problem solving the emotionally charged issues.

Planning

The initial plan was to provide medical care to stabilize Melissa after her overdose. She was admitted to the critical care unit for brief observation, due to changes in her liver enzymes. She was then transferred to the psychiatric unit for a brief admission. On admission to this unit a family history would be obtained to help to determine where there is support and what issues will further inflame the crisis.

In surveying the literature, one finds that there are a small number of articles relating to borderline families. Some of the highlights are presented here to broaden the understanding of the borderline individual in the context of his or her family.

Family Dynamics

Wolberg (1973) describes family dynamics that can contribute to borderline development as a hierarchy of acceptance-rejection patterns among family members, which reflect the attitudes of the parents. Wolberg proposes that "borderlines are less rejected than the schizophrenics, but more rejected than the neurotics." Wolberg reports that borderline clients have very disturbed mothers; she outlines four categories:

- The severe obsessive-compulsive mother
- The narcissistic, competitive mother with strong masculine qualities
- The paranoid mother
- The passive schizophrenic-like mother

Wolberg categorizes the fathers of borderline patients in the following manner:

- The passive-aggressive father who seems a schizoid type and withdrawn
- The hostile, aggressive, attacking, and controlling father
- The paranoid father
- The mildly psychopathic father

These descriptions of the parents' pathologic condition help Wolberg understand the client's acting out and sexual confusion as they relate to a reaction of the client's parents' behavior in the oedipal period. She outlines postulated behavior of the client during that developmental period, taking into account thoughts about which parent is more rejecting, which one more accepting, and what that does to the client's personality development.

Shapiro et al. (1977) described the borderline client's ego deficits to determine appropriate therapeutic interventions that would be most effective for the client. They describe splitting as a defense against an unconscious perception that the aggressive drives are so powerful that the internalized "good" object will be destroyed. They state that limit setting will correct this perception by providing structure and support for negative transference responses and that these do not destroy the actual object relationship. These authors worked with families of borderline adolescents, and they report that the adolescent period brings a time of family regression while the borderline personality struggles with the issues of separation-individuation. The families show a tendency towards splitting, which parallels that of the borderline personality. "Within the family group attributes of 'goodness' (providing, gratifying, loving) and 'badness' (depriving, punishing, hating) are separated one from the other and reinvested in different members so that each family member appears relatively preambivalent and single-minded in relation to the troubled adolescent." The authors state that parents of the borderline adolescent had difficulty in their own separation-individuation phase, and unconsciously see themselves as autonomous, or "good," or as dependent, or "bad." The negative self-perception is denied and projected onto the borderline child. The child's ego formation is developmentally impaired due to the intensity of the interrelated system of splitting and projective identification.

The authors state, "Motivated by his inability to tolerate either parental anxiety or his own anxiety over the possible loss of parental love, the borderline child unconsciously attempts to modify his subjective experience in accordance with these projections." The authors point out that the therapy process intensifies these dynamics in the transference. The therapist must assist the patient in distinguishing reality from overwhelming fantasy. Shapiro et al. (1977) believe that family therapy is helpful in assisting the client to develop an observing ego. In the family setting, the therapist can focus on the projective identification between the parents and the adolescent by using the therapist's ability to observe. Objectivity is maintained, and the therapist can clarify the nature of the family dynamics for interpretive use in managing the individual transference. The information about the family interactions is used in individual sessions where the interpretation assists client understanding and psychologic growth. It is important to note that during the individual sessions, the therapist does not take sides with the adolescent or the parents but assists the adolescent to observe his or her own part in the dynamics, so that the client can determine the reality of the regressed family behavior from the projected distortions and unconscious fantasies. A second therapist is used to provide marital therapy for the parents. In this way the parents can use the second therapist's observing ego in the same way the adolescent uses the individual psychotherapist.

Gunderson et al. (1980) studied characteristics of the families that had a member that was diagnosed as having a borderline personality. They conducted a study comparing variables, such as marital difficulty in the parental dyad, discomfort with the parental roles, psychopathologic conditions of the mother and father, alliances and splits among family members, turmoil among the siblings, and nonprotective, unstable family unit, which included such items as family rules and enforcement of them, alternate periods of withdrawal and intrusiveness, loss of parents, volatility of affects of family members, and active efforts of the family members to prevent the client from separating. There were 72 items in total, and the study population consisted of 12 families with a borderline member, 12 families with a schizophrenic member, and 12 families with a person diagnosed with a neurotic personality disorder. The parents' marriage in borderline families was characterized as having a "rigid tight bond, to the exclusion of the attention, support, or protection of the children." Neglect was seen as a major family theme. Another important characteristic of the borderline family was the use of projection or splitting. The employment of the projection to the children is consistent with tight nonconflictual marriages, because the unwanted and hostile aspects of the parents would be projected onto the children. Splitting can be recognized in the family when one child is described as the "good" child and one the "bad" child. These roles may change depending on the child's needs and how disruptive he or she is in terms of needing attention or support from the parents. "This pattern may be similar to the pattern seen in families where dependent demands by borderline adolescents are repudiated, denied, or withdrawn from." In fact, it seems that families with a member who has borderline personality disorder frequently ignore that member's acting out, which can become severe at times. This study found more psychopathologic conditions in the mothers, but not in a pattern as suggested by Masterson, who states that all those with borderline personalities have mothers with borderline personalities. One similar characteristic of the mothers in Gunderson's study (1984) was the denial of the psychopathologic condition of their borderline children. Gunderson et al. (1980) do not recommend family therapy in the early therapeutic work with the borderline individual. They believe that the borderline individual will heighten the parents' anxiety by their blaming and may promote a volley of accusations that may jeopardize the therapeutic alliance and the therapeutic work.

Herman et al. (1989) reported on their hypothesis that a history of childhood trauma is very common in clients who have a borderline personality disorder. Their sample consisted of subjects in a longitudinal study of borderline personality disorder, who they compared with subjects with related diagnoses of schizotypal personality disorder, antisocial personality disorder, and bipolar II affective disorder. Childhood histories were obtained by a 100-item semi-structured interview administered by Herman and van der Kolk. These interviews were scored for positive indexes of trauma in three areas: physical abuse, sexual abuse, and witnessing domestic violence. In addition to the structured interview, the subjects completed the impact of event scale, which measures current symptoms of posttraumatic stress disorder, and the dissociative experiences scale, which quantifies familiarity with dissociative states.

These authors found that the borderline subjects "suffered from abusive experiences more commonly than others but also reported more types of trauma, beginning earlier in childhood and repeated over longer time periods, resulting in higher total trauma scores." They conclude that childhood abuse is an "important antecedent to the development of borderline personality disorder." The reason for the higher incidence of women with this disorder is thought to be that sexual abuse is prevalent and more prolonged than is physical abuse and occurs more often to females. They discuss conceptualizing the borderline personality disorder as a complicated posttraumatic syndrome. This has implications for the treatment of these clients.

Goldstein (1990) identified three types of borderline families after conducting a study that involved administering the Kernberg structural interview and Gunderson's diagnostic interview for borderlines. Evaluation of the families were made in four areas: parental attitudes toward the identified patient, the nature of parent-child relationships, the nature of family conflict, and the nature of the parents' marital relationship. This study identified three family types: the overinvolved family, the rejecting family, and the idealizing or denying family. The overinvolved family is intense and overtly hostile and demonstrates a conflict that involves the client. These families are tightly enmeshed. Splitting is evidenced by one parent who was idealizing, needy, and overprotective of the client, while the other was devaluing, aloof, and rejecting. The parents have difficulty separating from the client. The alienated or rejecting families view the client as different, unwelcome, "bad," or the "enemy." The family believes that life would be peaceful if only the client would not disrupt it. The parents did not acknowledge any marital difficulties and seemed to have a tight bond that excluded the client. Marital problems were blamed on the client. In the idealizing or denying families, the family members view each other as perfect. There was minimizing of the client's difficulties. There is complete denial of any family or marital problems; there is a perceived complete harmony in this family. Goldstein (1990) points out the importance of recognizing the pathologic traits of borderline families; the use of primary defenses such as splitting, denial, and projective identification; conflicts around autonomy and dependence; and the presence of archaic self-object needs. Looking at the family patterns she has identified, as well as understanding the importance of the primary defenses, has implications in promoting a psychotherapeutic alliance with both the client and the family members.

Assessment of Family System

To significantly intervene in helping a person make important and lasting change, the nurse must assess the family system. The concepts employed here are from Bowen's family systems theory. Bowen (1976) described a theory that was based on observation and conceptualized behavior as part of a scientific system. He described systems thinking as focusing on what happened, how, when, and where, as opposed to why. This was viewed as a means of separating the functional facts from the subjectivity of emotional systems. This discipline of focusing on the facts of the relationship system assists the therapist not to get tangled in the emotionally charged content of the communication.

There are two main variables in Bowen's systems theory: the degree of integration of self and the level of anxiety. The ability to define one's self in the family system is a main concept in this theory. This definition includes a sense of self, as well as the abilities to problem solve and separate emotional and intellectual functioning. The more fusion, or lack of differentiation in the family system, the more decisions are made based on emotions, rather than cognition. Individuals in such a system are less flexible, less able to adapt to changes, easily stressed, and seem to have more problems. The borderline family falls in this category, because the fusion in the family system is extensive and problem solving is done more impulsively and based on emotions, as opposed to thinking through options. The anxiety in this family is quite high, because most of the energy is focused on seeking love and approval and in keeping chaotic relationships in balance. Another important concept is triangles. Bowen states that a triangle is a "three person emotional configuration, is the molecule or the basic building block of any emotional system, whether it is in the family or any other group." The movement of communication among the members of a triangle is predictable. In a period of a low anxiety, two members are comfortably close, with the third a less comfortable outsider. Movement is always occurring in a triangle — even in periods of calm — as the twosome strive to maintain the comfortable balance, while the third attempts to get close to one member of the twosome. In periods of moderate tension, one of the twosome feels uncomfortable, while the other is unaware of this feeling. The person feeling the tension moves toward a more comfortable space — one where self-integrity can be maintained. In periods of stress, the outside position is the most favored, because it provides an escape from the tension of the twosome. When there is not an opportunity to obtain the distant outside position, one member of the twosome involves a fourth person in the triangle, leaving the former third person aside for reinvolvement later. A common example that occurs frequently in borderline families is that there is a distance in the marital dyad and the child tries to get close to the parents by doing more than his or her share of responsibility around the house, and one of the parents becomes overinvested in the child, further distancing the spouse. Boundaries are blurred, and the child is treated similar to an adult in the system. When tensions in this type of system become high, the child is likely to receive blame and the emotionality that should be dealt with in the parental dyad. The concept of triangles gives the therapist an opportunity to observe and predict the family communication patterns over time, because triangles repeat their processes in a predictable pattern. Cain (1976) highlights the importance of this concept by saying, "If one can modify the functioning of one member of the triangle, and the other members of that system stay in emotional contact with each other, one can effect change in the whole system."

Case Study

Julie, a 24-year-old married mother of one child, described herself as the parent of all six of her siblings and a mother to her mother. Her father was often drunk or angry, and people stayed out of his way. Julie noted that she was often overwhelmed currently and expected her 3-year-old daughter to sit quietly and read "like a good girl." Her daughter was unable to do that, and Julie would become verbally abusive. Her husband stayed late at work or would leave the house when Julie's screaming became loud. Julie would then become even more upset and angry. Her daughter would cry, and soon Julie would feel like hurting herself. The pattern in this family is evident. Julie was the focused child in her family of origin. She had more than her share of responsibilities yet was unable to mother appropriately in her own family of procreation. Julie's husband took the outside position and became unavailable to both his wife and his daughter.

The first therapeutic goal with this family would be to reduce the anxiety in this system, observe the triangles, and assist Julie to observe her current mothering to decrease the verbal abuse and feelings of being overwhelmed with responsibility. Julie gave a history of having to parent her siblings, as well as "mothering her mother." It would be important in the early part of therapy to obtain a three-generational history. This would give an opportunity to observe how the people in this system relate to one another, as well as any patterns that occur within one generation or between generations. Pay particular attention to a history of family members with personality or psychiatric disorders, as well as conflictual, hostile, or abusive interactions within the family. Questions that relate to early loss or separation are important, because most theorists view those with borderline personality disorder as having a deficit in completing the separation-individuation stage of development, particularly around the rapprochement subphase (15 to 22 months of age). Ask questions about any violence in the family, including whether there had been any incest or early sexual molestation. When obtaining information about the client's parents, ask about the marital interaction: Did the parents talk to one another? What did they talk about? Was there arguing? What was that like? Did either parent drink alcohol or use drugs? How often? What was their behavior like when they were intoxicated? Was there any violence in the family? What was that like? How often did it take place? Who was involved in the violence? Was anyone ever injured? Did the parents' marriage ever end in separation or divorce? When assessing these variables, it is helpful to keep in mind some of the research about borderline families.

Gunderson and Zanarini (1987) studied the possible antecedents of the development of borderline personality disorder. In the family incidence studies, he found a strong association between family members with the "dramatic" personality disorders (antisocial, borderline, histrionic, and narcissistic) and a family member with borderline personality disorder. In the reconstructions and family studies, he found that a psychopathologic condition in the mother was strongly associated with the development of borderline personality disorder. This finding builds on the earlier works of Kernberg, Masterson, and Gunderson by further emphasizing the difficulty an individual with borderline personality disorder has in the early ego development phase. Masterson (1976) indicates that the inability to successfully complete the rapprochement subphase reflects failures of the mother to provide sufficient support and consistent nurturing. Kernberg (1984) points out that developmental failure in this phase may be due to either insufficient or excessive maternal support. Gunderson's work (1980) shows that family influence plays a big role in the development of borderline personality disorder. He describes two major family patterns: one in which there is lifelong unavailability or neglect and one in which parents actively withdraw or whose presence is inconsistent during critical times of personality development. This is substantiated in the retrospective surveys and family studies that are reported by Gunderson and Zanarini (1987), who found that the family that fails to provide attention and support is strongly associated with the development of borderline personality disorder.

Stone (1990) described a longitudinal study of 500 patients who were hospitalized from 1963 to 1976 at New York State Psychiatric Institute. In this study, he described the following statistics of psychiatric illness in the parents of clients with a borderline personality disorder. Out of a total of 395 clients with such a disorder, 50 had at least one parent who was an alcoholic, 32 had a parent with a major affective disorder, and 10 had a parent with a borderline personality disorder. Stone studied the impact of life events—such as early loss, incest, and parental brutality—on the development of borderline personality disorder. He divided the losses into several categories, such as death of a parent before the client was age 16; death of a parent within 2 years of the client's hospitalization; divorce of the parents before the client was age 16; abandonment by a parent; death of a primary caretaker other than a parent within 2 years of hospitalization; suicide of a parent; adoption; critical illness of a parent, where death was imminent at the time the client was hospitalized; placement in foster care or in an orphanage; death of a sibling who had been alive for more than 5 years of the client's life; separation(s) of more than 6 consecutive months from a primary caretaker; birth out of wedlock, where the client never knew the father; and death of a stepparent before the client was age 16. Using early loss statistics based on studies conducted in the United States from 1963 to 1976, Stone found that clients in the study group had approximately double the average number of losses when compared with the control group.

Stone interviewed his clients to determine the incidence of sexual abuse and molestation. Half of the female clients in his study had been victims of incest. The severity of the abuse ranged from forced intercourse with a father to unforced petting with a sibling or another family member or known adult. There was a lower incidence of male clients having experienced incest in this study; however these data were collected early in the study, before the development of in-depth understanding of the sequelae of childhood sexual molestation. Stone states that incest and its psychologic side effects play a definitive role in the development of borderline personality disorder. Incest survivors often demonstrate the symptoms of borderline personality disorder because of the object-relational attitudes that grew out of the incest experience. The other important issue that Stone raises is that the incest survivor has often kept the sexual molestation a secret and subsequently has grave mistrust of others. This may account for other important secrets that are not brought up in psychotherapy. The client may misrepresent his or her own real history because of this mistrust.

Stone sees the effects of parental or caregiver brutality as one of the important environmental factors in the development of borderline personality disorder. He identifies "inappropriate anger" as one of the key symptoms of clients with the disorder. An assessment of early parental brutality is essential in caring for such a client. Questions about this topic must include those about verbal abuse and witnessing any physical or emotional abuse of other family members.

As the therapist begins to obtain information about Julie, she learns that Julie has problems sleeping and strange dreams that she is reluctant to share. As Julie begins to be less anxious and overwhelmed with her daughter, she tells the therapist that her dreams have been about an early memory of her father, with liquor on his breath, demanding that she kiss him in the mouth and touch his genitals. While telling the story, Julie becomes withdrawn, draws into a fetal position, and wimpers. The therapist uses supportive verbal feedback to assist Julie to feel accepted and "heard." This is a lifelong secret, one she has not even said aloud to herself since childhood. Working through this incident will take time and a careful understanding of how this early abuse contributes to her adult behavior, particularly her mothering style. Assisting Julie to mother her daughter in a healthful manner will perhaps help her daughter in the future.

Because of the nature of the borderline family, as described previously, one can predict the family's response to the family member with the disorder when he or she demonstrates symptoms. If the family has been the type that withdraws or was unavailable when the client was a child, that behavior will persist in the future.

Melissa's family system was impoverished of warmth and emotional support. Her mother became dependent on alcohol as a means of coping when Melissa's sister died when Melissa was 4 years old. Her father is an angry man. He continues to blame the medical profession for the sister's death from cancer 18 years before. He spends many hours away from the home fishing with his buddies. Melissa does not remember her parents talking together about things around the house without an angry battle over who was right. Melissa used to try to protect her mother from her father's rage, only to have her mother disappear into her alcoholic haze. When Melissa was a teenager, she had problems in school. Her father was verbally abusive, calling her "stupid" and "dumb." He told her that she was a burden on the family and that she should have died, rather than her sister. Melissa took her first drug overdose at the age of 16, after receiving a failing grade and feeling scared that her father would beat her to death. She was not hospitalized. After a visit to the emergency room, she was discharged home to her parents. Her father was supportive of her for a few days after that episode, which reinforced this behavior.

The family would stay away from Melissa because of her fiery temper. This isolation further increased her anxiety and abandonment issues. The cycle was repeated in her relationship with her boyfriend. At first their relationship was very close, physically oriented, and passionate. After 2 months, when he would not call as she expected, she would fly into a rage, he would distance, she would escalate her anger, and he would give in to keep the peace. This pattern continued for some time until he became angry and decided to end the relationship, hence the acetaminophen overdose and hospitalization. Melissa needs nursing care that is theoretically driven to decrease her acute symptoms and increase her understanding of her illness.

Kreisman and Straus (1989) identified a three-part communication system— Support, Empathy, and Truth (SET)—as a means of assisting clients with a borderline personality disorder when they are most symptomatic. The support phase of this system is a statement of personal concern for the client. It must be heartfelt, because clients are very sensitive to any stimuli that they perceive as being a pretense. The empathy statement acknowledges the pain and inner turmoil that the client with such a disorder experiences. The truth statement is one where the client's responsibility for self is emphasized. The truth statement assists the client to identify the problem that created the current crisis and possible options to deal with the dilemma.

An intervention that is important in Melissa's care is to enter a contract with her for her safety. One needs to evaluate the client's suicide potential, and place the client on an appropriate level of suicide watch until his or her impulses are in control. Often, nursing staff members feel manipulated by a suicidal borderline client and wonder whether placing the patient on a suicide watch "feeds into" the client's illness. However, if the staff members consider the previous information about the borderline family, the intervention to place the client on suicide watch makes sense, because it is the opposite behavior of the family of origin. The client will begin to feel cared for, and a budding trust may develop.

Another important intervention to consider with this type of client is involving him or her directly in the planning of care. This empowers the client and places the responsibility for problem solving directly on his or her shoulders, rather than staff members' taking the lead. The client will initially resist this, because of difficulty with the separation-individuation phase of development. Taking this into account, continuing to assist the client to define problem areas—especially when very emotional—will make a lasting impression for client growth. When staff members do not recognize the process of the client's psychopathologic condition, they tend to get caught in the emotional triangle and splitting occurs among them. The natural or emotionally charged staff issues are evident in staff meetings. An increase in the tension on the unit, as well as a rise in medication errors, occurs when staff members do not address and rectify the splitting. Morale decreases, and the staff system becomes a divided camp. The use of triangles and systems theory can assist staff members to look at the issues without the use of negative labels.

An important principle to keep in mind is boundary setting. The client needs to know consistent limit setting, such as the length of individual psychotherapy sessions, expectations for participation in the milieu meetings, medication compliance, and financial responsibilities. Family sessions may be helpful for the client to observe the role he or she plays in the family process, and the family members may learn a new way of relating to the client.

Providing psychotherapy to an individual with borderline personality disorder is a thoughtful process. Becoming tangled up in the emotional system often frustrates the therapist. The triangle runs a predictable pattern, and the client remains stuck in the symptom complex of anger, clinging, suicidal attempts, denial, withdrawal, and so on. Growth is painful, yet when taking into consideration some of the concepts discussed previously, psychotherapy with an individual with a borderline personality disorder can be rewarding for both the client and the therapist.

REFERENCES

American Psychiatric Association. (1987). *Diagnostic and statistical manual of mental disorders* (3rd Ed.). Washington, D.C.: American Psychiatric Association.

Bowen, M. (1971). Family therapy and family group therapy (pp. 42-88). In Kaplan, H.I., & Sadock, B. (Eds.), *Comprehensive group psychotherapy*. New York: Williams & Wilkins.

Bowen, M. (1976). Theory in the practice of psychotherapy. In Guerin, P.J. (Ed.), *Family therapy: Theory and practice* (pp. 42-88). New York: Gardner Press.

Brobyn, L.L., Goren, S., & Lego, S. (1987). The borderline patient: Systemic versus psychoanalytic approach. *Archives of Psychiatric Nursing, 1,* 172-182.

Cain, A. (1976). The role of the therapist in family systems therapy. *The Family, 3*(2), 65-72.

Freedman, S.K. (1988). Inpatient management of a patient with borderline personality disorder: A case study. *Archives of Psychiatric Nursing, 2,* 360-365.

Gallop, R. The patient is splitting: Everyone knows and nothing changes. *Journal of Psychosocial Nursing and Mental Health Services, 23,* 6-10.

Goldstein, E.G. (1990). *Borderline disorders: Clinical models and techniques.* New York: The Guilford Press.

Gunderson, J.G. (1984). *Borderline personality disorder.* Washington, D.C.: American Psychiatric Press.

Gunderson, J.C., Kerr, J., & Englund, D.W. (1980). The families of borderlines: A comparative study. *Archives of General Psychiatry, 37,* 27-33.

Gunderson, J.C., & Zanarini, M.C. (1987). Current overview of the borderline diagnosis. *The Journal of Clinical Psychiatry, 48,* 5-11.

Hartman, D., & Boerger, M.J. (1989). Families of borderline clients: Opening the door to therapeutic interaction. *Perspectives in Psychiatric Care, 25,* 15-17.

Herman, J.L., Perry, J.C., & van der Kolk, B. (1989). Childhood trauma in borderline personality disorder. *American Journal of Psychiatry, 146*(4), 490-495.

Hickey, B.A. (1985). The borderline experience: Subjective impressions. *Journal of Psychosocial Nursing and Mental Health Services, 23,* 24-29.

Higgins, C.V., Nihart, M.A., Buckwalter, K.C., & Stolley, J. (1987). Exploring the concept of manipulation in psychiatric settings. *Archives of Psychiatric Nursing, 1,* 429-435.

Kaplan, C. (1986). The challenge of working with patients diagnosed as having borderline personality disorder. *Nursing Clinics of North America, 21,* 429-438.

Kernberg, O.F. (1984). *Severe personality disorders: Psychotherapeutic strategies.* New Haven, Conn: Yale University Press.

Kreisman, J.J., & Straus, H. (1989). *I hate you—don't leave me: Understanding the borderline personality.* Los Angeles: The Body Press.

Masterson, J.F. (1976). *Psychotherapy of the borderline adult: A developmental approach.* New York: Brunner/Mazel.

Masterson, J.F. (1983). *Psychotherapy of the borderline adult.* New York: The Masterson Group.

McGlashan, T.H. (1985). *The borderline: Current empirical research.* Washington, D.C.: American Psychiatric Press.

McGlashan, T. (1986). The Chestnut Lodge follow-up study: Long-term outcome of borderline personalities. *Archives of General Psychiatry, 43,* 20-30.

O'Brien, P., Caldwell, C., & Transeau, G. (1985). Destroyers: Written treatment contracts can help curb self-destructive behavior. *Journal of Psychosocial Nursing and Mental Health Services, 23,* 19-23.

Piccinino, S. (1990). The nursing care challenge: Borderline patients. *Journal of Psychosocial Nursing and Mental Health Services, 28,* 22-27.

Shapiro, E.R., Shapiro, R.L., Zinner, J., & Berkowitz, D.A. (1977). The borderline ego and the working alliance: Indications for family and individual treatment in adolescence. *International Journal of Psychoanalysis, 58,* 77-87.

Stone, M.H. (1990). *The fate of borderline patients: Successful outcome and psychiatric practice.* New York: The Guilford Press.

Sweeney, D. (1987). Treatment of outpatients with borderline personality disorder. *The Journal of Clinical Psychiatry, 48,* 32-35.

Wolberg, A.R. (1973). *The borderline patient.* New York: Intercontinental Medical Book.

Chapter 20

Schizophrenia and the Family

Ann F. Baker

Case Studies

PAUL AND EILEEN K.

Paul and Eileen have been called to a family meeting with their son's (John, age 19) psychiatrist. Within the past year, John has been hospitalized three times for bizarre behaviors and aggression. After his last discharge, John stopped attending school and became agitated and hostile. Returning home one evening, he attacked his father; went on a violent rampage destroying appliances, windows, and furniture; and injured his sister Sally. John stated he "was told to do this by God." The treatment team has diagnosed John as a paranoid schizophrenic. The family is frightened by their inability to communicate with John and are especially afraid of the possibility of a recurrence of John's violent behavior. Ultimately, they want to know how this will alter his individual functioning and change their family life.

MEGAN B.

When her schizophrenia was stabilized, Megan, age 34, was very nurturing and caring toward her 3-year-old son Nick. However, protective services and other involved agencies monitored the home closely because of Megan's past neglect of her child when her symptoms intensified. Twice the child was involuntarily removed from the home due to safety, nutritional, and daily care deficits. Through the distractions of her illness, Megan continues to try to remain Nick's primary caregiver.

THE A. FAMILY

When Andrea married Bill, she was well aware of his past mental health difficulties but felt that their home life would be manageable as long as they closely attended to treatment issues. However, she has found that the lability of Bill's illness has made her dreams of a "normal," stable family life impossible. Exhausted, frustrated, and angry, Andrea sees herself as the caretaker and provider of a home with three children—their two daughters and Bill.

• • •

Although it is impossible to objectively rate the degree of stress, loss, and handicap resulting from any chronic illness, the impact of a family member suffering from a cyclic psychosis is particularly devastating for the ill individual and his or her family. The chemical balance that maintains a client's contact with reality is delicate; schizophrenia is marked by a cycle of exacerbations and remissions, with the frequency of remission periods diminishing over time — based on research review, Torrey estimates that only one third of those suffering a schizophrenic break can expect full recovery. With a recurring symptomatology of delusions, hallucinations, inappropriate affect, and defective abilities to interpret language and perceive reality, schizophrenia tends to distance, frighten, and offend society. Although the intensity and difficulties of a chronic illness in any other context would elicit social support and sympathy, the very nature and oddities of this illness elicit stares, avoidance, and embarrassment.

Because of the advent of more effective and manageable drug regimens, schizophrenics have been more stably maintained in the past 3 decades. Treatment venues have moved from long-term stays in state hospitals and institutions to periodic short-term admissions for chemotherapeutic adjustments and more intensive psychotherapeutic interventions. In addition to this, insurance companies have begun to implement stringent reviews and requirements as to the extent and level of services covered for patients. Many clients return home still symptomatic, requiring critical care, observation, and support (Anderson, 1983; Greiner, 1987). In this era of service curtailment, the family is replacing previously provided transitional care settings — step-down in-patient units, halfway houses, or foster care homes. The burden on families has increased exponentially; however, services, support, and education for these families have not (Bernheim, 1985).

Parents like Paul and Eileen K. in the previous case study have a significant impact on their child's progress and stability. The family will affect their child, and the complexities involved in caring for and working with him or her will have an impact on and change the family. Although the family may not yet fully understand the implications of chronic mental illness, they do understand the distress and disruption of an active psychosis. Treatment plans that focus solely on the individual are ineffective; to develop more comprehensive and appropriate family-oriented plans, nurses must understand family functioning and coping in this context and the critical role families play in the schizophrenic's attainment of personal stabilization and maintenance.

Conceptual Framework

The family system of the schizophrenic has a demanding amount of input with which to deal. Obviously, even before illness recognition, the family is bombarded with unusual and incessant input that requires constant system modification. This barrage of input does not decline after adjustment to diagnosis and initial treatment; rather, the family must continue to deal with changes in rule, role, and task structures. The demand for flexibility and adaptability is overwhelming; periods of constancy during remission are a much needed respite from this stressful variability.

Within the context of general systems theory, McCubbin's Double ABCX Model (1987) is useful in detailing a family's reaction to developmental transitions, stressors of daily living, and unexpected crises, such as managing the difficulties associated with a schizophrenic family member. In this model, "A" is the stressor precipitating the crisis. "B" represents existing family resources, both positive and negative. "C" is the family's perception of the situation. "X" is the crisis these factors lead to: situational family dysfunction, anxiety, and temporary immobilization as they seek to use resources and develop new coping responses.

For example, the timeliness and appropriateness of John K.'s treatment depended largely on his family's reaction to his symptomatology. When the "A" stressor recurred—John's aggression and delusions—the family formed the perception, "C," that John needed psychiatric intervention. Alternatively, they might have believed John needed to be criminally prosecuted and quickly emancipated from family connection. The family relied on their resources ("B")—strong family support, a sister with mental health work experience, good health insurance—to seek a solution through intensive in-patient treatment.

The model then delineates family progress after the crisis point. As the process of adaptation takes place, the factors "A," "B," and "C" change through family coping attempts. Stressors increase during the "X" crisis phase; the family is faced with many crucial choices and decisions, drawing heavily on their abilities and strengths, intensifying other troubled family areas, or wearing on family weaknesses. This stressor pile-up is denoted by "Aa." "Bb" represents new and old resources, including those learned and provided in the therapeutic setting, as well as those naturally developed during family transformation. The family's perception of the crisis will change as they move through adaptation—"Cc" marks this alteration. Positive or negative family adaptation is a product of the interactions of these factors, mediated by the use of coping mechanisms.

Again using the case study of John K., his family began to experience stressor pile-up (Aa) immediately after his hospital admission. Paul and Eileen found themselves split on the issue of John's treatment as Paul sublimated his feelings of failure and frustration into anger toward Eileen for "putting his son away." Because of the pressures at home and her need to focus more on John, Eileen quit work, resulting in her loss of support and social stimulation, as well as a substantial loss of income. However, through hospital referral, John's parents began to attend a local support group and eventually shared their troubles with their minister and church friends, thus developing new resources (Bb).

The family sought information on the diagnosis and began to understand schizophrenia, thereby diminishing their fears and misconceptions of the illness and John's behaviors (altered perceptions, Cc). All of these changes were linked together by new coping skills learned through therapy and in educational groups. For a family still newly christened to schizophrenia, they began to cope remarkably well.

Stressors

DEMANDS ON FAMILY RESOURCES

Caring for a chronic schizophrenic can be a continual burden and drain on family resources. Caretakers may curtail social and occupational activities to attend to the behavioral and observational needs of the client. However, this isolation from others eliminates sources of stress reduction and support, fueling burnout and exacerbating family tension and conflict. The schizophrenic's needs and issues become the sole focus of the family; they lack the energy or time to nurture or attend to other relationships. John's parents separated twice as they attempted to acclimate themselves to the impact of his illness; their daughter began to experience school and peer problems as her needs were neglected. Andrea and Bill A. in case study #3 believe the crucial factor in maintaining their marriage was the help of a family therapist who assisted them in focusing beyond the illness on to themselves, their marriage, and their children.

The continuing cost of medicine, therapy, and hospital stays taxes financial resources. Insurance policies often have a set cap for mental health services. Families must seek additional help from social services or private sources or face extreme financial hardship.

COMMUNICATION

The basis of all effective relationships is the ability to communicate clearly, openly, and honestly. Coping for the schizophrenic's family may be difficult due to impaired interactional patterns. Much research has focused on exploring the communication of families with a member at risk for or diagnosed with schizophrenia; these families have been assessed for four different variables: expressed emotion, emotional overinvolvement, communication deviance, and affective style.

Expressed emotion (EE) is an index of family members' emotional attitudes. High EE is characterized by higher amounts of criticism, hostility, and emotional overinvolvement (EOI). Communication deviance (CD) is an overall rating of a person's ability to interact clearly and coherently and includes items such as lack of commitment to ideas, unclear communication of terms, and disruptive speech. Affective style (AS) refers to the presence of statements of support, criticism, guilt induction, and intrusiveness.

Vaughn and Leff (1976) found that a critical or emotionally overinvolved family was a significant factor in precipitating schizophrenic relapse. Many studies have documented that vulnerable adolescents are more likely to develop a schizophrenic disorder if their families display high EE or EOI, poor AS, or high CD (Asarnow et al., 1982; Doane et al., 1981; Goldstein & Doane, 1981; Valone et al., 1984). Despite their best intentions to provide support care to the schizophrenic, families with a communication handicap may end up complicating the client's progress and suffer frustration, helplessness, and immobilization.

GUILT

Most families, and especially most parents, spend a great deal of thought and time attempting to discover a "cause" of their child's schizophrenia. If the family is somehow introduced to outdated theories, such as the schizophrenogenic mother or the double bind, their feelings of guilt and failure may prevent them from effectively adjusting to and working with the client. Some therapists sabotage family intervention because of their beliefs that family experiences or practices have caused or greatly complicated a client's schizophrenia (McFarlane, 1983; Terkelsen, 1983). Hatfield and Lefley (1987) point out that some mental health professionals distort the literature exploring family interactional patterns and covertly accuse families of providing an unhealthy and destructive home environment. Any implication may lead the sensitive family to withdraw from support and assistance necessary for treatment or may have a negative effect on their ability to provide behavioral structure, set limits, or develop realistic expectations for the schizophrenic (Bernheim, 1985).

If the illness predates a marriage, the spouse will have less guilt over the "cause" of his or her partner's schizophrenia. However, the spouse may feel guilty about normal family conflicts contributing to deterioration of illness stability. Also, the couple may struggle with the issue of procreation—not only considering the impact of the illness on the child, but also the possibility of a genetic component of causality. Indeed, children can struggle with the implications of having a schizophrenic parent; they too can experience guilt over angry thoughts, embarrassment, and feelings of responsibility for setbacks. Siblings of schizophrenics are not excluded from guilt—they suffer over the issues of their own survivorship and health, as well as their indifference toward the sibling (Samuels & Chase, 1979).

GRIEF

For young clients like John K., who are just beginning the transition into young adulthood with plans for college, career, and success, both the family and the client must accept that these goals may be unattainable. Although not unheard of, emotional and social stability are often not maintained at a level uniform enough to meet educational or employment goals. The family may experience chronic grieving and sorrow, because the cyclic nature of schizophrenia gives no definitive end point or lengthy respite to complete mourning. The loss is as enormous as and perhaps stronger than death—certainly the remainders of the "might have been" can be a vivid, distressing part of daily family life.

ROLES

Because of the schizophrenic's repeated exits and entries into the family system, role boundary ambiguity is often a problem. Even if a spouse or parent is physically absent for long periods, they still possess a psychologic family presence. Families may modify roles and boundaries during absences, only to have to realign the structure when the client returns and expects his or her roles, rights, and responsibilities to remain the same. In the case study at the beginning of the chapter, Bill A.'s children resented having to answer to a new, less respected, authority, while Andrea was unwilling to give up independent decision making when Bill reclaimed his family position.

Besides role ambiguity, schizophrenics and their families also struggle with functioning outside normal role expectations. During the normal developmental life cycle, parents work toward slowly relinquishing control and decision making to their children as they make the transition from childhood to adolescence to young adulthood. A schizophrenic's parents must cope with their child's being in a terminal state of adolescence. Just as an adolescent has immature decision-making and coping skills, so does a schizophrenic as his or her illness exacerbates or as he or she makes the transition toward a period of recovered stability. Parents of teenagers must judge when and where to allow for independent choice and self-accountability, allowing the child — in carefully controlled settings — to develop an understanding of the natural consequences of his or her decisions without risking serious repercussions or personal danger; the same is true for families of schizophrenics.

The adult schizophrenic wants to be respected and allowed to live a self-directed and fulfilling life. However, delusional thinking and the distractions of internal stimuli may interfere with planning, commitment, and rationale for actions. Families must negotiate a tenuous and sensitive balance between the need for protection and the need for independence. People can be especially uncomfortable with the parenting aspects of caring for a schizophrenic spouse. The transition through periods of limit setting and behavioral controls is a difficult and ambiguous time for the marital relationship. Andrea was required to monitor and guide Bill's behaviors — both of them resented this imposition on the previous equanimity of their relationship.

Chronic mental illness can interfere with a person's ability to parent his or her children effectively. As the illness worsens and a person's ability to attend to personal responsibilities and care diminishes, so does his or her ability to meet his or her child's needs. If the alternate parent or active extended family is available, the child's needs can be met by these sources. However, single schizophrenic parents may unwittingly put their children at risk. In the case study at the beginning of the chapter, Megan B. was a good mother, but with a limited support system and the intrusion of her symptoms, she did have problems maintaining a high-quality home life for Nick. Nick was confused by the changes in his mother's personality, her recurrent absences from home, and the involvement and attitudes of social service agencies.

STIGMA

The mass media have made a concerted effort to improve the understanding and acceptance of those suffering from acquired immunodeficiency syndrome (AIDS). However, this same source has dramatized and incorrectly portrayed mental illness as flamboyant and unmanageable, with none of the sympathy accorded in other chronic situations. It is no wonder that families are embarrassed and uncomfortable with the schizophrenic's difficulties during the exacerbation cycle, and it is equally understandable when they try to prevent this by withdrawing from social situations. Family education and changes in their perceptions can, in turn, lead to community education and changes — nursing can promote and provide the impetus to ease the burden of stigma and the complications of family isolation.

Dysfunctional Coping

Families often dismiss the first indications that a family member may be mentally unstable — facing the situation is, as pointed out, stressful and painful. Families deny, ignore, and minimize the patient's idiosyncrasies to maintain the family status quo. Although this coping choice delays intervention, it can provide a needed respite during which families can develop alternative strengths to deal with this chronic crisis. Bernheim et al. (1982) note that difficulty accepting a chronic, severe illness is normal. Acceptance of schizophrenia is especially difficult due to the cycle of severity — during periods of remission, it was hard for Megan B.'s family to believe she would ever experience decompensation again. These authors bring up another interesting point — professionals often are reluctant to "label" clients; however, the family can find it quite comforting to have a concrete explanation of the client's behavior, a platform from which they can begin to understand and plan for home care and support.

Coping and adjusting often result in anger, as family members try to avoid their fear and grief. Although anger can be used by the family to initiate action and temporarily avoid more dispiriting emotions, it can also undermine other sensitive family relationships when channelled into blame and conflict. Professionals might see this anger reflected in family comments and challenges about the efficacy and nature of the treatment.

Some families will ultimately be unable to overcome the extreme sense of guilt, shame, and failure this situation invites. Helpless and hopeless, they may feel that the schizophrenic would be better off without their interference and contributions to his or her symptomatology. This withdrawal eliminates a crucial center of support and stability in the schizophrenic's life and interferes with the family's obtaining therapeutic help and developing coping skills.

Functional Coping

SOCIAL SUPPORT

Anderson (1983) encourages the family to gradually "go public" with the nature of the family member's illness to decrease isolation. As their own comfort level with the facts increases, the family can introduce the diagnosis and issues to extended family members, then to friends, ministers, and other important support sources. Seeking additional social support from other families in similar circumstances is invaluable — to locate or initiate a local support group, families can be referred to the National Alliance for the Mentally Ill, 1234 Massachusetts, Ave., N.W., Washington, DC 20005. The intervention section of this chapter discusses nursing groups that would also provide this sense of connectedness and normalization.

COMMUNICATION SKILLS

As previously discussed, many of these families display dysfunctional communication patterns that can be linked to schizophrenic relapse. Introduction to and practice with assertive techniques will assist the family in simplifying and clarifying their interactions. Overall intervention helped Andrea A. move into a more "accepting" stage of Bill's illness; communication skill training helped her to alter her affective tone to positive, supportive, and encouraging statements and to express her feelings more honestly and clearly.

DEVELOPING REALISTIC EXPECTATIONS

The schizophrenic will not return home ready to resume his or her place in the family and society. The family should expect a continuation of the recovery period and should thus emphasize predictability and structure, encourage behavioral change and treatment compliance, and provide for gradual increases in autonomy and responsibility. Well-informed families will avoid disappointment and anxiety as the client slowly progresses and recuperates.

UNDERSTANDING PSYCHIATRIC TREATMENT

Many families feel isolated from the treatment effort. It is difficult to understand the structure and roles of the treatment team — and because psychiatric treatment is not nearly as defined as the treatment of such physical ailments as strep throat or ulcers, it may appear that the team is moving slowly or ambiguously in their efforts to meet the client's and family's needs. Hatfield and Lefley (1987) noted that families feel that psychiatrists fail to give practical or effective advice and that this lack of knowledge prevents them from providing effective continuity of care between hospital milieu and home environment. Education should therefore cover the facts of the illness and treatment, as well as the intricacies and vocabulary unique to the psychiatric treatment system.

SETTING LIMITS

In-patient or partial hospital settings provide a highly structured milieu. Many newly discharged clients are still unable to self-impose daily structure; therefore family members must be able to set limits with the client. Good limits are simple and predictable, specific and concrete. A behavioral contract, worked out with therapeutic assistance before discharge, is an effective way to eliminate guilt or inconsistency when setting and applying consequences for inappropriate behaviors.

Intervention

Although it would appear that many professionals and researchers recognize the significance of the family-schizophrenic relationship, it is painful to note that strong implementation of a treatment program geared toward the family is not the norm. Many professionals cite client confidentiality as a roadblock to meeting a family's need to understand and to cope; Bernheim et al. (1982) note that "[Families] . . . are asking not for a breach of confidentiality but simply for concrete advice." Others find family involvement a territorial threat and thus react defensively; sometimes a family's "contribution" or "dysfunction" is used to roadblock attempts to treat family issues and concerns respectfully and thoroughly.

Despite the research support that family-oriented, psychoeducational efforts do decrease relapse rates and increase remission times, most team focus is on the individual, with some ancillary, traditional family therapy (Anderson, 1983; Anderson et al., 1986; Falloon et al., 1982; Vaughn & Leff, 1976). Family issues and needs should be a priority in treatment; in conjunction with traditional family and individual psychotherapy and chemotherapy, a support and education group solely for family members can be developed and implemented by nursing personnel. This treatment modality provides these isolated and stigmatized families with the absolutely crucial aspect of peer support and normalization, while at the same time offering an efficient and cost-effective means of meeting families' needs. Intervention discussion will therefore focus on the skeleton structure and implementation of such a group.

The psychoeducational group for families of schizophrenics is a program designed for psychiatric nurses attempting to meet the needs of families coping with schizophrenia. The purpose of the group is to provide education and support in depicted areas of need in a family-centered format. Through group work, the family is empowered to deal more effectively with situational crises and chronic stress. Overall objectives of the group are the following:

• To foster mutual support and cooperation within the family
• To increase family and individual self-confidence
• To improve family communication skills
• To increase understanding and acceptance of the schizophrenic
• To introduce the family to community resources and available services
• To increase the family's efficiency in managing resources
• To provide support and normalization of feelings and experiences
• To improve behavioral management techniques
• To improve problem-solving and stress management skills

PARTICIPANTS/SETTING

Although ideally this group would be composed solely of families of schizophrenics, smaller units and hospitals may need to open the group to all families with a chronically mentally ill relative; the nurse clinician would then provide specific diagnostic and chemotherapeutic information in individual sessions. A family intervention program described by Anderson (1983) is

geared solely toward families new to schizophrenia and psychiatric treatment — again, practicalities may lead to a group composed of these new families
and those who have been through several hospitalizations and need the support
or skills and information never provided to them before. Preferably, the client
should be excluded from the family support group — this allows the family to
freely express themselves without guilt and fear of repercussion.

Recruitment to the group could be facilitated by scheduling a 1- to 1½-hour
time block immediately after a popular visiting hour. Even if a family does not
recognize a need for education and support, the convenience of already being
at the hospital and the encouragement of staff and other attending families
might entice them to sit in on the session. If the setting is out-patient or partial,
a weekend or evening time, coinciding with a client's therapy or activity might
boost attendance. Other members of the treatment team can encourage
families to attend during family therapy, and the client may also be an active
recruiter if he or she understands the importance of the group.

LEADERSHIP STYLE

Although the essence of psychoeducational technique is to provide both
support and education, Hatfield and Lefley (1987) note that professionals often
try to force families to fit a set model, holding to a highly structured content
and format, with little regard for the families' individuality. Time must be
allowed for families to express their feelings for the nurse to understand how
to meet each group's unique needs. The objectives may be best achieved by
accepting the following guidelines:

- Families can learn and benefit from sharing with each other in group.
- Group participants are basically in control of and responsible for their own
  learning in the group setting.
- A guided family support and education group will facilitate individual and
  family growth and understanding.
- The roles of the leader are to provide information and to facilitate discussion
  and structured learning activities.
- Each group member can and will speak up for himself or herself during the
  session.
- No group member has the right to speak for another during a session.
- The group leader will avoid introducing his or her own beliefs and values with
  the expectation that group members should or will agree with them.
- Group leaders will foster a supportive environment to maximize the potential
  for learning and sharing.
- Group leaders will refrain from offering unilateral advice or definitive
  answers; rather, as issues arise, they will focus on alternative approaches,
  encouraging the group and individuals to discuss and determine what works
  best for their particular situation.

ASSESSMENT

Although therapy often provides a thorough social and family history, the family
psychiatric nurse should further explore family attributes specific to the group

objectives: stressors, resources, perceptions, and coping methods. Obtaining this information assists in making appropriate treatment decisions and interventions and also demonstrates an interest and concern for the family. A strong therapeutic alliance with the families encourages openness to support and learning.

McCubbin and McCubbin (1987) detailed two tools that could assist the nurse in delineating a family's needs and increase the family's self-awareness of their adaptive state. Family Inventory of Life Events (FILE) is a 71-item, self-report instrument that records normative and non-normative family stressors, hardships, and strains experienced within the last year. Family members complete the form either together or separately, covering specific areas of illness, care-taking burdens, losses, financial or resource strains, and intrafamilial difficulties. The form is simple and easy and tests to high validity.

Family Inventory for Resources and Management (FIRM) assesses family resources, providing a basis for the practical guidance families cite as vital but lacking. Consisting of 98 self-report items, the instrument covers four major areas: esteem and communication, mastery and health, extended family support, and financial well-being. Again, the scales have high validity and stability.

CONTENT

Although the nurse leader will try to maintain flexibility in her or his response to participants' input, prepared content addressing crucial issues and skills will be used every session. Discussion about Paul and Eileen K.'s concerns regarding John's home behaviors involved group support and normalization, other participant advice, and then a short nursing presentation with handouts on behavioral management techniques. Ask families what their priorities are — if information is outside of the nurse's expertise, the concern can be placed on hold and an appropriate answer referenced and developed for the next session. The following topics can be considered as a beginning agenda for content development:

- Diagnosis and treatment information
- Purposes, actions, and side effects of psychotropics
- Functional and dysfunctional coping strategies
- Community resources for therapy, support, and assistance
- Grief — coping with chronic sorrow
- Assertive communication techniques
- Diffusing family energy — focusing on each member's needs
- Behavior management — the home milieu
- Monitoring the patient's progress — stress, symptoms, and early warning signs
- Coping with stigma
- Stress management and relaxation techniques
- Problem-solving skills

The nurse leader can promote use of content in several ways. By working with the team and staying abreast of the specifics of current cases, the nurse can avoid unwittingly alienating or angering a participant. This can also help the clinician in guiding discussion toward a topic that the team feels would be especially pertinent and helpful to a participating family; with practice, a group leader will be able to make a transition to certain educational material even tangentially linked to discussion. Ultimately, nurses can continue to promote and emphasize new skills by modeling them on the milieu and practicing them in individual interactions with clients and their families.

Another important agenda point is allowing open expression of family frustration and anger toward the mental health system. Although it may be difficult for a leader to remain undefensive, remembering that the anger is not personally — but instead universally — focused may help the leader to respond to these intense feelings with support and guidance, acknowledging the families' pain from powerlessness and grief. Finally, the families should be urged to continue involvement in support groups and referred to the level of intervention warranted by their progress.

EVALUATION

Group leaders can encourage participants to be open about both the positive and the negative aspects of the group process. The end of session input can involve goal setting for the next session, a time of closure, and feedback to and from participants and leader. An anonymous evaluation can be filled out at the end of each session or series of sessions, including such items as most and least valuable session, areas of improvement, and positive aspects of experience. Families also should be asked to rate and comment on leadership style and effectiveness. Pretests and posttests could be done to judge change in knowledge base before and after some of the more specific and complex content sessions. This would assist the nurse in determining whether more practice or discussion on the topic is necessary.

Ideally, a more in-depth evaluation could be implemented. Studies that support psychoeducational intervention follow both the families who attend and those who do not, assessing remission time and relapse rate. Other important variables are unexplored; a survey of family self-esteem and coping during treatment, both at time of discharge and at various follow-up contacts, would be a valuable perspective on treatment effectiveness. These studies could define whether this type of program helps families to achieve any of the following postprogram objectives:

- Full acceptance of the schizophrenia
- Resolution of anger and guilt related to the illness
- Recognition of and attendance to caregiver needs and issues
- Heightened sense of family self-worth
- Effective use of functional coping strategies

• • •

Families are placed in a pivotal, crucial role in the care of schizophrenics — psychiatric professionals should be exceedingly concerned about the family's abilities and appropriateness for the unfamiliar treatment regimen now introduced into their daily lives. The family and the schizophrenic are inseparable treatment entities — consideration of the family system in nursing care plans will produce more appropriate and effective care plans and interventions. Positive family adaptation can be facilitated by psychoeducational interventions that provide a strong foundation for more functional coping with this chronic stress. As family psychiatric nurses, we are challenged to recognize and advocate for the needs of these families by initiating the development of a family-based treatment approach, with an emphasis on education, empowerment, skill development, and support.

REFERENCES

Abramowitz, I.A., & Coursey, R.D. (1989). Impact of an educational support group on family participants who take care of their schizophrenic relatives. *Journal of Consulting and Clinical Psychology, 57*(2), 232-236.

Anderson, C. (1983). A psychoeducational program for families of patients with schizophrenia. In McFarlane, W. (Ed.), *Family therapy in schizophrenia,* New York: The Guilford Press.

Anderson, C., Reiss, D., & Hogarty, G. (1986). *Schizophrenia and the family.* New York: The Guilford Press.

Asarnow, J., Lewis, J., Doane, J., Goldstein, M., & Rodanick, E. (1982). Family interaction and the course of adolescent psychopathology: An analysis of adolescent and parent effects. *Journal of Abnormal Child Psychology, 10*(3), 427-442.

Bernheim, K.F. (1985). *Working with families of the mentally ill.* New York: W.W. Norton.

Bernheim, K., Lewine, R., & Beale, C. (1982). *The caring family: Living with chronic mental illness.* New York: Random House.

Clausen, J., & Runck, B. (1979). The mentally ill at home: A family matter. In Corfman, E. (Ed.), *Families today: A research sampler on families and children.* Rockville, Md.: National Institute of Mental Health.

Cook, B.J. (1990). *Schizophrenia and the family.* Seminar paper for Master's of Education degree. Athens, Ohio: Ohio University.

Doane, J., West, K., Goldstein, M., Rodnick, E., & Jones, J. (1981). Parental communication deviance and affective style: Predictors of subsequent schizophrenia spectrum disorders in vulnerable adolescents. *Archives of General Psychiatry, 38,* 679-685.

Falloon, I.R.H., Boyd, J., McGill, C., Razani, J., Moss, H.B., & Gilderman, A. (1982). Family management in the prevention of exacerbations of schizophrenia: A controlled study. *New England Journal of Medicine, 306,* 1437-1440.

Goldstein, M., & Doane, J. (1982). Family factors in the onset, course, and treatment of schizophrenic spectrum disorders. *The Journal of Nervous and Mental Disease, 170*(1), 692-700.

Greiner, D. (1987). Assessing families with chronic mental illness. In Leahey, M., & Wright, L. (Eds.), *Families and psychosocial problems.* Springhouse, PA: Springhouse.

Hatfield, A.B., & Lefley, H.P. (1987). *Families of the mentally ill: Coping and adaptation.* New York: Guilford Press.

Kreisman D., & Joy, V. (1974). Family response to the mental illness of a relative: A review of the literature. *Schizophrenia Bulletin, 10,* 34-54.

Lefley, H. (1989). Family burden and family stigma in major mental illness. *American Psychologist, 44,* 556-560.

Lukoff, D., Snyder, K., Ventura, J., & Nuechterlein, K. (1984). Life events, familial stress, and coping in the developmental course of schizophrenia. *Schizophrenic Bulletin, 10*(2), 258-289.

McCubbin, H., & Figley, C. (Eds). (1983). *Stress and the family: Coping with normative transitions.* New York: Brunner/Mazel.

McCubbin, M., & McCubbin, H. (1987). Family system assessment in health care. In McCubbin H., & Thompson, A. (Eds.), *Family assessment inventories for research and practice.* Madison, Wis.: University of Wisconsin–Madison.

McFarlane, W. (Ed.) (1983). *Family therapy in schizophrenia.* New York: The Guilford Press.

Raymond, M., Slaby, A., & Lieb, J. (1975). Familial responses to mental illness. *Social Casework,* October, 492-498.

Samuels, L., & Chase, L. (1979). The well siblings of schizophrenics. *American Journal of Family Therapy, 7*(2), 24-35.

Terkelsen, K.G. (1983). Schizophrenia and the family: Adverse effects of family therapy. *Family Process, 22,* 191-200.

Thompson, E., & Doll, W. (1982). The burden of families coping with the mentally ill: An invisible crisis. *Family Relations, 31,* 379-388.

Torrey, E.F. (1983). *Surviving schizophrenia: A family manual.* New York: Harper & Row.

Valone, K., Goldstein, M., & Norton, J. (1984). Parental expressed emotion and psychological reactivity in an adolescent sample at risk for schizophrenia spectrum disorders. *Journal of Abnormal Psychology, 93*(4), 448-457.

Vaughn, C.E., & Leff, S.P. (1976). The influence of family and social factors on the course of psychiatric illness. *British Journal of Psychiatry, 129,* 125-137.

West, K., Cozolino, L., Malin, B., Mcvey, G., Lansky, M., & Bley, C. (1985). Involving families in treating schizophrenia: The role of family education. In Lansky, M. (Ed.), *Family approaches to major psychiatric disorders.* Washington, D.C.: American Psychiatric Press.

Wynne, L. (1981). Current concepts about schizophrenics and family relationships. *Journal of Nervous and Mental Disease, 169*(2), 82-89.

Chapter 21

Dementia and the Family

Valerie Telford Cotter
Deanna Gray Miceli

Allowing for individual variations in the rate at which one ages, there are universal changes that one can expect as a part of the normal aging process. These changes are largely manifestations of physiologic change that occur in organ systems, tissues, and cells throughout the human body with age. These specific changes in organ system structure and function are considered part of the normal aging process when they encompass the global characteristics of being universal, irreversible, and decremental (Barrow, 1989).

Certain aspects of cognitive function seem to remain unchanged and may even improve with age, despite the normal physiologic age-related changes that occur in the brain structure (see the box on p. 357). Further results of studies that measure age-related changes in the human brain have failed to demonstrate that it is normal to experience a decline in cognition with age. In fact, the belief that it is normal to become "senile" with age is an erroneous myth that has no factual basis.

Research investigations have noted little decrease with advancing age in capacity to learn (Eisdorfer, 1977). Anecdotal observations reveal improvement in general information and wisdom as a function of age. Most researchers agree that general intelligence does not deteriorate with age (Bayles & Kaszniak, 1987). Intellectual function, as measured by the intelligence quotient (IQ), is subject to decline among aged persons when education, interests, and time necessary to complete the task are variables. Furthermore, a benign condition seen in healthy older adults termed benign senescent forgetfulness (BSF) is believed to be a normal age-related change in short-term memory. Older individuals with this condition usually report forgetfulness for names, dates, appointments, and where they placed objects. BSF is characterized by difficulty retrieving information, but not in learning new information, as observed early in dementing illness (Cummings & Benson, 1983). In addition, BSF does not progressively worsen nor does it interfere with one's ability to provide self-care. Individuals with BSF are acutely aware of their absentmindedness and may have instituted memory aids to assist in daily living. In addition, a loss of speed of response has been demonstrated with age because of the changes in the

---

Normal Age-Related Changes in Structure and Function of the Brain

Anatomic structural changes with age

Progressive loss of neurons
Decreased corticol area (atrophy), widening of sulci
Diminished synthesis and metabolism of neurotransmitter substances
Atrophy of axon and dendrites
Changes in periventricular white matter

Age changes influencing physical function

Decreased reflexes
Increase in reaction time
Improvement in vocabulary
Wisdom

---

central nervous system and transmission of neurotransmitter substances (Birren, 1974). It is therefore important to reassure healthy older individuals that some increased difficulty remembering events and retrieving information is to be expected with aging (Bayles & Kaszniak, 1987) but, as long as time is not a factor, older adults can learn and perform as well as younger adults on similar tasks.

Cognition is a global term used to describe the many areas in which the brain functions to enable humans to process information, remember, understand the written and spoken language, speak, write, reason, calculate, be oriented to present circumstance, and so on. All of these cognitive or higher intellectual functions are routinely performed and are necessary for one to live independently and safely. In the absence of certain diseases and irrespective of age, individuals are expected to perform well on all tasks that measure language, orientation, attention, calculation, memory, and judgment. Of course, educational background in terms of the location, grade completed in school, and any impairments in sensory function, such as vision and/or hearing, can influence individual performance.

If, for example, you interviewed a healthy 80-year-old person, you would expect this individual—when given sufficient time to respond—to be oriented to time, place, and location; to be able to recall immediate, recent, and past events; to calculate; to recognize and label familiar objects; and to execute written and verbal commands. If you learned that this older adult had a fourth-grade education from Baton Rouge, Louisiana, and was severely hearing impaired, it might explain errors in language or calculation. Overall, to have any clinical relevance, impairment in any of these higher intellectual functions must be considered in the context of what is considered to be a normal expectation among the older individual's cohorts. Once this is taken into account, if intellectual impairment exists, it should prompt further investigation.

Dementia is a disease that impairs cognitive function. It is an acquired condition and therefore represents a change in previous cognitive abilities. To meet diagnostic standards, the condition must also be progressive, with subsequent deterioration in cognitive abilities; interfere with work or usual social activities; be present for more than 6 months; and represent no change in level of consciousness. According to the *Diagnostic and Statistical Manual of Mental Disorders* (D.S.M.-III-R, 1987) the diagnosis of dementia is made when specific changes in cognition occur. Among others, the hallmark feature includes impairment in memory, both short-term and long-term. Because of the short-term memory loss that accompanies this disease, the ability to learn new information is thwarted. In addition, impairment must exist in at least one of the following areas: abstraction, judgment, personality change, language, or constructional ability. All of these changes can make daily living cumbersome for both the older client suffering from dementia and the family caregiver.

The incidence of dementia has been observed to increase with age among older Americans. Dementing syndromes have been reported among 5% of those 65 years of age and nearly 20% of those age 80 and over (Kane et al., 1984). Moreover, nearly 50% of institutionalized elderly persons have dementia (Gurland & Cross, 1982). These figures, however, might be underrepresentative of true incidence rates because of reduced recognition of dementing illnesses among health professionals who care for elderly persons, as well as failure of physicians to report the underlying causes of death, such as pneumonia, which may have originated from a bedridden state secondary to dementia. Of significance is the great numbers of older Americans with the type of dementia known as Alzheimer's disease (AD). By far, AD accounts for about 50% of the causes of dementia (Cummings & Benson, 1983; Kane et al., 1984). Current estimates are that approximately 4 million Americans currently suffer from AD (Berg, 1991), a figure which is much higher than previously estimated.

Because AD—similar to other types of dementia—is progressive, characteristic changes have been observed according to severity among the various stages. Overall, as with any other disease, the rate of progression varies among individuals. Those afflicted with AD may survive for many years (up to 20 years), or the course may be fulminating from the initial time of diagnosis and result in death very early after the time of diagnosis (a few years). For the purposes of discussion, the term *early* stage will be used interchangeably with *mild* dementia, the *middle* stage will be highlighting *moderate* severity, and the *late* stage will be synonymous with *severe* dementia. All of the changes associated with each stage are reflective of changes in higher cognitive function (to be further discussed in the section "Stages of Dementia").

The criterion for *mild* dementia is defined as significant impairment in work or social activities, but the capacity for independence in daily living remains. There is also adequate personal hygiene and relatively intact judgment (D.S.M.-III-R, 1987). *Moderate* dementia is associated with hazardous living and requires some degree of supervision. As dementia progresses, all previously learned skills—such as writing, reading, ambulation, and other self-care activities—become lost (*severe* dementia). Because of the impairment in language skills, clients with AD become mute and display an inability to understand what is spoken to them. Not only do these clients display loss of recognition of others, they also lose recognition of themselves. It is at this last stage of *severe* dementia that continual supervision is required.

From the time of onset to the final stages of AD, significant changes occur in the client and family caregiver and also between the client and family caregiver. Relationships and roles change alike. Family caregivers are often painstakingly confronted with the realization that their loved one is no longer able to safely or adequately care for himself or herself. Such unforeseen events as fires at home, wandering from home, or becoming lost in previously familiar places occur and signal cognitive impairment. Thus family members often must provide greater supervision. For some, this may involve rearranging work and leisure activities, travelling, increasing the frequency of contact, or forsaking other activities. For these reasons, it is usually during the *middle* stage that physician consultation is initiated by family caregivers.

Successful adaptation to changes in roles and relationships depends on individual personality and methods of coping, degree of burden, family resources, ability to access help through social support networks, and possibly stage of initial presentation. In addition to changes in cognition that are observed during each stage, there are some behavioral manifestations of dementia that family caregivers often have to manage. Investigations have shown that the most frequently occurring behaviors include wandering, acute and chronic types of agitation (restlessness and pacing), catastrophic reactions, "sundowning," suspiciousness and false accusations, hoarding objects, paranoid ideation, hallucinations, and delusions (Gwyther, 1985; Roper et al., 1991).

In many settings the nurse will encounter clients with AD and families who are the primary caregiver. Caregiver issues and conflict may develop that the professional nurse may encounter, and these will differ depending on the clinical setting. In both the ambulatory and home care setting, the caregiver may be more relaxed and have a greater sense of control over potential problems. Issues about safety and injury prevention, elopement, and assistance in daily living often surface as the degree of dementia progresses. In the institutional setting, family caregivers may be overwhelmed with guilt and feelings of family abandonment and even powerlessness as their loved one is cared for by strangers. In all clinical settings the role of the professional nurse remains the same: to enable family caregivers to provide the best possible care and to provide the best quality of care for the client's remaining years. This involves anticipatory guidance, ongoing education about the disease, and progress towards treatment; counseling; behavioral management; and client advocacy.

Family Caregivers

The majority of clients with AD live in the community, under the care of supportive family caregivers. Even when care is relinquished to professionals through institutional arrangements, families remain very involved and suffer many of the same effects of "caregiver burden." These "hidden victims" (Zarit et al., 1985) provide constant care and support to the ill family member for

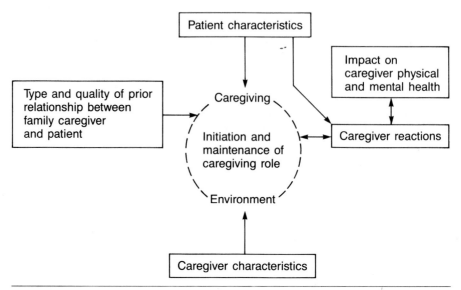

Figure 21-1   Factors influencing caregiver responses to the patient with AD. (From Given C., Collins, C., & Given B. [1988]. Sources of stress among families caring for relatives with Alzheimer's disease. *Nursing Clinics of North America, 23,* 69-82.)

prolonged periods, often with personal physical and psychologic compromises.

Over the past decade, considerable research has clearly defined these caregivers and the complexities of the caregiving process. Given and colleagues' model (1988) represents the dynamic interrelationships influencing caregiver responses: symptoms of the demented client, caregiver characteristics and social roles, social support, financial resources and health care services available within the caregiving environment, and the caregiver's emotional reactions to providing care (Fig. 21-1). The components of this model presented in Fig. 21-1 are discussed in further detail.

Client Characteristics

Symptoms and characteristics of the client with dementia vary, and as the dementia progresses, they can become more disruptive and distressing to family members. The decline in intellectual abilities and self-care skills and the deterioration in personality necessitate constant supervision. Clients often develop severe behavioral problems, such as combativeness, catastrophic reactions, inappropriate sexual behaviors, as well as nighttime wandering. As caregivers attempt to understand these problematic and unpredictable behaviors, they often experience feelings of guilt and inadequacy. There is also a tendency to personalize the client's words and actions, even when they are irrational. Nurses can anticipate these reactions and help families understand changes as they occur.

Although these symptoms and characteristics of the client with dementia — as well as the duration of the illness — are significant, George and Gwyther (1986) suggest that it is the characteristics of the caregiving situation and the resources available to the caregiver — rather than the condition of the client — that most directly affect caregiver well-being. Nurses must look beyond the client to understand the caregiver and enhance his or her effectiveness.

Caregiver Characteristics

The primary caregiver is usually a spouse or, if not available, a child, typically an adult child (Stone et al., 1987). Women — including wives, daughters, and daughters-in-law — are the largest group of caregivers (Brody, 1981; Cantor, 1983; Sommers & Zarit, 1985). Spouses and children assume the role of caregiver gradually as the dementia progresses, often without making a conscious decision to do so.

Adult children are more likely to have more role obligations caring for their own children and families, as well as their aging parents, and may experience higher levels of stress (Mace & Rabins, 1991). Johnson and Catalano (1983) suggest that elderly spouses experience role regression and role entrenchment, in which they forego their social and familial roles and focus almost completely on caring for their ill spouses.

When assessing the stressors of family caregiving, one must address other role obligations of the caregiver. Questions to consider include: What roles does he or she have within the family? How will changes and expectations of others affect each member in the family?

Reactions of Primary Caregivers and the Family

Even under the best circumstances, families develop conflicts about assuming new roles and/or relinquishing others. One member of the family, either the spouse or adult daughter, usually takes on the primary responsibility for direct care and coordinates formal assistance. As the dementia progresses, the caregiver spends more time providing personal care, such as bathing, dressing, toileting and feeding, and managing problematic behaviors. Caregivers are not able to cope with all the various tasks and look to the family for assistance. More importantly, caregivers search for social-emotional support from family members and friends. A multitude of such feelings as resentment, guilt, anger, and abandonment may surface. Unresolved family issues and conflicts of the past may develop into new crises and prevent the family from working together.

In addition to the primary caregiver, the nurse is concerned with how other members of the family perceive and interact with the client with AD. Creasey and colleagues (1990) studied relationships in families with and without an elderly parent with AD. Adult child caregivers perceived a poorer relationship with parents with AD when contrasted with couples with a healthy elderly parent. In addition, married women with a parent with AD also tended to have more negative relationships with their husbands than did those who had a healthy parent. Perceptions of burden were associated with poor spousal relationships for wives, but not husbands. In addition, grandchildren described a poorer relationship with their grandparent with AD, as compared with grandchildren who had a healthy grandparent (Creasy et al., 1989).

Nurses can work more effectively with caregivers if they understand family dynamics and individual coping skills. Additional areas to consider include a description of present family relationships, family members' ability to assist the

---

Table 21-1　Caregiver Strain Questionnaire

I am going to read a list of things that other people have found to be difficult in helping out after somebody comes home from the hospital. *Would you tell me whether any of these apply to you?* (GIVE EXAMPLES)

	Yes = 1	No = 0
Sleep is disturbed (e.g., because ___ is in and out of bed or wanders around at night)	_____	_____
It is inconvenient (e.g., because helping takes so much time or it's a long drive over to help)	_____	_____
It is a physical strain (e.g., because of lifting in and out of a chair; effort or concentration is required)	_____	_____
It is confining (e.g., helping restricts free time or cannot go visiting)	_____	_____
There have been family adjustments (e.g., because helping has disrupted routine; there has been no privacy)	_____	_____
There have been changes in personal plans (e.g., had to turn down a job; could not go on vacation)	_____	_____
There have been other demands on my time (e.g., from other family members)	_____	_____
There have been emotional adjustments (e.g., because of severe arguments)	_____	_____
Some behavior is upsetting (e.g., because of incontinence; ___ has trouble remembering things; or ___ accuses people of taking things)	_____	_____
It is upsetting to find ___ has changed so much from his or her former self (e.g., he or she is a different person than he or she used to be)	_____	_____
There have been work adjustments (e.g., because of having to take time off)	_____	_____
It is a financial strain	_____	_____
Feeling completely overwhelmed (e.g., because of worry about ___; concerns about how you will manage)	_____	_____
Total Score (count yes responses)	_____	

From Robinson, B. (1983). Validation of a caregiver strain index. *Journal of Gerontology, 38,* 344-348.

primary caregiver and provide emotional support, and individual strengths and weaknesses among family members.

One method of identifying caregivers at risk is to administer screening instruments, such as the caregiver strain index (Table 21-1) or the burden interview (see the box on pp. 364-365). These instruments provide an objective measurement of caregiver strain and are useful tools in conjunction with clinical assessment.

Psychologic and Physical Health Consequences

Individuals who assume responsibility for a family member with AD are at great risk for physical and/or psychologic illness. "Caregiver burden" refers to the physical, psychologic, social, and financial problems that may be experienced by family members. According to George and Gwyther (1986), caregivers average nearly three times as many stress symptoms, use a substantially higher number of psychotropic drugs, and are less able to pursue social activities, when compared with other family members. Pagel et al. (1985) report in a study of 68 family caregivers of clients with AD, 28 currently met the criteria for depression and 27 had met the criteria for diagnosis of clinical depression at an earlier point in the client's disease. Caregivers are also at risk of physical illness or injury as a result of caring for a relative with dementia (Yankelovitch & White, 1986).

Caregiver stress may exacerbate already existing chronic illness. Many caregivers forego ongoing health maintenance and primary medical care for themselves. Therefore it is not surprising that the cumulative effects of such stressors take their toll and can result in worsening of preexisting caregiver illness.

Although it is not clear whether caregiver stress plays a role in the development of caregiver alcohol or drug abuse, one can assume it contributes to addictive behaviors. Drug abuse in the older adult typically involves the inappropriate use of prescription drugs—such as tranquilizers, hypnotics, and narcotics—rather than illegal drugs. Nurses should include questions about alcohol and drug abuse in the caregiver and family as part of the overall assessment.

Social Supports and Financial Resources

Even with family involvement in caring for an elderly client with AD, caregivers need additional support. Acceptance of assistance can be difficult for many caregivers. Yankelovitch and White (1986) report that the expense associated with services was the most frequently cited reason for non-use of services, but reasons such as client refusal to accept the service was also cited. Likewise, paranoid and agitated behaviors and dependency on the primary caregiver make new routines and unfamiliar caregivers difficult for the client to accept. A common reaction of the caregiver is to withdraw and become isolated from friends, family, and social activities. It is often a crisis, such as severe behavioral

Burden Interview

INSTRUCTIONS: The following is a list of statements that reflect how people sometimes feel when taking care of another person. After each statement, indicate how often you feel that way: never, rarely, sometimes, quite frequently, or nearly always. There are no right or wrong answers.

1. Do you feel that your relative asks for more help than he or she needs?
   0. Never 1. Rarely 2. Sometimes 3. Quite frequently 4. Nearly always
2. Do you feel that because of the time you spend with your relative that you don't have enough time for yourself?
   0. Never 1. Rarely 2. Sometimes 3. Quite frequently 4. Nearly always
3. Do you feel stressed between caring for your relative and trying to meet other responsibilities for your family or work?
   0. Never 1. Rarely 2. Sometimes 3. Quite frequently 4. Nearly always
4. Do you feel embarrassed over your relative's behavior?
   0. Never 1. Rarely 2. Sometimes 3. Quite frequently 4. Nearly always
5. Do you feel angry when you are around your relative?
   0. Never 1. Rarely 2. Sometimes 3. Quite frequently 4. Nearly always
6. Do you feel that your relative currently affects your relationship with other family members or friends in a negative way?
   0. Never 1. Rarely 2. Sometimes 3. Quite frequently 4. Nearly always
7. Are you afraid what the future holds for your relative?
   0. Never 1. Rarely 2. Sometimes 3. Quite frequently 4. Nearly always
8. Do you feel your relative is dependent on you?
   0. Never 1. Rarely 2. Sometimes 3. Quite frequently 4. Nearly always
9. Do you feel strained when you are around your relative?
   0. Never 1. Rarely 2. Sometimes 3. Quite frequently 4. Nearly always
10. Do you feel your health has suffered because of your involvement with your relative?
    0. Never 1. Rarely 2. Sometimes 3. Quite frequently 4. Nearly always
11. Do you feel that you don't have as much privacy as you would like, because of your relative?
    0. Never 1. Rarely 2. Sometimes 3. Quite frequently 4. Nearly always
12. Do you feel that your social life has suffered because you are caring for your relative?
    0. Never 1. Rarely 2. Sometimes 3. Quite frequently 4. Nearly always
13. Do you feel uncomfortable about having friends over, because of your relative?
    0. Never 1. Rarely 2. Sometimes 3. Quite frequently 4. Nearly always
14. Do you feel that your relative seems to expect you to take care of him or her, as if you were the only one he or she could depend on?
    0. Never 1. Rarely 2. Sometimes 3. Quite frequently 4. Nearly always
15. Do you feel that you don't have enough money to care for your relative, in addition to the rest of your expenses?
    0. Never 1. Rarely 2. Sometimes 3. Quite frequently 4. Nearly always

From Zarit, S.H., Reever, K.E., Bach-Peterson, J. (1980). Relatives of the impaired elderly: Correlates of feelings of burden. *The Gerontologist, 20,* 649-655.

Burden Interview — cont'd

16. Do you feel that you will be unable to take care of your relative much longer?
    0. Never   1. Rarely   2. Sometimes   3. Quite frequently   4. Nearly always
17. Do you feel you have lost control of your life since your relative's illness?
    0. Never   1. Rarely   2. Sometimes   3. Quite frequently   4. Nearly always
18. Do you wish you could just leave the care of your relative to someone else?
    0. Never   1. Rarely   2. Sometimes   3. Quite frequently   4. Nearly always
19. Do you feel uncertain about what to do about your relative?
    0. Never   1. Rarely   2. Sometimes   3. Quite frequently   4. Nearly always
20. Do you feel you should be doing more for your relative?
    0. Never   1. Rarely   2. Sometimes   3. Quite frequently   4. Nearly always
21. Do you feel you could do a better job in caring for your relative?
    0. Never   1. Rarely   2. Sometimes   3. Quite frequently   4. Nearly always
22. Overall, how burdened do you feel in caring for your relative?
    0. Not at all   1. A little   2. Moderately   3. Quite a bit   4. Extremely

---

problems of the client or illness of the caregiver that finally permits the caregiver to accept assistance. Nurses need to educate families on various supports in the community and give anticipatory guidance before a crisis develops.

Respite is available in many forms, depending on the availability and cost of services. Services most valuable to families caring for someone with AD include adult day care and such in-home services as home health aides and companions. In the majority of cases, these community services are not covered by Medicare, Medicaid, or other third-party payors. For most families the financial responsibility of caring for someone with AD is a significant strain. Fear of ultimate long-term care placement of the client and the associated expenses influence the family's ability to pay for in-home services.

Support groups that deal with issues associated with aging and AD have been beneficial in easing the caregiver's sense of burden (Barnes et al., 1981; Grad & Sainsbury, 1968; Wilder et al., 1983). They provide emotional support, education, and referral to various community resources. Nurses should contact the county area Agency on Aging or local Alzheimer's Association chapter to learn about support groups and local social supports. Other resources include university-based geriatric assessment or Alzheimer's disease diagnostic programs. The accompanying box provides a list of services that may be needed by clients with AD and their families.

Nursing Interventions

EARLY STAGE

The early stage of AD may last from 2 to 4 years. Short-term memory loss, lack of initiative, and poor judgment are characteristic symptoms. Subtle changes in

Services That May Be Needed by Clients with AD and Their Families

Services for Patients

Health care services
In-patient
Out-patient
Emergency
Crisis teams
Research
Case management

Socialization, nutrition
Senior centers
Drop-in centers
Friendly visiting/
  buddy systems
Stroke clubs
Parkinson groups
Congregate meals
Meals On Wheels

Transportation and escort services
Senior centers
Red Cross
Community programs
Dial-A-Ride
Office on Aging

Respite, home care, and day care
Home attendants,
  housekeepers,
  homemakers
Visiting nurses
Rehabilitation
Nursing Home
  Without Walls
Day hospital
Day programs

Residential programs
Adult homes
Foster care
Board and care
Intermediate care
Nursing homes
VA long-term care
Psychiatric hospitals

Entitlement programs
Medicare
Medicaid
Social Security
  disability
Veterans' benefits
Other health and
  disability insurance

Services for families/caregivers

Health and mental-health services
Refer to *Services for patients*
Family/mental-
  health agencies
Private practitioners
Crisis teams
ADRDA support
  groups

Socialization, nutrition
Senior centers
Drop-in centers
Friendly visiting/
  buddy systems
Stroke clubs
Parkinson groups
Congregate meals
Meals On Wheels

Information, referral, and advisement
Office on Aging
Help line/hot lines
Self-help/
  clearinghouses
Practitioners/advisers
Legal services
Clergy
Patient advocate/
  ombudsman

ADRDA
Local chapter
Support groups
Self-help groups
Telephone help line
Autopsy Network
National office
1-800-621-0379

Respite services
Day programs
Respite care
Hospice
Temporary placement
Senior vacations/
  camps
Friendly visitors
Home care

Entitlement and government programs
Medicare
Medicaid
Social Security/
  disability
Veterans' benefits
Other health and
  disability insurance
Protective services/
  State Department
  of Social Services

From Alzheimer's Disease and Related Disorders Association, (1985). *Understanding Alzheimer's disease: What it is, how to cope with it.* Fort Lee, N.J.: Future Directions.

behavior and personality may go unnoticed by the family and are often dismissed as "old age." The client recognizes changes within himself or herself but has little awareness of the implications. Depression is common in the early stage and may be the presenting symptom that initiates evaluation. Diagnosis of AD is not usually established in this stage. Clients are still able to live independently but, as time wears on, need assistance with finances, driving, and day-to-day functioning.

Family reactions vary but are frequently marked by denial, frustration, anger, and bewilderment. Tasks the client was once able to accomplish are assumed by the spouse or other family member. This process occurs so gradually that often the caregiver is unaware of the client's actual deterioration. Other family members or friends who have infrequent contact with the client may be the first to recognize the client's disabilities and identify that there is real illness.

Most clients are still driving their cars in this stage, yet – with poor judgment and visuospatial disorientation – can lose their sense of direction and precipitate motor vehicle accidents. In the case of an elderly couple where the affected individual is the primary driver and the spouse does not drive, this disability can be very problematic. How then will the couple do grocery shopping, meet medical appointments, or socialize? Likewise, if the affected individual is not aware of his or her disabilities, how does the family explain to him or her that he or she should no longer drive? This issue alone can precipitate family conflicts over whether the client should continue driving, who will explain the limitations to the client, and then how transportation needs will be solved.

The relationship of a parent with AD and his or her adult children has to change. As the adult daughter or son gradually assumes increasing responsibility for the parent, he or she may feel sadness over the loss and guilt about "taking over." The process of "role reversal," although a positive adaptation, is very stressful and often leads adult children into counseling. Caregivers need support about such decisions as living arrangements, legal and financial plans, and employment. Issues of individual autonomy, competence, and family reciprocity are important ethical questions common in caregiving.

Spouse caregivers become increasingly isolated from friends and social activities toward the end of the early stage. The affected spouse prefers familiar environments and routines, communicates in generalities, and often has difficulty with word finding. These changes make any activity away from home a stressful event for both partners.

The spousal relationship begins to change as the affected spouse loses his or her mental and functional capabilities. A symbiotic partnership becomes one of unequal responsibility and roles. Expectations and hopes for the future take unforseen directions as the healthy spouse begins to make decisions and choices that will affect them both.

MIDDLE STAGE

The middle stage of dementia (of moderate severity) is characterized by significant changes in higher cognitive function. Both recent and remote memory worsen. Typically, clients are unaware of recent events — such as those which occurred within a few minutes of time — and have an inability to recall events in which they participated — such as what they did for the day or what they had for lunch. Events of the distant past — such as anniversary dates, birthdates of children, or their own birthdate — may also be forgotten. As in the early stage, clients with middle-stage AD may fabricate answers to questions posed in an attempt to explain their lapse in memory.

The ability of the client with AD to learn new information continues to worsen. Family members typically comment on the client's inability to learn how to use a new appliance, such as a microwave oven, despite repeated instruction. Even previously acquired knowledge can become lost. Frustration and agitation can easily arise among family members who relentlessly and vigorously try to "teach" the client how to operate the appliance. Failure of the family caregiver to recognize that the client with AD is incapable of learning can jeopardize family relationships. Family caregivers may try harder to teach the client, which can lead to further stress, or they may give up and disinvest from the client altogether. In the latter instance, families may become uninvolved and believe their efforts to be futile. This belief is potentially dangerous, because it can lead to withdrawal and/or dissolvement of family relationships.

Families must be taught to develop an awareness of what the client is capable and incapable of achieving, supervising activities and then offering praise for successful accomplishments. In this regard it is often best to advise family caregivers to simplify tasks and present activities that the client can successfully accomplish. Each activity — such as cooking, telephoning, bathing, or dressing — should be modified for better understanding. The client in the middle stage of AD is unlikely to be able to cook a meal. Therefore eliciting the client to cook a meal will only lead to errors and potential frustration by both client and family caregiver. Rather, direction should be given step by step, such as "First, let's get the recipe; now, let's get the ingredients; next, get the utensils," and so on. Every activity must be simplified, while also allowing the client the opportunity to participate in the task. This approach is time consuming and for some family members may be overwhelming. Therefore support services may need to be accessed to assist in caregiving and to prevent the development of stress, especially if family members report or demonstrate difficulty coping with behavioral problems. Most important, however, this approach discourages family caregivers from "doing for" the client, especially if the client maintains the capacity for self-care with supervision.

Moreover, health care providers, as well as family caregivers, are vulnerable to display paternalism for clients. This is especially true when caring for those with dementia, because it takes much less time for caregivers to perform the same task. Maintainence of a sense of "self," however, is an important concept to engender to family caregivers in this stage.

In addition, it may be difficult for family caregivers to reflect on their own pattern of behavior and to change it constructively. Patience, guidance, and continual reinforcement can assist the professional nurse to enable family caregivers to provide the best possible care.

Language significantly deteriorates during the middle stage of AD. There is a reduction in vocabulary and often a paucity of speech. Words may not make sense or be recognizable as part of the English language, such as those words fabricated by the client. Speech can become unintelligible. Clients are observed to develop pet phrases or words that are repeatedly uttered throughout the conversation. Sentences and stream of thought may make little sense to the listener. The middle stage of dementia has been further characterized, in terms of language function, by anomia, paraphasia, impaired comprehension, and difficulty to engage in conversation (Cummings & Benson, 1983). Anomia is an inability to call an object by name. Common examples include asking the client to identify such items as a ring, watch, telephone, door, or even a person whom the client should know (spouse, child). Clients can demonstrate frustration at their inability to name common objects or persons. Because of these changes, communication becomes difficult. Family caregivers may try to clarify or "teach" the client the correct word. Because of the impairment in cognition and learning, these efforts are futile. Often both written and verbal language are impaired. This creates significant difficulties for family caregivers. Often, labeling can assist in cueing clients; however, as language function further deteriorates, it may be of no benefit. Instead family caregivers must be taught to rely increasingly on observation of behavior and patterns of behavior demonstrated when trying to decipher what the client is indicating. In particular, clients with dementia who develop a decline in health, such as an infection, are often unable to adequately communicate their concerns. An increase in agitation or worsening confusion or cognition signal medical problems. In addition, family caregivers are encouraged to observe behaviors because hidden meaning can be evident in the manifested behavior.

Concentration or attention span and calculation deteriorate from the client's baseline cognitive function. Because of decreased concentration, clients are unable to complete a thought or sentence and are unable to execute activities without frequent repetition with direction. The sense of time and place is lost, resulting in clients' inability to recall the day of the week, month, or date. Once told the correct information, clients may even perseverate the month or day repeatedly throughout your interview, even to unrelated questions. The ability to perform arithmetic calculations—as evidenced by asking the client to add, subtract, and perform other simple calculations—becomes impaired. Family caregivers may first notice that the client has difficulty balancing a checkbook or with the bills. In addition, writing becomes impaired because of the changes in motor function. Writing can become illegible, as can the content of what is written. Motor coordination, as demonstrated when clients are asked to copy simple designs, can reveal errors. Because coordination and motor skill eventually become impaired, clients in this stage are at risk for falls when misperception of environmental cues occurs.

Mood swings and changes in personality often occur during the middle stage of AD. Family members may comment on their inability to understand why their loved one is responding in such a way. Clients with AD have been observed to be more irritable, teary, or even silly; most importantly, there has been a change from the client's baseline. Behaviors such as suspiciousness, restlessness, pacing, and catastrophic reactions typically develop in this stage. A catastrophic reaction is a sudden, emotional outburst that is often short lived and results from confusion or misinterpretation of what is said or perceived in the environment. Clients with AD become overwhelmed and then extremely upset and may cry, scream, swear, or strike out at others in close distance. They display both fright and mistrust, which makes this reaction difficult to manage. The best approach is to reassure the client gently and remove him or her from the situation. Family caregivers find themselves asking, "What did I say, what did I do to cause this to happen?" Measures should be taken by health care providers to teach family members that many times events in the environment become overwhelming to the client suffering from cognitive impairment, because there is difficulty interpreting environmental stimuli, assimilating and processing new information. Catastrophic reactions are best managed by following simplistic routines, thereby eliminating choices that can further contribute to confusion. When a catastrophic reaction has reoccurred, family caregivers and health professionals usually can identify trigger events and patterns of behavior that reproduce these reactions. It is important to identify catastrophic reactions, because with change in approach and/or environment these overwhelming events can most always be prevented.

Other behaviors often become manifested during the middle stage of AD, including chronic agitation or motor restlessness, which is often manifested by frequent pacing or wandering away. Clients with AD may become extremely fidgety, performing repetitive activities or motions, including rocking in place, pacing, or performing constant hand motions. Because of the motor restlessness and disorientation, clients with AD are likely to wander and potentially elope, especially in the evening. Family caregivers may be awakened by their loved one's roaming around because he or she is lost or packing his or her bags in the early morning and eloping and ready to leave. Alterations in the sleep-wake cycle characteristically occur, and clients may have daytime drowsiness and even napping. Interventions by family members to restrict daytime napping and encourage structured activities during the day and even before bedtime can include walking, which can reduce boredom during the day and promote nighttime sleeping, and elimination of caffeinated beverages before bedtime.

It is not uncommon for clients with middle-stage AD to develop hallucination and delusions. Fearfulness and paranoid ideation also occur, which may be directed toward the primary caregiver or significant other. Family caregivers may feel overwhelmed when the client with AD relentlessly follows or "shadows" the caregiver, because of loss of recall for familiar events and disorientation at home. In addition, because clients with AD have difficulty interpreting reality, they can misinterpret daily events such as radio broadcasts, television programs, and even general conversation. Communication by family caregivers can easily become misinterpreted, and disputes can arise between family members when the client with AD misinterprets conversation.

Because of the significant deterioration in cognitive function that occurs during the middle stage of dementia, the ability to care for oneself becomes impaired. Basic self-care activities (that is, activities of daily living [ADLs]) such as dressing, bathing, ambulation, toileting, grooming, and feeding can be too complex for clients with dementia. All of these activities require an ability to assimilate information, including gathering the necessary articles to complete the task, recalling how to execute the task, and then successfully completing the task. When short-term and long-term memory and/or reasoning become impaired, basic self-care activities are also likely to become impaired. Family caregivers can provide assistance by directing and guiding the client with simple instruction and even demonstration. Nurses working with family caregivers must be certain to query them about the client's ability to perform basic ADLs, because impairments are unlikely to be reported by the client with dementia. On the other hand, family caregivers are often acutely aware of deficits in instrumental activities of daily living (IADLs) (Lawton & Brody, 1969). They include the ability to travel or access transportation; administer medications; handle the finances; prepare meals, including shopping and cooking; and use the telephone, to name a few. Deficits in any of these activities are likely to be noticed by caregivers. For instance, if a client who manages the finances forgets to pay a bill or forgets to sign the check needed to pay the bill, services can be interrupted. Family caregivers may notice changes in cooking or discover fires on the stove. Safety issues can also arise in regard to driving and medication administration.

The overall management of clients afflicted with AD encompasses a general principle of care that is directed toward individualizing a plan of care for each client, familiarizing the client during all phases of care, and empathizing with the client. Clients with AD are human beings who must be treated with dignity and respect throughout all stages of cognitive loss. The manifestation of behavior and cognitive loss is individualized. Personality, coping styles, family caregiver support, and adaptation to the environment are all factors that contribute to disease presentation, as well as management. Therefore successful management should reflect client wishes, including incorporation of previous hobbies, skills, and/or favorite activities. A holistic plan of care that reflects client interests is one that can provide for a sense of mastery in the client's own care.

Likewise, every effort should be made to maintain personal and social integrity. Repeating instructions to clients with AD with simple sentences and using a soft voice and gentle approach and incorporating the use of touch can help to establish a sense of trust. This is an important intervention strategy for those experiencing a loss of safety or security, such as the elderly client who repeatedly cries, "I want to go home to my mother," or the client with AD who becomes acutely agitated because he or she no longer recognizes once familiar faces. Development and enforcement of a structured routine can also create a sense of mastery and control over one's environment.

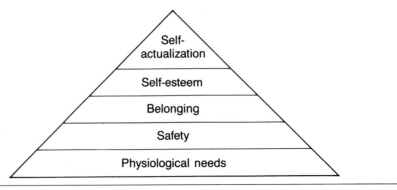

Figure 21-2   Maslow's hierarchy of needs.

As AD progresses, clients are less able to verbalize thoughts, thus creating difficulty in communication, interaction with clients, and subsequent management of behavioral problems. Foremost, however, physical illnesses can be missed or behavioral problems escalate. Because of this, family caregivers must be taught to carefully observe and interpret the client's behavior. For example, a client who holds his or her face and stops eating can be indicating a toothache. Likewise, a client who suddenly develops urinary incontinence and increased agitation may have a urinary tract infection.

Management of behavioral problems can be accomplished best by first performing a comprehensive assessment that is based on Maslow's hierarchy of basic human needs (Maslow, 1970; Fig. 21-2). This theory is based on the assumption that all human beings have physiologic, safety, social, and self-actualizing needs. When caring for clients with dementia, family caregivers must first ascertain whether the basic physiologic needs of hunger, thirst, and elimination have been met. Clients with AD often demonstrate signs of discomfort by restlessness or agitation, as opposed to stating that they are hungry or thirsty, because of the deterioration in language. Once these needs are met, then the next stage is to assess the client for alteration in safety. This often develops as loss of recognition of caregivers or surroundings increase. Reacquainting the patient to his or her environment by use of name tags, labeling objects, and displaying familiar items can allay insecure feelings clients may experience. Once safety needs are met, individuals should be assessed for social needs. Social needs include love and belonging and the need to be a part of one's environment and peers. Because of losses in recognition of others, self, and environment, disassociation or reduced socialization occurs. Self-actualization requires cognizance of oneself, goals, environment, and the resultant interaction. As the dementia progresses, self-actualization may have less meaning.

LATE STAGE

The late stage of AD is short, typically less than 2 years. So much of the brain is affected that the person is confined to bed and is unable to express himself or herself or take care of his or her personal needs. Hughes and colleagues (1982) delineated a five-stage Clinical Dementia Rating (CDR) scale in which the last stage "severe dementia" is described as the following:

- Severe memory loss, with only fragments remaining
- Orientation to person only
- Inability to make judgments or solve problems
- No pretense of independent function outside the home
- No significant function in the home or outside the client's own room
- Much help required with personal care, and frequent incontinence

Heyman and colleagues (1987) added the following two stages to the CDR scale to classify later stages of dementia frequently seen in those in nursing homes and other chronic care facilities:

- "Profound dementia," in which clients have "severe impairment in language or comprehension, inability to walk unaided, and problems in feeding themselves, recognizing their family, or controlling bowel or bladder function"
- A "terminal" stage, in which clients require "total care because they are completely uncommunicative, bedridden, vegetative, and incontinent"

Although some clients in this stage are cared for at home, most are placed in a long-term care setting. The decision of whether to continue care at home or use long-term care is a significant stressor for caregivers. Caregiving at home is often continued until the point of physical and mental exhaustion to avoid placement. Feelings of guilt, family caregiving obligations, and fears of transferring care to strangers prevent families from accepting support from the long-term care system.

In the late stage, families face the finality of AD with grief and a sense of powerlessness over their inability to control the progressive deterioration and inevitable demise of the dying relative. For some elderly spouses, the realities of independent living and insecurities about their own future have significant implications during this period. Nurses should focus on the needs and reactions of the caregivers and include options for them in planning care for the client. Opportunities for guidance and support through counseling should be made available to the family on a consistent basis. The focus of counseling is situational coping, rather than correcting long-standing maladaptive family patterns.

Sources of conflict common in this stage are quality of life decisions — such as withholding or withdrawal of specific treatments, artificially provided fluids, and nutrition — and whether to hospitalize the client for acute illnesses. These ethical dilemmas place a considerable burden on the family, especially if end-of-life treatment preferences were not expressed by the client, if there is disagreement among family members, or when the client's previously stated wishes conflict with those of the family. It is imperative that nurses and other members of the health care team provide an environment for open discussion with family members to help them reach responsible decisions. Legally recognized advance directives for health care can now provide clear guidance to family members, caregivers, and health care professionals in many states about these issues. Unfortunately, unless these documents are prepared early in the course of AD, while the client still has decision-making capacity, they are invalid. If advance directives were not prepared by the client, then the health care team needs to assist the family in surrogate decision making.

• • •

Once dementing illnesses are better recognized, nurses will face the challenge of providing care to this group of older adults and their families in a variety of clinical settings. The continuum of care afforded to the client with dementia is no different than the provision of care to any other group of clients; however, involvement of families is the key to successful nursing care with this group of individuals. Providing care to an older adult with a progressive illness such as dementia depends on caregiver resources, coping abilities, and adaptability. The nurse's role encompasses a wide range of health care services available within the caregiving environment directed toward both clients and families. It is paramount for professional nurses to recognize and provide support to caregivers who are at great risk for physical and/or psychologic stress.

REFERENCES

Barnes, R.F., Raskind, M.A., Scott, M. (1981). Problems of families caring for Alzheimer patients: Use of a support group. *Journal American Geriatric Society, 29,* 80.

Bayles, K.A., & Kaszniak, A.W. (1987). *Communication and cognition in normal aging and dementia.* Boston: Little, Brown.

Berg, L. (1991). Special care units for patients with dementia. *Journal of the American Geriatrics Society, 12,* 1229-1236.

Birren, J.E. (1974). Psychophysiology and speed of response secondary to age and changes in central nervous system and neurotransmitters. *American Psychology, 29,* 808-815.

Brody, E.M. (1981). Women in the middle and family help to older people. *The Gerontologist, 21,* 471-480.

Cantor, M.H. (1983). Strain among caregivers: A study of experience in the United States. *The Gerontologist, 23,* 597-604.

Council on Alzheimer's Disease. U.S. Division of Health and Human Services, January, 1991.

Creasey, G.L., Myers, B.J., Epperson, M.J., & Taylor, J. (1989). Grandchildren of grandparents with Alzheimer's disease: Perception of grandparent, family environment, and old people. *Merrill-Palmer Quarterly, 35,* 227-237.

Creasey, G.L., Myers, B.J., Epperson, M.J., & Taylor, J. (1990). Couples with an elderly parent with Alzheimer's disease: Perceptions of familial relationships. *Psychiatry, 53,* 44-51.

Cummings, J.L., & Benson, D.F. (1983). *Dementia — a clinical approach.* Boston: Butterworth Publishers.

Diagnostic and statistical manual of mental disorders (3rd Ed.), Revised. (1987). American Psychiatric Association.

Eisdorfer, C. (1977). Intelligence and cognition in the aged. In E. W. Busse, & E. Pfeiffer (Eds.), *Behavior and adaptation in later life.* Boston: Little, Brown, & Co.

George, L., & Gwyther, L. (1986). Caregiver well-being: A multidimensional examination of family caregivers of demented adults. *The Gerontologist, 26,* 253-259.

Given, C., Collins, C., & Given, B. (1988). Sources of stress among families caring for relatives with Alzheimer's disease. *Nursing Clinics of North America, 23*(1), 69-82.

Grad, J., & Sainsbury, P. (1968). The effects that patients have on their family in a community care and a control psychiatric service—A two-year follow-up. *British Journal of Psychiatry, 114,* 265.

Gwyther, L. (1985). *Care of Alzheimer's patients: A manual for nursing home staff.* Fort Lee, N.J.: American Health Care Association and Alzheimer's Disease and Related Disorders Association.

Gurland, B.J., & Cross, P.S. (1982). Epidemiology of psychopathology in old age: Some implications for clinical services. *Psychiatric Clinics of North America, 5,* 11-26.

Heyman, A., Wilkinson, W.E., Hurwitz, B.J., Helms, M.J., Haynes, C.S., Utley, C.M., & Gwyther, L.P. (1987). Early-onset Alzheimer's disease: Clinical predictors of institutionalization and death. *Neurology, 37,* 980-984.

Hughes, C.P., Berg, L., Danziger, W.L., Coben, L.A., & Martin, R.L. (1982). A new clinical scale for the staging of dementia. *British Journal of Psychiatry, 140,* 566-570.

Johnson, C.L., & Catalano, D.J. (1983). A longitudinal study of family supports to impaired elderly. *The Gerontologist, 23,* 614-618.

Kane, R.L., Ouslander, J.G., & Abrass, I.B. (1984). *Essentials of clinical geriatrics.* New York: McGraw-Hill Book Co.

Lawton, M.P., & Brody, E.M. (1969). Assessment of older people: Self-maintaining and instrumental activities of daily living. *Gerontologist, 9,* 179-187.

Mace, N., & Rabins, P. (1991). The 36 hour day: A family guide to caring for persons with Alzheimer's disease. Baltimore: Johns Hopkins Press.

Maslow, A. (1970). *Motivation and personality.* New York: Harper & Row.

Pagel, M.D., et al. (1985). Loss of control, self-blame, and depression: An investigation of spouse caregivers of Alzheimer's disease patients. *Journal of Abnormal Psychology, 94,* 169-182.

Robinson, B.C. (1983). Validation of a caregiver strain index. *Journal of Gerontology, 38,* 344-348.

Roper, J.M., Shapira, J., & Chang, B.L. (1991). Agitation in the demented patient: A framework for management. *Journal of Gerontological Nursing, 17*(3), 17-20.

Sommers, T., & Zarit, S. (1985). Seriously near the breaking point. *Generations, 10,* 30-33.

Stone, R., Cafferata, G., & Sangl, J. (1987). Caregivers of the frail elderly: A national profile. *The Gerontologist, 27,* 616-626.

Wilder, D.E., Teresi, J.A., & Bennett, R.G. (1983). Family burden and dementia. *Advances in Neurology, 38,* 239.

Yankelovitch, K.S., & White, I. (1986). *Caregivers of patients with dementia.* Washington, D.C.: Office of Technology Assessment, U.S. Congress.

Zarit, S., Ory, N., & Zarit, J. (1985). The hidden victims of Alzheimer's disease: Families under stress. New York: New York University.

Zarit, S.H., Reever, K.E., & Bach-Peterson, J. (1980). Relatives of the impaired elderly: Correlates of feelings of burden. *The Gerontologist, 20,* 649-655.

Chapter 22

The Substance-Abusing Family

Christine S. Fawcett

Family theorists and therapists agree that the issue of substance abuse is one in which all members of the family are participants. With that in mind, this chapter focuses on the patterns, dynamics, and themes of the family in which an individual or individuals experience substance abuse.

Much research has been completed on the biologic model of the substance abuser (U.S. Department of Health and Human Services, 1987). Also, much research has been done on the stress factors to be considered when analyzing the psychologic contributors to substance abuse. Sociocultural determinants have also been studied. However, the family and its maladaptive behavior toward the substance abuser may be the greatest factor in facilitating sobriety and then assisting to maintain it.

Family Patterns

GENERATIONAL REPETITION

The substance abusing family usually does not form itself by chance. In the majority of these family systems, there is a generational repetition. Guerin (1979) indicated that in many families of Irish descent there are themes of alcoholism. This is not unique to Irish families but is shared by many other cultures.

The ongoing pattern is one in which drinking is a major issue. An example of a variation of this theme is when one generation is a drinking generation and another is a sober generation.

Current research on genetics certainly reinforce this pattern (U.S. Department of Health and Human Services, 1987). Research has shown not only that sons of alcoholics are more likely to become alcoholics than sons of nonalcoholics, but that sons of alcoholics who were adopted by nonalcoholics were more than 3 times as likely to become alcoholics as sons of nonalcoholics who also were adopted by nonalcoholics.

Susan is one of four siblings who all experienced severe problems with alcohol. They had been raised in a household in which their father was constantly inebriated. His father, also, was an alcoholic. Her brother and sisters all attended AA and worked on their sobriety. She stated to them that she couldn't change because drinking was "genetic."

EMOTIONAL VARIABILITY

Members of these families describe the family emotional system as having wide extremes and variability. At one moment the family appears to be doing well — is processing and communicating information openly. All members know not to count on the situation remaining stable and describe their feelings during this time like "walking on eggs." Inevitably, the abusing member will become drunk or high and become abusive, either hitting one particular member or verbally accosting someone or the entire group.

Growing up with emotional lability may be a way of life for many in these families. Upon hearing good news, abusers sometimes respond with joy or sorrow; accolades or crying. And many times both of the responses are expressed. Others relate that when they brought home good report cards, nothing was said or done, but when they did something minor and childlike, it was met with undue emotional response.

Certain times of the year are high-anxiety times for most of the population. Also, special days, such as Christmas, birthdays, and anniversaries, are dates that substance-abusing families associate with intoxication and extremes of emotionality.

Connie remembers that she and her brother Andy would dread the annual Christmas tree. They both shared memories of their drunken father tearing down the tree limb by limb and destroying all of the ornaments. She remembers that her "best" Christmas was when she and Andy secretly bought a tree, hid it in her room, and decorated it on Christmas Eve in her room. Her father never knew about it and didn't destroy it. They each still cherish the ornaments they saved from that tree.

BEHAVIORAL EXTREMES

Along with the emotional variants just mentioned are concomitant behavior excesses. Examples of these include severe beatings of certain family members, usually spouses or "identified" children, and ritualistic practices, such as requiring that a family member repeatedly scrub a floor or bathroom.

Connie relates that she proudly ran home and showed her mother her straight "A" report card. A family celebration was planned. During that party her father slapped her severely for "trying to be someone she wasn't."

NO MODEL OF NORMALCY

Each of the two patterns just mentioned, the emotional variance and the behavioral extremes, indicates that many of the families do not grow and develop with the knowledge of what is normal and what are expected responses to aspects of life.

Susan, the daughter of an alcoholic, believes that she married her ex-husband because she was overwhelmed by the peacefulness she experienced when she visited his family's home. Dinnertime at her in-laws was calm and happy. Disagreements were talked out and resolved by discussion. It appeared to her to have a Disney-like quality, which greatly contrasted with the chaotic, unpredictable family dinners in her household.

DEPRESSION

The family and its membership appear at times to be hopeless, helpless, incapacitated by small stressors, and generally depleted in carrying on everyday life. Depression and all of its side effects may be experienced and felt by any or many members of this family.

The members may also be "constantly grieving" for the loss of their happy childhood memories, their positive emotions, and their dignity.

RESPONSIBILITY

Many members of these families grow into individuals who believe that they are responsible for the actions of the other members of their family. This develops when certain children take over the parental responsibilities from incompetent parents. These children do not lead lives of children, but rather as "parentified children." In these roles, they are consistently accountable for the maintenance of the household, the rearing of the children, and the caretaking of the parents.

Sandra remembers that her older brother was like "a mother hen" to her sibling set of 8 brothers and sisters. He would awaken and make their lunches and check to make sure that all had their homework completed and with them. It was her brother who checked in with each of their teachers, requesting that he be notified if there were any problems. It was also her brother who cared for their sickly mother and who was certain that when their father came home drunk, no harm would come to him or other family members. Sandra wondered why he had so many problems with adult relationships.

Another term, *codependency*, is consistent with the family perspective of this disabling illness. This concept views the behavior and significance of the nondrinking or abusing member(s) of the family. A codependent may be as limited in growth potential as the abusing member. This dynamic is newly and not readily recognized by outsiders because these are not the abusing members of the family.

The following characteristics describe the role behavior of these family members:

1. They are addicted to offering a helping relationship. At times, codependents do not know the limits of their boundaries or where others begin. Because much of their life has been spent in the care of others, much of their self-esteem comes from the offer to others. "Their main goal in life is to figure out what others want and then deliver that to them" (Schaef, 1986).
2. As caretakers, co-dependents make themselves indispensable. This portion of the characteristic moves into qualities of martyrdom; that is, the caretaker is keeping the family together for the good of the children.
3. Codependents frequently suffer from physical illness. These illnesses may go unattended because the codependent is focusing so much on the care of the abuser.

4. Codependents frequently are disconnected from their own feelings or have distorted their feelings because of a lack of self-esteem, poor ego boundaries, or just genuine fatigue. They literally do not consider their feelings to be worthwhile; their joy comes from ameliorating the feelings of the other person.

ENABLING

Enabling describes how many families manuever in response to an addiction or abusive process. The abuser drinks, and the enabler or enablers allow the process to continue. At times the enabler appears to be facilitating the abuse. Because of depression, shame, codependency, and other factors, the family continues the same process because either they feel they are powerless and cannot stop or they know how to behave as such and are fearful of what the requirements would be to change their behavior.

A major portion of the process of enabling is to maintain the family's status quo. Many view this not as stabilizing, but as another expression of depression.

SHAME

Fossum and Mason (1986) offer a definition of shame that is portrayed in families who are moving out of the trap of abuse. They say the following:

Shame is an inner sense of being completely diminished or insufficient as a person. It is the self judging the self. A moment of shame may be humiliation so painful or an indignity so profound that one feels one has been robbed of her or his dignity or exposed as basically inadequate, bad, or worthy of rejection.

It is these feelings of worthlessness, loss of dignity, internalized as well as externalized humiliation, and vulnerability that keep many families stuck in the trap of the abusing family.

There are also family rules (Fossum and Mason, 1986) for maintaining the shameful systems. They are the following:

- Control
- Blame
- Perfection
- Incompleteness
- Noncommunication
- Unreliability
- Denial
- Disqualification

Once put into operation, these rules will perpetuate an ongoing family ritual. Many family members want to change the tradition of their abusing family but feel powerless against the motivation to "drink."

Intervention

Motivating that desire to change is one of the initial strategies used in assisting the abusing family. A prime example of motivation is the valuable resource of social support. Groups such as Alcoholics Anonymous offer a tremendous amount of interpersonal growth to the abusing individual and enabling family system.

The support is of assistance if it targets feelings of depression, helplessness, and powerlessness in allowing the family to recognize that they are not unique. Relearning coping strategies and decision-making abilities to correlate with optimism and powerfulness is extremely helpful and necessary. Realignment of strengths and establishment of foundation is essential.

Ultimately, each individual and the family need to deal with aspects of anger and shame. The family will require new rules to replace those of the shame-bound system.

With each step, each family member and the family collectively need to applaud themselves for moving out of unhealthy but "secure" patterns of living together. It takes much energy and fortitude to take the steps to stop abusing.

REFERENCES

Bean-Bayog, M. (1991). *Children of alcoholics,* New York: Haworth.

Berenson, D. (1986). Alcohol and the family system. In Guerin, P.J. (Ed.), *Family therapy: Theory and practice.* New York: Gardner.

Bowen, M. (1986). *Family therapy in clinical practice.* Northvale, NJ: Jason Aronson.

Elkin, M. (1984). *Families under the influence.* New York: W.W. Norton.

Fossum, M.A., & Mason, M.J. (1986). *Facing shame: Families in recovery.* New York: W.W. Norton.

Guerin, P.J. (1979). A Systems View of the Alcoholic. *The Family, 4*(1), 134-141.

Lederer, G.S. (1991). Alcohol in the family system. In Brown, F.H. (1991). *Reweaving the family tapestry.* New York: W.W. Norton.

Pickens, R.W., & Svikins, D.S. (1985). *Alcoholic family disorders: More than statistics.* Center City, MN: Hazelden.

Schaef, A.W. (1986). *Co-dependence misunderstood-mistreated.* San Francisco: Harper & Row.

U.S. Department of Health and Human Services. (1987). *Alcohol and health.* Rockville, MD: National Institute on Alcohol Abuse and Alcoholism.

Wood, B.L. (1990). *Children of alcoholism: The struggle for self and intimacy in adult life.* New York: New York University Press.

Chapter 23

The Impact of War on Family Functioning

Laila Farhood

Over the past decade, research on the epidemiology of disasters has emerged as an area of special interest. Wars are occurring more frequently around the world, causing psychologic and social damage and impairment. Wars cause significant crises in human conditions, and interest in studying their effect on health is growing. Increasing emphasis is placed on understanding the impact of disasters. Such understanding is vital to the psychiatric nurse and the mental health team to improve preparedness of the populations, particularly vulnerable groups, in management of disasters to minimize negative effects.

The term *disaster* has most often been associated with sudden natural happenings outside of human control, such as floods, earthquakes, hurricanes, storms, and drought. The short-term and, to a lesser extent, the long-term health effects of natural disasters have been extensively studied and documented, particularly the mental health and psychologic dimensions. Man-made disasters, such as wars and technologic accidents, have generally been less studied. Investigations of the effects of war on health, for example, have tended to concentrate on combat veterans and refugees (Shisana, 1987).

It is believed that war experiences provide material for research about life experiences, their effect, and demographic changes occurring under such war conditions. It is logical to assume that during war times, exposure to stressful life events increases. Moreover, the types and impacts of stressful events are expected to change under different circumstances and for different cultural groups. These stressful life experiences have been shown to be related to several somatic disorders (Dohrenwend B.S. & Dohrenwend B.D., 1978; Farhood, 1986; Finlay-Jones & Brown, 1981), as well as a wide range of psychiatric disorders, such as depression, anxiety, and interpersonal problems (McCubbin et al., 1980; Mueler et al., 1978; Rabkin & Streuning, 1976).

In their review of literature, Logue et al. (1981) pointed out that it is important to distinguish between natural and man-made disasters because each may be associated with different health problems. Man-made disasters as such might threaten the ecologic balance of the community. Also war-related disasters produce long-term health sequelae. Among symptoms after human-induced violence are guilt about other victims, blame, hostility, and identification with the aggressor (Logue et al., 1981). Moreover, the extra family events, such as war bombing and political persecution, seem to solidify the family in the long run (Hansen & Hill, 1964). The purpose of this chapter is to critically review the nursing and related literature on impact of war on the mental health and psychologic functioning of family members.

Research Findings

Research findings of incidence of psychologic impairment in war-related disasters are grouped into three areas: general impact on civilian population; impact on children; and impact on the family. The literature is described and critiqued in each area.

GENERAL IMPACT ON CIVILIAN POPULATION

General impact of war stress is described in five studies (Aubrey, 1941; Hourani et al., 1986; Lyons, 1979; Murphy, 1977; Saigh, 1988). All but one of the studies were surveys, and only one used random sampling (Hourani et al., 1986). Studies are presented separately because of diversity in the methodology and findings.

A descriptive study was conducted of 3000 private patients after direct exposure to air raids and bombs during World War II, with data obtained from a physician in general practice (Aubrey, 1941). The patients were considered "middle class," with a ratio of two women to one man. One third of the female patients complained of neurotic disorder, whereas one fifth of the men did so. Reports of anxiety states, mild depression, and states of transient confusion and mental exhaustion were found specifically among the elderly, adolescents, and women of middle age. Psychologic symptoms were found to be aggravated in those persons who had damage to the home (58%) or absence of domestic shelter (74%).

The author concluded that severe neurosis rarely occurs as a war phenomenon except in people who are neurotic before the war. Although the results were interesting, the study presented crude figures from hospital and out-patient clinics. There were no design or operational definitions of the terms, and results were not statistically tested for significance. Validity and reliability of measurement tools were not addressed.

Results from a survey of 102 households of Vietnamese civilian evacuees from a battle front (Murphy, 1977) suggest that 65% of these evacuees had high stress levels based on the self-anchoring scale (SAS) and the health opinion survey (HOS) 5 years later. The sample was primarily women and children, because men were either fighting or had been killed in action. The high levels of tension, depression, and anxiety suggest that the psychologic effect of adverse circumstances may persist over an extended period. Analysis of variance showed that age was not significant, but that stress and gender were. Women displayed a higher level of psychologic disturbance and were more prone to depression than men. Also, there was a positive relationship between hardship levels, such as family being broken up because of war separations, deteriorating economic situations, and psychologic disturbance. The study presents interesting results by use of control groups and significant statistical finding. There were no conceptual framework or operational definitions of terms. Moreover, the questionnaires were not designed to fit this particular population, which poses questions about validity and reliability.

Similar results were reported by Hourani et al. (1986) in a household surveillance of 5788 (random sample) displaced and nondisplaced civilians during the Israeli invasion of Lebanon in 1982. Using the Red Cross checklist on emergency psychiatric care during disasters, individuals were asked to report symptoms of inappropriate or unusual behaviors that had occurred only since the beginning of the invasion (June). Approximately 8.3% reported at least one symptom of psychologic distress and unusual behavior. The highest concentration of symptoms reported was in adults age 34 years and older, followed by children 10 years old and younger, with the least concentration in preteen and teenage individuals. Females reported higher symptomatology, with the highest risk score associated with loss of physical health and with the second highest risk category those displaced before the June war. The authors reported relatively low incidence of psychologic disorder during war. Loss of home and property was positively related to psychologic distress. The authors suggest that the study is best viewed as hypothesis generating because of its limitations in that it is a descriptive study and was meant to provide information on health status of Beruit residents during war time for relief purposes.

In another report about psychologic impact of civil violence in Belfast, Lyons (1979) in a community study reported about affective disturbance, such as fear, anxiety, irritability, and depression, in a sample of 217 patients (162 women, 55 men) from a physician's office. Women in this sample were found to be more vulnerable to stress than men. Approximately 50% of patients were age 14 to 44 years. Somatic symptoms, such as abdominal pain, chest sensation, headache, sweating, and trembling, associated with the feeling of anxiety were reported. There were no psychotic symptoms or suicide attempts. Insomnia and situational state anxiety were experienced by more than 149 patients (68.7%). Admission rate to psychiatric hospitals did not increase, and there was a significant decrease of depressive illness during periods of violence. This finding was more pronounced in men.

In another longitudinal study of Beirut population, Saigh (1988) administered STAI state, BDI, and RAS to 12 female students (6 undergraduate, 6 graduate) at the American University of Beirut. The tools were administered to students 63 days before they were exposed to a significant war-related stressor, as well as 8, 37, and 316 days later. The majority of respondents reported higher levels of anxiety and depression, as well as lower levels of assertiveness 8 days after the trauma. Students did not develop chronic post-traumatic stress disorder (PTSD) after they were exposed to an intense and prolonged bombardment. The author suggested that singular traumas of this sort may not be generally associated with the development of chronic PTSD. The sample was a small one, and all female. Because of the size, the study may not offer reliable and valid predictors.

IMPACT ON CHILDREN

Two studies focused on children (Bodman, 1941; Punamaki, 1988), and two others reported about children as part of a study (Aubrey, 1941; Hourani et al., 1986). The impact of war conditions on the mental health of the child was reported in a survey of British children during air raids in World War II (Bodman, 1941). Approximately 4% of a large sample of school population showed signs of strain, either purely psychologic or else psychosomatic. Among the psychologic symptoms noted were general nervousness, trembling, crying, and aggressive behavior. Among the psychosomatic symptoms were headaches, anorexia, indigestion, neurosis, soiling, pallor, and epistaxis. These psychologic symptoms occurred twice as often in the 5- to 7-year-olds as in the senior group (ages 11 to 14 years), whereas psychosomatic symptoms were common in the older group, which was interpreted by the author as disguised anxiety. The study reported that younger children were found to have felt the strain and lack of sleep more readily than older ones, who have developed more control and can repress their feelings to conform with adult standards. The study also reported another survey on 54 in-patient children after more time elapsed and during a period of freedom from the raids. The hospital was damaged and children evacuated. Findings showed persistent signs of stress between ages 1 and 5½ years and greater chance of infection, which suggests a lowered resistance at stressful times. The symptoms of stress persisted after 7 months. The author concluded that children have extraordinary flexibility in adapting to threatening situations.

Punamaki (1988), in a study of Palestinian children in the West Bank and Beirut refugee camps, hypothesized that factors affect the coping modes, fears, and psychologic responses of children. Qualitative and quantitative analyses were used on 66 children in 1982 before the Lebanon war; a group of 42 children in 1985 in the West Bank; and a group of 31 children from the refugee camp in Beirut in 1984. All children were from 8 to 14 years of age, with an equal number of boys and girls. Structured interviews and analysis of variance with factorial designs were carried out. Older children showed more active, purposeful, and cognitive coping modes than did younger children and girls. Traumatic experience correlates with active coping modes, and girls expressed more fears than boys and levels of fears were higher among young children. The place of residence (Beirut or West Bank) had a very significant effect on coping modes. Those residing in a refugee camp (Beirut) employed more passive and helpless coping modes, but place of residence was not related to the cognitive level of coping. The good design — attention to reliability and validity, definition of concepts measured, and analysis of data, both quantitative and qualitative — lends credibility to the findings.

Two other articles reported findings about children as a part of a larger study. In a large sample, children mostly between the ages of 7 and 11 years, it was reported that approximately 2.8% of the children who were evacuated after severe air raids during World War II had nervous disturbance, depending on the fear experienced by the child and his or her mother. The symptoms reported were neurosis, hysterical vomiting, sleepwalking fits, tics, and anxiety and depression (Aubrey, 1941). Increased frequency of shouting and bed wetting was also reported in children exposed to war in Lebanon (Hourani et al., 1986). The literature on children does not reflect the intensity of war on the mental health of the child. The figures presented are not compared with finding of children's symptomatology in the general population. Thus further research is needed in this area.

IMPACT ON THE FAMILY

The literature on impact of war-related stress on the family was the focus of five studies (Bryce, Walker, Ghorayeb, & Kanj, 1989; Bryce, Walker, & Peterson, 1989; Farhood, 1986; Farhood et al., in press; Rosenheck, 1986). The focus was either on mother, mother-child, family members, or the next generation. All studies utilized self-report or mother reporting for the child and studied relationship between life events, coping styles, and psychologic functioning. A conceptual framework was used in two studies (Bryce, Walker, Ghorayeb, & Kanj, 1989; Farhood et al., in press). All studies reported acceptable validity and reliability, and one study used random sampling (Farhood et al., in press).

In a study of 192 mothers in Beirut, Bryce, Walker, Ghorayeb, & Kanj, (1989) found that the number of environmental problems, level of crowding, and number of children under the age of 15 years at home positively correlated with increased levels of depressive symptoms among the women. Educational level and household income were negatively correlated with women's score on the BDI scale, indicating that women with higher levels of income or education reported fewer depressive symptoms. Multiple regression was used to predict women's depression. Variables explaining 20.6% of the variance were emotional coping, life experiences relative to problems in interpersonal relationships, and social coping. Results suggested that events associated with the ongoing war in Lebanon were not strongly linked to depressive symptoms. The finding is similar to what Farhood, et al., (in press) reported in a study of a random sample of 1159 members of Beirut families (525 mothers, 413 fathers, and 221 adolescents). Multiple regression explained 40% of mothers' depression using the following variables: by-product of life events during the past 6 months with behavioral coping pattern, 30%; dissatisfaction in interpersonal relationships, 5%; network support, 4%; social support, 1% (inversely related). Stressful life events past 6 months were not considered war-related. This suggests that war is not different in kind from other events, but creates the kinds of conditions that in turn create depression (Bryce, Walker, Ghorayeb, & Kanj, 1989).

In another advanced study by the same authors (Bryce, Walker, & Peterson,

1989), a sample of 152 mothers in Beirut were studied to determine the relationship between life experiences, mothers' depression, and children's health and behavior. Measures of the perceived negative impact of both war-related and non-war-related events, measures of available social support, sociodemographic variables, coping responses, and displacement were conceptualized to predict mothers' depressive symptomatology and their children's health. Results suggest that the level of perceived negative impact of war-related events was strongly associated with higher levels of depression. This is contrary to earlier findings (Bryce, Walker, Ghorayeb, & Kanj, 1989; Farhood et al., in press). Mothers who reported more emotional coping response were found to have the highest levels of depression. This might be that the measurements of depression and emotional coping overlap. Size of social network was positively correlated with education and income levels. Levels of satisfaction with the support decreased as the number of residential relocations increased.

Mothers' level of depression was the most important predictor of reports of child morbidity. In addition, the number of environmental threats in the home was significantly related to the children's behavior. Also, the perceived impact of experiences was found to be a more powerful predictor of mental disturbance than were the number of events. Among limitations of the study as discussed by authors are (1) reports of child illness by the mother possibly being biased by memory and social desirability and (2) interaction of different measures, such as depression and emotional style response. The sample size, the conceptual framework developed, design, and recommendation lend credibility to the findings.

In a descriptive study of 78 families in Beirut (Farhood, 1986), findings suggest a strong tendency to use somatization as a way to deal with stress. Approximately 80% of the sample interviewed suffered from musculoskeletal symptoms, digestive symptoms, depression, metabolic symptoms, impaired interpersonal relationships, and a high tendency to use alcohol and smoke cigarettes. These results are associated with increased war-related events occurring within the family. The results should be interpreted with caution because of the descriptive and exploratory nature of the study.

The last study focused on family and war stress (Farhood et al., in press) with a large random sample ($n = 1,159$). The study measured the effect of perceived life events and background variables on the physical and psychologic well-being, including interpersonal and marital relationships. A questionnaire consisted of six different scales focusing on the family members (parents and an adolescent at random), individual child, coping, stressful life events, and fertility. Validity and reliability were accounted for. Dependent and independent variables were defined, and multiple classification analysis (MCA), multiple regression, and prevalence rates were performed. Findings suggested that psychologic symptoms were high in both males and females and in all age groups. Approximately 10% of the sample reported clinical depression, and there were more female depressives than males.

Anxiety and physical symptoms were reported by mothers and fathers, but females tended to have higher levels, especially those ages 29 to 59 years. Low back pain tended to be higher in males ages 40 to 59 years. Results of regression analysis for both males and females showed that life events during the past 6 months were the first predictor for depression and psychologic symptoms ($P = .000$). Severed interpersonal relationship were high predictors of depression in adolescents. Social support appeared as an important mediating factor in depression and psychologic and physical symptoms for the family as a unit. Marital relationships showed strength in general. The study poses interesting and reliable findings.

In a clinical study of offspring of combat veterans of World War II, subjects were adults at the time of the study and had no combat experience on their own. Rosenbeck (1986) found that the psychologic scars of post-traumatic stress disorder (PTSD) persisted throughout life and into the next generation.

• • •

A summary of findings from research literature on war suggests that there is a low incidence of psychiatric illnesses and admissions during war time (Aubrey, 1941; Hourani et al., 1986; Lyons, 1979). This might be because individuals need all their energy to survive. Most studies report high prevalence of anxiety symptoms and depression (Aubrey, 1941; Farhood, 1986; Farhood et al., in press; Hourani et al., 1986; Lyons, 1979; Murphy, 1977; Rosenheck, 1986; Saigh, 1988). Loss of property was correlated to increase in psychologic impairment (Aubrey, 1941; Hourani et al., 1986; Murphy, 1977). Perceived negative life events were associated with depression in mothers and in other members of the family (Bryce, Walker, & Peterson, 1989; Farhood et al., in press). Stressful life events concerned with life and property loss were found to be significantly related to depression in the victims at large (Aubrey, 1941; Bryce, Walker, Ghorayeb, & Kanj, 1989; Farhood et al., in press; Hourani et al., 1986). Findings also suggest that the more intense the exposure, the lower the ratings for mental health (Bryce, Walker, Ghorayeb, & Kanj, 1989; Farhood et al., in press). Of the children studied, the most vulnerable to war stress were those in the younger age group (Bodman, 1941; Punamaki, 1988). All studies reported women's vulnerability to depression. Such findings should be interpreted with caution. The need is evident for future research in this area.

The most striking characteristics of the review of literature on war-related disasters is that it is a growing field in its first developmental stages. The nursing literature did not address such concerns at all. This might be because of the novelty of the field and because nurse scientists who are involved in research live in war-free countries. There is a growing concern for the relief of victims of disaster, and nurses should be able to provide nursing care based on sound scientific knowledge in order to help inflicted victims to adapt. The current state of research on war-related disasters in nursing and in other disciplines to a lesser degree does not provide a consistent body of knowledge that will guide sound nursing practice in the physical and emotional well-being of war victims. Replications are needed with major improvement in sampling, methodologic designs, and adequate control groups. The reviewed literature points to difficulty in measuring mental health variables and constructs; most of the studies are descriptive, symptom oriented, and based on the medical model. Findings from the reviewed research on impact of war on family members strongly support the idea that war stress and resultant negative life events produce psychologic symptoms and scars that persist over time.

More information is needed about the nature of war stress and the variables that mediate such stress. There are many conflicting claims regarding the relationship of war-related activities and psychologic symptoms. We need to acknowledge that the researchers have used different methods in designing studies and consequently have chosen different measurement strategies, which tend to yield uncomparable results. Furthermore, these studies depended largely on victim self-report and clinical interviews as a measure of psychologic impact. The concept of social desirability is in effect. Also, most studies utilized measurement of psychologic consequences of the war, which resulted in inappropriate conceptualization and operationalization. Thus the definition of anxiety in one study might not be the same in another. The nature of war stress and psychologic sequelae cannot be explained in a simple linear model. We need conceptual models depicting the factors that affect the psychologic consequences of war stress. Such models should consider (1) the duration, time, and type of war; (2) the characteristics of the social system in its ability to play a role in mediating the psychologic impact; and (3) the characteristics of the individual. Control groups could be helpful in such comparisons.

Most of the studies had adequate sample size, but a major weakness in the designs was that age groups or vulnerable groups at risk were not specified. Some authors included samples from different age groups, cultural backgrounds, or any convenient sample available. Authors in most cases did not discuss limitations of these studies.

The findings indicate a need for further investigation on the impact of war on the family as a unit, taking into account personal as well as social factors that do mediate in the outcome of stress and mental health. There is a need for conceptual framework development that isolates important variables and specifies the channels through which war impact infringes on individuals and families and might produce psychologic consequences, whether positive or negative. In addition, it is important to know how war-related disasters associate with long-term health sequelae. The nature of future studies should be designed to allow room for such differences. Another factor is the prevalence of such psychologic and emotional symptoms among women in most of the studies presented. They all present women as a high-risk group. Studies with improved design and sampling methodologies are needed to further understand reasons for this finding.

A major strength of the findings is the presence of such studies. What is needed is to build on such knowledge base with improved methodologies. Also needed are intervention studies with control to exclude the personal variables that could affect the outcome of the study and identify those at a higher risk for psychologic impairment. There is a need for longitudinal and evaluation-intervention studies that follow up the victims with matched control groups for an unlimited period of time. Such studies are needed to determine individuals' and families' adaptation over time, to observe actual change and identify the variables involved in such change.

War-related research represents a unique field for the community. Nursing must assume a more vigorous role in this area. It requires the expertise of all branches and disciplines, and it needs the contributions of all fields: medical, psychologic, and social. A multidisciplinary research team could answer some of the questions still unanswered.

REFERENCES

Aubrey, L. (1941). Incidence of neurosis in England under war conditions. *Lancet, 2,* 175-183.

Beck, C. Rawlins, R. & Williams, S. (Eds.). (1984). *Mental health: Psychiatric nursing.* St. Louis: Mosby–Year Book.

Bodman, F. (1941). War conditions and the mental health of the child. *British Medical Journal, 2,* 486-488.

Bryce, J., Walker, N., Ghorayeb, F., & Kanj, M. (1989). Life experiences, response styles and mental health among mothers and children in Beirut, Lebanon. *Social Science and Medicine, 18*(1), 685-695.

Bryce, J., Walker N., & Peterson, C. (1989). Predicting symptoms of depression among women in Beirut: The importance of daily life. *International Journal of Mental Health, 18*(1), 57-70

Dohrenwend, B.S., & Dohrenwend, B.D. (1978). Some issues in research on stressful life events. *Journal of Nervous and Mental Diseases, 166*(1), 7-15.

Farhood, L. (1986). *Family structure and sociocultural change in Lebanon: Its effect on mental health.* Presented at 8th International Congress of Cross-Cultural Psychology. Istanbul, Turkey, July 6-10.

Farhood, L., Zurak, K. H., Shaya, M., Meshefedejian, G., Saadi, F., Ismail, R., & Sidani, T. (in press). *War effects on the physical and mental health of the family as reported by the Beirut population.*

Finlay-Jones, R., & Brown, G. (1981). Types of stressful life events and the onset of anxiety and depressive disorders. *Psychological Medicine, 11,* 803-815.

Hansen, D.A., & Hill, R. (1964). Families under stress. In H. Christensen (Ed.), *Handbook of marriage and family.* Chicago: Rand McNally.

Hourani, L.L., Armenian, H., Zurayk, H., & Afifi, L. (1986). A population-based survey of loss and psychological distress during war. *Social Science and Medicine, 23,* 269-275.

Logue, J.N., Melick, M.E., & Hansen, H. (1981). Research issues and directions in the epidemiology of health effects of disaster. *Epidemiologic Reviews, 3,* 140-162.

Lyons, H.A. (1979). Civil violence. The psychological aspects. *Journal of Psychosomatic Research, 23,* 373-393.

McCubbin, H., Joy, D., Cauble, A., Comeau, J., Patterson, J., & Needle, R. (1980). Family stress, coping and social support: A decade review. *Journal of Marriage and the Family, 42,* 855-871.

Mueler, D., Edwards, D., & Patients, C. (1978). Stressful life events and community mental health. *Journal of Nervous and Mental Disease, 166*(1), 16-24.

Murphy, J. (1977). War stress and civilian Vietnamese: A study of psychological effects. *Acta Psychiatrica Scandinavica, 56,* 92-108.

Punamaki, R.L. (1988). Historical-political and individualistic determinants of coping modes and fears among Palestinian children. *International Journal of Psychology, 23,* 721-739.

Rabkin, J., & Streuening, E. (1976). Life events, stress and illness. *Science, 914,* 1013-1019.

Rosenheck, R. (1986). Impact of past traumatic stress disorder of World War II on the next generation. *Journal of Nervous and Mental Disease, 174*(6), 319-327.

Saigh, P. (1988). Anxiety, depression, and assertion across alternating intervals of stress. *Journal of Abnormal Psychology, 97*(3), 338-341.

Shisana, O., & Celentano, D. (1987). Relationship of chronic stress, social support, and coping style to health among Namibian refugees. *Social Science and Medicine, 24*(2), 145-157.

Index

A